D1830726

CORPORATE GOVERNANCE AND SOCIAL RESPONSIBILITIES

CORPORATE GOVERNANCE AND SOCIAL RESPONSIBILITIES

H.C. Mruthyunjaya

Consultant (Corporate Systems) Bengaluru

KALPAZ

©Author

All rights reserved. No part of this work may be reproduced, stored, adapted, or transmitted in any form or by any means, electronic, mechanical, photocopying, micro-filming, recording or otherwise, or translated in any language, without the prior written permission of the copyright owner and the publisher. The book is sold subject to the condition that it shall not, by way of trade or otherwise, be lent, resold, hired out, or otherwise circulated without the prior publisher's written consent in any form of binding or cover other than that in which it is published.

The views and opinions expressed in this book are author(s) own and the facts reported by them have been verified to the extent possible and the publishers are not in any way liable for the same.

ISBN: 978-93-5128-109-2

Price : ₹ 1490

First Published, 2016

Published by

Kalpaz Publications
C-30, Satyawati Nagar,
Delhi – 110052
E-mail: kalpaz@hotmail.com
Ph.: 9212142040

Printed at: G. Print Process, Delhi

Cataloging in Publication Data—DK
Courtesy: D.K. Agencies (P) Ltd. <docinfo@dkagencies.com>

Mruthyunjaya, H. C., author.
Corporate governance and social responsibilities / H.C. Mruthyunjaya.
pages cm
ISBN 9789351281092

1. Corporate governance—India. 2. Social responsibility of business—India. I. Title.

DDC 658.400954 23

To
My Parents
and
Teachers

Contents

Preface

The history of industrialisation across the world as well as the innovative practices of the industrial community ever anxious to address the never satiable hunger of the ambitiously evolving knowledge society for newer and newer products and services provide ample instances and examples that failed to prick the conscience of the inner mind that has a natural tendency to align with the higher bandwidth of *virtues-spectrum*. For a long-time, the society, as a whole, did not suitably respond for the innumerable numbers of unholy practices that a sensitive civilised society would ever be prepared to accept. If the nature and magnitude of some of those non-acceptable practices are analysed and carefully evaluated for their cumulative adverse impacts, whether on people or on the surroundings or on the environment around, one might readily be tempted to label many of them as heinous crimes committed against society and the mankind as a whole.

It is also a known fact that the fast-evolving society has also, periodically, witnessed many scams and scandals of varying magnitudes resulting either cumulatively or singly from those malpractices. The nature of impacts and their coverage profile also varied from one scam to another. Over a period of time, some of the scams and scandals that carried a high potential to create a severe adverse impact on the social-economy and/or on community health and wellbeing, did induce intellectuals across the society to ponder over those issues and to explore the phenomenon from different perspectives and to find ways and means to identify suitable control measures that could help in preventing recurrence of such unfortunate events and incidences.

Soon, socially conscious intellectuals and social ethicists pressed themselves into action and attempted to identify the root cause for some of those widely prevalent malpractices. This was a very tough job for these social-ethicists. The knowledge available did not help them in establishing a direct and precise correlation between many of the unacceptable observations and the operation environment that prevailed in many industries. It was, similarly, not possible to quantify and accurately measure the magnitude of contribution to different observations and their corresponding adverse impacts made by any specific industry. As such, social scientists and ethicists could not come to the rescue of industrial workers, the surrounding environment and the society at large for a long-time. Social scientists were, however, sure of adverse impacts of certain activities if not properly executed. They were also equally sure that some of the impacts seen across the society and the surroundings were the result of cumulative effect of a large number of precisely non-quantifiable work environments and work methodologies, though they were not able to provide a ready formula to either correlate a specific element of work environment or precisely extrapolate and work out a future impact. One more uncertain element that made the issue more complicated was the fact that work environments varied from one industry to another and no industry could be singled-out for a specific observation.

Social ethicists, however, did not give-up their efforts but continued to pursue the phenomenon with the objective of identifying nearest acceptable remedial and/or mitigatory measures. They continued to work in close collaboration with scientists. Intensive studies and aggressive exploration into the realm of knowledge did help these scientists to identify a close relationship between certain observed impacts and their correlatable work environments. This analysis and cause identification, in turn, ensured that the society would act on those observations and conclusions through appropriate control measures. Thus born the concept of *Corporate Governance and Social Responsibility*. Societies all over the world started responding to this newly evolved concept. Necessary legislations were framed and implemented. Further, as and when additional and/or supplementary knowledge got generated; legislative stipulations were also accordingly modified and strengthened including by incorporating additional requirements as felt necessary. However, depending on its socio-economic and cultural backgrounds, the degree of response varied from one society to another.

Most unfortunately, in spite of much legislation, even today, the society continues to witness scams and scandals now and then. This is primarily because the ever corrupt human mind always keeps exploring innovative ways and means to maneuver situations by taking shelter either under lapses and short-falls in enforcement/administrative mechanisms or by leveraging the missing links within the legal framework. As such, *Legislative Controls* alone cannot totally rescue the society. Such unfortunate incidences keep occurring till the human race itself undergoes a permanent *psycho-emotional-genetic-transmutation* where both the first concern as well as the last concern of all individuals would always remain well being of the society, environment and the mankind as a whole!

Bulk of the information available in published literature emphasises on the basics of corporate governance and social responsibility. The concept of corporate citizenship has also been introduced to highlight the requirements of corporate social responsibility and to emphasise certain requirements under governance. Published literature also lays fairly good emphasis on the observations made by various committees constituted for purposes of evaluating and identifying the role of business corporates in the field of *Corporate Governance* and *Social Responsibility*. However, necessary emphasis does not appear to have been laid on specifying what needs to be done to ensure that business corporates make a smooth start and take active part in this critical area and to highlight what is expected of them and to define what needs to be specified and/or prescribed for them. This book is configured to address this area and to help practicing executives and administrators in marching systematically towards a *Ready-to-Start (Take-off) Position* and to ensure that they do not get stuck at the start itself.

The book is designed to give a skeletal presentation of some of the key aspects generally associated with the subject of *Corporate Governance and Social Responsibility* and is configured to suitably support shop-floor executives particularly from different types of processing and/or manufacturing industries who are willing to check their governance skills and would like to add to their skill-kit. Discussions open with a brief insight into industrial development process and attempt to identify the key forces and root causes that induce different types of malpractices. This is followed by a brief description of how intellectuals across the society worked towards building public conscience against corporate malpractices by creating global awareness against harmful effects of some of those malpractices. The type of hurdles that this movement faces is also presented here. Response of society towards some of the known adverse effects of corporate malpractices leading to evolving a control-framework for corporate governance and social responsibility is also discussed.

Discussions next present a global view of the basic governance process. Mechanism of conceptualisation of different components of governance is briefly presented. This is followed by identifying means and methods to satisfactorily translate the key requirements of governance to actual shop-floor practices. This presentation is supported by appropriately designed spreadsheets that highlight the nature of more frequently encountered malpractices in different activity areas and are further supported with suitable mechanisms that could help corporates in translating governance requirements to practical reality in a true sense. Readers' attention is also drawn here to a strange phenomenon namely the hurdles posed by the society itself for satisfactorily practicing good governance in certain activity areas. Nature of some of these hurdles posed by the society is also briefly discussed. A few typical check points to identify a few non-wholesome situations are also given. The chapter concludes with a schematic conceptual model for managing governance mechanism.

The third chapter opens with a short description of certain key issues associated with ensuring full compliance to all the applicable legal requirements. Opening with a brief reference to merits and advantages of satisfactory law abidance, the types of hurdles normally faced by business corporates in this process are also briefly touched-upon. This is followed by a skeletal cross-sectional view of the requirements under *Companies Act, 2013* and also a few other laws that one should normally consider for their applicability before proceeding further. These tabular presentations help companies in identifying most of the key requirements under different acts and laws so that they could comfortably make a start without much difficulty and then proceed for detailed study and exploration of applicable acts for purposes of fine tuning their compliance operations. Next, a few typical worksheets are presented to help different activity centers to carefully identify applicable acts and their relevant clauses for ensuring total compliance at their respective work centers.

The next chapter highlights a basic truth that executing certain pre-identified activities under the head social responsibility is never a favour that corporates do to the society, but, on the contrary, they form a part of their basic duty towards society under the principle of reciprocity. These discussions embrace the mandatory components under the companies act. A mechanism for satisfactorily administering different CSR projects is also briefly presented here.

The fifth chapter dwells into an activity area which, unfortunately, is not normally considered under governance, though the harsh truth of the fact remains that in the absence of this activity, the very purpose of governance and social responsibility may get defeated more often than not. This area stands for accident management and emergency preparedness both of which together guard the long-term interests of people (entire cross-section of stakeholders), society and the environment at large. Starting with a brief description of the nature of corporate accidents under different operating environments, the discussions also present a few worksheets that would come handy for practicing professionals in designing an accident free safe-activity domain.

The last chapter gives a skeletal description of auditing of governance area and to identify the lapses in the same. The discussions also highlight the significance of elaborate preparation for carrying out satisfactory audits. A few typical audit checklists are also presented to help governance-auditors in making a good preparation and in carrying out satisfactory governance audits. The chapter concludes with a brief presentation of a ten step audit process.

Some key features of these discussions are:

- Good support from many schematic diagrams that give a clear picture of the concept being discussed.
- Suitably designed spreadsheets to support careful identification of legal requirements under different acts and rules together with methods to ensure compliance.
- Tabulated presentation of a cross sectional view of the requirements under the Companies' Act and other acts that helps new entrepreneurs in directly taking-off in the beginning.

- Suitably configured malpractices' spreadsheets that help system-designers in readily identifying and recognising non-wholesome activity areas.
- Discussions on one of the significant activity areas that are not normally considered under governance administration but are very critical to uphold the process of governance and social responsibility.
- Step-wise guidance for carrying out satisfactory governance audit.

Suggestions for making the book more useful to a larger section of users are welcome (drmruthyunjaya@gmail.com).

Efforts of the publisher in bringing out this book are deeply appreciated and gratefully acknowledged.

H. C. Mruthyunjaya

Evolution of the Concept

Nucleation

The history of industrialisation in general and the methods followed by industries for productivity enhancement, product development, expansions, diversifications and building competitiveness, etc. in particular, offered innumerable numbers of opportunities for the onset of the concept of *Corporate Governance (CG)* and *Corporate Social Responsibility (CSR).* However, this concept could not take off in a big way for long for many reasons governed by the then prevailing industrial and socio-economic environments. The severe jolt that shook the commercial and the economic world in 1929 through *Wall Street Collapse* appears to have triggered the onset of this concept. Since then the world has been witnessing, now and then, many corporate scams and scandals. Such scams and scandals are not confined only to industrial operations but embrace all types and forms of commercial establishments and other activities across the world. Similarly, corporate scams and scandals are not confined to any particular society. In fact, it has become universal in nature though the frequency of appearance may not be same in different parts of the world. Over a period of time, most unfortunately for the society, different wings of public administrative machinery and service systems, either solely or in collusion with other wings and divisions also entered the race. The same mischievous human psychology works everywhere. These scandals have shaken the confidence of the general public in corporate affairs and activities as well as in public administration and service provision establishments. Whenever a scandal comes to knowledge of the general public, there will be a series of discussions and trading of different thoughts across different cross sections of the society regarding different useful and desirable control measures that could be introduced to both corporate and public life to prevent occurrence of such unfortunate events.

Nature of Frauds

If we carefully dissect these scandals and try to understand their nature, we realise that most of these scandals have their roots, either directly or indirectly, in different forms of financial malpractices. The types of economic frauds that we come across in those scandal situations generally belong to the category of *Accounting Malpractices* which manifest in different ways. Among them, following three types are more common.

- ➢ Resorting to preparation of fraudulent balance sheets of companies with an objective to keep the business investors, financiers, government agencies and the general public in darkness regarding actual practices and true facts.

  For this purpose, people involved in activities leading to scams and collapses resort to some of the following measures to address their needs:

  - Under-billing or overbilling of products and services.
  - Under-valuing or overvaluing of company's assets and liabilities.
  - False reporting of profits and losses under different activity heads.
  - Manipulating stocks in trade and false reporting of stocks.
  - Resorting to showing notional income and expenditure:
    - Showing false income and imaginary receivables.
    - Showing false expenditure and false payables.
  - Generating fraudulent records about expenditure and/or commitments made to workmen, on their welfare and development activities including workmen's retirement benefits like provident funds, gratuities, or pension funds, etc.
- ➢ Manipulating company's share values.
- ➢ Directly participating and/or supporting internal trading.

History of corporate scams reveals that we do come across many live instances under each one of these malpractice categories. On all such situations, accounts executives liberally collude with company auditors, sales and purchase executives and with many external executives including many officers of the administrative machinery. Such unholy collusions will also be entered into with some opportunistic crooked financiers, investors, stock-brokers and stock agents. Under-valuing and overvaluing is specifically resorted to address many of the unholy practices including supporting heavy bribery and kickbacks and/ or other unethical favours. Generating unaccounted money (black money) through most of the above malpractices and using the same for financing and supporting all forms and types of unfair and unethical activities including pumping of company money for personal welfare is almost a standard practice in many corporates. Internal trading in particular is practiced in collusion with many key executives from accounts and finance divisions and some key intellectuals in the company and also some opportunistic financiers and bankers, to make quick bucks at the cost of the general public. Scams involving legal offences are generally carried out in collusion with public administrators and law enforcement authorities. In fact, in many of these corporate scams it is hard to find as to who is not involved in the process. Many times corporate finances are utilised for perpetrating certain heinous crimes like spying, financing terrorist activities, etc.

Macro Frauds

Generally, these are the types of scams and scandals that carry high potential to come to the knowledge of the general public. This is just one apparent category. These are generally known as *Macro-frauds.*

There is one more latent category of fraud under this macro fraud class. This refers to those marketing and/or public goodwill development activities which eventually lead to causing severe damage to company's name and fame and the image in the society. These frauds, which involve huge amounts of corporate money being used for bribes and kickbacks, could go unnoticed for long but always carry a high potential to cause the damage.

There is yet another macro-fraud category. Many giant corporates control most of the other smaller business establishments, administrative systems, procedures and controls in the region without any accountability as they always remain behind the screen and are not visible to the public. They also ensure that they are not on records anywhere in the fraud chain. Many rules and regulations and also control mechanisms are framed as per their directives at the cost of the society and the environment. Is this a small fraud? Such a phenomenon is not limited only to giant business establishments having big monetary muscle power. It also embraces many political bigwigs in the society who control administrative machinery itself to perpetrate malpractices in many offices who would be directly involved in designing and managing many scandals. But the real culprits namely those political bigwigs who would be the key beneficiaries would ensure that the scandal-chain is designed, organised and managed in such a way that they generally remain safe. Whenever such scandals come to the knowledge of the general public, political bigwigs behind the entire activity chain go scot-free as it would not be easy to link them to the scandal chain and their image will not suffer any dent. All these macro-frauds gave rise to concept of *Macro-Governance*.

These corporate scams and scandals induced the society to frame, from time to time, many rules, regulations and acts and some control measures for enforcing them on corporates. Separate administrative machineries were also established to supervise corporate operations. Some of the major legal controls that came to existence from these scams are the company law, stock exchange rules and regulations, financial rules and regulations, guidelines and/or standards for accounting practices, and some personal laws, etc.

Micro Frauds

There is one more latent category of corporate malpractice. This may not directly involve financial malpractices. This category of malpractice refers to rampant prevalence of malpractices associated with activity execution schemes and mechanisms. This category of frauds carries the potential to make the workmen or the environment suffer silently. The macro category carries the potential to cause financial harm while the micro ones the potential to harm health and general welfare of people. At times, cumulative and collective financial harm or loss from micro frauds would be of similar magnitude or even more depending on the nature of cumulative harm. In many situations, this group would even harm many innocent lives.

Yet, this group does not glaringly come to public knowledge except in cases of major accidents. What a pity! Even during accident situations, people rarely identify system failures and execution lapses as the root of problem. On the contrary, failure of a control mechanism or a mechanism in the operation chain would be identified in isolation as the sole reason for accident. As such, they are normally described as unwelcome malpractices or simply as unethical practices. However, from broader perspectives of corporate health and social health, we could describe both apparent and latent categories of malpractices as corporate frauds. The methods followed by industries to ensure their continued and/or sustained productive growth and prosperity traversed different routes differently and at different stages of their development and implementation ever since the beginning of evolution of industrial era. Different philosophies and different approaches were entertained by people who were directly involved in governing and directing prosperity trajectories for industries they were controlling. This trajectory, which gave rise to practice of different types of large numbers of mini- and micro-malpractices, in turn, has triggered the concept of *Micro-Governance.* The nucleus that has triggered this concept has its base in the knowledge emanating along the traverse-trajectory followed by industries across the world at different stages and at different times.

The Seed

Corporate output is actually a form of wealth for the society. Corporate output could be both material wealth as well as knowledge wealth. As business entities, corporates generally work towards transforming both these forms of wealth to monetary wealth form. Thus, corporates ultimately generate monetary wealth for the society through their activities. All societies across the world whole heartedly welcomed wealth generation process through industrialisation and encouraged and supported all types of industrial ventures.

With the advancement of industrial development, social requirements and demand for newer products and services also changed and steadily a new life pattern emerged. This new social-life pattern that emerged depended very heavily on innumerable numbers of diverse industrial products and less on natural products. For a long time industries focussed on the greater cross section of the society and on the bulk outlet for their products. The common man or the general public were the main targets for industrial products. Focus of industries, for a long time, was mainly on large volume production and marketing the same. During this period of development and growth, industries, the world over, had not visualised that they could also add on another activity that may not be based on weight or volume production but on number production to create a hi-end niche market in the society. Development of electronic gadgets, entertainment facilities and utility products started at this stage. Industries started developing products which did not belong to the category of basic necessity of the bulk cross section of the population but belonged to the category of add-on-comfort products. Industries had, then, hardly realised that such add-on-comfort products would gradually manoeuvre the general outlook of the population in such a way that, over a period time, they would get shifted to the basic necessity category as people get addicted to those gadgets. This situation ensured that need based market demand gradually transformed itself to a desire-based market demand. Products aimed only at serving the hi-end markets became the focus for development and soon hi-end products started invading the market. Ironically enough, some industrial products that are acquired by certain cross sections of the society just stand for competitive comforts (A Status Symbol!) of people rather than meeting a dire necessity of those who acquired the same. The society totally got wedded to industrial products in all walks of life. This tendency also ensured that people steadily drifted from virgin nature and natural products and on their own personal skills and abilities and drove the society to a point of no-return namely a situation where it is just not practical for anyone to lead a normal comfortable life without industrial products at every stage and at all stages and walks of life. This tendency grew exponentially in the society in a competitive spirit across the world and societies went on acquiring different types of industrial products for different applications including for those applications which the societies had been comfortably managing earlier without much difficulty or fuss about the same. All along, since the society was primarily concerned with products at its disposal, production methodologies and practices never caught the attention of the society. Micro-malpractices liberally proliferated.

Thus, we have two basic types of corporate frauds:

1. Macro-impact frauds.
    - Triggered the onset of Macro-governance aspects or issues.
2. Micro-impact frauds.
    - Triggered the onset of Micro-governance aspects.

From governance viewpoints both these areas are equally critical. An interesting observation here is that control measures referred earlier (company law, stock exchange rules and regulations, financial rules and regulations, guidelines and/or standards for accounting practices, etc.) cannot come to the rescue of silently suffering workforce or the surrounding environment. Fighting these frauds call for a different set of control measures.

The Root

It is a well understood fact that along with industrial progress, all societies also progressed well in many spheres including in the knowledge-sphere to transform themselves to knowledge societies. Over a period of time, knowledge-societies also started building social conscience. With the steady evolution of social-conscience, intellectuals realised that industrial/corporate activities are camouflaged with both the welcome aspects as well as unwelcome aspects. Welcome aspects referred to those obvious positive contributions of adding to the material comforts of the society and unwelcome aspects referred to all activities which contributed, either directly or indirectly, to deprivation of some of the comforts of people and the society.

Intellectuals from across the society started carefully observing and identifying the various unhealthy and unwelcome/unacceptable aspects and/or practices that were normally associated with different manufacturing activities and their impact on industrial workmen in particular and others in general. They did realise that certain work situations created by industrial work practices carried high potential to cause a severe dent in the health of industrial workmen and some works practices carried equally high potential to cause damage to public health as well.

Such a realisation induced intellectuals to build an intense desire to suitably sensitise people regarding those non-satisfactory activities and their adverse impacts on people and the environment, whether direct or indirect. A sensitisation movement was soon initiated. Like many other conscience-driven international sensitisation movements, this movement also aimed at drawing the attention of the society across the entire world regarding rampantly prevalent unwelcome and/or unacceptable practices of different manufacturing and/or product or service generation activities and to create awareness about the same.

However, before we try to traverse through the sensitisation movement, it would be useful to take a quick traverse through the industrial trail. Business Corporates came to existence with the sole objective of meeting certain needs and requirements of the society by way of identifying prevailing gaps in supply-demand position and potential opportunities for development and expansion. All such gaps and opportunities generally hover around one basic aspect namely enhancing the material-comforts of society. With a view to addressing this need, corporates work towards generating and establishing some new and innovative product supply chain or some service supply chain which, either directly or indirectly, contribute towards enhancing the material comforts of the society. And, in this process, they also address their own business needs and interests.

If we carefully examine the history of industrial revolution through the ages, we would realise that all the revolutionary changes that have taken place all over the industrial world have one common force directing, guiding and controlling them, namely, to meet the ever growing demands of the society which is ever anxious for better quality and better performing products that could enhance the ever growing and never satiable demand for extra material comforts of man. In their pursuit of developing and introducing better performing products to the market, industries all over the world extended good support for intensive development works. But in their zeal to industrially progress faster than others by achieving quicker commercial breakthrough, none of them seriously viewed associated issues of impact of their activities on their workforce, the society and the environment.

While some development projects fulfilled their basic objectives of adding to the material comforts of man and some could not, most of them certainly contributed to deterioration of the environment and deterioration of general health standards of the society. This was the direct result of industries' not attending to provision and/or maintenance of healthy and safe work environment for the workmen who were engaged in generating the products of utility to the society and through merciless throwing of generated by-products having varying degrees of harmful side effects on the environment around.

It is also a well recognised fact that industrialisation across the world ushered in a new era that laid great emphasis on generating large numbers and large volumes of consumer products and to make the same available to larger cross sections of the global society and to give a boost to their living comforts and/or standards. As the demand for more and more utility consumer products started gaining momentum, the emphasis steadily got shifted and got focused only on the product generation aspect. Industrial activities symbolically stood for product or service generation. As a natural consequence, means and/or methods followed for product generation got least importance and significance. *Some-how Generate the Product* was probably the thought that used to guide and control all product generation processes. The methods followed by manufacturers also did not attract the attention of many, rather none in the society (!). With the result, manufacturers explored and innovated many ways (rather, many ignoble ways!) of generating their end products more competitively and much ahead of the rest in the field. Their emphasis naturally got shifted on speed and operation economy. Naturally, the finer, more sensitive aspects, associated with the product generation process got totally ignored, rather neglected.

It is needless to say that profit-motif remained the key driving force behind all manufacturing activities. The profit-motif, in turn, ensured that manufacturers did not care to recognise the unwelcome aspects that got ingrained and integrated to their activities in stages. Over a period of time, many of their unholy/ignoble practices appeared as routine ones, if not as standard ones. The society comfortably accepted industrial environments without reference to any of the unholy or ignoble practices that were adopted by industries during their product generation process. The society was made to believe that generation of different utility products that could add to its material comforts at competitive prices can take place only through such (ignoble) methods as otherwise product generation costs would go up and they (society) have to pay much higher price for the same product, a situation which the society was never prepared to accept. General society believed with a conviction that some of the unfair practices are inherently integral to product generation and they have to willingly live with necessary compromises.

Proliferation

As the manufacturing activities got expanded, unholy/ignoble practices also grew exponentially. Neither the manufacturers nor the consuming general public bothered about such unholy/ignoble practices. The net result was uncontrolled proliferation of unsafe working conditions inside manufacturing premises, unhygienic living conditions in workers' colonies, miserably poor wages to industrial workers, rampant child labour and women labour hired most of the times at a pittance, liberal employment of women for carrying out strenuous physical labours, highly discriminating employment and compensation practices, liberally widespread environment pollution, free dumping of industrial wastes and debris including highly hazardous wastes, merciless butchery of virgin environment, etc, etc. In fact, such industrial environments became the order of the industrial era!

Activity Dissection

It is needless to say that overzealous, uncontrollable, greed-driven desires, rather wants, of people was the key driving force for onset of all types of ignoble practices during product generation and distribution stages.

A broad categorisation of different ways in which human desire manifests is typically presented in schematic diagram, figure 1.1. A careful analysis of different mechanisms and means of proliferation of corporate malpractices as seen in the industrial world is briefly summarised in table 1.1. The details given in this table are neither exhaustive nor designed to make the same comprehensive and there could be many other types of observations made by the society in different situations, environments and locations and at different stages of industrial revolution. The details given here just present a broad spectrum of major drive-forces that operated across the bulk cross-section of industries and other manufacturing units across the world at different stages of evolution of industries.

A word of caution! One should, however, not immediately construe that all the malpractices presented in this table are simultaneously practiced by all industries and at all times. Similarly, one should also not construe that at one time or the other all industries do take to these malpractices. Temptation to take to these ignoble routes is primarily decided by many other factors that rule the situation. There could always be some exceptions.

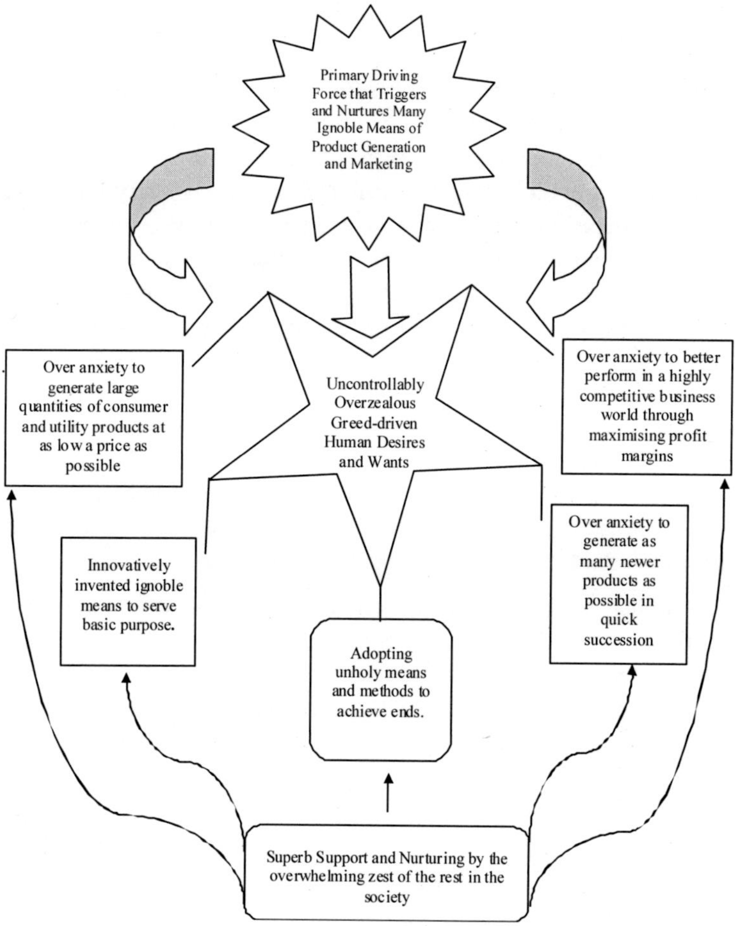

Fig.1.1 Factors that Nucleated and Supported Unholy Practices

We should also not forget here that such observations depend only on the degree of evolution of the thought process and the degree of sense of social-conscience among the industry managers as well as the intellectuals in the society. Only when the intellectuals in the society build some degree of social-conscience regarding the after-effects of product generation and post-generation activities, they can make certain observations and draw suitable inferences regarding their impact. Otherwise, many facts go unnoticed even when they are practiced brazenly in the open.

We can see from this table that it is not practical to draw a clearly defined demarcation border line between different key drive forces and secondary forces. The basic reason for such an inherent ambiguity is the fact that these forces acquire different significance in different operation environment contexts. A specific primary force in a particular operation environment context can function as a secondary force in a different operation context and vice-a-versa. Further, some of the resulting actions can themselves become a major force to drive some other unforeseen/unprojected reaction chain. Also there are many chain reactions involved in these areas. An action or an apparent outcome of a response to an action driven by a specific motivation force can, by itself, trigger another action and the chain can continue by many steps leading to an altogether different observation. Also many of these drive forces are intricately interlinked with each other and cannot be separated from each other. As such, they are diffusive in nature and one should not get confused regarding the nature or types of forces that work behind all forms and all kinds of industrial malpractices.

Another striking feature that stems out from this table to draw our attention is the fact corporate malpractices find no borderline to operate within a specific activity sphere but extend their wings to practically all activity areas both within the corporate premises and beyond.

Table 1.1 Key Forces that Induced Proliferation of Industrial Malpractices

Sl. No.	Primary Forces	Induced Complementary Forces	Net Result (Revelation)
1.	Perennial market demand for a wide variety industrial products that could serve different applications	Perennial survey of market gaps and voids open for potential business opportunities	Intensive exploration of the opportunities open for business transactions Steady industrial growth across the world
2.	Over anxiety and over eagerness of industrialists to generate large quantities of consumer and utility products at as low a price as practical.	Ever eager society to acquire industrial products at very economic/ competitive prices!	Exponential growth of market demand Intensive growth of industrial activities ever eager to meet the market demand Steady growth in both demand and supply position
3.	Steady development of specific demands by certain market segments	Too many suppliers vying with each other to supply their products to the same market segment	Onset of high competition between different business establishments for capturing specific/ target market segments
4.	Growth of competition camouflaged with growing concept of profitability Key driving force being *'Make Hay While the Sun Shines'*	Public apathy to identify shortcuts and malpractices that are open to business executives	Innovative inventions of many operation shortcuts and malpractices to face competitive challenges and to serve business purpose
5.	The over anxiety and over eagerness of business executives	Self-interest driven gross negligence by individual members	Onset of unholy marketing practices with no bounds and limits and without

	to better perform in a highly competitive business world through maximising profit margins.	of the society and the public in general to observed malpractices practiced by business executives	exception in all market segments
			Innovating ways and means to exploit the ever helpless consumer segments in Society
6.	Tolerance by the society to all forms of industrial malpractices either out of sheer helplessness or out of '*Unconcerned Attitude*' or out of ignorance of what happens in an industry	Encouragement, support and nurturing provided by the society through ignoring even apparent and obvious malpractices	Innovative inventions of many ignoble or unholy means by industrial/business houses to serve their purpose
		Total negligence of the society to all forms of unwelcome and unholy practices that ruled industries and business houses	Cashing-in on the helplessness of customers and unconcerned attitude of society
		Lack of concern for the general welfare of the society through totally unconcerned attitude towards means and methods adopted by industries to promote business interests	Business houses got wedded to innumerably large numbers of unholy means and methods to achieve their ends and executives made them an integral part of their profession.
7.	Overwhelming zest of the rest in the society towards addressing self interest even at the cost of others in the society	Catalyst for inventing different cards to be played at different market segments	Individual efficiency depended very heavily on how people would manoeuvre an issue
		Natural shift of emphasis in industries and all manufacturing units to product generation speed and operation/ process economy	Invention of innovative unholy strategies to play around in different market segments and with different customers
8.	Ever uncontrollable greed-driven desires of mankind to	Intellectuals overpowered with development biases	Development of knowledge only to serve quick

	quench self ego and to project self image (status symbols) through acquiring as many newer and different products as possible and as are made available	focussed only on self growth and self-image projection	commercialisation of the same without reference to any of the associated and/or inherent harmful side effects on workmen, people in the region and the environment whether immediate or long-term
9.	Extra heavy business pressure from business promoters and business managers on product development technologists to quickly develop newer and newer products	Succumbing of product development technologist to business pressures for personal gains	Resorting to quick commercialisation of scanty developmental/ experimental observations
		Dancing to the tune of business bosses	Incomplete development of knowledge
			Competitive launching of newer and newer products to the market in quick succession by different manufacturing units
		Product performance life-cycle or utility life-cycle (Long-term application validity) never remained a criteria for designing development experiments	Immediate application including a one-time application suitability became the only criteria for marketing a product
10.	Innovative inventions of ways and means to quickly translate knowledge under development without reference to impact/implications of practicing incom-pletely developed knowledge	Society remained ever anxious to welcome newer products	High frequency of a large number of newer and newer products entering the market at competitive speeds, many times with very short application/utility life-cycles

11.	Product and application development without knowing disposal of the same after use/ service	Society unhesitatingly continued to accept any new product or application development	Used and/or outlived product was simply discarded, ignored and thrown
12.	Strong urge to maximise business returns	Unconcerned attitude of society towards industrial activities other than their direct products in the market	Unsafe working conditions inside manufacturing premises Unhygienic living conditions in workers' colonies Miserably poor wages to industrial workers Rampant child labour Women labour hired most of the times at a pittance
		The society comfortably accepted the situation as it was made to believe that economic generation of different products that could add to society's material comforts always demands certain compromises in practices	Liberal employment of women for carrying out strenuous physical labours Highly discriminating employment and compensation practices
13.	Development of various electronic gadgets, test instruments, medical diagnostic and treatment gadgets that work on different wave-lengths and different frequencies of the entire bandwidth of the radiation spectrum	Society's concern only towards application of a product without reference to adverse side effects of using a product	Exposure to different frequencies and different wavelengths of radiation spectrum having different damage potential Working on the risk border line zone of potentially harmful radiation including nuclear radiation

	The development also included nuclear-gadgets and devices		
14.	Unconcerned attitude of Society towards industrial activities other than their direct products in the market further strengthened and catalysed industrialists' reckless attitude towards everything other than mere product generation and marketing	Unconcerned attitude of business establishments towards all types and forms of unsafe and harmful industrial work environment	Industries had a free go in all their activities
		Work environment safety issues remained at the mercy of business bosses Work nature dependent heavy pollution of work environment did not catch anybody's attention	Steady increase in different types of industrial accidents
			Exposure of industrial workmen to varying types and magnitudes of work-related hazards such as physical hazards, chemical hazards, biological hazards, stress & fatigue induced workplace hazards and electrical & mechanical hazards and silent suffering of industrial workmen became a routine
			Work-nature-dependent varying magnitudes of damages to lungs, liver, intestine, eyes, ears, nasal membranes, certain vital normal body metabolisms, etc. of industrial workmen became a routine
			Injury to workmen varied from instantaneous fatality to varying degrees of

			metabolic failures causing mild to severe damages to normal body functioning that lead to varying degrees of health problems, short duration, long duration, permanent, etc.
			Steady march towards fatality due to complete loss of natural-Immunity
			Varying degrees of physical deformation and incapacitation resulting from failure of normal metabolic functions
			Negligible compensation for even permanent and major damages to workmen
15.	Work-nature dependent and industry-practice dependent pollution of both micro-and macro-environment	Liberal emission of poisonous and harmful gases to the environment	Industrial workmen and people in the immediate vicinity of industries became direct victims of exposure to toxic vapours and harmful gases
		Diffusive nature of gaseous matter Steady traverse in all the directions depending on the direction of wind drift	All forms of life on earth including man, animals, plants and other micro- and macro-organisms find it difficult to breathe the contaminated air as they cannot live comfortably due to varying degrees of interference with the normal body metabolism.
		Steady and long exposure to toxic and poisonous vapours and gases	
16.	Total negligence towards side effects of toxic and poisonous emissions, discharges, and wastes, etc.	Liberal and unrestrained discharges and/or disposal of toxic and poisonous gaseous	Industrial workmen became the first direct victims of all forms of malpractices practiced by manufacturing units
			Direct exposure to all sorts of adverse and unhealthy

		emissions, toxic effluents, washouts and solid wastes, fine particulate matter etc. in and around the work premises	work conditions ensured a steady fall in workmen's health
		Heavy contamination/pollution of breathing air in the work premises	
17.	Society remained a silent spectator for total unconcerned attitude of both development technologists and industrialists towards exploring and/or evaluating all other associated aspects and/or adverse impacts of their processes and process outputs on the surrounding environment	Steady butchery of the serene virgin environment with no concern for the same by anybody	Serene virgin environment became the immediate next victim
			Materials and machinery used in many abandoned projects, except where an alternative outlet readily existed, were simply thrown in the open or dumped in the backyard
			Merciless dumping of industrial debris, non-salvageable process wastes, etc. to the land either at the backyard of the premises or away from the premises or dumped in the sea wherever there was scope for the same
			Huge mounds of industrial debris came up at many places including public places in and around industrial towns to remain as an eyesore for some sensitive people
		Many industries ensured that their liquid effluents and discharges are stealthily channellised into nearby water bodies to keep	Uncontrolled discharge of highly contaminated process fluids, effluents, washouts, etc. to the land
			Pollution impact horizon literally moved away from industrial premises wherever there was scope

		their premises clean	for the same to cause harm to even those who were not part of the industry
18.	Carrying out scanty development works to generate highly non-reliable data to extrapolate and project unknown phenomenon particularly regarding long-term adverse impacts of their aggressive contribution to environment pollution and attended harmful effects	Uncontrolled discharge of highly toxic effluents to the land and nearby natural water bodies	Transformation of most of the natural water bodies including underground water bodies totally unfit for drinking Direct victimisation of animals, birds, all forms of mobile and migratory macro-organisms and economically weaker sections of the society which cannot afford to drink processed water Transformation of large chunks of natural land into barren land due to total elimination of natural micro-flora and micro-fauna of the region
19.	Highly biased development to induce short-term soil productivity enhancement at the cost of long-term irreparable damage to the natural soil	Temptation to liberally use readily available synthetic chemicals to mercilessly pump the same to soil for quick and/or enhanced return	Transformation of large belts of virgin fertile land to virtually barren land that can no more support natural flora and fauna and becoming unfit for growth of natural vegetation
20.	Uncontrolled and senseless meddling with virgin nature under the cover of experimentation for knowledge generation and/or under different development pretext	Temptation to liberally meddle with nature for some form of immediate gains including certain (occasional) hypothetical gains	Frequent occurrence of manmade near natural disasters and calamities Steady change in natural weather and climatic cycle.

21.	Liberally widespread exploitation of scarce natural resources	Heavy demand by the society either directly for some form of precious but scarce natural material or indirectly for a product made using the same	Nature steadily got deprived of most of its precious/scarce treasures!
			The posterity is totally robbed of its treasure and deprived of its rightful entitlement to *Nature's Gift including denial of the* virgin natural environment.
22.	Liberally widespread and uncontrolled environment pollution	Steady change in Nature and Natural Environment	Steady increase in the earth's atmospheric temperature adversely affecting people all over the world
			Liberal proliferation of certain toxin generating macro-organisms in tropical countries.
			Frequent flash floods, landslides, change in weather and monsoon pattern, change in natural vegetation pattern
			Drastic change in natural biodiversity and the eco-balance of the environment triggering many newer health and food problems
			Extinction and/or heading towards extinction of many virgin vegetative and micro- and macro-bio-species
	Denudation of forests and drastic reduction of earth's green coverage		Forests became inhabitable for many virgin wild life and other forms of macro-life and forced them to steadily migrate to cities, towns, villages and other human habitats in search of food and safe shelter;.

			Steady decrease in natural immunity levels of people culminating in frequent succumbing to different forms of illness
			High economic costs to the society to maintain normal good health
			Environmental change induced steady change in living habits of people and their social life (See Figure 1.2)
23.	Society's failure to recognise observed ecological changes as a result of deteriorating environment's health	Deterioration in natural environment's health started taking its toll in the society	Many live members of the virgin eco-biosphere underwent mild to violent degrees of mutations or metabolic changes and deformations for their own survival, in turn, making it difficult to manage for the rest of the bio-life on earth including man, animals and plants as a result of severe non-compatibility with normal life pattern and/or life process.
			Perennial struggle between different members of the virgin bio-sphere and changed bio-sphere for survival
24.	Steady butchery of virgin nature and nature's configuration	Total tolerance by the society	Evolution of new micro-organisms including evolution of a host of new human-health-impacting pathogenic micro-organisms evolved due to steady mutations resulting from steady ecological changes
			Never ending, ever growing necessity to identify and/or develop

	newer bio-active organic molecules to fight the hitherto unknown newer forms of health problems originating from newer forms of micro and macro-organisms

Realisation

The society was overpowered with uncontrolled desires for material comforts for a long time. Most unfortunately for the society, this desire is ever growing and ever exponentially. Such desires ruled all forms and types of social activities as well as corporate activities. Naturally, this situation did not permit the society, for a long time, to critically examine and dissect the ways and means followed by industries and other business establishments for achieving commercial breakthroughs and performance achievements. With the advancement of knowledge and its percolation to different levels in society, intellectuals started exploring corporate activities from holistic perspectives, uninfluenced by the uncontrolled desire for extra material comforts. This intellectual exploration resulted in society's steadily becoming more knowledgeable about many associated unwelcome aspects of corporate activities. The society soon realised that industrial activities are generally abreast with both welcome aspects and unwelcome aspects (Figure 1.2). However, the society could not overcome its desires for enhanced material comforts for a long time to interfere in industrial activities and their methodologies. Manufacture and supply of general utility products including hi-tech electronic add-on-comfort products continued unabated without much reference to most of the associated adverse effects. The net result is that the society landed itself at apoint-of-no-return.

Catalysts for Corporate Malpractices

Industries and business corporates always remain under heavy pressures from different corners. The following are some of the key factors that exert heavy pressures on business establishments. Each of these pressure fronts carries a high potential to catalyse different forms of corporate malpractices. The unconcerned attitude of the society provides an extra incentive for proliferation of the same and catalyses the process. When the entire scenario is examined from holistic view points, we realise that most of them would be practiced in connivance with each other though not publicly admitted but practiced with mutual consent and concurrence of varying degrees between investors, investment managers and shop-floor executives as may be appropriate to the type of malpractice.

- ➢ Fast changing technology environment.
    - o Development of technology at galloping speeds to push the one that is being currently practiced towards obsolescence.
    - o Fast changing demand for newer technology and infrastructure up-gradation.
    - o Fast changing demand for skill updation to match technology innovations.
    - o Fast changing demand for higher finances and other resources to address the requirements of developments and innovations taking place in the area of technology.

⇩

Good inducement for making quick bucks

(Target Group: Enterprise Managers/Investment Managers)

- ➢ Fast changing market and social environment resulting from ever growing competition.
    - o Competition induced need for better trained skill power.
    - o Competition induced heavy brain drain.
    - o Competition induced demand for higher wages and compensation packages.
    - o Competition triggered ever increasing demand from customers for price reduction.
    - o Competition triggered ever increasing demand from customers for immediate product and service delivery.
    - o Competition triggered ever increasing demand from customers for better service provision.

- o Competition triggered heavy demand for better performing products.
- o Competition triggered heavy demand for newer technology products.
- o Competition triggered ever growing demand from business investors for better returns.

⇩

Triggers many unholy practices across the organisation
(Target Group: Business Managers)

➢ Competition triggered ever growing demand from the ever sensitive society for higher investment in social development and infra-structure development activities.

- o Heavy pressure to earn higher profits.
  - Heavy pressure to reduce product or service generation costs.
  - Heavy pressure to make the product/service more appealing and price-wise highly competitive.
- • Options explored: Increasing productivity coupled with reducing generation costs.
- • Options examined further: Reduction in product/service generation life cycle with reduced manpower and reduced consumption of inputs materials and services.

⇩

Induces many unholy practices across the shop-floors
(Target Group: Business Managers)

➢ Heavy pressure/demand from enterprise managers for:

- o Increasing productivity.
- o Reducing production cost.
- o Increasing efficiency and reduce staff.
- o Reducing product generation life cycle time.

- o Innovating and upgrading technology and to ensure absence of technology obsolescence.
- o Identifying highly profitable products that can capture the market and bring better returns.
- o Strengthening and boosting market goodwill.
- o Enhancing product quality and meeting customer demands.
- o Ensuring quick delivery and ensuring immediate service to customers

⇩

Each and every individual shop-floor executive would be tempted to invent, innovate and identify a novel means of cutting short some of the procedural steps and sequences, skip some operations, etc.

Catalyst Promoters

Shop-floor malpractices are further promoted by some of the following factors which are generally ignored while exerting extra production pressure on shop-floor executives.

- Job dissatisfaction among staff who can desert the company any time.
- Prevalence of high rigidity in certain operation quarters.
- Absence of freedom of expression.
- Non-timely supply of input materials and services.
- Supply of sub-standard inputs.
  - Replacement with good quality inputs not readily available.
- Outdated process facilities.
- Paucity of funds.
- Not-updated technology status.
- Shortage of skilled manpower.
- Worker absenteeism and skill inadequacy.
- Brain drain and staff turnover.

- Workers' reluctance to stretch working hours.
- Migration of trained and skilled people.
- Short supply of critical input materials and other service provisions.

Net Result

All these inducement forces collectively manifest themselves in one or more of the following forms of corporate malpractices:

- People would innovatively identify that facet of knowledge including part developed and/or part understood knowledge that can leverage some unholy results or leverage competitive advantage.
- People would invariably look for some form or other of escape route from legal clutches/social issues which divert their attention from production activities.
- People would innovatively identify wrong methods to do right things and to leverage quick commercial advantage.
- People would invariably identify unholy means for handling unacceptable by-products and process-wastes and rejects of business activities.
- People just do not bother about any of the hazardous process-wastes and other hazardous process-inputs and other materials that carry high risk-potential while storing and/or handling or while disposing them off.

  None of the safety-precautions are taken care of and personnel-protection gadgets are never provided to workmen. Safe design and safety-infrastructure is not heard of by anybody.
- People innovatively invent means to conceal different types of shop-floor mishaps and process mishaps. Most of the times even the next executive would not even come to know about such things.

Sensitisation Movement

Intellectuals who realised the adverse impact of corporate malpractices on the workforce as well as on the environmental health felt an intense desire to build a strong public opinion against all types of corporate malpractices with a view to bringing a global change in the manufacturing environment and approach towards product generation and management. Building a strong public opinion that would ensure that all manufacturing premises would get transformed into fully workforce friendly as well as environment friendly is an onerous task. The difficulty stems from the fact that the general public comprises of very broad cross section of people with varied personal and/or group interests. The highly stratified social structure also contributes to such interest variance. We should not forget here that the general apathy, tolerance and unconcerned attitude of self-centred general public is one of the key reasons for prevalence of many unacceptable practices in many spheres of life including in corporate environments (Mruthyunjaya, 2013).

Building a public opinion against certain practices/operations is actually a conscience building movement. Like many other conscience-driven international movements, this movement also aims at sensitising people across the entire world regarding rampantly prevalent unacceptable and unholy practices of different manufacturing and/or product or service generation activities which carry a high potential to cause harm or damage of varying degrees and magnitudes to people around and the society in general. Such a sensitisation mechanism is, therefore, basically building a consensus-driven approach towards industrial/corporate activities and their outcome through careful observation of all activities and to identify if there are any, unacceptable, hidden or latent malpractices associated with them and to draw the attention of many more people in the society by raising an immediate alarm against the same and to ensure that together they resist such practices.

This movement has a central theme to eradicate all sorts of unacceptable practices associated with and/or prevalent in manufacturing and product generating environments to give the required relief to society. With a view to meeting this end-purpose, it works towards achieving the following key objectives:

- Creating a global awareness among conscience intellectuals in particular and the public in general regarding various unacceptable and unholy aspects normally associated with different product generation, distribution and management

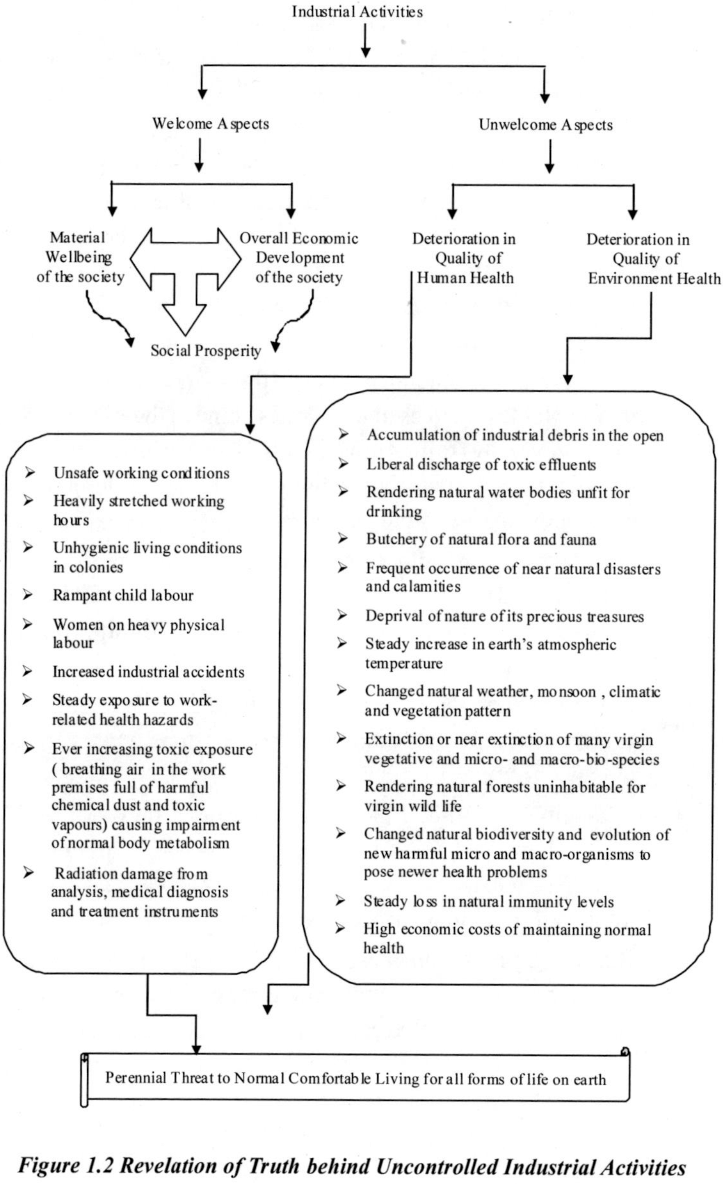

Figure 1.2 Revelation of Truth behind Uncontrolled Industrial Activities

practices followed by different manufacturers and their adverse effects on people and environment.

- Highlighting the unhealthy and unacceptable aspects associated with those activities that carry high potential to leave an adverse impact on people, the surroundings, and the environment (either immediate or long time) and creating awareness in people on those issues.
- Building an internal drive (conscience development) in people to consciously look for such unacceptable practices and trigger the process of further sensitising a larger cross section of the society on the issue with a view to building high-magnitude pressure on corporates to refrain from unacceptable practices and save the mankind.
- Sensitising the general public to the extent, that whenever unacceptable practices of corporates come to their knowledge, they never refrain from sending warning signals to manufacturers, that the society would not tolerate their hazardous/unacceptable practices.
- Sensitising all manufacturers regarding normal performance requirements of their operations and activities by building the necessary public willpower clubbed with appropriate monitoring controls.
- Educating people regarding highly desirable conditions, environment and omissions and commissions while carrying out an activity.
- Educating the general public to ensure that they realise that unless they exert necessary pressure business corporates and industries, unhealthy, risky and unacceptable practices continue to prevail in all industrial premises.
- Educating people on these issues is a very arduous task. It calls for great patience and perseverance attitude from those concerned. As indicated earlier the key reason for this situation is the configuration-complexity of different cross sections of the society.

- Educating the general public to ensure that they realise that unless they exert necessary pressure on business corporates and industries, unhealthy, risky and unacceptable practices continue to prevail in all industrial premises.

Hassles

Sensitising the general public cannot be readily achieved through mere conveying and/or communicating certain relevant, useful and/or important information or data to the public.

In order to achieve success in this activity, social scientists and technologists have to successfully tunnel through many powerful fortresses and barricades across the society. Each cross section would have built its own unique fortress founded on its own perceptions, views, interests and priorities, evolved and entertained based on its own cultural, educational and socio-economic backgrounds. As such, each of these cross sections offers different types and natures of resistance in building a powerful, convinced force, committed with a clear conviction, to fight all forms and kinds of industrial/corporate unholy and unacceptable actions, operations and practices and save the society. Social scientists and technologists have no option but manage to surmount all these hurdles. Table 1.2 gives a brief description of the different types of barricades offered by different cross sections of the society.

Sensitisation Process

This activity needs to be carried out in two stages. The first one is to convince all the intellectuals across the society and then to approach and/or appeal to other cross sections of the society. Though intellectuals do not constitute a bulk cross section in the society, they do pose major hurdles because of their all powerful fortress. But winning over of this smaller cross section of the society is very crucial and critical for achieving true progress and success as this specific cross section of the society belongs to the category of people who make things happen essentially because it is this cross section of the society that normally guides, directs and controls the rest of the society in all key areas and aspects of public life.

Table 1.2: Types of Barriers encountered by Conscience Building Movement

Sl. No.	Fortress Owners	Key Barriers		Nature of Resistance
		Fortress Category	Nature of Barricade	
1	Intellectuals	Professional Biases	Ego Filters	Intellectuals tend to believe that the knowledge generated and/or being communicated is too inadequate from true knowledge viewpoints to convince them on the issue.
			Command Filters	Hence they do not recognise the many associated limitations of others in generating more data on the issue being conveyed. Therefore they would not be prepared to receive the message being conveyed.
		Personal Biases	Comfort Filters	Intellectuals would invariably love to receive a message the way they would love to practice it by applying their own interpretations, explanations and emphasis and from their own professional and/or personal comfort view points and perspectives about the issue in a way that suits them best.
			Opinion & Impression Filters	Depending on their own exposure to different aspects of knowledge of different subjects and areas, intellectuals tend to build their own personal views, opinions and impressions on the message being conveyed and ascribe professional competence limitations of the technologists who have generated the data and information being communicated.
				As such, they would not receive the message in its true perspectives.
2	Capital Investors & Shareholders (A select cross section of the general public)	Investment Biases	Monetary (Return) Filters	The primary interest and key concern of this category would exclusively be the net monetary return from capital they have invested.
				Other forms of returns including name and fame would also be of some concern as long as it would not be at the cost of net monetary returns.
				Would not be interested in any system till it starts openly digging into its basic credibility and profitability

3	Investment managers or Enterprise managers (A select intellectual cross section of the general public)	Performance Biases	Business Turnover	This is a unique category that is primarily concerned with net business turnover and net business returns.
		Expenditure Biases	Tight Control over Expenses	Tight war against all forms of expenditures including investing on certain basic facilities and to hold them at minimum levels
				Would be least anxious to establish any system of administration and management that does not directly add to profitability and that may not discredit them.
		Credit/Acclaim/ Image Biases	Name of the Industry in the Society	Returns for this specific group is not limited only to monetary form but also includes forms like personal names, fames and global acclaim for self but would always hesitate to proceed with anything that demands additional investment.
			Complex Return	
4	Suppliers (A select cross section of the general public)	Performance Biases	Monetary Returns	Interest is confined exclusively to net price/profit realised for goods/materials/facility or services supplied
		Credit Biases	Credit Complex	Equally interested in making big name in the field but not at the cost of monetary returns.
		Competition Biases	Commercial Advantage	Interested in leveraging the competitive advantage
				Least concerned about any of the activities of the company
				But would definitely welcome any management/administration system that can add to their comfort levels.
5	Process Managers & Activity Managers (A select cross section of the general public)	Performance Biases	Enhanced Efficiency and Productivity Filters	Interest is confined exclusively to net credit and accompanying benefits and monetary returns realised for goods/materials/facility or services generated
		Credit Biases	Credit and Accompanying Monetary and Benefits Returns	Would be least interested in practicing any other system of operations that would not directly add to productivity.

6	Employees (A select cross section of the general public)	Monetary Returns linked Performance Biases	Competitive Merit and Advantage Gained	Interest confined only to leveraging merit and/or situation to competitive advantage of self. Not bothered about other issues.
				Interest confined exclusively to net monetary returns with minimum efforts. As such allergic to all forms and types of add-on works that cannot bring extra returns.
		Net Benefits linked Performance Biases	Cumulative Benefits Returns	Concerned exclusively with performance efficiency improvement linked returns
				Centred only on all forms of benefits, both direct and indirect or monetary and perks, derived from the employer and nothing beyond
				Other activities would be considered only if they add to net benefits and returns
				Least concerned about taking up any other non-remunerative activity.
7	Customers (A select cross section of the general public)	Net Competitive Advantage and Merits	Direct Monetary Advantage and Benefits	Interested exclusively on holding their purchase prices at minimum levels
				Concerned only with net performance advantages from goods or services purchased
				Net overall higher competitive benefits in the market.
8	The Public (The bulk of the general public)	Totally unconcerned Attitude	No Barrier what-so-ever	This cross section of the society that constitutes the bulk of the general public is least participative in company's activities.
				Dedicatedly concerned with just its own affairs and interests
				This section neither supports nor resists any movement.
9	Local Society	Different Social and public Establishments	Overall Benefits	The general society is concerned with overall benefits it derives from an industry/corporate in terms of employment potential for local talents
				Liberal contribution from corporates to the overall welfare of the society and the region
				Would insist that corporates meticulously follow all the norms set by the society
				But would appreciate the corporate establishing all types of good administration and management systems.
Which particular cross section of the general public is specifically concerned about harmful side effects of some industrial/corporate activities or their output?				

People can be placed in three classes: The few who make things happen; The many who watch things happen; And the overwhelming majority who has no idea what has happened.
- N.M. Buttler.

The goodwill of intellectual cross section of the society can be achieved only through intellectual appeal with as much quantitative and verifiable data as practical together with well established or well recognised 3D models or image projection.

- The objective of educating the general public should be to convey the following key information to them, though it need not be confined only to the following information. Any other useful information and/or data that intellectuals feel would help in readily convincing the general public could also be included:
  - o Detailed information on unsafe practices prevalent in manufacturing environments with specific reference to those components that carry a potential to cause harm to human (workforce) health.
    - In contrast with this, desirable safe practices should also be highlighted for each of the unsafe practices explained above.
  - o Information on the harm potential of industrial activities should include the following:
- Nature and magnitudes of harm and its variation limits where quantified.
  - ♦ Wherever the impact is visible or obvious and apparent, how it can be seen or identified.
  - ♦ When and where all should one look for the same.
  - ♦ When should one look for indicative signals and signs.
  - ♦ How to check the impact coverage width and magnitude.
  - ♦ How long does the effect of impact persist and how to check its active-life-cycle.
  - ♦ How to measure the harm magnitude.

- Qualitative explanation or description of the nature of harm wherever quantitative data is either not available or not practical to generate.
    - Wherever the impact is not directly visible but the impact is obvious how it can be identified or recognised.
        - By a feel or through observations of something happening elsewhere.
        - What type of observations should one make to identify the impact.
        - Do these impact-affected centres give any warning signals to indicate or announce that they are affected.
        - Wherever the impact centre lies elsewhere away from work station or work centre how to recogninse its coverage profile.
        - How to evaluate its active-harm-potential-life-cycle and harm magnitudes of indirect impacts.
- Examples of similar impacts and their presence or feel.
- Wherever the harm impact is not spontaneous but becomes effective or noticeable only after some time, what are the signs one should look for during the period before such delayed effects make their presence notably felt or glaringly visible.
    - How to identify and recognise delayed impacts.
        - Can the harm-impact magnitude be measured.
        - If so, how to measure.
    - How long such delayed impacts persist and how to identify that the impact effect has ceased to persist.
    - Wherever the delayed impacts take place, what happens between harm incidence and impact appearance.
    - If the impact is directly on human beings, what type of damage it can cause.
        - What is the degree or intensity of the impact.
        - How long does the impact persist.

- If repetitive or multiple incidences resulting in multiple exposures take place, can it cause any permanent damage to any of the natural organs of the body.
  - Can the same incident cause any damage to any of the natural body metabolisms.
  - How long such impaired condition of body metabolisms persist.
  - Do those impaired metabolisms need external rectification/correction programmes or would they undergo self initiated auto-corrections and do those impaired metabolisms positively respond to rectification programmes to render the life-cycle once again normal.
  - If so how effective they are.

o Even if a person does not directly encounter or get caught in a situation that can directly cause harm, can the harm be still caused because of other changes taking place in the surroundings and the environment.

o Building an internal drive (conscience development with a clear conviction) in people to consciously look for unacceptable practices.

Thus, when translated to action, this movement refers to generating a committed society that has a strong desire and an equally strong will-power to root-out all malpractices to cleanse the industrial environment with a view to transforming the entire society and the social environment to become safe, healthy and friendly for a normal comfortable living for everybody. This is achieved through the following latent objectives behind the movement:

➢ Creating a social environment where unsafe, unholy practices of industries and business corporates that carry high adverse-impact potential, have no place.

➢ Sending severe warning signals to all manufacturers that they should attend to certain safety and other unwelcome aspects of their operations.

- Sensitising all manufacturers to safety requirements of their operations through building necessary monitory public pressure on them.
- Ensuring that manufacturers understand and realise that unless they build appropriate response to safety demands of their activities and operations they would be wiped out of business.

Sensitivity Base

Any cross section of the society, at any given point of time, comprises of people of widely varying age-groups. Therefore, any cross section of the society would encompass a wide spectrum of intellectuals with widely differing exposures to prevailing realities of different aspects of life, and with an equally wide spectrum of personal interests, priorities, approach and attitude. As such, any attempt to create a ready impact on the minds of people in the society would prove futile unless such an attempt is able to appeal to the conscience sensitivity of public intelligence. Such an attempt has to be an intellectual appeal. Any sensitisation movement, therefore, should have a firm intelligence base. An intelligence base, in turn, can be developed only with established and well proven facts and figures.

Since the concept of *Public Sensitisation* is triggered from a *Knowledge* that emanates from the after effects of industrial malpractices and their proliferation as can be seen and/or practiced across the industrial world, its evolution also follows the typical three stage development as followed by knowledge evolution (Mruthyunjaya, 2011) (Figure 1.3).

1. Conceptualisation
2. Nucleation
3. Crystallisation

These three stages should, automatically, lead intellectuals and the concerned cross sections of the society to an action point, a result of effective sensitisation.

Similar to the mechanism of *Knowledge Evolution*, the *Knowledge* that governs industrial growth and prosperity, knowledge that periodically emanates from industrial malpractices and its proliferation is also an ever continuous, transformative evolution process. Here, the concept of ever continuity has its roots in the following reasons:

- Knowledge that guides and operates behind many newly innovated types and kinds of industrial activities is always ever continuous in nature.
    - o Therefore, provision and/or means and opportunities that are open for associated malpractices are also ever continuous in nature.
        - Naturally, the knowledge that gets generated from all those newer methods and means of industrial malpractices is also ever continuous in nature.
- The data or the information on different aspects of undesirable impacts on either the workmen in particular or on the environment in general is not a one time fully generated data.
    - o Different aspects or facets of different types of adverse impacts of industrial malpractices on people or on the environment get periodically unfolded and expounded.
        - Impact-knowledge also gets generated periodically in tune with newer observations made.
- Conclusions drawn and inferences made on certain impact-obsererrvations could by themselves undergo minor changes and/or refinements as and when finer elements/aspects of certain theories and/or hypotheses are better understood.
    - o Impact-knowledge also gets periodically refined in tune with refinements made in understanding, and/or applying relevant theories.
- While some observations are obviously visible and their impacts could be identified almost instantaneously with the incident, some observations can be identified only after a lapse of some time, whether on workmen or the environment.
    - o Full bandwidth of delayed impact-spectrum may not become identifiable concurrently. The same could be understood in stages.
        - Impact-knowledge governing a delayed appearance of an impact also gets added-up only with some time-gap and probably in stages.

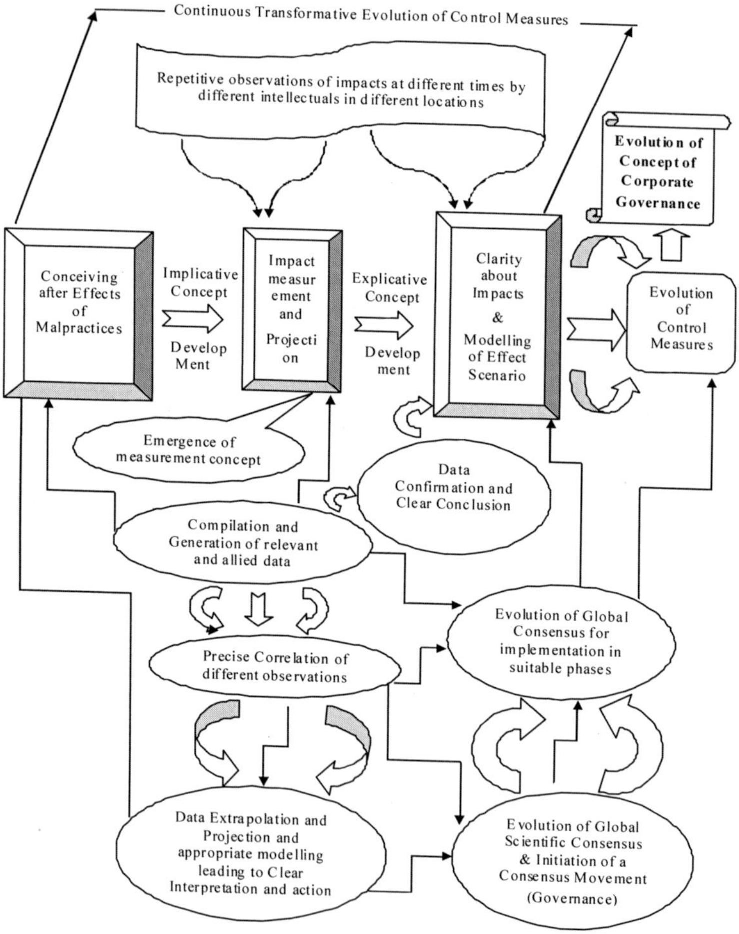

Figure 1.3 Evolution of the Concept of Corporate Governance

- o Impacts of some other incidents are cumulative and complexly interdependent in nature such that it may not be practical to precisely define the number of independent incidents and their relative individual damage component in an overall observed damage situation.

- Impact-knowledge gets generated in bits and pieces making it difficult to present a comprehensive impact-knowledge package.

- In the absence of an established direct correlation between certain observations and corresponding malpractices' incident, associated impact-knowledge also would not become immediately identifiable.
    - o There could always be a time gap between incident occurrence and understanding the impact nature and profile.

Thus, all the three stages of *Concept Evolution* namely, conceptualisation, nucleation and crystallisation add-up newer dimensions to their development profile. Such periodical additions of newer dimensions at some unspecified intervals make it an ever continuous phenomenon.

It is also for this reason that it is not practical to draw a precise demarcation border line between these three stages of concept evolution.

Conceptualisation stage, basically, comprises of the following steps:

- ➢ Careful observation of all types and natures of corporate activities with specific reference to their associated unhealthy and unacceptable elements or practices carrying varying degrees of risk-potential.
- ➢ Repeating those observations as many times as practical and at as many different locations and at as many different times as practical to ensure that no element of chance error or individual biases enters the observation cycle and the inference there from to render the same non-reliable. Also to confirm that the observed unacceptable malpractice does not belong to one time exceptional category to ignore the same but actually a regular practice.
- ➢ Further ensuring that observations are made by as many different intellectual teams as practical to build a large cushioning factor to those observations that would nullify the contribution from individual and personal errors.

- Doubly ensuring and confirming that observations are free from all sorts of omissions and commissions and influence from external parameters.
- Suitably segregating and grouping corporate activities into appropriate categories based on their adverse-impact potential and nature.

  Basic grouping or categorisation could be as follows but need not be confined only to these. Any other logic developed based on scientific facts and acceptable to a larger cross section of the intellectual society, could be applied for this purpose. Basic guidelines could be the risk potential, nature and magnitude of associated risk, life-cycle of the risk and the risk impact-horizon.

  i. Activities which are ever abreast with adverse-impact potential.
  ii. Activities that can create an immediate adverse impact.
  iii. Activities that would certainly have an adverse impact but only over a period of time and cannot be noticed spontaneously or immediately.
  iv. Activities that can create an adverse impact depending only on the magnitude/concentration/dosage, degree of inherent impact potential and/or duration of exposure to those unacceptable environment conditions.
  v. Activities that would adversely impact only those workmen who directly handle the activities or physically present in the immediate vicinity of the work centre and not others.
  vi. Activities whose adverse impact horizon is confined only to the work centre or premises and not beyond.
  vii. Activities whose adverse impact horizon extends beyond the manufacturing/work premises.
  viii. Activities where impact profile or horizon cannot be precisely identified because of its diffusive nature.
  ix. Activities which can cause severe to major damage and/or permanent damage to workmen if not either averted or not appropriately handled.

x. Activities whose adverse impact extends beyond the manufacturing/work premises and is readily seen or felt.

xi. Activities whose adverse impact extends much beyond the manufacturing/work premises but not readily seen or felt.

Nucleation process takes-off from this base. The following are some of the key steps that contribute to thought nucleation.

- Correlation of different observations coupled with detailed analysis of the data/observations to interpret the data based on available scientific facts to understand the phenomenon and to identify the principle that governs all those observations of after-impact effects.
- Identification of the principle that governs all those observations of after-impact effects.
- Translation of the guiding principle (behind observations and the data) to identify the indicative and/or latent meaning (outcome of malpractice) that could emerge from those observations.
- This is further supplemented by similar interpretations and similar inferences drawn by different teams for similar contextual operations and/or for similar observations made under different but equivalent and/or allied situations of impact-effect.
- Applying all the available knowledge in the field and projecting the indicated and/or latent meaning or outcome to visualise a somewhat hazy picture of *What Happens in this Specific Situation of Impact Scenario of Malpractice* over a broader impact horizon.
- The next crucial step is essentially a theoretical/scientific exercise of extrapolating the data to carefully project the impact trend on a time scale to arrive at most likely outcome, namely *What Could Happen* if similar impact creating situations continue to prevail uninterrupted for a long-time.

Crystallisation stage takes-off from such a scientific projection and reasoning followed by a visualisation. Following steps play the key role at this stage.

- The first key step is also a theoretical exercise.

  Computing and preparing different but precise mathematical models to embrace the entire bandwidth of impact horizon with specific reference to each of the individual constituent members using different permutations and combinations of available theoretical inputs and concepts to precisely project the outcome of the situation and quantifying the same on a relative time scale.

  Modelling and quantifying the impact on various elements/ constituent components of the impact horizon with specific reference to *pros and cons* as related to varying degrees, severity and durations of the specific situation under consideration.

  Careful examination of these mathematical models by the entire scientific community across the world with the help of different theoretical inputs to identify and select the most realistic model that would represent the situation to project the most likely outcome of the phenomenon or the specific situation under consideration on a time scale.

  Computing and preparing consequential impact outcome models for all the affected members of the regional or global biosphere as may become necessary.
- Segregating those observations that do not carry any ambiguity and uncertainties together with their relevant data to conclude about the outcome of the situation.
- Generating necessary support data through suitably designed and carefully conducted simulation experiments, where practical and where desirable and to confirm the inference drawn from different mathematical models.

Outcome of Concept Evolution

We can thus see that *Crystallisation* stage that evolves from conceptualisation followed by nucleation embraces two distinct activity spheres.

i. The first impact sphere stands for all those inferences that do not carry any element of uncertainty and ambiguity due to their inherently obvious nature, directly visible or felt. These inferences can be drawn almost in situ with the incident.

a. Therefore this category of inferences could be easily conveyed to the general public without much difficulty.

b. They do not pose any problem in initiating the necessary action plan.

ii. The second impact sphere stands for all those inferences which carry a certain degree of in-built uncertainty due to limitations in understanding and interpreting the data and due to the fact that projecting a precise 3D model of their outcome is fairly complex. As such, arriving at a consensus scientific reasoning and visualisation also is a delayed process.

a. It is not easy to readily convey these inferences to the general public in the society. One has to struggle very hard with great perseverance to do so.

b. Adequate base work needs to be carried out to prepare a conducive reception environment among the general public.

This stage, thus, provides the required intelligence base for social scientists to initiate the process of building desired public opinion and consensus on various issues and observed phenomenon and industrial malpractices. Through incessant efforts these social scientists could build a strong conscience-driven public opinion in the society.

Net Revelation

With the evolution of social intelligence and social conscience, intellectuals across the society recognised some of the following striking facts that emanated from the *Net Result (Revelation) Column* of industrial malpractices shown in Table 1.1:

- Safety of industrial workforce is always under severe threat.
- Accidents taking place in industrial workplace causing varying degrees and magnitudes of damages to the workforce are not properly addressed.
- Work environment would pose severe challenges to health of industrial workforce
- Rampant child labour prevails.

- Women are engaged for carrying out heavy physical labour.
- Industrial workforce does not get compensated commensurate to their contribution to growth of industry.
- Industrial work environment parameters carry a high potential to pose severe challenges to maintain good health of the society.
- Gaseous emissions from industries carry a high potential to cause acid rains that causes severe damage to natural eco-system, vegetation pattern and soil fertility.
    - Natural flora and fauna find a way towards exit and total disappearance.
- Comminuted, carbonaceous and other fine chemical particulate matter oozing-out from factory chutes/exhaust towers, deposit on historic and architectural monuments to pose a severe threat to their aesthetic appeal.
- Toxic industrial effluents and discharges carry a high potential to spoil the quality of water bodies and to pose a severe threat to the very survival of aqua-life and to render natural water unfit for drinking.
    - Only weaker strata of the human population animals and the helpless bird folk drink this highly polluted toxic water and continue to suffer.
- Industrial process parameters carry a high potential to spoil the health of the environment.
- Some of the industrial process parameters carry a high potential to spoil the health of global environment.
- Deterioration in the quality of global environment causes severe damage to configuration of the virgin nature.
- Damage to virgin nature, in turn, steadily alters all processes of Nature.
- Climatic changes in the global environment, in turn, severely damage the natural biosphere on earth.
- Changed, rather damaged, natural biosphere, in turn, results in dangerously harmful multiple mutations of many micro and macro-bio-species to pose a perennial threat to normal comfortable living of man and all other forms of life on earth.

Response of the Society

Birth of Basic Concepts - Corporate Governance & Corporate Social Responsibility

Once these revelations were made and social scientists and technologists worked strenuously towards building global awareness about corporate hazards and ensured that a good degree of social conscience is developed in the society, the bulk cross section of the society conceived the same to build certain convictions about realities of industrial/corporate life, again with specific reference to associated harms and hazards, whether direct or indirect or whether immediate or long-time and cumulative. Societies had to respond to the situation and control the situation to ensure overall safety and welfare of the population.

Ready response from societies faced certain hurdles in the beginning. All societies encountered one common problem of uncertainties and ambiguities associated with many of the inferences drawn from a dissection of unwelcome industrial activities. Further, even in the case of many obvious inferences, it was not practical to prove and evidence the adverse impact on the spot or on a clearly defined time scale. This was primarily because they belonged to the category of *Indirect-in-Nature, Slow-in-Nature and/or Slow-and-Cumulative-in-Nature* and escalation of the situation depended exclusively on the intensity and duration and also frequency of occurrence of such incidents. Further, modelling of 3D images/pictures of the most likely non-desirable outcome-situation on a time scale was further complicated and was not practical because the impact and its magnitude also depended on many other variable surrounding parameters prevailing at different incident time intervals. Elimination of all associated uncertainties was, therefore, not as simple as conceived and projected. Therefore, the society found it difficult to directly buy many of the inferences which environmental scientists and technologists had arrived at since a direct correlation and relation of a delayed impact to a specific corporate activity was not available. Scientists and technologists could also not readily come to the rescue of the society in this regard. All these issues compounded together, rendered the situation a fairly complex one for the society to handle and respond spontaneously in spite of the fact that it was seriously concerned about the same.

Left with no alternative, the society had to go slow and cautious on these scientific observations, inferences and projections. However, it did not find it difficult to readily embrace those inferences that were very obvious and were totally free from all types of uncertainties and ambiguities. All societies started responding positively on these areas and aspects. Some societies responded fast and some took a little more time depending on their socio-economic and cultural backgrounds. In fact, all societies across the world did not simultaneously work on these areas. Societies, whose socio-economic and cultural backgrounds were favourable, designed and formulated necessary controls to prevent industries/business corporates from some of the known misdeeds and malpractices. Some other societies carefully watched the effectiveness of control measures that were practiced in other societies and learnt from their experience before implementing similar or improved measures at their own place.

However, as explained earlier under creation of a *Sensitivity Base,* all the three stages of conceptualisation, nucleation and crystallisation do not belong to the category of onetime process leading to a onetime action plan. All these stages are ever continuous and ever evolutionary processes. As such, additional data and information that would further support some of the inferences drawn earlier would keep getting generated continuously. Similarly, as the technology advances, new observations would also be made leading to newer inferences necessitating newer control measures. Societies also started responding to those additionally-strengthened inferences and additionally generated newer inferences in stages and in phases at suitable intervals.

Societies soon realised that mere designing and formulating appropriate control measures and providing necessary guidelines would not serve much purpose in effectively controlling unacceptable practices of industries and business corporates and the basic objective would get defeated. True take-off action point demanded an enforcement mechanism to derive associated benefits and to give necessary relief to society. Necessities for an enforcement mechanism, in turn, lead all societies to free the process from all forms of uncertainties and ambiguities of freedom of choice. Appropriate legislative norms and guidelines together with control/assurance measures were formulated and put to mandatory practice.

When industrial activities are examined from the view points of enforcement of controls, we realise that they embrace two inseparably integral activity spheres. One of them refers to *practice methodology* purely from technology translation view points of achieving set corporate goals and the other one refers to the details of actual *execution methodology* followed. The two activity spheres are complementary to each other and together they address the pre-set business purpose.

It goes without saying that pre-defined goals of industries/ corporates can be met by a set of activities only when they are designed in accordance with the technology that governs those activities. Governing technology provides the necessary norms and control measures for designing and conducting those activities. If those activities are not carried out precisely as per technology norms, they do not yield expected results and the exercise becomes futile. As such, their controls are invariably identified internally by concerned industries based on governing technology being practiced. Therefore, those activities do not need any external control measures. In fact, no industry would accept external controls on their technology practice as the same is generally considered as confidential information of the organisation. Also, if an external control authority or administrative agency attempts to enter the technology domain, the authority or the agency would be lost in an ocean of total confusion and chaos. Such a control is neither practical nor desirable or required. While it is generally believed that technology translation methods do not normally change with many of the visible parameters, in reality it is not totally so. Following are some of the *Parameters* that could influence some of the finer details of technology translation methods as well.

- Changes in Practice Environment.
- Changes in Skill Level Variation and/or Advancement.
- Changes in Infrastructure Environment and/or Advancement.
- Changes in Time Induced Demand for Performance changes.
- Changes in Technology Environment.
- Changes in Socio-economic Environment.

Each one of these variable parameters carries a high potential to adversely affect objectives of industries with special reference to productivity and profitability. But corporates would never like that their goals should get defeated. As such, industries would, immediately, re-design their technology translation methodology and refine the same in tune with impacting parameter.

Naturally, external control authorities should look into only the finer elements, rather, lapses in execution methodology with specific reference to unwelcome outcome that can periodically creep into operations and could keep varying over a wide range of entire activity spectrum. Since it is only the society that decides about unwelcome nature of an activity and operation lapses from broader sociological perspectives, society alone should decide about acceptability or non-acceptability aspects of corporate activities. This is the key reason for why certain types of industries are allowed to be established only in some pre-identified or pre-notified areas and not in any place at the sole discretion or choice of business promoters.

On a careful examination of corporate activities from broader perspectives, one would realise that there is an inseparable intricate relationship between business corporates/industries and the society. Such an inseparably integral relationship renders the same as mutually accountable and responsible to each other. It is this aspect of mutual accountability and responsibility that gives rise to the birth of *Corporate Governance* and *Corporate Responsibility* concepts.

Figures 1.4 – 1.7 explain different facets of interdependence and/or interrelationship between the society and a business corporate. As can be seen from these schematic diagrams, the intricacies associated with the practice methodology provide the necessary base for the concept of *Corporate Governance (Ruling a situation with authority to enforce control measures).* Similarly, the means of expressing corporate gratitude towards society for all the favours and support it has received from the society has given rise to the concept of *Corporate Social Responsibility!* These two concepts namely *Corporate Governance* and *Corporate Social Responsibility* could be described, respectively, as the reactive component and the pro-active component of corporate response to social demands. The concept of reactive component stems from the fact that the society positively wants elimination of all unwelcome aspects of corporate activities and therefore mandatorily enforces certain performance guidelines and requirements through appropriate control mechanisms. The concept of

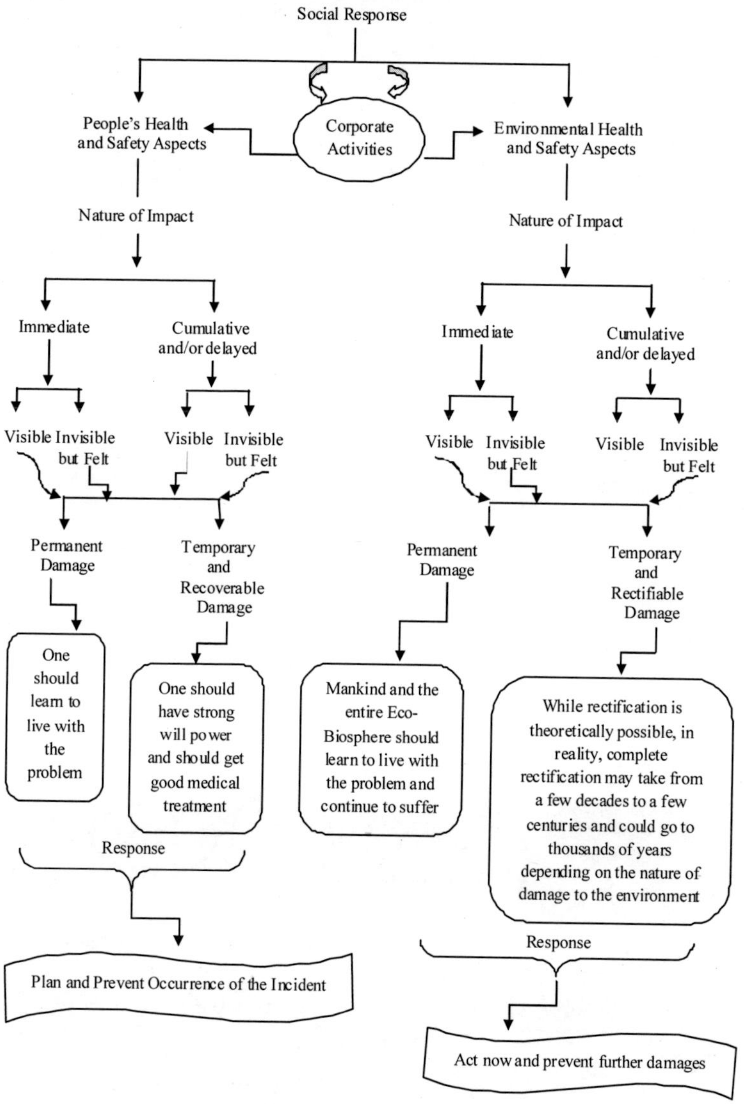

Figure 1.4 Response of Society to Unacceptable Practices of Industries

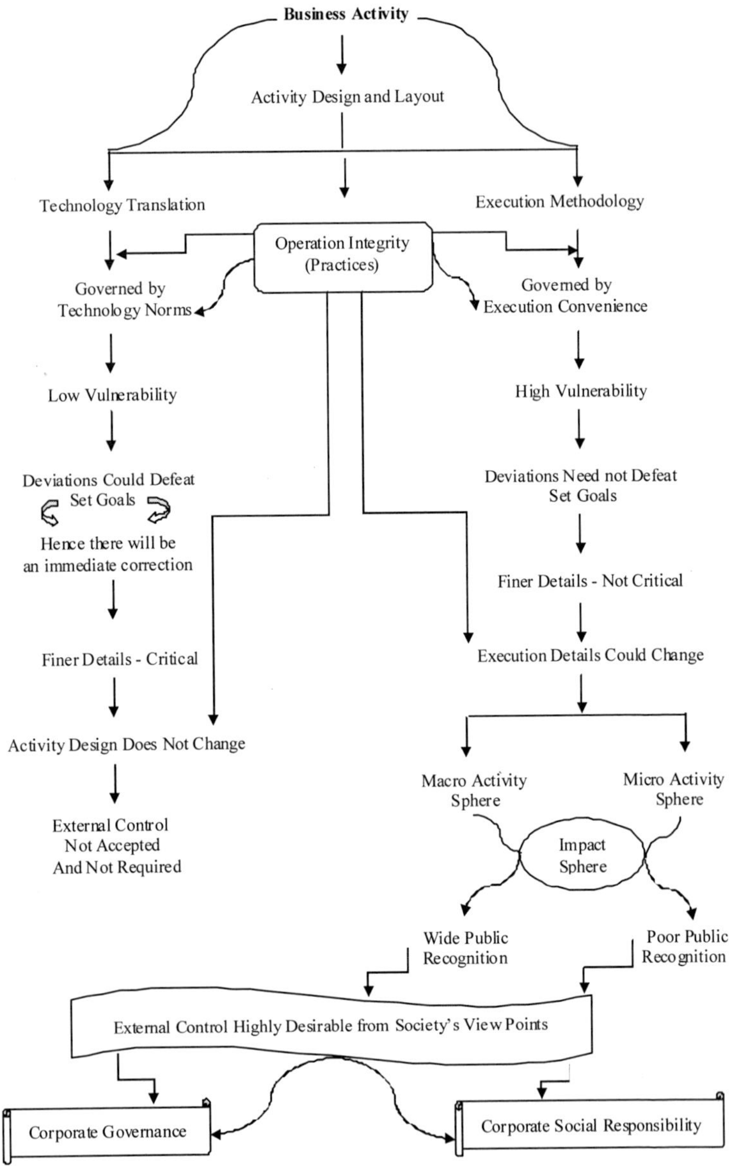

Figure 1.5 Vulnerability Potential of Business Activities

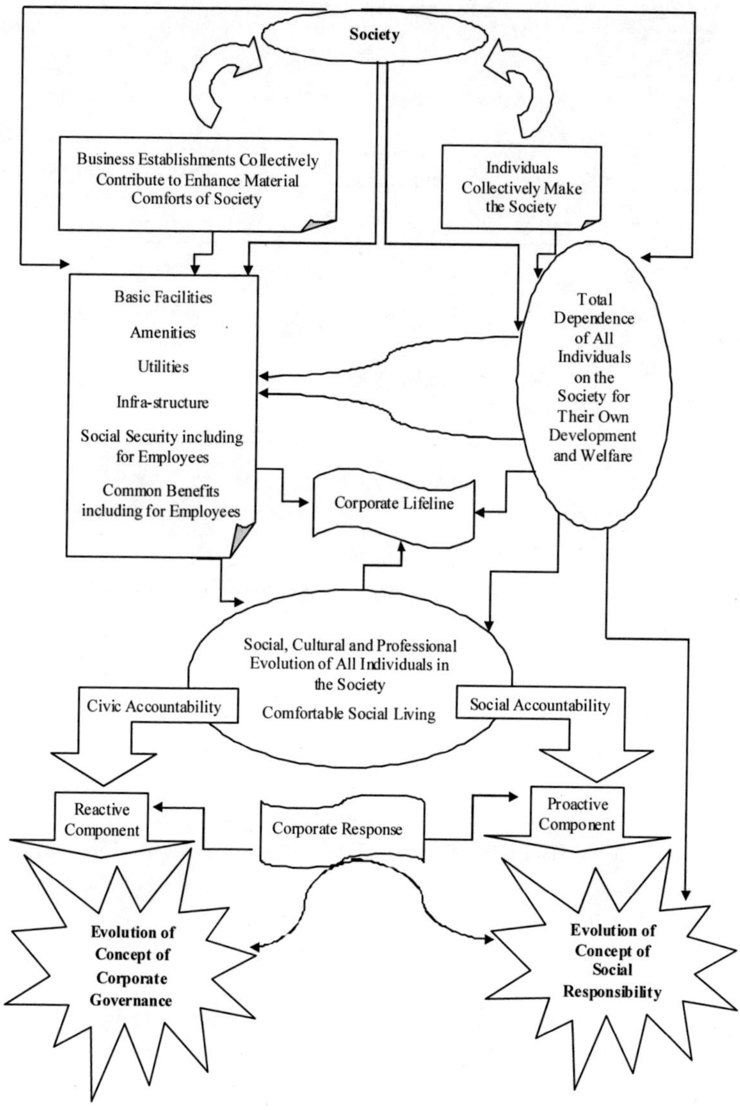

Figure 1.6 Total Dependence of Corporates on the Society Nucleates the Concepts of Corporate Governance & Social Responsibility

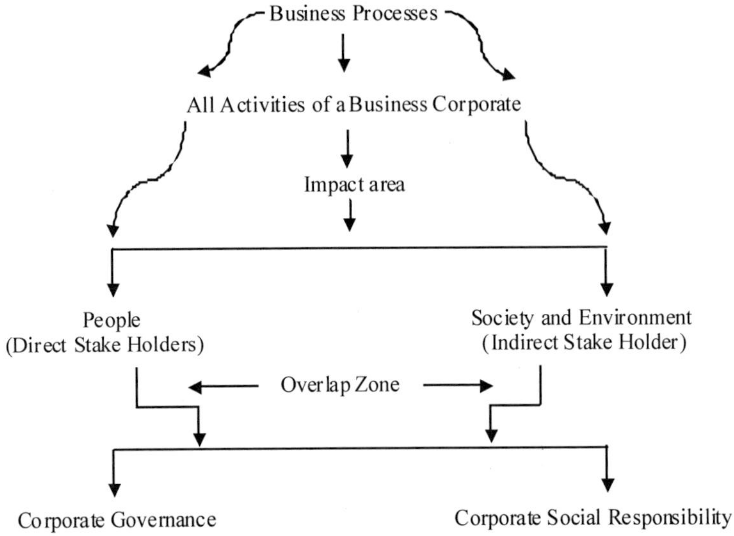

Figure 1.7 Impacts of Business Processes Trigger The Concept of Corporate Governance and Social Responsibility

pro-active component stems from broader perspectives of general social wellbeing and social welfare. Such broader social perspectives have their roots in the fact that industries and business corporates totally owe their very existence to the society and draw very heavily from the same and hence in order to ensure satisfactory maintenance and sustained continuity of social infrastructure, corporates have to liberally contribute towards those causes. While the implementation of the governance aspect does not pose much problem because of its mandatory nature, the practice of social responsibility aspect remains far from satisfactory as it continues to remain voluntary at the discretion of business corporates. However, of late, societies are seriously exploring means to ensure positive and committed participation of corporates in social development and welfare activities through suitable legislative directives and guidelines.

Regarding mandatory aspects of performance requirements, societies readily embraced following two basic categories of corporate activities that carried high potential to adversely affect the immediate workforce or the surrounding environment and/or the general public and necessary statutory guidelines were framed.

a. Apparent category:

- ➢ Poorly designed and poorly managed and very casually handled work conditions that lead to accidents and/or loss of health of industrial workforce.
- ➢ Poor compensation to the industrial workforce coupled with poorly designed pattern of hiring the workforce.
- ➢ Poorly designed and poorly managed and very casual handling of proven/established dangerous/risky operations and/or handling, storing and disposal of toxic and poisonous materials.
- ➢ Liberal discharge of toxic and/or poisonous effluents and emissions.

b. Latent category:

- ➢ Merciless exploitation of *Nature and Natural Resources* that has lead to slow and steady deterioration in environmental health, which, in turn, has lead to a host of other unwelcome outcome.
    - o Steady deterioration in normal health levels of people.
        - • Steady surfacing, including occasional outbreak, of many newer forms and types of diseases.
            - \- A result of steady changes taking place in micro-bacterial and macro-organisms' life-style and order.
    - o Perennial search for newer bio-active organic molecules to fight newer micro-organisms and also to erase the menace of newer macro-organisms.
    - o Steady increase in the cost of normal living on earth.
    - o Steady changes in global climatic pattern.
        - • Steady changes in natural vegetation pattern.
            - \- Changes in micro-bacterial life-style and order
            - \- Changes in natural soil micro-flora and micro-fauna.

→ Changes in food habits and social order of global population

- Totally robbing of the posterity of its natural right to Nature's Precious Gifts.

Societies soon formulated and put to practice many legal stipulations (acts, rules, regulations and guidelines) to control and administer satisfactory system of corporate activity management.

However, as explained earlier, with the passing of time and with gaining of more experience with the mode of operations practiced by different industrial establishments, the data and/or information on different aspects of corporate activities to be covered under formal rules, regulations and control measures steadily got expanded. Requirements grew several fold. Many more unforeseen and not-anticipated types of unacceptable practices crept into corporate activities. Societies soon realised that corporate malpractices were not confined only to a few well understood areas directly related with production and/or manufacturing environment but also to a wider spectrum of activity profile that had not at all been visualised earlier as carrying any potential for malpractice.

Over a period of time many more malpractices came to the knowledge of the general public. These areas, though were not directly affecting the health or safety of the workforce or the surroundings, were greatly affecting the morale of both the workforce as well the general public. Some of the activity areas under this newly invented category belonged to one or more of the following:

- Fraudulent Accounting Practices

  Inaccurately prepared balance sheets of companies prepared exclusively to give a wrong presentation of companies' working and performance, under billing/overbilling of products and services; false reporting of stocks; false reporting of profits; Fraud in provident fund, gratuity and/or pension money and their records; under valuing/over valuing of assets; showing false income; showing imaginary receivables; showing false/ highly inflated expenditure; manipulating stocks in trade, etc, etc..
- Fraudulent marketing practices including marketing of dangerous and/or potentially harmful products.
- Direct or indirect involvement in different kinds and magnitudes of spying against other commercial establishments.

- Financing anti-social activities, directly or indirectly, knowingly or unknowingly, with specific intention or out of sheer helplessness in the hands of some people or organisations.

None of these was an acceptable situation to the society. Suitable control measures had to be introduced. Societies did not shy away from shouldering their increasing responsibilities. More and more amendments to established legal norms and stipulations were framed and introduced as and when situations/work-practices/work environments warranted the same.

While the area of work-conditions-related or manufacturing-environment-related aspects did not pose much problem for framing and introducing necessary legislative measures/controls at appropriate stages, bringing all the activity areas related to deteriorating environmental health and associated impacts on the general public did pose many hurdles. Societies had to go through many platforms to manoeuvre some of these situations. Wherever direct correlations were not practical, societies had to pass through different national and/or international, intellectual and/or administrative consensus-development forums before introducing necessary legislative control measures. Global societies are still to achieve complete success in this area.

Thus, in conclusion, we can say that, in a broad sense, the two basic concepts, *Corporate Governance* and *Corporate Social Responsibility* embrace the following two broad activity spheres.

Corporate Governance:

- Abidance to norms and guidelines set by the government and other local administrative bodies for the activity purpose.
  - o Should uphold all norms set by the government for environment protection and health and safety requirements or any other norms as may become applicable to the product/by-product/service/activity at all stages including generation, handling, storage, packing and transportation.

    Achieved through:

    - Establishing a strong performance base for the corporate.

- Establishing fair means of product/service generation and distribution with equally good fair practices across the corporate.
- Creating safe and healthy work environment.
  - Equipment design and layout should be such that operation ergonomics is well taken care of.
  - Ensuring that people have necessary education and training in handling processes.
  - A high degree of automation is introduced wherever monotonous repetitive movements are involved.
  - Lifting and movement of heavy weights is organised through suitable mechanised operations that have been approved for their safe working.
  - Activity area should be well lit as per lighting standards. Brighter and more reflective colours should be used rather than glaringly brighter lights. Activity area cleanliness is well maintained.
  - Good ventilation and free flow of natural air is provided wherever natural air is allowed. Otherwise, good, breathable-quality filtered air should be provided.
  - Breathing air should be maintained free of all types of airborne respirable chemical dusts and other suspended particulate matter, fumes, chemical vapours, smoke, mists/aerosols, suspended droplets, obnoxious/toxic/pungent gases, etc.

Corporate Social Responsibility:

➢ Guarding the genuine interests and/or requirements of the society, both local & global, and the mankind as a whole.

  o Ensuring that moral ethos of the society and the general public is not jeopardised through their operations and activities or output.

Achieved through:

- Conserving Social Wealth and Developing Infrastructure.
- Conserving Nature's Precious Resources.
  - Taking utmost care to ensure that all resources are very conservatively used and very productively engaged in generating only useful output.
  - Conserving nature's wealth through development and adoption of resource conserving technologies.
  - Educating the society to conserve nature's wealth by judiciously demanding for newer products.
- Protecting Environment and Promoting Environmental Causes.
- Preventing Greenhouse Gas Emissions.
- Protecting Ozone Layer.
  - Controlling contribution to ozone depletion, green-house gas emission, developing and adopting clean technology to avoid generation and emission of green house gases.
- Respecting Posterity's Right.
  - Upholding nobility of the eternal universal value system namely all ensuing generations on earth *(the posterity)* has as much right to enjoy and benefit from natures' bountiful gift as the present generation has.
  - Ensuring that none of the natural product is exploited till the end but ensuring that the posterity is not robbed of its right to the same.

The Fillip

Although the spade work done by intellectuals and sociologists from across the world, did initiate the concept of *Corporate Governance,* it did not take-off in a big way for long. However, economic liberalisation and globalisation of trade and technology across the world changed the scenario and this movement received a big boost in most of the organisations that went aggressively in globalisation programmes. The changed business scenario intensified interactions between industries and business establishments from different parts of the world for pursuing a common cause of growth and expansion. Such interactions, in turn, lead business establishments to realise that differences in work methodologies and work philosophies and also the work environment, if any, could pose many hurdles for a smooth sailing in the long run. This realisation, in turn, induced business corporates to establish good governance mechanism.

Organisations started demanding this requirement from their venture partners or from their collaborators. International business cooperation and transactions also catalysed this process. The net outcome is that many business establishments are seriously working towards designing and establishing good corporate governance systems. Sarbanes-Oxley Act of the U.S. which was formulated for restoring public confidence in companies with regard to saneness and honesty (soundness) behind all their activities, whether product generation or marketing, gave the necessary forceful support for practice of good corporate governance in companies.

Corporate Governance

Views of Different Schools of Thought

The interest in the subject of *Corporate Governance* is universal in nature. This is basically because, whether or not a person is directly interested in a business corporate and its activities, a business corporate always caries a high potential to create an impact on a large cross section of the society. Yet, it is hard find a common consensus among different cross sections of intellectuals regarding the description of *Corporate Governance*. The key reason for prevalence of such a situation is the fact that different schools of sociologists and social ethicists view this subject from different perspectives. Perception alignment between different schools is not practical because each school would have explored this subject in the background of prevailing social, education and cultural background of the local society. As such, different schools identify different aspects as integral to corporate governance. There is a wide variation in the degree of emphasis laid on different aspects of *Corporate Governance* due to widely varying differences in the cultural, educational and socio-economic backgrounds of different societies across the world. Similarly, different cross sections of global intelligentsia dwell into different depths of constituent components of *Corporate Governance.*

However, all schools agree that a good governance system would bring the following advantages to the corporate:

- Ensures good stability and competitive growth of the company.
- Builds a high degree of confidence and trust amongst present and prospective stakeholders.

- Investors do not hesitate to pay a higher premium especially when governance practices are on par with best known international norms.
- Ensures a significant reduction in potential risk levels and a consequential reduction in capital cost and thus enables the directors of the company to take quick and better decisions that could result in quicker growth of the company.
- Ensures long-term sustainability through sustained growth and strong stakeholder relationship.
- Company's image is always held high in the public.
- Ensures a highly respectable status in the society.

It is a well established fact that socio-economic development status prevailing across a good cross section of the society moulds the impressions and opinions of sociologists and social ethicists regarding impacts of corporate activities on the society. At the same time, it is also an equally well known fact that there is a wide variation within many micro-and sub-micro-cross sections of the same society in terms of its socio-economic development status as well as in terms of its educational and cultural development status. Very unfortunately, such micro and sub micro variations prevail across all regions of the world to make it almost the order of global society. Naturally, socio-economic-cultural integration across the world is far from the reach of sociologists and social ethicists! Variations in their perspectives continue to prevail and the phenomenon of corporate governance has to continue to develop in this background of widely differing perspectives.

Let us examine the following popular descriptions from different schools of thought regarding corporate governance:

1. *Corporate Governance* embraces the area of how corporate activities are designed, conducted and regulated, consistently at all times in such a way that it satisfactorily addresses the requirements of its stakeholders.
2. *Corporate Governance* is a set of systems, processes and principles which would ensure that governance of the corporate would be in the interests of all its stake holders.
3. *Corporate Governance* is a well defined frame work under which the board of directors as well as administrators ensure that satisfactory accountability, fairness and transparency prevails in all its decisions and actions.

4. *Corporate Governance* is a system of rules, practices and processes that direct and control the governance mechanism to achieve satisfactory balancing the interests of all its stakeholders.

From these descriptions it becomes clear that the concept of *Corporate Governance* is, by itself, a subjective area and provides for accommodating as many useful concepts as practical under its fold.

Let us examine the following description form yet another school:

> "*Corporate Governance* is a work discipline in corporate governance means and methods that keep constantly reminding all its senior managers that their actions and behaviours should be such that it is universally recognised and accepted as correct and proper."

When we examine this description, we realise that it opens-up a totally flexible, boundary-less open-ended approach to the subject. And it is this thought that enthused many sociologists and social ethicists to explore this subject from globally wide considerations to bring everything under the sky under its coverage.

The fifth description, particularly the use of two adjectives, namely *Correct* and *Proper,* provides so much scope for interpretation that it is hardly possible to specify and/or prescribe a set of activities that one could readily embrace under the head *Corporate Governance.* Further, it is this boundary-less approach that renders the subject 'more subjective than what it should be' for any business corporate to put to practice. Such a global coverage has also induced many intellectuals to play around a few idealistically hypothetical issues and to examine corporate activities from those hypothetical angles. Naturally, this was not what was expected by those who conceived the concept of *Corporate Governance* and propagated the same. Post SOX (Sarbanes-Oxley Act) era has given rise to emergence of one more description namely corporates can display good governance practices through good corporate citizenship, environmental awareness and concern and through good ethical practices. Published literature on business ethics clearly tell us that good ethical practices always stand for good governance practices (Mruthyunjaya, 2013).

Evolution of CG Components

We have seen above that one basic fact that stems out from these descriptions is that *Corporate Governance* is essentially a system of rules, regulations and guidelines set by a corporate for itself to govern the mechanism of administering and conducting all its activities in such a way that its practices always uphold certain basic performance requirements of satisfactorily addressing its stakeholders' requirements. Here, the description 'performance' invariably refers to that aspect or area of corporate activity profile which has no direct relationship with either product generation or its distribution but stretches far beyond these two areas.

All corporates know for themselves as to what they should do for improving their product generation process and what should they do for capturing a larger segment of the market. These are the bread winners for all corporates and they do not look for a lesson from sociologists or social ethicists in this regard! In fact, sociologists and social ethicists enter the fray only to handle this area of great vacuum which corporates have not looked into seriously.

This is the starting point for the evolution of the concept of corporate governance. We can further see from the above descriptions that with "Stakeholders' Interests" at the centre of focus, the first stage of evolution of constituent components of corporate governance represents five key aspects shown in Figure 2.1. This is the first breakthrough in the evolution of the concept of corporate governance.

Sociologists did not stop at this. They continued to explore these five components to examine whether they could be further strengthened by incorporating some more features to support them and to ensure that the concept of governance would better serve the purpose for which it was originally conceived. Different schools probed this area from different perspectives and identified a few more components which they felt would further strengthen the basic purpose. These schools strongly opined that *Corporate Governance* should stand for governance of all corporate processes based on ten specific aspects shown in Table No. 2.1.

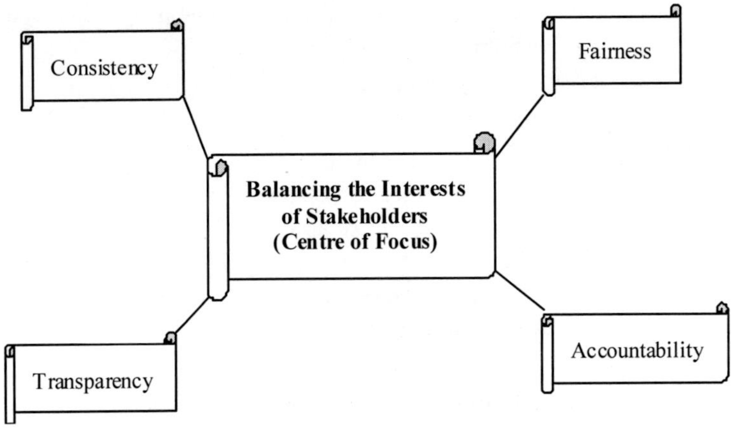

Fig. 2.1 Key Components of Governance

Table 2.1 Second Phase of Evolution of CG Components

Sr. No.	CG Components
1	Clear Strategy.
2	Work Discipline.
3	Effective Risk Management.
4	Independence.
5	Transparency
6	Responsibility
7	Accountability
8	Fairness
9	Social Responsibility
10	Self Evaluation

Basic Premise

These ten aspects have been identified based on the following premises:

- o Unless a proper work discipline prevails to bind everybody to follow set procedures and guidelines, organisations cannot pursue their strategic approach towards market capturing, product development, productive financial management, developing market goodwill, etc.

- Origin of the concepts of *Work Discipline* and *Strategic Operations*.

o Business strategies also include effective risk management and decision independence because in the absence of these two criteria, corporate decisions and actions may come under heavy influence of vested interests of a hand few of its senior executives or major shareholder groups and such conflicting interests could lead to a miserable performance in a globally competitive market environment.

- Origin of the concepts of *Effective Risk Management* and *Decision Independence*.

o In the absence of the concept of transparency, namely allowing independent competent authorities to critically examine all decisions and actions of executives and ensure that they are free from all sorts of personal biases and interests, organisations cannot hold their executives accountable for their actions and performances/results. In such situations, business prospects itself would be at stake.

- Origin of the concept of *Transparency*.

o If corporates have to enforce concepts of responsibility and accountability to their actions and performances in the direction of achieving corporate goals, the element of transparency should be fused to corporate activities to help them in independently verifying their actions and approaches and to ensure that they are free from biases and vested interests.

- Origin of the concepts of *Responsibility* and *Accountability*.

o In order to continue to perform well to achieve competitive excellence in an ever dynamic and globally challenging market environment which is flooded with innumerable numbers of hi-tech-driven products and services resulting from ever potential and evergreen innovative technological breakthroughs, corporate decisions and actions have to remain, forever, free from all sorts of biases, favouritisms, creating situations that ensure unfair advantage to a selected few people, groups or organisations.

- Origin of the concept of *Fairness*.

o A business corporate is an integral entity of the society. Therefore, as consciously good citizens of the society, corporates have to reciprocate the favour they receive from the society and remain forever non-discriminatory, non-exploitative and ever sensitive to environmental issues and human rights' issues.

- Origin of the concept of *Social Responsibility*.

Incidentally, this concept also incorporates the post SOX description of environmental awareness and concern and also good ethical practices.

o Irrespective of the degree of meticulousness and the execution discipline with which corporates pursue their objectives in an ever vibrant and ever dynamic global market, there could always be an element of failure associated with their decisions and actions. And, as soon as they realise their failure and trace it to some mistake committed at some point in the execution chain, they should immediately respond positively to the situation and correct their mistake and strive to better their performance.

- Origin of the concept of *Self-evaluation*.

If we carefully examine these ten aspects or requirements of corporate governance and compare them with the first set of elements stated earlier, we do realise that they are not different from the first set of five elements in their true meaning and scope of interpretation. The second group of ten requirements either re-identify themselves with one or more of the first five elements or get integrated with one of them as schematically shown in Figure 2.1.

Concept Correlation

Let us briefly examine each one of these concepts.

o Consistency in operation and performance levels can be achieved only when people follow certain strict work discipline superimposed with periodical review and self correction to fine tune their operation strategies.

- Thus, the three elements of *work discipline, operation strategy* and *self evaluation* integrate with the concept of consistency.

o The concept of accountability can prevail only when people assume full responsibility for their non-interfered (unbiased) decisions and actions. Accountability for performance results calls for effective risk management and reformulating operation strategies based on self evaluations as and when required.

- Thus, the concepts of *responsibility, independence, effective risk management, self evaluation* and *operations strategy* all integrate with the concept of accountability.

We can, thus, see that there is not much difference between the first set of five elements and the second set of ten elements that different schools of sociologists and social ethicists have evolved independently. All of them are inter-related in a true sense of their application scope and profile and none of them can be completely independent of others to be effective. It is just an issue of interpretation and explanation. Foregoing discussions, thus, help us in realising that irrespective how the constituent components of *Corporate Governance* are viewed by different schools of thought, it is essentially built around the central

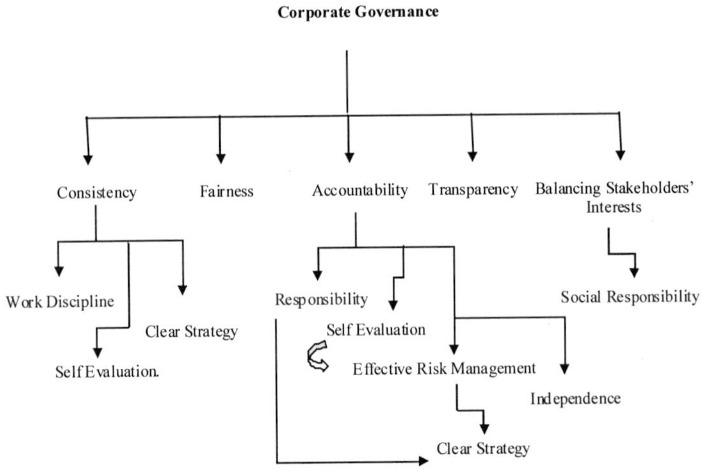

Figure 2.2 Integration of Basic Concepts of Corporate Governance

theme of upholding certain basic values of the society together with ensuring that the basic comforts of society are never put at stake.

A Realistic Approach

When we explore the subject of corporate governance from the viewpoints of feasibility of its direct translation to regular practices and actions, we realise that none of the constituent components of governance identified earlier, could be verified for its satisfactory compliance status because most of them are highly subjective both in interpretation and in scope. Therefore, neither the corporates can claim to satisfactorily address the requirements under any of the constituent components of governance, nor the few sociologists who vociferously advocate them and are seriously concerned about it. Though it is very unfortunate for the very concept of governance, it remains a harsh truth of reality. Therefore, unless either the society or corporates themselves identify an area that could be comfortably verified and ensured for satisfactory implementation or for satisfactory compliance, and also simultaneously address the requirements of most of the governance elements, the phenomenon of corporate governance would continue to remain a hypothetically wishful desire of a small intellectual cross section of the society!

Fortunately, however, knowledge society has not kept silent on these issues. It has been continuously exploring different facets of knowledge and has been evolving means and methods to identify types and nature of different types of adverse effects of corporate work environment, work methods/practices and their outputs including some of their unwanted outputs can have on people working inside corporate premises and also outside in the society. To counter all those adverse effects, knowledge society has been evolving different mechanisms, from time to time, to ensure general welfare of people and the society. It started framing different guidelines to help corporates in satisfactorily addressing the needs of the society. Many rules and regulations were framed and legalised through legislative approvals. Thus, emerged many acts, rules and regulations to be complied with and the concept that corporate governance is a system of legal compliances which direct and control its activities! These rules and regulations embrace practically all aspects of a good, comfortable social living. Further, the society has always been conscious and is suitably responding to corporate realities and has addressed most of the issues that periodically make their presence felt. These rules and regulations are framed in such a way that they embrace a very broad spectrum of corporate realities' profile with respect to social life and collectively they ensure that many of the requirements of corporate governance elements are fairly well addressed to ensure welfare of a good cross section of the society.

Therefore, though *Corporate Governance* has always remained a subject for debate among intellectuals and sociologists and social ethicists due to prevalence of different and divergent views on this subject, in common parlour, it is generally understood as standing for sincere abidance to all applicable laws and legal processes of the land that could be formally administered, operated, regulated and controlled. The key reason for this approach to the subject of corporate governance is that unlike most of the other areas, this description does not give scope for uncertainties and ambiguities regarding compliance to requirements. Abidance to laws and satisfactory compliance to the same can be independently checked, verified and audited by suitably trained system auditors. Periodical audit verification would generate a base for identifying activity areas that pose threat to law abidance and/or established norms of the society, and that are required to be carefully controlled. Such audits, popularly known as diligence audits, would also help in identifying activity areas that carry good potential for further improvement in law abidance provision.

Element of Uncertainty

According one of the thought schools, *corporate governance is a system of structuring, operating and controlling the activities of a company with a view to achieving long term strategic goals with respect to the following four key aspects*. When we carefully examine accomplishing these four aspects we realise that all of them are ingrained with a high degree of uncertainty. The element of uncertainty here refers to our inability to measure precisely the degree of accomplishment of meeting the requirement on a well defined scale which can be cross verified by any other person and confirmed to be an accurate measure. All these measures are only qualitative and just descriptive and therefore are subjective measures. We also know that when the measure itself is subjective, it would always remain a debatable issue. People would always have a question mark on its reliability.

i. Satisfying the needs of its direct stakeholders:
   a. Investors/Promoters/Business Partners/Financial Partners/ Shareholders.
   b. Financiers – Banking institutions who function as transient or financial partners with limited interest.
   c. Enterprise Managers (Investment Managers or Business Managers).
   d. Employees.
   e. Customers.
   f. Suppliers.
   g. Public Infrastructure Administrators.

ii. Complying with statutory regulations and norms as applicable to the operations and activities of the corporate, and as amended from time to time, provides corporates an opportunity to express its concern to society and mankind and keeps the morale of people always high. Not only that, a good system of compliance to all the requirements of statutory guidelines prepares the necessary background for establishing a good governance system.
   - Enables people to feel proud of their organisation.
   - Enables people to feel proud of their own social conscience through expressing respect for the law of the land.

iii. Complying with the requirements of environment protection as stipulated by law and the society.
   - Giving an extra comfort to the society.
   - Addressing the requirements and expectations of ensuing generations.

iv. Addressing the requirements of the local community.
   - Keeping the society comfortable and happy.
   - Fulfilling conscience commitments to the society.

Generally, the first one of these strategic goals starts with just a qualitative description. However, organisations should not stop at mere qualitative descriptions but should transform all the subjective elements (qualitative descriptions) to objective parameters (quantifiable and suitably verifiable parameter). Wherever only qualitative descriptions prevail performance compliance cannot be properly administered. Similarly, performance achievement cannot be confirmed or certified due to the fact that any such attempt would just be an expression of personal opinion of the individual.

When a system administration mechanism itself cannot be defined with desired clarity of process, clarity of purpose and above all a measure of outcome, it is just not practicable to ensure fulfilment of activity purpose with any degree of certainty. This is where sociologists and social ethicists had to get back to technologists to identify a satisfactory administration mechanism. The following descriptions give one such mechanism that can be used for transforming different subjective components to objective verifiable parameters and to fuse some degree of certainty to the process.

Quantification can be achieved by following a few transformation steps as briefly explained below:

- Understand each of the qualitative description in totality
  - o Carefully analyse and identify all the associated elements of *'Full Satisfaction"* namely those parameters, which in the opinion of stakeholders themselves can lead to satisfying each of the stakeholders' categories.
  - o Interact with a large cross section of stakeholders under consideration and generate similar views.
    - Compile the views together and statistically analyse them to identify parameter distribution among different cross sections of stakeholders.
    - Prepare cause-effect diagrams.
    - Correlate effects with causes for different impacting parameters and different levels of satisfaction.
    - Identify and arrange the best combination of causes and effects in such a way that a very high degree of satisfaction of target stakeholder category is achieved.
  - o Understand the contributory parameters/requirements of each of the associated elements namely understand what needs to be done under each of the contributory parameter

head to achieve targets on a suitably defined competitive performance scale.

- While such performance scales could also be qualitative in nature to some extent, the rating on a graded scale with specific reference to a pre-identified reference standard would always provide a base with a reasonably good reliability.

- Project performance/achievement levels on a mutually acceptable timescale.
  - o This is a fairly complicated area due to the fact that the description, performance/achievement levels' has many facets, each one representing the views of a specific class or category of stakeholders.
  - o Therefore, corporate performance is viewed not by its mere product performance and the extra popularity it has gained in the global market but precisely in terms how it has been able to meet the specific interest/interests of the stakeholder.
    - Governance process does not embrace product performance sphere but refers to *meeting of stakeholders' interests*.
- Prepare appropriate action plans that could lead to achieving projected levels.
  - o This is again not totally at the discretion of corporates.
    - Action plans should be developed, preferably in consultation with the concerned stakeholder.
    - Where practicality does not exist, it could be prepared based on suitably (statistical) analysed data output.
  - o Corporates should never forget that time element is an essential component of 'stakeholder satisfaction'.
    - Therefore, unless strict time-bound and time-targeted action plans are designed and implemented to ensure early returns to its stakeholders, stakeholders would not feel comfortable and the entire activity could go against the first requirement of 'full satisfaction' of stakeholders.

- Earnestly implement the plan.
- Periodically verify target achievement to identify gaps, if any.
    - o Analyse reasons for deviations and identify factors (processes and their individual and/or relative contribution) responsible for deviation. Quantify the relative contribution of each of the contributrory factor.
    - o Identify appropriate corrective actions to eliminate such deviations in achievement.
    - o Suitably implement identified corrective actions.
    - o Re-verify, at suitable intervals, performance and refine identified corrective actions as may become necessary.
- Generate necessary feedback from concerned stakeholders through well laid-out interactions and re-refine all the above steps to achieve set, long-term strategic goals.
    - o Stakeholders' feedback should be generated with specific reference to fulfilment of his expectations.

The next two strategic goals namely compliance to legal requirements does not generally carry uncertainty elements. These requirements could be clearly defined and prescribed and periodically refined and up-dated as and when additional knowledge gets generated. The concept of improvement in law abidance provision should, however be properly understood and correctly interpreted. This qualitative description refers to situations where the law does not specify any specific boundary line for compliance but carries a good scope for performance Betterment. This aspect of corporate governance could be described as *Conscience Promoters or Conscience Guarding Transparency.* The element of total transparency generates an environment where many intellectual inputs become possible for bettering performance levels.

The following are a few typical corporate activity areas which are not specifically covered directly by the law of the land but only under a unique administrative mechanism that aim at achieving one or more of the following objectives:

- ➢ Ensuring a high degree of social security.
- ➢ Ensuring uniform socio-economic development of different locations of the region.

- ➢ Ensuring uniform social justice across different cross sections of the society.
- ➢ Preventing continuance of butchery of sensitive environmental parameters of the location or the region.
- ➢ Minimising generation of hazardous by-products or waste-products that pose severe threat to local environment, environment health and for disposal.
- ➢ Avoiding technologies which are not energy-efficient, material conversion efficient, etc., namely avoiding resource guzzling technologies in the interest of mankind and posterity.
- ➢ Recognising and respecting environmental sensitivity issues of different regions.

A governance mechanism demands that corporates should prepare suitable action plans to address each one of these issues in such a way that people dedicatedly work on a well identified, time-targeted plans and achieve the following. It is equally desirable that such action plans are made public knowledge and periodic progress notified.

◆ Totally avoid using a technology that carries a high potential to generate hazardous wastes or by-products. ◆ Wherever it is not practicable to totally eliminate hazardous waste generation, minimise their generation. ◆ Wherever generation takes place, identify methods to dispose-off the same in an environment-friendly way. ◆ Phase out all resources-guzzling technologies and replace with environment friendly, clean and nano-technologies.	Technology Innovation

While the activities that fall under conscience promoting category, they are generally guided by administrative controls and mechanisms which have been designed to guard the overall interests of the local society from the view points of both general social welfare and also in terms of environmental welfare. These administrative control mechanisms ensure that they identify different categories of industrial activities that carry a high sensitivity against one or more of the above factors and classify them according to their region-friendly or location-friendly nature. Formal permission to establish industrial activities are accorded based only on these criteria. Naturally, some reservation categories have come to existence with the objective of ensuring satisfactory distribution of socio-economic development opportunities across different geographic locations of the region and to ensure that further interference with the local environment which has already been heavily manipulated by all sorts of human interferences. Similarly, some restricted/limited access categories also have come to existence.

Therefore, when we explore the issue of satisfactorily addressing statutory requirements and fulfilling their expectations, corporates should specifically ensure that they comply with the following two requirements which speak high of their social conscience:

- ➢ Ensure that you do not, either directly or indirectly, get into an activity (manufacturing and/or processing) which is not friendly with the local society or with the local environment or is not compatible with national or international interests.
  - o Before identifying an industrial activity for the corporate, either as a part of expansion or as a part of diversification and/or acquisition, do not hit-upon a technology which is not open for the general public, but in the interest of national security and/or social security, are reserved only for exclusive-dedication and/or captive alignment with defence establishments.
    - ◆ Identify if there are any administrative and/or procedural restrictions for your contemplated activity.
  - ◆ If there are any, make sure that you are willing to get bound by all those additional restrictions and stipulatory protocols.
  - ◆ Any non-compliance of those additional stipulatory constraints will be treated directly as a serious legal offence and necessary actions will be initiated.
- o Before finalising a technology for adoption, check whether the contemplated activities carry any regional/location

restriction tag due to the nature of activities (output product and/or intermediate product nature, input resources nature, nature of execution mechanism details, etc.).

- o Before importing a technology, check thoroughly the credibility of the exporter under consideration.

  Make sure of the following aspects:

  - No pirated technology is being exported to you.

    Otherwise you are likely to be entangled in an international legal offence/nexus.

  - Ensure that you are not tempted to import some hazardous material together with processing technology and prove yourself to be anti-national and anti-social.

    - A few exporters manoeuvre to transfer their risk and liability onto your shoulders!

      Processing of those hazardous materials could have been banned in their countries.

      Disposal of those hazardous materials could pose them severe challenges due to highly environmental sensitive nature of local population or governmental agencies.

      You should never put to risk your own fellow citizens or your serene environment.

  - Similarly, high-sea hijacking and robbery is not uncommon. Do not get tempted to purchase high-sea-hijacked equipment and machineries or raw materials that are not readily available for purchase through proper channels for many reasons including for reasons of rationing of the same by the original manufacturers/ distributors and their refusal to accommodate your request.

    You will be caught under vicious international punishable offence/nexus.

- o Before importing a technology and also the specific input to the process that is being imported, carefully check the viability of the technology and its environmental and social performance nature and status.

Social performance status here refers to involvement of inputs, intermediates or outputs that carry high potential for use in anti-social activities.

- Make sure that you are not getting an outlived and outdated technology.

  It would be anti-social basically because out-lived and out-dated technologies would be heavily material/ resource oriented and carry heavy environment pollution potential.

- Carefully check whether a technology or input raw material is already a banned item anywhere across the world for reasons like
  - Eco-unfriendliness
  - Workforce unfriendliness
  - Local society-unfriendliness
  - Natural resources unfriendliness
  - Heavy consumption of scarce natural resources, or heavy consumption of material inputs in the background of ready availability of proven-material technology conserving, clean technologies, etc. } Heavy Resource Guzzling Technology

    ⇩

    Law does not fix any cut-off levels for any of these parameters. Socially conscious corporates should work out strategies to phase-out all such activities.

➢ Ensure that you carefully identify all laws and regulations that are applicable to your activity and install a mechanism to comply with those requirements.

- o You cannot take to shortcut on basic infrastructure on environmental performance requirements.
  - If you do not have certain minimum in-house facility, people would evade such activities. You will become a non-compliant party.

- You can take help from external agencies only for some analysis purpose but not for all.

From the view points of ensuring that law abidance is consciously practiced by people, it is advisable that organisations should prepare formal documents giving details of all applicable laws together with their relevant sections, clauses and sub-clauses and also the scope of their application as applied to activities of the corporate. Wherever, there would be need or scope for preparing time targeted achievement targets, such time targeted tasks or goals should be fixed for verification.

Consensus Components

Evolution of a high degree of social conscience among the public in general and among intellectuals in particular triggered the process of evolution of the concept of developing consensus among intellectuals in general and sociologists and social ethicists in particular, as to what all should corporate governance really comprise of. This was not an easy task particularly because different schools of thought continued to view the constituent components with differing degree of emphasis. This sort of a situation of differing emphasis continued to prevail on them basically because of the wide variation in the development status of socio-economic environment of different societies across the world. Sociologists and social ethicists soon realised that it is just not practical to achieve a uniform level of socio-economic development status at any given point of time and therefore, one has to compromise on the basic issue of recognising constituent components of corporate governance and arrive at a consensus opinion on the issue.

Some of the activity areas that are considered as integral parts of *Corporate Governance* (CG Components) by different schools of thought and by a good cross section of intellectuals across the global society are shown in Table 2.2.

Table 2.2 Consensus CG Components

Sr. No.	CG Components
1.	Law Abidance
2.	Operation Integrity
3.	Conscience Keeping Operation Transparency
4.	Decision Pattern
5.	Health and Safety Aspects
6.	Compensation Package
7.	Discrimination
8.	Participative Management & Freedom of Expression
9.	Time Targeted Response Mechanism
10.	Stakeholders' Interest Protection
11.	Expansions, Diversifications, Acquisitions and Takeovers
12.	Corporate Citizenship (Corporate Social Responsibility)

While discussing these aspects of governance, we should not forget that except the first CG component namely, 'Law Abidance Aspect', practically almost all the remaining CG components (aspects) have retained their ever-live status and are always open for discussions, negotiations and compromisation. This is basically because details under any of these aspects cannot be defined and specified in such a way that it can be precisely measured and therefore cannot be challenged. Answers to each one of them are qualitative descriptions and could be arrived at the discretion of people. At the same time, very strongly divergent views on these issues prevail in the society. Therefore, business enterprises have to work towards maintaining certain minimum performance levels in these areas and continuously work towards accommodating as many additional divergent views as practical and maintain a good dynamic balance between performance levels and the expectations of the society. Most unfortunately, the phenomenon of *Corporate Governance* has to continue to live with this situation.

A very interesting observation that one could make from the ensuing discussions is the fact that most of the components of governance issues are interdependent and/or interrelated with each other so intricately that some of them can hardly have an independent existence in the absence of the other. Many times, it would even appear that practically none of them could have an independent existence. Interrelationship of some of the components is so intricate and inseparable that when one component is properly established the other one automatically comes to existence. Similarly, requirement details of some components are such that when they are satisfactorily established they pave way for smooth installation of the other component. Some components function as complementary to the other one and most of them support each other. Incidentally another interesting observation would be that if an organisation successfully goes through the establishment of all the applicable legal requirements, it would automatically pave way for easy establishment of many other governance components. Organisations should, however, not forget that establishing total compliance all the legal requirements is basic to establishing good governance system.

Table 2.3 gives a proximate correlation between different consensus, constituent components and the components evolved in earlier stages. The correlation shown in the table is just an approximate relation,

Table 2.3 Correlation Between different CG Components

Basic Components				Distribution of Consensus CG Components across Basic Components			
First level		Second level					
Component	Degree of Non-specificity	Component	Degree of Non-specificity	Component	Degree of Non-specificity	Component	Degree of Non-specificity
Consistency	High	Work Discipline	Medium	Operation Integrity	High	Conscience Keeping Operation Transparency	Medium
		Clear Strategy	High	Decision Pattern	High	Conscience Keeping Operation Transparency	Medium
				Participative Management & Freedom of Expression	Medium	Time targeted Response Mechanism	Medium
		Self Evaluation	High	No Equivalent Component			

<table>
<tr><td rowspan="4">Fairness.</td><td rowspan="4">High</td><td rowspan="4">Fairness</td><td rowspan="4">Medium</td><td>Law Abidance</td><td>Nil</td><td>Conscience Keeping Operation Trans--parency</td><td>Medium</td></tr>
<tr><td>Decision Pattern</td><td>Medium</td><td>Discrimination</td><td>Medium</td></tr>
<tr><td>Compensation Package</td><td colspan="3">Medium to High</td></tr>
<tr><td>Participative Management & Freedom of Expression</td><td>Medium</td><td>Health and Safety</td><td>Medium</td></tr>
<tr><td rowspan="6">Accountability.</td><td rowspan="6">Medium to Nil</td><td rowspan="3">Accountability</td><td rowspan="3">Medium</td><td>Decision Pattern</td><td>Medium</td><td>Discrimination</td><td>Medium</td></tr>
<tr><td>Corporate Citizenship</td><td colspan="3">High</td></tr>
<tr><td>Stake-Holders' Interest Protection</td><td>Medium to High</td><td>Health and Safety</td><td>High</td></tr>
<tr><td rowspan="3">Responsibility</td><td rowspan="3">High</td><td>Law Abidance</td><td>Nil</td><td>Conscience Keeping Operation Transparency</td><td>Medium</td></tr>
<tr><td>Compensation Package</td><td>High</td><td>Time Targeted Response Mechanism</td><td>Medium</td></tr>
<tr><td>Participative Management & Freedom of Expression</td><td colspan="3">Fairly High</td></tr>
</table>

Accountability.	Medium to Nil	Account ability	Medium	Decision Pattern	Medium	Discrimination	Medium
				Corporate Citizenship	High		
				Stake holders' Interest Protection	Medium to High	Health and Safety	High
		Responsibility	High	Law Abidance	Nil	Conscience Keeping Operation Transparency	Medium
				Compensation Package	High	Time Targeted Response Mechanism	Medium
				Participative Management & Freedom of Expression	Fairly High		
		Clear Strategy		Decision Pattern	Medium	Conscience Keeping Operation Transparency	Medium
		Independence		Participative Management & Freedom of Expression	Fairly High		
		Effective Risk management	Medium	Operation Integrity	High	Time targeted Response Mechanism	Medium
				Decision Pattern	Medium	Expansions, Diversifications Acquisitions and Takeovers	High
		Self evaluative	Medium	No Equivalent Component			

<table>
<tr><td rowspan="3">Trans-parency</td><td rowspan="3">High</td><td rowspan="3">Trans-parency</td><td rowspan="3">High</td><td>Decision Pattern</td><td>High</td><td>Conscience Keeping Operation Transpa-rency</td><td>Medium</td></tr>
<tr><td>Compensa-tion Package</td><td>Medium to Nil</td><td>Expansions, Diversifica-tions Acquisi-tions and Takeovers</td><td>High</td></tr>
<tr><td>Discrimi-nation</td><td>High</td><td>Time targeted Response Mechanism</td><td>Medium</td></tr>
<tr><td rowspan="5">Balancing Stake-holders' Interests</td><td rowspan="5">High</td><td rowspan="5">Social Responsi bility</td><td rowspan="5">High</td><td>Law Abidance</td><td>Nil</td><td>Conscience Keeping Operation Trans-parency</td><td>Medium</td></tr>
<tr><td>Decision . Pattern</td><td>Medium</td><td>Stake Holders' Interest Protection</td><td>High</td></tr>
<tr><td>Discrimi-nation</td><td>Medium</td><td>Time Targeted Response Mechanism</td><td>Medium</td></tr>
<tr><td>Health and Safety</td><td>High</td><td>Compensat-ion Package</td><td>High</td></tr>
<tr><td>Corporate Citizen-ship</td><td>High</td><td>Expansions, Diversifi-cations Acquisitions and Takeovers</td><td>High</td></tr>
</table>

because, in the absence of specific prescriptions of requirements under each one these components, only a qualitative assignment can be made. As such, other intellectuals may like to work out different combinations for this analysis depending on their views on the subject.

An attempt is made here to present the highlights of some of the normal performance expectations under each of these CG component categories.

Governance Issues

Let us now examine the broad implications of each of these CG components.

Law Abidance: This CG component refers to ensuring total compliance to all relevant and applicable acts, rules, regulations and statutory guidelines at all times without exception. Such compliance ensurances should become a standard operation practice and execution norm for the organisation because the law does not accept exceptions and non-compliances would lead to punitive consequences. Compliance prescriptions under the law generally do not carry ambiguities and uncertainties except in areas where the guiding knowledge itself is not fully developed but sufficient degree of clarity or international consensus has emerged. Wherever applicability of a legal requirement exists, the law clearly specifies *'what needs to be complied with'*. Further, the law also prescribes standard formats in which records of compliance should be maintained and submitted to the department at pre-specified time-intervals. In addition, the government ensures that compliance of legal requirements is always maintained by business corporates through regular inspections and verifications from its own officers. In fact, corporates hardly get a chance to skip these requirements. Uncertainties therefore do not have any scope to prevail in this specific CG component area. Since this is the only component which is completely free from uncertainties and can be precisely verified for conformance and also carries a high potential to invite punitive measures in situations of compliance failure it has to be explored from a broader perspective. Some of these aspects are discussed with the help of a few spread-sheets in the next chapter. Incidentally, we should always bear in mind that total compliance to all the requirements of the law speaks high of corporates' commitment to good governance.

Operation Integrity: This is one of the key CG component areas that are always viewed with great suspicion by the public in general and intellectuals in particular. Why such a suspicious air pervades across the society? The onus for creating this sort of a suspicious environment rests primarily with business corporates especially because the industrial development history, growth and proliferation over the past several decades, and the various activity designs and execution mechanisms evolved from time to time by business corporates did support generation of such an unpalatable impression among the general public. Operation integrity generally remains as a questionable area in most of the business establishments. Until business enterprises make it a point to dedicatedly work towards changing this scenario, they will have to continue to live under the blanket of a suspicious air.

This CG component speaks volumes about the guiding philosophy that drives and directs all work-execution methods and practices of an organisation. As such, it is very important that corporates come clean on this issue. Once corporates achieve a major break-through to set a new milestone in this direction, most of the other remaining CG components automatically get reset and fine-tuned to resonate to the tunes of the society and the general public, thus creating the necessary base for corporates to carve a better picture for themselves.

The word *Integrity* means soundness or wholesomeness or honesty. It also means sincerity in approach towards various activities and their execution methodologies. Sincerity in approach, in turn, refers to total reliance on pure unadulterated or non-modulated knowledge that governs the process or phenomenon for all activities of a business corporate right from conception to product or service generation and delivery at customers' place. Such an honest approach does not give room for inclusion of any type of macro- micro- or sub-micro-unethical practices at any of the stages involved in an execution chain/mechanism. Therefore, in order to ensure that operation integrity never becomes a questionable area to be challenged now and then by the general public or the intellectuals across the society, organisations should doubly ensure that motivation induced modulated knowledge or pre-designed/ formulated biased opinions configured for leveraging a pre-conceived unfair advantage just has no place anywhere in the organisation and its activities whether carried out inside its own premises or outside anywhere in the society. Further, if organisations can successfully establish an operating system completely free from the influence of negative components of knowledge namely intentionally modulated pre-meditated perverted knowledge and can successfully maintain the same forever, then all discussions on corporate governance aspects would automatically become an academic subject for mere hypothetical discussions of not much practical relevance to realities of business life!

Corporates normally keep continuously exploring improved methods for more effective translation of guiding technology with a view to achieving better operation efficiency, better process-time management, better process-economy, etc. and keep evolving newer and/or improved methods periodically. The question of micro-operation integrity here refers to the meticulousness and the execution discipline with which shop-floor people implement those practices.

An ever-burning issue for this particular CG component is:

"Are there are any *Latent* and *Undisclosed Objectives* or motives behind any move of the corporate, whether inside its own work premises or outside in the society, that might prove unfair to any of the cross-sections of the society or stakeholders of the corporate?"

If the answer to this issue happens to be *'Yes'*, then conclusion would be that the corporate lacks integrity of operations.

But the question here is "*Who would give **Yes** answer to this question*?" None! No senior management member or the enterprise managers of any organisation would give such an answer. Then, can *Diligence Auditors* unearth the truth and declare whether the answer is definitely *"Yes or No?"* Certainly not! If diligence audits could identify such undisclosed and latent facts or situations, then how could so many corporate scandals and scams take place? In fact, it is a harsh truth of the fact that now and then we do come across mind-boggling scams and scandals. Society has to live with this situation.

Can there be any solution to this problem?

"Total transformation of the human mind, rather thought processes to stay true to the core or stay true to their conscience is probably the only solution for this corporate malady!"

The solution should, therefore, emanate from within. If operation integrity has to find a safe place and has to stay in an organisation, it has to start only at the top. Only then, it can comfortably percolate down and spread its roots across the entire organisation and not otherwise. Business managers should never expect that while they could continue to remain exceptions to rules, everybody else down the line should be honest to them. If such attitudes prevail in any organisation, then there would be only pretence of honesty and sincerity everywhere but not true honesty! Staying honest always calls for extra will power, firmness and courage to face consequences of remaining honest, where as becoming dishonest does not call for any extra efforts. If operation honesty has to find a permanent place, it has to happen in a natural way and not always with extra efforts or through coercion. If we look at Professor Bertrand Russell's viewpoints from slightly different contextual perspectives, we do realise one of the harshest facts/truths of life namely *collective integrity of intellectuals could vary from zero to minus infinity!* This is primarily because all individuals tend to follow the law of nature namely randomness of orientation or orderliness. Dishonesty stands for the *randomness* or *disorderliness* in the order of *activity orientation* whereas operation honesty or integrity demands a specific orientation and/or alignment. When this law of nature is additionally powered and supported with another law of nature namely the law of entropy (one of the laws of thermodynamics) which states that all systems tend to acquire the status of least energy levels (As if to become and stay least active!). These two laws of nature clearly tell us that disorderliness and random orientation of activities is natural to any organisation and all orderly operations will have to be specifically managed with extra efforts. What an unfortunate thing! All business managers should realise this basic truth, rather law of nature, and suitably manage appropriately to administer operation integrity throughout the organisation.

There would be innumerable numbers of micro and sub-micro-malpractices in all organisations. However insignificant they may appear to be, if all such things could be put-an-end-to with an *Iron Will Power*, then all activity shop-floors could be transformed to stay clean. We should never forget the basic truth *Drops of Water Make the Ocean!* Organisations can maintain operation integrity only when each and every individual activity centre, irrespective of wherever it is located, is transformed to become and stay clean. We have already realised that this is not an easy task. Business managers should personally take responsibility to ensure that they provide necessary infrastructure and facility and the required skill power to all work centres and help them in staying clean. This is the starting point for an organisation to install and uphold operation integrity.

Evidencing satisfactory compliance to all the applicable legal requirements through appropriate practice methods of addressing them and demonstrating proof of achievement is probably one of the best means of establishing a high degree of operation integrity. The basic premise here is the belief that laws of the land are generally framed to embrace a broad spectrum of corporate activities that are required to be performed in such a way that the welfare of the society is never put at stake.

In fact, one of the first elements of non-integrity in this area stems from non-identification of some of the applicable clauses and sub-clauses of the law under the cover/pretext of 'being unaware of the same'.

The next most commonly noticed *Non-integrity* is the fact that many corporates have specialised in manipulating their records in such a way that *'They always Stay Clean on Records'*. Many corporates have also intricately specialised in ensuring proper interrelationship and correlation between different types of records supposed to be generated at different activity centres. This type of an unholy activity is resorted only to show an external agency that they are true to the requirements of technology norms or norms set by professional bodies, etc. Incidentally, this approach is not restricted only to legal compliances but spans over the entire activity spectrum especially because any inspection agency can go only by records of action and their outcome. Occasionally they can even ask for a physical demonstration of a particular execution for conformance verification or an interview like interaction with people at random wherever technical and practical feasibility exists and not beyond. Manipulation is not restricted only to records; it extends far beyond to almost all activity areas of corporates. It is not a surprise that many corporates specially train and tutor some of their selected few executives and corresponding other members of their workforce to put-up such impressive shows and to confidently face randomly addressed interviews and to present a picture that appears very natural in the regular routine. Nobody can make a comprehensive list of such malpractices of corporates. Marketing area, business expansions, diversifications, acquisitions, etc., suitably supported by other activity groups together carry an invisible but highly potential goldmine with them for malpractices. In fact, the types and nature of different kinds of malpractices that stand to the core, the degree of operation non-integrity can only be left to people's imagination!

No inspection agency can physically install himself/herself inside a corporate to check day and night as to what all happens there.

As such, the concept of operation integrity should actually stem from consciously sensitive human mind within the people and cannot be enforced from outside.

Open access to all concerned stake holders to verify practices, records, facts, and the governing knowledge behind decisions that could affect their immediate and/or long-term interests.

Some Common Hurdles for Practice of Integrity

It is a fairly well understood fact that practice of *Total Integrity* is not easy in many corporates. This is primarily because there would be many obstacles for the same. These obstacles are generally not confined to any one particular level of operation front. In fact, they would be present at all levels though the degree of obstacles offered by different levels could vary from one organisation to another. Similarly, different activity execution divisions might have different types of obstacles. Only those organisations that would carefully identify all such obstacles and successfully eliminate the same could successfully practice *total integrity* in their operations.

What are the common obstacles that one would come across for practice of integrity?

- ➢ Most of the organisations face two types of operation hurdles.
    - The first of them is people's inability to identify the various statutory compliance requirements. Multiplicity of these requirements would generally induce a confused state of mind in people because they would be lost in their plurality.
        - Many times, the root of problem for confusion lies in people's inability to properly interpret the true compliance requirement as stipulated by the law.
    - Lack of necessary infrastructural facility for complying with those statutory requirements is the next hurdle which many people face in their pursuit of ensuring compliance to statutory requirements.

- One should not construe here that the complete range of compliance requirements would call for special types of facilities. It is not so. Only some compliances call for certain facilities. People should carefully identify those requirements and identify those facilities and pursue with concerned people in the organisation and organise their procurement and installation.

➢ Many of the compliance procedures call for a good working knowledge of certain aspects of technology practice. Similarly use of some facilities that would help in ensuring compliance would also call for some additional skills in people.

- Occasionally this aspect of acquiring a good working knowledge of technology practices also poses challenges to people. There is no option for this. People may have to struggle a little in the beginning but have to gain sufficient expertise in handling those technologies.

➢ A clear conviction and a firm determination superimposed with an earnest, innate desire to comply with all the legal requirements is the secret of success to stay clean.

➢ All this is only the first phase of the hurdle. The real crux of the problem, in some organisations, could lie in the next phase namely people's inability to cope with all these requirements.

- When people lack the basic competence, all other limitations could even prove to be just an imaginary problem, wrongly visualised and wrongly projected.
- Organisations may have to carefully identify the real root of problem and work towards finding solution to the problem at root.
- Therefore, as a pre-requisite for establishing a good practice of operation integrity, organisations may have to start with building necessary competence in people.
- This is not an easy task. It is a highly involved process and generally takes more time.

- Equally critical is the next stage of follow-up, namely building the necessary confidence in people in suitably handling those infrastructural facilities and operation technologies.
    - Equipment handling comprises of two aspects namely effective handling to ensure compliance of a stipulated requirement and also the care necessary in handling the equipment in such a way that it does not pose maintenance problems.
    - The other aspect of equipment handling refers to acquiring necessary competence to correctly identify maintenance activities, its frequency, etc. to ensure that equipments always stay reliable.
    - If adequate competence is not built in people, installed facilities could go waste or could remain idle, either for want of proper maintenance or for want of appropriate skill for handling them. In either situation, statutory compliances suffer.
- The next major hurdle one would come across in many organisations is fairly complex and intricate.
    - In many activity centres and in many organisations, this hurdle mostly works beneath the surface and may not appear obvious.
        - Nature of this problem is generally unique. People rarely admit that they pose hurdles for others.
        - This is the problem of lack of co-operation and co-ordination and prevalence of friction between different people or between different work centres.
        - People like to lock-up a facility for themselves for two reasons. One of them is that whenever they would be required to use a facility, they want it to be readily available for them without having to wait or asking someone for the same.
        - The other one is that they do not like others also to perform as good as they do and that they always like others to keep struggling for completing their tasks. In such situations, intermediate job-halts become

frequent. Some groups feel bad about it while some other groups feel comforted.

- Frictional hassles are, thus, man-made and intentionally created.
- Organisations can eliminate frictional hassles by going very cautious and very systematic basically because it hurts peoples' ego and sentiments. Organisations can get over ego-issues when they can install a high degree of performance temperament across the entire organisation.

• This is typical interface problem and cannot be overcome by organisations by mere interventions and till people go through all the three evolutionary stages of interface to finally evolve into the integrated-interface level (1993) where a complete sense of realisation that they can only collectively address end-users' application requirements satisfactorily and not otherwise. Similarly, it is only when people evolve into this interface level that they treat others' problems as their own and jump to help others to ensure that they collectively uphold organisations' commitments.

  - The entire organisation works as a single workforce and therefore incidental limitations of either a skill or a facility seen in a particular work centre would never pose problem to anybody because organisational facilities would be treated as common for all.

• Some of the other more frequently encountered reasons for such an observation could be: practice of favouritism, biases, non-sharing of credits and or returns between people or work centres, non-recognition of new and novel ideas, and accomplishments, absence of open communication and prevalence of high rigidity, absence of freedom of expression, lack of mutual trust and confidence, etc. practiced by many people in the organisation including the top.

- The next major hurdle that one might come across in many organisations is the lack of a collective and co-ordinated approach towards organisational issues.
  - This sort of a non-conducive environment prevails in many organisations as a result of different work centres or different people entertaining differing approach towards organisational commitments and goals.
    - This is also due to lack of activity alignment between different work centres.
    - People think that their work is more important for the organisation than that of others. Occasionally they even think that it is only their work which can ensure customers' comforts and not that of others. Hence, they try to exert supremacy over others or exert monopoly over issues of common concern.
    - Naturally, people do not weigh others' requirements as valuable.
    - Concept of collective responsibility finds no place in the organisation. Therefore, problems keep floating but solutions do not find a place.
    - The net result could be stretched delays in job executions and final output which has to reach external customers suffers.
    - This hurdle is an extension of the previous one.
    - Many organisations fail to realise that this sort of alignment problems have their roots in management's practices of holding people accountable for specified and isolated activities and not for collective accomplishment.
- The next common type of hurdle that one might come across is the prevalence of knowledge pockets and knowledge voids.
  - This hurdle is generally recognised as due to absence of proper knowledge-deployment across the organisation.
    - When knowledge deployment does not take place, many work centres are likely to dope in darkness and suffer for want of right type of knowledge or skill.

- Many a time, people would not even be knowledgeable about job requirements and their individual role in fulfilling organisational commitments. Such situations come-up when corporates fail to share their goals, missions, commitments, etc. with the entire cross section of the work force. This is very dangerous for any organisation. This situation could also be described as self-created hurdle.
- Activities do not get transformed to one of total package of activities aimed at addressing customers' requirements.
- Overall effectiveness takes a dip.
- People do not become true self-driven *Knowledge Workers* but continue to function as mere proficient job workers.
- People's true latent potential remains unearthed forever. Break-through does not take place.
- The result is that building of all the requisite features to the job under consideration may not take place.

➢ Another major hurdle that one could come across in many organisations is the absence of whole heartedness and dedicated approach to work or unflinched willingness of people in accomplishing the breakthroughs.

- Though this specific parameter is not considered by many as a true hurdle in the practice of integrity, it is a known fact that true secret of success for any organisation lies in this critical parameter.
    - Unless people wholeheartedly and willingly participate in all executions, how can there be any operation integrity or transparency?
    - Integrity calls for proper execution of jobs. Proper execution of jobs, in turn, calls for willingness to do so. Therefore, involving people's willing participation is very critical for any business.
    - How to invoke people's willing participation in all activities?

  - This calls for boosting of their morale and confidence in themselves as well as in the organisation.
  - Though it is a harsh truth, this requirement can become a practical reality only when people get good rewards for their good work.
  - The basic human psychic parameter namely *Rewards act as Performance Catalysts and Efficiency Promoters* holds good in all organisations and in all operation situations irrespective of the cross section of the society to which the workforce belongs.
  - Such appreciations contribute to liberally strengthening people's internal reasons or desires to perform better and to out-beat others through achieving their personal best over collective excellence.
  - Most unfortunately, organisations tend to forget that if not carefully handled, in spite of appreciations, this can also act to butcher people's enthusiasm to perform better.
  - A transparent appreciation mechanism is a basic requirement for leveraging true benefits from this process.

- An uninvolved participation is the next major hurdle for practicing total integrity. Non-involvement, which is also understood as unwillingness to work, brings many unexpected situations that could pose challenge to operation integrity.
  - Organisations hardly realise that non-involved participation is more dangerous than many other forms of hurdles.
  - Involvement refers to two specific modes of participation.
    - One of them is emotional involvement.
    - Emotional involvement refers to that aspect of human participation which is driven by an intense internal desire to participate in the activities to make them a success.

- Since this is a desire triggered process, participation mode becomes more critical than participation level.
- Emotionally involved people jump with enthusiasm and identify themselves with any work centre that might need their help.
- This situation induces people to liberally practice multi-directional, multi-tunnelling of different activity spheres. Totality approach rules the situation.
    - o No one needs to hide any information or data.
    - o How can non-transparency find a place in such environments? Global transparency has to prevail.
- These people transform themselves as emissaries of corporate value systems and try to install a *knowledge-based value-driven performance culture* across the organisation. Because they understand what do corporate goals mean in terms of commitments to customers and therefore they uphold the same through their actions and output.
- Each and every individual member of the knowledge workforce understands what corporate targets and goals mean in terms of one's own contribution to corporate output.
- This enviable enthusiasm induces them to acquire the required knowledge and to disseminate and/or deploy the same across all levels to ensure that the entire workforce is steadily transformed to knowledge workforce, the ultimate in TQM (Mruthyunjaya, 2001).

• The other one is intellectual involvement.
  - In this mode people participate with a full understanding of what is expected of them and what is expected of others in the activity chain.
  - People build an intense desire to acquire the required knowledge and skills and transform themselves to an independent invincible business force for the corporate.
  - The executive would then successfully install himself at each and every individual work centre within the organisation to render it a very effective work centre, always striving hard to beat the competition and to excel the same.

- Naturally people ensure that all activities are well-designed and well-planned and well-executed and that they are in line with corporate goals.
- People would be able to beat the competition through swiftness and speed with which they execute the job to full satisfaction of customers and other beneficiaries in the activity/process chain.
- This becomes a practical reality because knowledge which has no space and time boundaries freely traverses and pervades throughout the organisation.
- As such, no work centre would suffer for want of a data or information or a skill or facility for completing their part of the job. The entire knowledge workforce will be there to solve their problems. Concept of highest degree of *Self-accountability* and *Collective Responsibility* pervades everywhere.
- This mode is always backed-up with emotional participation mode.
- Therefore, in an intellectual participation mode, people go out of the way to make others understand the details of what needs to be done. They will not stop at this. They will go further to help and ensue that others do their part of the job well so that cumulatively organisational output satisfactorily meets external customers' requirements. They fuse the required operation comfort in those who lack the same. Concept of individual *Process Ownership* pervades to ensure that no process centre suffers because knowledge-deployment takes place very effectively.
- Operation integrity and total transparency rules such a scenario!

➢ The last category of major hurdle that poses far greater challenges to practice of integrity in any organisation, whether public sector or private sector, big or small, whether manufacturing or non-manufacturing, is the *Allurements* to which executives succumb to and fall prey either knowingly or unknowingly.

- Under the influence of allurement, a form of intoxication, people resort to modulating activity details to suit the contemplated requirement.
    - Activity integrity would be outright given a death blow.
- There would be innumerable numbers of allurements for executives' right from simple operation short-cuts to save a little extra exertion for self to taking to intentional deviations from the set process path or execution scheme in exchange for a personal or official favour.
    - This tendency ensures that people mortgage their integrity and honesty for the sake of a favour.
    - When personal integrity itself is under stake, how can process integrity be practiced?
    - Challenged personal integrity arising from lack of will-power of people, nucleates operation non-integrity.
- Organisations can effectively fight this situation only when people inherently carry a high degree of personal morale and ethos.
    - This can become a practical reality when people can well cultivate and well nourish their mental attitude in an honest and sincere environment.
    - This attitude should be well supported with a high degree of professionally conscious sincerity of people. When people are professionally conscious and professionally sincere, they refuse to budge to allurements and attractions. Naturally, this situation leads to upholding activity integrity.
        - o Operation transparency would never go under challenge.
    - Organisation's value systems can never face a jolt when people hold themselves morally responsible for ensuring and upholding organisation's image, glory, name and fame in the society. Executives become extra cautious and ever remain accountable

to the corporate and the society. Therefore, they go out of the way to keep their activities and transactions extra honest and extra transparent.

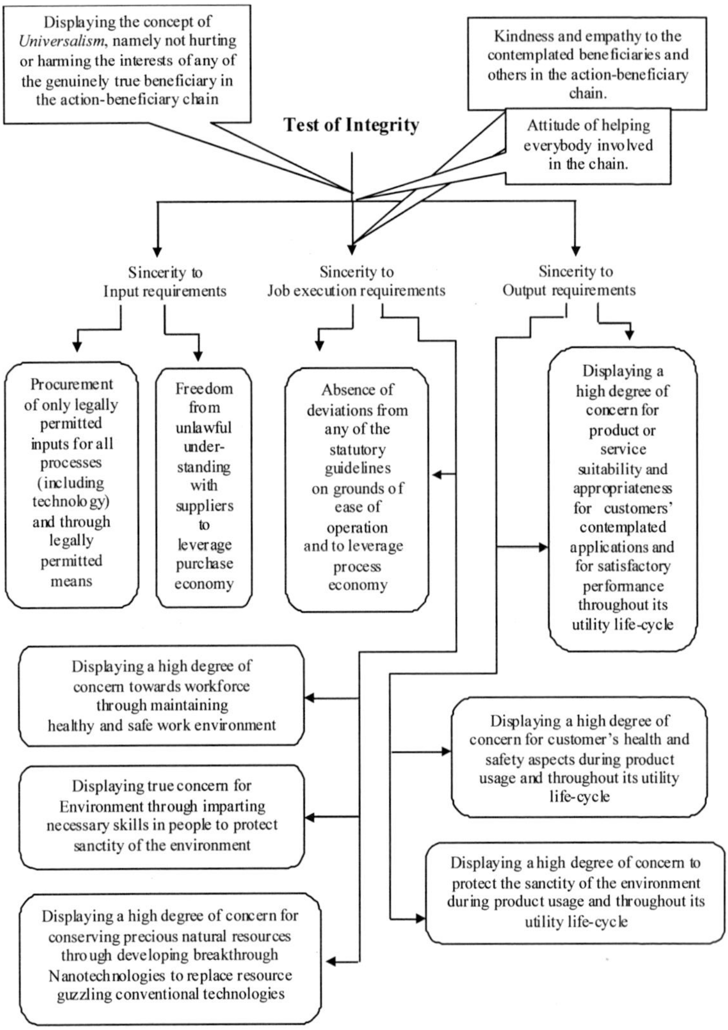

Fig. 2.3 Key Components of Test of Integrity

Elements of Fairness

Marketing Practices

- Products and services of the corporate are always priced most competitively.
- None of the following unfair means are entertained by marketing executives at any stage for any reason and in all situations.
  - Hoarding
  - Black-marketing.
  - Discriminatory distribution of products and services among needy customers.
  - Floating prices to suit the situation and to leverage the same to address personal interests of many.
  - Preparing false invoices and to leverage the difference to address personal interests of many
  - Buying goodwill and favours of corporate customers, government officers, etc. through liberal offering of luxurious gifts, cash gifts, sponsoring of personal events and programmes including private tours and travels, etc.

Distribution of Returns

- Wealth generated by the corporate is equitably distributed among all the stakeholders.
- People do not practice discrimination and take shelter under innumerable numbers of flimsy grounds.
- Ensuring that all stakeholders of the enterprise always remain comfortable.
- Responding suitably to feedback generated through interactions and investigation of reasons for dissatisfaction and satisfactorily addressing those reasons to stakeholders' satisfaction.
- Displaying a high sense of corporate citizenship.
  - Ensuring that social development and welfare activities are suitably identified, encouraged and supported.
  - Responding with a great sense of involvement to issues of social/national importance.

Fig.2.4 Fairness Components of Marketing and Wealth Distribution Activities

Test of Integrity

Though the subject of operation integrity appears vague and highly subjective, corporates cannot continue to stay in darkness forever. Otherwise, the concept of installing and/or evolving a good corporate governance mechanism can neither take a firm seating nor a take-off in any establishment. It is therefore necessary that, wherever required, corporates should take a thorough introspection of their activities and their impacts from different perspectives and prepare the necessary background for making a start in this direction.

A few quick-check-points could help corporates in identifying the lapses in their systems and in fine-tuning the same. The following descriptions have been developed to help corporates to take a good introspection of their activities and to carefully check some of the key areas where operation integrity becomes very critical for successful performance in the fast-emerging present day social context. An attempt is also made to suggest a few remedial measures that could help them in fine-tuning their modus-operandi so that they can confidently move on to installing a good governance mechanism.

Let us start with identifying the *Key Components of Test of Integrity.* Figures 2.3 and 2.4 spell out some of these critical areas which corporates cannot afford to neglect.

Three of the components shown in Figure. 2.3, namely the concept of *Universalism, Kindness and Empathy and Attitude of Helping* call for some explanation. These three components together embrace two specific areas, namely, *Fair Marketing Practices* and *Fair Distribution of Returns*. Figure 2.4 gives a brief presentation of elements of fairness associated with these activity areas.

A Quick Checklist

From the view points of establishing a good governance mechanism, it is always advantageous to identify means of finding a satisfactory answer to the question *How to identify a situation of Non-wholesomeness or Dishonesty associated with corporate activities?* In fact, if we carefully explore this area, we do realise that such an exploration is extremely critical for designing a good governance system.

Most of the members of the workforce in a corporate would always be busily engaged in carrying out some activity or the other. A sizeable cross-section could even be completely lost in their race against time in completing their part of the assignment well in time. Some of them would be so grossly involved in carrying out their routine activities that it appears that they are performing their works almost robotically by virtue of customary habituality. Many of them may not even try to find out the significance of their part of the work. In such situations, it is hard to believe that non-soundness or non-wholesomeness could camouflage their thoughts and actions. This is because they conceive execution mechanisms either just before starting their work or only once at the beginning of understanding the entire process. Subsequently, their concern would only be to execute the job and complete the same within the time allocated for the purpose. They may not even care to know as to what would happen if they fail to complete their part of the job or what would really happen if they do their job well though the general belief is that people generally understand the details of works they execute. Then, except in situations of intentional wrong conception of the execution mechanism primarily for reasons of operation convenience triggered by investment shyness of higher-ups, where does the element of non-wholesomeness come from? And when and at which stage of execution it would happen?

Fortunately enough, finding satisfactory answers to these questions are not as complex as solving the basic puzzle that hovers around the concept of *Integrity* itself. Table 2.4 gives a brief bird's-eye view of different cross-sections of society that entertains questions camouflaged with doubts and uncertainties regarding corporate integrity. It also refers to key areas where, given an opportunity, they like to probe into depths.

A careful examination of this table reveals that almost all key activity areas of corporates are abreast with an air of suspicion. Though it is regrettably very unfortunate for corporates, it is indeed a harsh fact of life. All business corporates have been continuing to live with this situation for long. While some organisations have managed to come out of this suspicious air most of the organisations have not done so. It is high time that business corporates change this situation and clear the air of suspicion around them. If a corporate likes to clear such airs of suspicion that prevails in the society and likes to come clean and stay clean forever, it has to identify reasons for prevalence of such a suspicious environment and find answers to them. Only then it can successfully design a satisfactory *Corporate Governance* mechanism.

Table 2.4 Some Activity Areas that Always Remain Challenged

Sr. No.	Corporate Activity Area	Challenged By
1	Organisations' General Administration and Mechanisms followed in Their Pursuit of Business Objectives	Sociologists and Social Ethicists
2	Managing Stakeholder Values - Distribution of Returns	Business Investors Employees
3	Accounts and Finance Practices	Intellectuals across the society in particular and the public in general. Public Administration System. A Good Cross-section of Organisation's Workforce. Competitors
4	Knowledge Management – Technology Source	Competitors
5	Knowledge Management – Technology Identification	Business Managers Business Investors in some unique situations
6	Knowledge Management – Technology Practice	Systems Administrators Systems Auditors
7	Knowledge Management - Manufacturing Environment and/or Output Generation Activity	Systems Auditors
8	Marketing Activities – Managing Customer Values	Customers
9	Marketing Practices	Competitors General public
10	Managing Employee Values	Organisation's Workforce
11	Managing Stakeholder Values – Supply Chain Management	Suppliers
12	Managing Stakeholder Values – Social Obligations	Society

Some of the issues presented in Tables 2.4 – 2.11a could help organisations and also diligence auditors in identifying activity areas that carry a high potential to create an impression in certain cross sections of the society that they are full of non-wholesome executions. We should, however, not forget here that what is presented in these tables just refer to some of the more frequently challenged activity areas of business corporates. As such, they are neither comprehensive nor exhaustive. It may not, therefore, be a surprise, if any of the cross sections of intellectuals or diligence auditors would come across instances of altogether different types and natures of non-wholesome situations.

Non-wholesomeness of corporate activities has its origin in the following four parameters:

- Incidental in nature due to very casual approach and not being serious about certain requirements.
- Accidental in nature due to lack of adequate skills on the part of some people handling certain jobs.
- Inevitable in nature because people do not have the knowledge of actual requirements.
- Intentional in nature due to dishonesty by design. In fact, wherever corporate governance would be at its infancy or has not yet made a start, this would be the case.

A good number of business establishments across the society belong to this category.

The element of dishonesty stems basically from the following:

a. Non-provision of adequate processing equipments or instruments or facilities.
b. Tolerance to operation shortcuts and omissions.
c. Improper/ineffective time-management.
d. Not taking system requirements seriously.
e. Not taking end-use application requirements or customer requirements seriously.
f. Not taking statutory requirements and/or guidelines seriously.
g. Overconfidence in self-manoeuvrability capabilities.

It is a well known fact that whenever someone speaks of dishonest activities of corporates, the first activity area that flashes across

Table 2.5 Checkpoints to identify Non-wholesome Situations (Accounts and Finance Practices)

⇩

The Starting Point

Sr. No.	Frequently Encountered Types of Non-wholesome Operations ⇩ Key Areas of Concern	Can this be Tried? ⇩ Key Routes to Build Wholesomeness to Accounts and Finance Practices
1.	Dishonesty in preparing company's annual Balance Sheet for purposes of the general public, business investors, financiers, etc. ⇩ A result of ⇩ Buying the Goodwill of Company's Auditors	➢ Carefully design a system of management of all financial and accounts matters of the company taking care to ensure that system procedures and practices follow the standard norms of the profession set by appropriate professional bodies and also other statutory guidelines laid down for the purpose as well the industry norms established, if any. Standard international practice should be followed.
2.	Root cause for such a fraudulent behaviour ⇩ Collusion with marketing executives and others in improper/inaccurate billing for company's products and services – *A glorious platform for Proliferation of Corruption.* ⇩ ◆ Under-billing with an objective to receive, in return, some direct favours from target customers or indirectly through their contacts and/or a say in those organisations and/or establishments or influence in other organisations and/or in society. ◆ Over-billing of products and services: - To generate additional (black) money required to offer favours, including monetary favours, or favours in kind (under the guise of *Gifts*) for all those executives who helped in generating purchase orders from customer centres.	➢ Ensure that the system package specifically addresses methods to capture and classify all types and forms of expenses incurred by the entire organisational workforce including senior executives and business managers. It is always good to prepare a ready base for classification of different types of expenses into appropriate groups. Such a documented comprehensive reference matrix of different types of expenses incurred by different activity centres ensures that uncertainties do not exist in this regard. ➢ Ensure further that before finalising the system design, you carefully identify all forms and types of expenses that take place across the organisation.

- To generate additional money required to spend on extra efforts to be put including bribing concerned people for realising payments against supplies made to them.
- To generate additional money required to spend on purchase of goodwill of all those public administrative executives who could help the organisation in smooth running of their activities.
- To generate additional money required to spend on extra efforts to be put for creating or generating additional market potential
3. like product campaign, product promotion, moulding public opinion, public goodwill, etc.
- To generate additional money required to spend on publicity activities and public relation activities-universally accepted form of collectively and indirectly bribing many people in the target platform or field including buying the goodwill of larger cross sections of the society.
- Incorporation of notional income and expenditure that cannot be readily challenged.
- Shifting/transferring all forms of bribes and gifts to generally accepted public relations and product promotion categories.- Shifting/transferring all forms of unaccounted and non-admitted expenses incurred by business managers and selected few others including some popular public personalities, under the guise of business promotion, to generally accepted public relations and product promotion categories.

◆ Can any organisation be subjected to an honest "Product or Services Generation Cost Audit?"

➢ Summarise the information so generated and get the same verified by a good cross section of workforce and correct the summary-list where necessary. A brain-storming session with sizeable cross section of workforce would always help in minimising periodical revisions of expenses list.

➢ Doubly ensure that no other form of unaccounted expenses prevails in the organisation.

➢ Taking into consideration the types of formal expenses that industry norms or professional norms or standard international practices accommodate while preparing organisational finance statements classify and group the types of expense into appropriate categories. Do not hesitate to modify and update the list as and when necessity arises.

➢ Accuracy of this list helps you in generating reliable expenses' statement for the organisation.

- Ensure that the system design and its periodical audit verification mechanism does not provide any scope for executives to play into each others' hands and to manipulate expenses or income figures to mutual comforts.
  - This aspect will have to be doubly ensured in the case of repetitive and large volume purchases as well as in the case of repetitive and large volume sales to some customers.
  - Legal affairs, personnel welfare, and public relations activity divisions carry a high potential to live with many non-wholesome activities. This should be carefully guarded.

- Never! With so many reasons that force organisations to increase product/service price, how can any audit reveal the true add-on-component of "Uncalled for Increment" to price structure?
- The society has accepted many other similar costs which get added up to product cost, as inherently integral to product generation cost.

- Another unique fraudulent accounting feature seen in many organisations is the shifting of the bulk of actual expenses incurred particularly by the legal affairs cell and the public relations cell to other expenses head like equipment repair and maintenance, staff welfare expenses, sales promotion expenses, social welfare expenses, etc.
- System design and verification mechanisms should carefully address these issues.
- Another unique area of this category is intentional meddling with both expenses figures as well as income figures at the instance of senior management to inflate certain figures and to shrink certain other figures to suit their comforts and convenience. Occasionally such fudged accounting practices would also accommodate many unlawful and unfair expenses.

➢ Also identify source of data and methods to ensure its accuracy.

➢ Since expenses summary or statement is generally a questionable area, ensure that the element of doubt is completely eliminated by all possible means.

➢ Some extra efforts put at this stage will ensure that the entire workforce builds full confidence in organisational accounting system. Once convinced, organisational workforce which carries great potential can positively catalyse spreading such a confidence in the society around.

➢ Introduce a system of good control on expenses. Define methods of control including clearly identifying limits for expenditure for different activities and authorisation levels.

It is a good practice to clearly define discretionary expenditure powers of people at different levels together with details of records and/or supporting documents to be

4.	• Purchasing the goodwill, including comfort levels, of business investors, financiers, etc. - Playing into the hands of all key executives (purchase, marketing, production, process and product development, legal and personnel, public relation and estate maintenance, etc.) to manipulate figures to mutual comforts and to identify false grouping and wrong classification of expenses figures by clubbing together expenses of different sections to bring alignment with budget estimates. - Resorting to preparation of false statements of goods in stock, goods in process and goods in transit embracing both process input as well as process output. - Resorting to preparation of false statements regarding payments receivable from different customer centres against different supplies made to them and at different times. - Undervaluing or overvaluing company's assets as may be felt beneficial in the context of overall situation. - Resorting to showing false facts/ information about company's profits and losses. - Hiring only such company auditors who would formally approve all sorts of fraudulent expenses and incomes to prepare equally non-wholesome annual balance sheet of the company.	submitted. Such clarities will eliminate all sorts of ambiguities and associated elements of doubts in people's mind. You can thus eliminate instances of uncontrolled expenses in some areas or by some individuals as it could otherwise lead to doubting its genuineness. ➢ Keeping a comprehensive reference matrix that briefly describes the nature of expenditure incurred by each of the activity centres in the organisation will help to a great extent in expenses control. Such lists could be collectively and jointly reviewed periodically and revised. ➢ All activity centres should consciously concur with expenses summary shown against their names and wherever they find differences, they should be free to point out the same and get the summary corrected to their satisfaction. Revised summary statements should be kept open for scrutiny and comments. What is more critical for organisations is that the entire cross section of organisational workforce should consciously concur with the expenses summaries and statements. If the entire workforce enjoys the freedom and keeps periodically challenging expenses incurred under any of the expense heads by different departments and individuals and offer proposals to make the same more competitive and economical, such proposals should be openly welcome and necessary refinements should be incorporated in the control mechanism. ➢ Practice of an "Open-Score-Board-System" is an indispensable tool for building total trust

		across the entire cross section of the organisation and other directly involved stakeholders like investors and financiers. ➢ For this purpose you introduce a system of periodical reviews or audits of expenses summary by a good cross section of workforce as well as by representatives of other directly involved stakeholders like investors and financiers as may become necessary and beneficial in fusing the desired degree of trust and confidence in accounting practices. ➢ Periodicity and randomness for such cross verifications could be fixed based on reliabilities established for expenses' summaries. ➢ The general industrial psychology is that people would be concerned more about expenses incurred by higher-ups. Keeping such summaries open for verification by other employees imparts great confidence in the accounting systems of organisations.
5.	Purchasing the goodwill of general public, administrative executives, etc. by presenting rosy pictures of workforce compensation packages and workforce appreciation and satisfaction levels even in situations where certain basic infrastructural and support facilities including the critical ones necessary for comfortable execution of different jobs are ignored and neglected.	➢ Purchase prices of goods and services, valuation of goods in stock and trade, wages payables and wages paid, incentive and staff welfare expenses, etc. also would trigger questions in many minds. Find acceptable ways to ensure that there is no undervaluing or overvaluing anywhere in the chain and that there is no fudging of any of the figures and things always remain completely non-challengeable and stand for true facts.
6.	Resorting to appropriate manipulation of records to ensure that collectively they speak of good coordinated work across the organisation. • Wherever feasibility exists - carrying out either small corrections in the same (record sheets) or for replacing just a couple of sheets with fresh records	➢ Expenses incurred by public relations people and marketing people are yet another area that is always challenged by others across the organisation. ➢ Based on past experience, prepare a master list of standard forms of expenditure for people to refer to and abide by. Introduce a counter-check point at this stage. Introduce methods to check details of their expenses and ensure that they do not spend money,

ensuring required interlinking and alignment between them. • Resorting to preparation of altogether fresh records that would exhibit the required interlinking and alignment between different records.	either directly or indirectly, in any form of non-obligatory expenses, bribery and kickbacks. ➢ Can you ensure that such indirect expenses are not covered under different non-challengeable heads like tours and travel expenses or product promotion and product development expenses, etc? If feasible, introduce multi-stage and multi-level scrutiny of such expenses and build full trust among people.

anybody's mind in the society is the area of organisational finance and accounts management practices. This is next followed by marketing activities. In some contexts these two activity spheres vie with each other for the first slot. Often they interchangeably interchange their significance positions. All other activity areas carry different degrees of contextual and/or consequential non-wholesomeness potential. Organisational work culture decides the degree of their non-wholesomeness.

Table 2.5 identifies key activity areas of finance and accounts operations of corporates which collectively carry the potential to lay a strong foundation for practice of all other forms of non-wholesome activities across the organisation. In fact, it may not be a surprise if one would be tempted to infer that it is this group of dishonest activities that trigger all other forms of non-wholesome activities across the organisation.

- ➢ Even if business corporates want to come clean and stay clean forever, would the corrupt social environment engulfing them ever permit them to do so?
- ➢ Would the corrupt policy making body and corrupt policy implementation systems configured of multiplicatively proliferating corrupt officials whose appetite for money can never be whetted to their satisfaction or comfort level as they perennially keep haunting business executives and keep extracting money (extortion) from them ever permit business corporates to come clean?
- ➢ Would the corrupt social (pressure) groups and public societies configured exclusively to extract, rather squeeze, money from business corporates through different forms of harassment

Can Business Corporates Come out of this Vicious Corruption Circle?

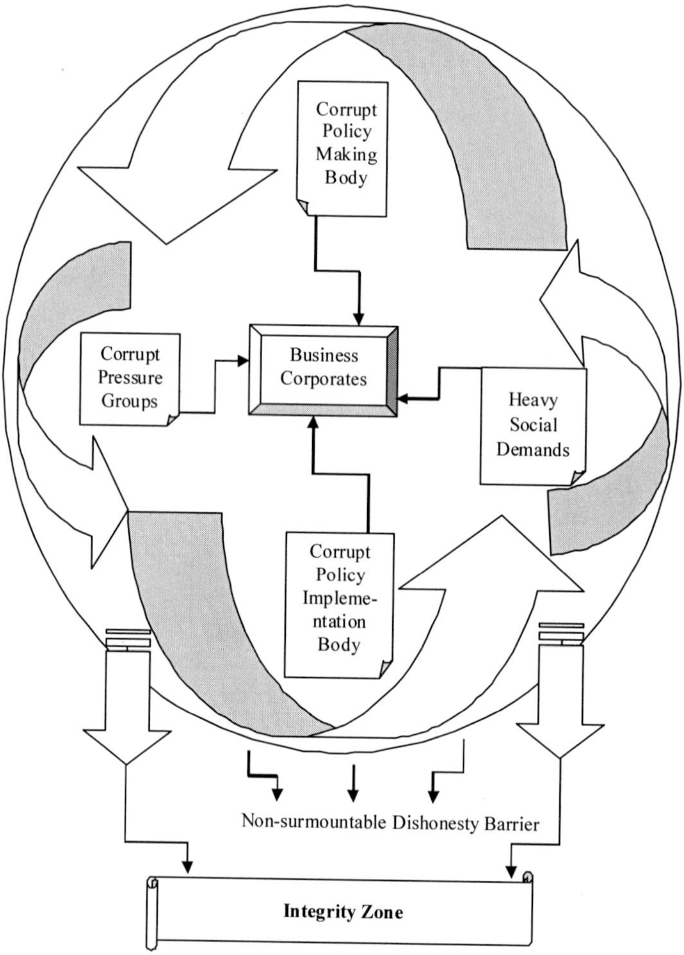

Fig. 2.5. Dishonesty Barriers that Haunt Business Corporates

including psychic harassment and/or informal blackmailing of widely varying nature and magnitudes ever allow business corporates to stay clean?

- Can the root cause for all fraudulent practices seen in business corporates explained above be traced back to corporates alone?

- Does the society not have a share or a role in the blame game?

⇩

  - Do sociologists and social ethicists have an answer to this ever-live and an ever–burning question?
  - Can they rescue business corporates out of this vicious corruption circle and help them in coming clean?

Table 2.6 Checkpoints to identify Non-wholesome Situations (Public Relations Activities)

Sr. No.	**Frequently Encountered Types of Non-wholesome Operations** ⇩ **Key Areas of Concern**	**Can this be Tried?** ⇩ **Key Routes to Build Wholesomeness to Public Relations Activities**
1	Randomly conducted activities with no rhyme or rhythm. Acting on information generated from different quarters or under somebody's suggestions or instructions. A result of ⇩ Not having any set public relations' programme for the company ⇩ Attempting to buy goodwill of the general public or some VIPs and influential people in the society whenever an opportunity arises.	➢ Prepare a well thought-out Public Relations' Policy and practices for the company. Spell out goals and objectives for public relations activities of the company. ➢ Ensure that public relations policy and practices are so designed and developed that it never allows people to use this platform to buy the goodwill of political and public administrative bigwigs or the executives of public administration to curry some favours in return from them. ➢ Define standard but acceptable methods to translate the policy to actions. ➢ Ensure that practices do not provide any scope for bribing any public figure in anticipation of return of official favours. ➢ Formally declare the means and methods of extending normal courtesy to visiting VIPs or residential bigwigs and executives in power. ➢ Define the types of proposals/suggestions or requests for support/favours from social organisations or event organisers which the company would not entertain. ➢ Include a formal definition of identifying visiting or residential VIPs or other events for offering company's general courtesies. ➢ Also include a clear definition (identification) of public or social events, a calendar of events for the year where company would generally like to participate. Do not forget to include the modes or methods and magnitudes of such public participations. ➢ Prepare an annual budget for all public relations activities and get the same formally approved from appropriate authorities.
2	Root cause for such a random behaviour ⇩ ⇩ ⇩	

<table>
<tr><td></td><td></td><td>➢ Prepare a well thought-out Public Relations' Policy and practices for the company. Spell out goals and objectives for public relations activities of the company.</td></tr>
<tr><td></td><td></td><td>➢ Ensure that public relations policy and practices are so designed and developed that it never allows people to use this platform to buy the goodwill of political and public administrative bigwigs or the executives of public administration to curry some favours in return from them.</td></tr>
<tr><td>3</td><td>Absence of annual plans, absence of a clear definition of purpose, scope of activities, budgeting, etc. for public relations activities.</td><td>➢ Define standard but acceptable methods to translate the policy to actions.
➢ Ensure that practices do not provide any scope for bribing any public figure in anticipation of return of official favours.</td></tr>
<tr><td>4</td><td>Identification and selection of social development projects only to suit the tastes and desires of some local bigwigs or some other influential people in the society and not necessarily on the true and relative merits of those projects.</td><td>➢ Formally declare the means and methods of extending normal courtesy to visiting VIPs or residential bigwigs and executives in power.
➢ Define the types of proposals/suggestions or requests for support/favours from social organisations or event organisers which the company would not entertain.
➢ Include a formal definition of identifying visiting or residential VIPs or other events for offering company's general courtesies.</td></tr>
<tr><td>5</td><td>Focussing only on managing to buy the goodwill of VIPs and other influential people in the society as and when need arises through offers of fabulous gifts (depending on the quantum of contemplated return of official favours)</td><td>➢ Also include a clear definition (identification) of public or social events, a calendar of events for the year where company would generally like to participate.
Do not forget to include the modes or methods and magnitudes of such public participations.
➢ Prepare an annual budget for all public relations activities and get the same formally approved from appropriate authorities.
➢ Ensure that the organisational workforce, local society and also the local administration is kept well informed of company's public relations policies, practices, annual plans, budget and means or modes of participation in public relations activities, etc.</td></tr>
<tr><td>4</td><td>Keep innovating newer and novel methods to ensure that public figures and executives in authority remain always happy with the company through all forms, kinds and means of bribery on a sustained basis</td><td>➢ With a view to upholding the noble concept of corporate citizenship, define the types of social welfare and development projects where the company generally participates. Also define scope and mode of participation and cut-off levels, if any. Identify projects that would speak high of your commitment to the local society and its welfare.
Also identify projects that would stand for your commitment to environment.
Keep proper records of all activities and expenses incurred on them and make the same totally transparent and verifiable by public figures in the society.
Similar to any other activity of the company, institute a mechanism to periodically verify and review the progress on on-going social-development projects and suitably reorient them to achieve set goals as may become necessary and ensure that company's precious resources do not go waste.
Devise a mechanism to ensure that pressure groups never get an opportunity or scope to influence company's public relations activities to alter or reorient the same towards achieving their-own preconceived goals.</td></tr>
</table>

Table 2.7 Checkpoints to identify Non-wholesome Situations (Marketing Activities)

Sr. No.	Frequently Encountered Types of Non-wholesome Operations ⇩ Key Areas of Concern	Can this be Tried? ⇩ Key Routes to Build Wholesomeness to Marketing Activities
1.	➢ Carrying out marketing activities in such a way that everybody has a free hand in the process. Such practices liberally operate under the cover of professional freedom for executives. ➢ Not laying down any specific set of guidelines, rules and regulations for people to follow thus ensuring that they have sufficient scope to play around with human sentiments, market sentiments/situations and the prevailing competitive technology environment. This is supported by: • Open pricing policy clubbed with open product distribution policy under the cover of serving the customer better.	➢ Can corporates develop and establish a system of management which would ensure that marketing executives do not have any scope to deviate from set procedures and fair marketing practices? ⇩ • Does the system ensure that marketing executives do not have scope to entertain temptations to play with product or service prices to leverage a prevailing situation to corporates' advantage or for self advantage? - Customer sentiments regarding product/service of the corporate. - Urgency in customer requirements. Pushing to market those products that have not undergone full cycle of specification checks. - Customer application environment badly affected for want of a specific product or service in their application chain. - Short-supply of similar products from competitors in the field. - Shooting prices in the market for similar products due to short supplies. - Offering price incentives for opting for non-standard products.
		➢ Does the system define details of mechanism to be followed for fixing price of different products and services? Does this mechanism clearly spell out the types of variable parameters that will have to be considered for price fixation?

2.	➢ Allowing the market forces to decide on the price structure of corporates' products and services as well as product distribution pattern without trying to exert any control over the same.	➢ Does this mechanism also spell out details for identifying factors and situations that demand price revisions for products? • Are factors which cause an impact on the product price identified? • Does the mechanism also provide for fixing the magnitude or quantum of contribution towards price change from each of the impacting parameters? • Is a clear guideline, formulae and calculations details available for preparing a price-change-impact-matrix that gives the relative contribution of different parameters with respect to each other namely a price-change-correlation-matrix? • Does the mechanism provide for fixing differential price levels between corporate and non-corporate customers due to differences in payment patterns and the efforts needed to collect payment? • Does the mechanism ensure that similar prices are fixed at base levels for similar customers and that there is no scope for giving differing treatment to different customers? • Does it also spell-out the formulae for working out variable component in the product price structure together with details of identifying and quantifying the impact of those variable parameters? Do these details specifically include impacts of capital-goods lock-in-period, payment pattern, extra efforts needed to be put-in for realising the price, etc.? • Does the price fixing mechanism provide for customers to know the reasons for price variations between two different customers or between two different geographic locations, etc.? ➢ Can the system ensure that products of the corporate are always priced most competitively and people do not take to any

type of unfair means in price fixation, product distribution, etc.

- Unwarranted product supply control.
- Taking shelter under discriminatory distributions.
  - Resorting to controlled product distribution to different market segments to match the situation.
- Nil supplies/short supplies to create artificial scarcity and to generate extra heavy demand for the product with a view to jacking-up the prices or to push non-standard products to market.

  Accepting bribes and other personal favours for effecting supplies.
- Leveraging the situation to either promote other products or for personal gains including true scarce situations of short supplies of process raw materials, service inputs, etc.
- Hoarding products under heavy demand and resorting to short-supply to boost induced-scarcity to be followed by leveraging the situation to jack-up the price or for other gains. Black Marketing.
- Resorting to floating prices in tune with vibrant market situations and to leverage the situation to corporates' advantage whenever an opportunity opens-up.

➢ Does the system design and administration mechanism specifically identify the following types of unfair/unwholesome practices seen in many organisations and address them with well defined control measures to eliminate scopes for practicing the same:

- Playing with invoice figures (under-invoicing, over-invoicing, nil-invoicing, preparation of non-taxable service invoices against actual products supplied, etc.) to leverage the difference between true prices and invoiced prices for purchasing the goodwill of prospective customers including direct bribes and kickbacks or personal favours.
  - Leveraging the price difference to buy goodwill of political groups, pressure groups, faith groups, etc.

3.	➢ Accepting and accommodating all forms of unfair practices of marketing executives under the cover that they are all standard features in marketing operations and a basic requirement for product promotion and/or for boosting sales of corporates' products and services.	• Aligning product price-structure with local market environment of different geographic locations. Flexible, rather non-standard price policy. • Aligning product distribution pattern with local market environment of different geographic locations to accommodate mutual/personal favours. – Flexible, rather non-standard, product distribution policy. - Makes room for personal assessment and interpretation of the situation to be followed by self directed actions. • Differing product pricing and distribution to different category/class/groups of customers within the same geographical location for leveraging some non-specified benefits either to self or to corporate and to favour a target segment. - Highly flexible, non-uniform product pricing and distribution policy full of provisions to practice biased/differential treatment to customers depending on other impacting parameters.
4.	➢ Giving a totally free hand to marketing executives to work out their own strategies regarding all aspects related to product marketing as long as they manage to earn good returns for products of the corporate. • Freedom enjoyed by marketing executives is so unique that in spite of huge product stocks, they can decide to withhold supplies to certain selected market segments or can mix both sub-standard and	➢ Does system design provide for rooting-out of following types of malpractices? • Mixing of standard products and non-standard or sub-standard products together in such a way that it would not be readily recognised by customers. An activity carried out in collusion with product generation centre and/or product evaluation centre. • Playing into the hands of production executives to withhold supplies of good quality products for a market segment where there is a heavy demand for company's products followed by leveraging the induced starvation situation to clear factory's huge stocks of non-standard products by pushing

	standard products together while effecting product supplies. • And in this process and depending on the market starvation magnitude and seriousness, if they are tempted to accept some personal favours including cash gifts, from prospective customers notably the giant corporates and other big customers, ignoring the same.	non-approved and/or sub-standard goods to customers together with approved goods. • Resorting to offering extra price incentives to customers and to manoeuvre some situations in such a way that customers are induced to accept sub-standard products by sacrificing some of their product specification demand or application requirements. • Resorting to creating unhealthy competition between different major customer centres from different market segments by intentionally withholding or delaying supplies to certain pre-targeted market segments for different periods to suit the convenience and comforts of other pre-identified market segments thus raising the starvation level to leverage the situation for an extra *Premium* on the standard price from starved market segments.
5.	➢ Extending liberal support and encouragement for activities that would promote purchase of customers' goodwill. ➢ Encouraging executives to innovate in this area so that they could establish extra high degree of customer goodwill.	➢ Does the system design and administration mechanism specifically identify different types and modes of goodwill gestures practiced by marketing executives? Has the system addressed satisfactory measures to prevent the same? • Footing personal bills of corporate customers. • Organising different types of service facilities for prospective customers depending on their purchase decision potential or purchase quantum potential. • Offering different types of informal service facilities like sponsoring certain events, sponsoring individuals for some events, etc. • Offering extra price-discounts. • Offering free gifts of service package or product package. • Liberally sponsoring customers or their pre-identified representatives for

		different social, cultural and/or academic/semi-academic programmes, visits, etc. without reference to whether they are of professional interest or of personal interest.
6.	➢ Allowing the market forces to decide on the media promotion of corporates' products and services without restrictions and/or constraints. ➢ Executives are encouraged to innovate and identify novel methods to promote products and services.	➢ Are product promotion measures like advertisements and media campaigns in different media carefully controlled to ensure freedom from attempts to create false impression or appeal in the general public? • Do people take to false propaganda? • Do product literatures give true facts about the product and its serviceability or application suitability features or about productively active utility-life cycle? - Or do they give only part information aimed at implanting a false confidence in the minds of anxious customers? - Are the descriptions deceptively framed in such a way that they hide certain true facts but give only a qualitative exaggeration of certain non-critical features? - Are words and sentences coined in such a way that they could be interpreted either way to suit the comforts of marketing executives? • Is sales campaign free from raining false and/or fake promises and assurances regarding service quality, product performance quality and competitive merits, etc.? • Does product literature or product campaign aim at speaking low or ill of competitive products in the market? • Are these activities guided by well defined policies? - Do well framed control measures exist to ensure that actual practices would always guard executives against resorting to misrepresenta-

		tion of facts and product performances, biases in selection of media, public forums etc.,? - Do these control measures also ensure that none of their ad-activities aim at maligning competitors' products and services to create a biased impression among the general public? - Do these control measures keep a strict vigilance on diversion of ad-funds for purposes of buying goodwill of government officers, political leaders, prospective customers and others who could favour the corporate in some areas? - Do these control measures also keep an eye on installation and commissioning of full-product-range at customers' place under the cover of demonstration models? - Do people sponsor development projects primarily for the purpose of building intellectual appeal and/ or intellectual soft-corner – a form of goodwill?
7.	➢ Allowing the market forces to decide on the strategies and modus operandi to be adopted for effecting product sales.	➢ Do marketing executives take to mere brain wash or manoeuvre prospective and anxious customers? Do they get involved throughout the activity cycle right from concept promotion to actual installation and commissioning of the product at customers' place including pre-delivery and post-delivery activities that would ensure satisfactory use of product supplied to customers and also throughout its productive service life? ➢ Do marketing executives exhibit a sense of total commitment to customers' cause without reference to his personal status or without reference to whether he is small customer or a big customer and irrespective of whether the sales activity takes

		place at corporate headquarters or at individual sales and distribution centres? • Are these executives committed to correctly understanding customer application requirements before recommending a particular product or combination of products for the purpose or they simply force their own views? • Or do they focus only on generation of a purchase requirement/order and nothing beyond? • Do marketing executives generate the required knowledge package regarding safety and/or other legal aspects' related issues during handling, storage and usage as may be applicable to instil the necessary confidence in corporates' products and services?
8.	➢ Allowing the market forces to decide on the strategies and modus operandi to be adopted while participating in big-value tenders and purchase orders.	➢ Are system elements and control measures designed in such a way that they close all routes for malpractices in competitive marketing like for example in participation in huge value/large volume tenders, finalising purchase orders in giant corporates or politically or socially important customers through: • Under cutting the competition. • Digging into competitors' confidential information with a view to manipulating their own data. • Reaching into a mutually agreeable product tender allotment/distribution scheme. • Misguiding customers regarding competitive products and their performances, etc.?
9.	➢ Allowing marketing executives to act as per need of the situation but ensuring that they bring satisfactory results.	➢ Does the system design provide for periodical auditing of all activities of the marketing division to verify and confirm that practices do not violate laid-down policies and procedures and corporates' image would not be at stake at any point of time and at the same time no customer would be at risk?

Table 2.8a Checkpoints to Identify Non-wholesome Situations (Technology Identification)

Technology Identification Oriented Non-wholesomeness				
Sr. No.	**Key Driving Force**	**Checkpoint**	**Element of Non-wholesomeness**	**Non-sincerity towards**
1	➢ What is the true driving force behind the activity?	Check and confirm that it is only the virgin knowledge and principles that governs the process or phenomenon.	➢Non-identification of fully developed and well proven technology. ➢Pretention/Projection of State-of-the-Art-Technology.	➢Business investors and financiers – Major category. ➢Product or service end-users – Minor category. ➢Self.
2	➢ Does the knowledge provide total package of processes that could lead to transformation of all involved or concerned or associated intangibles to tangible products or services?	Check and confirm that no ambiguity prevails in any of the activity areas as to how it should be carried out.	➢Non-identification of all critical intangibles. ➢Total translation of knowledge to useful tangibles does not take place. ➢Pretention/Projection or belief of wholesomeness.	➢Business managers. ➢Product or service end-users. ➢Self
3	➢ Does the available knowledge package help in correctly identifying all other associated activities to be managed to complete main activity cycle?	Check and confirm that all associated activities have been correctly identified including correctly identifying their .entry point to the main stream of activity chain.	➢Non-identification of all critical activity stages/steps. ➢Pretention/Projection or belief of wholesomeness.	➢Business managers. ➢Self. ➢Product or service end-users.
4	➢ Does it identify what needs to be done under each of those micro-processes?	Check and confirm absence of uncertainties.	➢Prevalence of non-clear zones or pockets here and there, but a false notion of full clarity. ➢Pretention of total clarity.	➢Business managers. ➢Self. ➢Product or service end-users.

<table>
<tr><td>5</td><td>➢ Does it identify principles behind different associated activities or micro-processes or incidences associated with the main process?</td><td>Check and confirm that people know why and how all those associated activities should be carried out.</td><td rowspan="2">➢ People do not have the right kind of execution skills.
➢ Or right kind of execution skills are not provided at all work centres.</td><td rowspan="2">➢ Business managers.
➢ Self.
➢ Product or service end-users.</td></tr>
<tr><td>6</td><td>➢ Does it define skill, experience, expertise, etc. required for effectively completing the process cycle?</td><td>Check and confirm that right skill has been identified and provided at the respective work centres.</td></tr>
<tr><td>7</td><td>➢ Does the practice stand for norms set by the virgin technology?
➢ Does the practice stand for norms set by Industries?
➢ Does the practice stand for norms set by professional bodies?
➢ Or any other recognised bodies or international standards?</td><td>Ensure that activity sequence and details are designed in such a way that they always uphold standard norms set by technology, industries in the field, professional bodies or any other national or international bodies set for the purpose?</td><td>➢ Not in line with the guidelines set by basic knowledge, industries, professional or other standard bodies.</td><td>➢ Business investors and financiers.
➢ Product or service end-users</td></tr>
<tr><td rowspan="3">8</td><td rowspan="3">➢ Is the knowledge identified or developed keeping an external customer at the centre of focus?</td><td rowspan="3">Make sure that it is only the external customer for whom the product or service is being developed and no other incidental or ancillary interest in the process.</td><td>➢ Non-identification of total knowledge or information package regarding end-users' application requirements and utility profile.</td><td>➢ Product or service end-users.</td></tr>
<tr><td>➢ Knowledge based complete translation does not take place.
➢ Product or services are ingressed with some inherent but latent shortcomings or lapses.</td><td>➢ Organisa-tion
➢ Product or service end-users.</td></tr>
<tr><td>➢ Non-identification of market potential for a particular product or service.
➢ Improper identification of knowledge package regarding what exactly the market is looking for.
➢ Pretention of total clarity regarding market needs.</td><td>➢ Business investors and financiers – Major category.
➢ Product or service end-users – Minor category.
➢ Self.</td></tr>
</table>

Table 2.8b Checkpoints to Identify Non-wholesome Situations (Technology Execution)

<table>
<tr><th colspan="3">Technology Execution Oriented Non-wholesomeness</th></tr>
<tr><th>Sr. No.</th><th>Element of Non-wholesomeness
(Technology Modulation)</th><th>Non-sincerity towards</th></tr>
<tr><td>1</td><td>Intentionally modulated and/or pre-meditated perverted knowledge used to prepare activity execution design with some kind of ulterior insane motives namely leveraging some unfair benefits to:
- Self.
- Self-group.
- Self organisation.
- Pre-identified external target or external beneficiary.</td><td rowspan="3">• Self conscience.
• Genuine interests of many innocents.
• Virgin nature
• Society and mankind.
• Trust and confidence in execution integrity.</td></tr>
<tr><td>2</td><td>A situation where a person is being influenced through offers of money or other forms of inducements to persuade him to do a dishonest job or to render an illegal service.</td></tr>
<tr><td>3</td><td>A situation where a person is being influenced through offers of money or other forms of inducements to persuade him to do an honest job which he is expected to do in the normal course as part of his legitimate duty and/or responsibility but is reluctant to do so.</td></tr>
<tr><td>4</td><td>Wrong interpretation and/or intentional misinterpretation of data, information or a particular available knowledge. to convey intentionally distorted facts about things or to convey pre-conceived or pre-designed messages for leveraging some unholy gains for:
- Self.
- Self-group.
- Self organisation.
- Pre-identified external target or external beneficiary.</td><td>• Self Conscience.
• Genuine interests of many innocents.
• Virgin nature
• Society and mankind.
• Trust and confidence in execution integrity.</td></tr>
<tr><td>5</td><td>An action carried out at one's whims and fancies not being guided by any rhyme, rule or sane reason and without reference to adverse impact on others whether a self group, self-organisation or an external end-user.</td><td rowspan="4">• Professional requirements.
• Self conscience.
• Social/human values
• Trust and confidence in people's integrity.</td></tr>
<tr><td>6</td><td>Interpretation of knowledge out of context to convey wrong and/or pre conceived/pre-designed messages.</td></tr>
<tr><td>7</td><td>Influencing thought processes of intellectuals to achieve some preconceived or pre-contemplated objectives.</td></tr>
<tr><td>8</td><td>Taking undue advantage of a prevailing situation of lack of information or knowledge or skill or helplessness or in dire need of a product or a service to leverage an unholy result or benefit to:
- Self.
- Self-group.
- Self organisation.
- Pre-identified external target or external beneficiary.</td></tr>
</table>

9	➢ Buying the goodwill of intellectuals and pressing them to do insane activities including propagating wrong thoughts or information to gain some unfair benefits to: - Self. - Self-group. - Self organisation. - Pre-identified External target or external beneficiary. - Or for sabotaging of human values. ➢ A sold-out intellectual would focus on development and/or propagation of knowledge only to support and uphold the concept (biased objectives) he has been sold to. ➢ He would be obsessed and builds biases and gets tempted to ignore contradictory observations as mere exceptions in his pursuit to develop knowledge, including focusing only on part development and propagates the ideas he has been sold to. ➢ He would focus on development of knowledge in certain areas including the one that is exclusively meant for insane or unholy activities.	• Professional requirements. • Self conscience. • Trust and confidence in people's integrity. • Organisational and national interests. • Social and human values.
10	Leveraging available knowledge exclusively for personal benefits/gains at the cost of self group, or self organisation.	• Professional requirements. • Self conscience.
11	Not sharing due credits with source with selfish motives.	
12	Innovating a physically non-existent and a totally notional entity to project its pseudo-existence, followed by aggressively propagating the concept to nucleate an endless chain of such propagation cycles to trade and generate a non-existent or notional physical wealth.	• Self conscience. • Social/human values • Trust and confidence in professional integrity.

Table 2.8c Knowledge and Technology Management (Technology Source)

Sr. No.	Frequently Encountered Types of Non-wholesome Operations ⇩ Key Areas of Concern	Can this be Tried? ⇩ Key Routes to Build Wholesomeness to Knowledge Management Practices
1.	Practicing a unique system of remote technology control throughout the organisation including technology modifications, improvements and refinements. ⇩	➢ Can the corporate generate records that would prove beyond doubt the sources of different technologies that are being practiced at different work centres? ➢ Can extracts of such records or categorical statements regarding the same be publicised in different forums like annual reports or house magazines etc.?

	• Ensuring that only a selected few control centres know the source of different technologies. • Ensuring that nobody knows the exact source of technology which they are practicing? • Training people to work almost robotically with knowledge of just "*What-to-do* and *What-not-to-do*." • Ensuring that people are not fully equipped with the knowledge of "Why and Why-not" of whatever they are working with. • Ensuring that data generation and analysis is carried out by independent teams that do not have any contact with the regular execution teams. • Ensuring that data analysis outcome and consequent process refinements are handled by independent technical teams.	➢ Wherever the records belong to the category of "*Confidential*" in nature, can such records be suitably listed and/or labelled and marked for restricted/limited access? Can the corporate define people eligible to access confidential records? Can it define mode and authorisation for getting access to confidential records? Can it also define mode of confirmation of purpose for which access could be granted? Do such permissions incorporate generation of declarations to the effect that the information referred will not be misused or used against the corporate? ➢ Can the corporate generate a reference correlation matrix with respect to each and every individual item of its product range or service range and the source of its governing technology/knowledge? Can this matrix be marked as to whether it is meant for open access to the general public or has a limited accessibility? ➢ Wherever the source of technology happens to be a combination of in-house development together with some element of externally acquired technology or exclusively from in-house development, can the corporate maintain records to evidence the two components independently? ➢ In cases of in-house developments, can the corporate evidence the credibility or proof of proficiency/competency (publications, books, review articles, conference/seminar proceedings, patents, awards, recognitions, etc.) of technologists/scientists involved in those developments to justify its claim for originality?
2.	• Total absence of the concept of knowledge/ technology inventory and its management.	➢ Does the corporate appreciate the concept of maintaining an ever-updated knowledge inventory of all technological practices operating in the corporate?

	• Nobody knows who is who in the technology-hierarchy in the organisation and people do not know the type of technology that operates at different work centres.	➢ Does it translate this inventory to an ever-updated knowledge-wealth and intellectual-capital inventory for the organisation? ➢ Does it maintain an ever-updated knowledge-wealth and intellectual-capital inventory across the organisation or across the intellectuals in the organisation?
3.	• The corporate does not believe in periodical verification of its technologies for their updation-status. • People are not aware of whether their technologies are compatible with other contemporary technologies or whether they would be taken over by the emerging technologies. • Concepts of *Green-technologies* or *Eco-friendly technologies* do not carry much weight in the organisation. People continue to work the way that suits them without reference to side effects and/or after effects of their activities.	➢ Does the corporate verify at regular intervals updation-status of its different technologies? ➢ Do such verifications lead to identification of obsolete technology, technologies on-par with other contemporary technologies, emerging technologies, etc.? ➢ Do such identifications or listings lead to phasing-out of obsolete technologies? ➢ Wherever phasing-out is decided, would the same be done in consultation with concerned stakeholders? ➢ Does the corporate maintain an inventory of those external factors which influence its phasing-out programmes? ➢ Does the corporate appreciate the concept of *Green-Technology* and has it established a method to periodically evaluate and fine-tune different technologies being practiced at different work centres for *their Eco-Compatibility Status*? ➢ Does the corporate prepare a matrix showing eco-compatibility of its different technologies and keep the data open for public view? ➢ Is there a mechanism to phase-out all non-eco-friendly technologies?
4.	Practice of pilfering either the full technology or part thereof from other organisations is rampant. ⇩ • Institutes an informal mechanism that would provide for systematic	➢ Can the corporate design a novel mechanism that would ensure that their executives do not take to technology piracy? Would the design incorporate methods to monitor the same? • Instead they focus their efforts on unearthing their own latent skill potentials and knowledge potentials to achieve technological breakthroughs

siphoning of information or data that could lead executives to comfortably re-configure technical details of competitors.

- Executives keep constantly exploring means to trap experienced technologists from other organisa-tions and work towards buying their professional integrity to ensure that those technologists part with their company's technology for a price.
- Experienced technologists from other organisations are lured with attractive baits to desert their parent companies and to join the organisation.
- Inward migration of technologists from other organisations in suitably spread-out stages is liberally encouraged and practiced.
- All migrated executives are assigned the job of immediately putting to practice all the good and beneficial technological practices like critical control parameters, critical success factors, process recipes and formulae of their earlier companies (knowledge espionage).

or innovate novel methods of enhancing process effectiveness/ efficiency rather than attempting to get those details through their own contacts elsewhere.

- The mechanism ensures that executives from competitive organisations are never hired for doing either similar works or alternate works.
- Whenever executives are hired for some other reasons, their previous employer/employers are informed of the same and their concurrence is obtained.

➢ Does the design ensure that competitive intelligence activities do not cross the limits of published literature available to the general public and nothing beyond?

➢ Would the mechanism also provide for preventing executives from extrapolating and projecting competitors' strategies with a view to evolving their own strategies to counter those of competitors?

➢ Does the corporate have a mechanism that can convincingly prove/establish with adequate documentary evidences that it has not pirated any of the competitors' technologies, either directly or indirectly through professional agencies specialised in technology piration, but on the other hand, has either fully developed the same in-house or formally purchased the technology through well established and well recognised sources?

➢ Does the system design provide for generation of latent/potential innovation-inventory-matrix of intellectuals across the organisation?

➢ Does it also provide for periodic assessment of emotional balance of intellectuals and suitably encourages them to innovate into areas of achieving breakthroughs in technology development and/or refinement in tune with contemporary technologies as well as with emerging technologies?

• Wherever direct import of technologists is not practical, the company engages the services of external agencies or intermediaries for knowledge espionage purposes.	➢ Does the system management instil sufficient confidence in people so that they do not hesitate to face any audit regarding verification of "Technology-Integrity?" Do people know how to guard critical technological secrets of their operations and processes?

Table 2.9 Purchase Activities

Sr. No.	Frequently Encountered Types of Non-wholesome Operations ⇩ Key Areas of Concern	Can this be Tried? ⇩ Key Routes to Build Wholesomeness to Purchase Activities
1.	This is one of the activity areas in many corporates that carry a very high potential for carrying out only non-wholesome activities.	➢ Designing and establishing carefully thought-out purchase procedures to ensure an ever dynamic balance between procurement and its productive utilisation. ➢ Ensuring that purchase design identifies all the necessary controls on purchase process to ensure that organisational resources do not go waste because of dynamic imbalance between input and output requirements. o Establishing reliability and capability of Suppliers' with respect to each of the output utility parameters as well as
2.	Root cause for such inherently random behaviour ⇩	
3.	Randomly conducted purchase activities with no rhyme or reason arising from instantaneous response to information generated from different quarters or acting on somebody's suggestions or instructions. A result of ⇩ Not having any set purchase programme or a *purchase-vision* for the company	
4.	Roots for such non-wholesome actions ⇩ o Absence of specific correlation between purchase activity and total utility of purchased products.	

- Absence of controls on purchase specifications and their conformance. Verification of specification conformance is never taken serious.
- Not identifying and/or addressing safety aspects of purchased products during transit, handling and storage leading to creation of highly hazardous situations at the premises.
- Absence of correlation between competitiveness and performance suitability of a purchased product.
- An unconcerned attitude towards maintaining a dynamic balance between input consumption and procurement.
- Not serious about identification of appropriate controls that are required to ensure satisfactory utilisation of purchased products.
- Absence of specific correlation between purchase requirements and suppliers' capabilities with specific reference to material quality and suitability for designated application, maintaining contemplated delivery schedules and target quantities (weight or volume or numbers).
- Playing into the hands of suppliers and creating near crisis situations by ensuring that certain materials or services are not available to consumption centres in their need. Or due to absence of effective purchase plans followed by leveraging the situation to push sub-standard or non-standard materials of some suppliers.
- Absence of the concept of *self-responsibility* and passing on the responsibility for establishing product suitability conformation to users' discretion.
- Playing into the hands of suppliers and continuing to procure materials which exhibit a widely varying coefficient of specification variation (Cv).
- Playing into the hands of suppliers and manipulating purchase price structures in

with respect to product competitiveness and also maintaining a minimum inventory at any point of time at the procurement centre for ensuring that no corporate activity would suffer for want of an appropriate input.

- Maintaining ever dynamic minimum stock levels in such a way that at no point of time there would be an idle inventory.
- Establishing a system that would ensure that material/service consumption centres do not carry any risk in using a purchased material or service.
- This, in other words means that the purchase executives themselves take full responsibility for ensuring that they supply only reliable materials to all consumption centres.
- Establishing a purchase mechanism that would ensure that no supplier could manage to purchase the goodwill of purchase executives.
- Ensuring that the purchase mechanism is designed in such a way that it always

	such a way that routine audits cannot dig into true depths to unearth such unholy arrangements. o Absence of specific mechanisms that could effectively prevent suppliers from buying the goodwill of purchase executives. o *Playing Lord* by squeezing small suppliers on price, deliveries and on payment terms. Enforcing harsh terms and conditions.	remains totally transparent and is always open for cross-verification and scrutiny and hence remains ever challengeable.

Table 2.10 Human Resources Development and Skill-Power Management Activities

Sr. No.	Frequently Encountered Types of Non-wholesome Operations ⇩ Key Areas of Concern	Can this be Tried? ⇩ Key Routes to Build Wholesomeness to HR Activities
1.	HR activities, full of fraudulent practices and procedures resulting from one or more of the following malices:	➢ Developing a deep sense of realisation that this activity area carries a high potential to make or mar an organisation and its competitive progress in a globally wide, vibrant technology and market environment.
2.	➢ Rampant practice of parochialism in practically all areas of their activity spectrum. One can see in many places just a pretention; rather show, of a good professional HR management.	➢ Can such a realisation lead to designing of an effective operating system that would ensure practice of the following? • Preparation of a company-wide skill-power-matrix with specific reference to the following: - Talent distribution across
3.	➢ Most of the times, and in many organisations, HR executives act only as per their own whims and fancies and to suit their comforts and convenience without much reference to shop-floor realities of skill demands. • This is basically because; from recruitment to retirement, HR executives will have the last laugh.	

- They are typically known for their highly discriminatory practices that are deep rooted in their highly biased views based on caste, creed, race, region, language, gender, religious faith, culture, etc.
- All such unholy practices would generally be covered with a blanket laced with false claims of certain unique merits and long-term interests of the organisation.

4. ➢ It is not a surprise that in many places, HR executives participate in certain activities almost robotically and without much technical or intellectual involvement.

5. ➢ As a result of such practices shop-floors continue to suffer for want of appropriate support from HR, notably among them are:
   - There will be hardly any match between actual job-content and professional background and experience of new-recruits.
   - Identification of right type of Skill-power required by different activity centres will not take place.
     - Skill development programmes hardly match the true skill gaps in people.
     - Wherever imparting necessary technical skills is called for, it would just be a formality and nothing beyond.

6. ➢ Appreciations and promotions, job allotment and assignment of responsibility are two other areas where HR executives rarely go by true utility values or effectiveness values of the work-force.
   - They either act on their own impression or opinion based on some scanty information generated through their own contacts within the organisation.
   - Realities of shop-floor contributions or work effectiveness or execution economies need not always have a direct

the organisation.
- Talent distribution across different work-centres
- Talent requirement across different work centres.

- Would such matrices be periodically updated to identify talent gaps across the organisation?
- Would this gap identification lead to designing of appropriate skill training programmes that would positively ensure that the target workforce would indeed be imparted the required execution talents or skills?

➢ Can the system design ensure that talent distribution and/or updation will match exactly what is projected in skill-requirement-matrix for the organisation?

➢ Would the system design ensure that HR practices always lead to creation of knowledge workers who, in turn, steadily get transformed to

	bearing with the measures invented by HR executives for this purpose. - Expression of displeasure or discomfort in this regard would never be tolerated. • They act only at the instance of higher-ups or selected few key personalities in the organisation.	process owners to uphold organisatinal commitments?
7.	➢ One more activity area where HR practices would be far from general expectation could be typically seen in some of the following: • Total mismatch between supervisory skill training with shop-floor requirements of process control and techniques, risk management, process related safety, health and hazards management, counselling and coaching in leadership skill requirements, etc. • Redistribution of skill available across the organisation is one more area where HR executives would generally fudge and fumble. • Most of the times such skill-redistributions carry the potential to reduce the effectiveness levels of many work centres both individually and collectively.	➢ Can the system design ensure that HR practices are completely free from all sorts and forms of biases and prejudices or discriminations based on caste, creed, race, region, language, gender, religious faith, culture, etc. at all stages from recruitment to retirement, periodical appreciations, promotions and rewards, etc. and that training programmes are made more relevant to job demands and inherent potentials of people?
8.	➢ Professional and social wellbeing of organisational workforce is another grossly ignored or neglected area in many organisations.	➢ Would the system design encourage and support HR executives in indulging in overall development of organisational workforce and their personal, professional and social wellbeing?

Table 2.11 Manufacturing and Output Generation Activities

A good cross-section of intellectuals across the society including quite a few diligence auditors does not view the following issues as part of *Corporate Governance* for any business establishment. This cross section views these aspects as belonging to *Productivity and Profitability Management*. As such, this cross section builds a firm conviction that all business establishments automatically address these areas though the degree of satisfaction could vary from one organisation to another.

This view is further supported by the fact that these aspects form part of independently certifiable management systems' design and system administration (ISO 9000, 14000, 18000, 22000, etc.). However, the harsh truth of the fact is that the belief of the above intellectual cross section is far stretched and is actually far from reality. This is because the bulk of audits under any of these certifiable system standards, rely heavily on records prepared for the purpose. For those who have had good exposure to live realities of activity-shop-floors, it is a well known fact that records are just a formality and are prepared at will and they need not always stand for virgin truth. This situation forces shop-floor executives to hide many facts which, in turn, ensure that operation transparency would always remain a questionable area. Naturally, integrity of operations would also be under constant challenge. It is for this purpose of minimising such open challenges, that one should identify the following aspects while designing a good *Corporate Governance* mechanism.

Most unfortunately, on certain occasions, even if there are a couple of manufacturing executives who might like to comply with necessary conformances, they may not get the required support. They may have to face two types of hurdles. One of them is lack of necessary and adequate infrastructure. The other one is resistance from bulk of the workforce who would directly equate the extra efforts they are required to put-in for ensuring certain compliances with the remuneration they get from the organisation. The psychology that rules the workforce in this regard is that most of these compliances activities do not form part of manufacturing activities and hence they do not contribute to increased production. On the contrary, they call for extra time and efforts to be put-in without any direct additional return. Hence they are non-remunerative activities. If one can manage to avoid them, why not? This is *execution shyness.*

The counterpart of this psychic barrier is the *investment shyness* exhibited by some senior managers. They also view investment in additional infrastructure as non-remunerative because they do not directly contribute to enhanced production or improved productivity. And hence if we can manage without them, why not? A good design of *Corporate Governance* mechanism therefore calls for carefully identifying the requirements of various compliances and provide necessary infrastructure support. Another support that is necessary in this regard is making provision for required time element without resorting to exerting undue pressures on the workforce for additional productions. One should, however, not forget that many compliance do not call for too much of extra time element and could be readily integrated with regular manufacturing activities without any sacrifice on production volumes. Shying away from making provision for adequate time element for job execution is another component of *investment shyness* of senior managers.

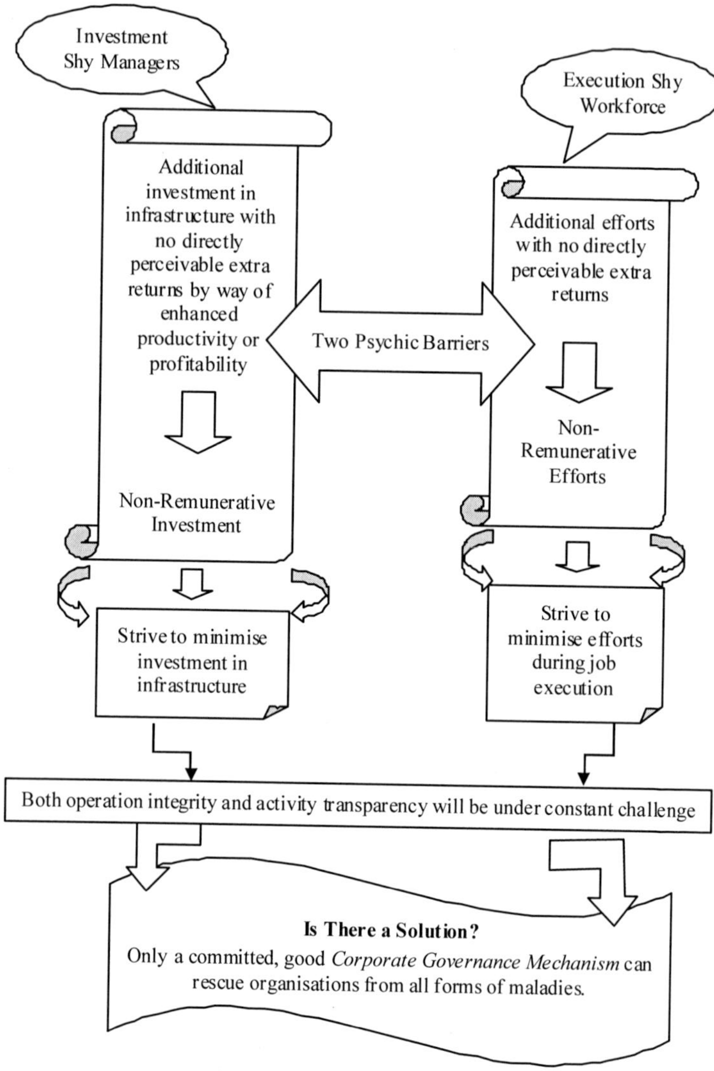

Fig. 2.6 Two Facets of Psychic Barriers that Haunt Business Corporates

Further, one should also not construe that all the types of malpractices that are discussed here below are seen in all types of organisations engaged in manufacturing activities. It is just not practical in this present globally competitive market environment. Magnitude of malpractices could vary from one organisation to another. What is important for us here is that the design of *Corporate Governance* mechanism should carefully address all these issues. By identifying these issues under *governance* area, organisations would always stand to gain maximum benefits.

When we explore these issues from broader perspectives of shop-floor realities, it becomes clear that most of these malpractices have their roots in the following two critical psychic parameters or psychic barriers that generally govern any industrial establishment.

The description *Investment Psychology*, here, precisely refers to that part of investment managers' views that guide their decisions with regard to investment in infrastructure necessary for establishing certain compliances. This cross section as well as some members of senior management in the shop-floor opines that some of the infrastructure elements are really superfluous and one can always manage without them. In their opinion, any investment in an infrastructure component that cannot bring a significant change in performance levels either in the process or in its output but can only add to incremental, but not significant, benefits is not worth (an idle investment or a non-remunerative investment!). Naturally, they shy away from certain investments, thus forcing active shop-floors to live under certain infrastructure vacuum.

Such infrastructure vacuums, force production executives to take to what is popularly known as *Manoeuvrability Skills*. This skill actually stands for their skills in manipulating various records and different elements of manufacturing environment in such a way that no auditor would normally get a doubt about their integrity. In addition, one more equally powerful psychic parameter operates in active shop-floors. This is popularly known as *Execution Psychology*. This psychic parameter actually refers to views that generally rule the bulk of industrial workforce namely *minimum exertion with maximum returns*. None in the industrial workforce would like to put-in extra efforts, however insignificant it may be, that would not directly bring additional monetary benefits. This psychic parameter would be so deep rooted that, in many situations where a specific infrastructure is available; the workforce would love to skip an additional execution step if they can manage to do so.

Design of a good *Corporate Governance Mechanism* should find ways and means to overcome both these two psychic barriers.

Table 2.11a Manufacturing and Output Generation Activities

Sr. No.	Frequently Encountered Types of Non-wholesome Operations ⇩ Key Areas of Concern	Can this be Tried? ⇩ Key Routes to Build Wholesomeness to Output Generation Activities
1.	All forms and types of non-wholesome practices and procedures seen in manufacturing shop-floors and/or in output generation workshops, basically result from one or more of the following malices: ⇩ ⇩ ⇩	➢ Can organisations fuse total integrity to all activities/operations that are being carried out by the organisation? ➢ Can such integrity be seen from activity transparency? ➢ Can organisations strive hard to remain absolutely clean in the eyes of employees, customers and other stake-holders?
2.	People have not developed a high degree of duty-bound consciousness which could ensure that they put-in earnest efforts to satisfactorily uphold corporate commitments to its stakeholders. - Total absence of good manufacturing planning including identifying and planning of associated ancillary activities and services and leading to considerable increase in manufacturing life-cycle thus adversely affecting stake-holders' interests in organisational activities. - Not identifying even certain basic critical-process-steps and operation criticalities adding to customers' risks in products and services of the organisation.	➢ Can organisations ensure development of a deep sense of realisation that this activity area carries a high potential to make or mar an organisation's image in the society? ➢ Can development of such concepts ensure its competitive progress in a globally wide, vibrant technology and market environment?

3.	Not developing the sense of job-execution based exclusively on the knowledge that governs the said activity.	➢ Can organisations ensure that each and every individual activity step is designed and configured or formulated in such a way that only the unadulterated latest knowledge about the process guides them?
4.	Developing an intense sense of achievement by mere addition to extra production volumes without much reference to any of the other standard performance requirements associated with job executions and job-execution environment. Like for example: • Not concerned/serious about maintaining workforce-friendly production environment. - Lack of concern for health and safety requirements of operation environment. - Absence of meticulous attention to regular maintenance of production machineries and equipments forcing production staff under heavy tension. - Forceful stretching of production times beyond people' tolerance limits. - Pressing uneducated and unskilled workers to handle intricate jobs, full of risks. - Not making any provision for safety devices and/or personal protection gadgets for people handling jobs carrying varying degrees of risks. - Not attending to even basic minimum safety devices like automation, partial or semi-automation that could reduce workers' stress levels through	➢ Can system design ensure the following? • People are seriously concerned and work towards maintaining workforce friendly job-execution-environment? • Equipment lay out is such that it fully addresses operation ergonomics and workforce comforts. • Job execution environment is configured in such a way that there will be no health and safety issue? • All the critical process steps and controls thereon have been carefully identified and put to place. • Maintenance of processing equipments is promptly attended and there will be no stretching of work hours or equipment utility hours. • System design is configured in such a way that it identifies right type of skills required to carry out different

elimination of certain monotonous and repetitive body movements related to job executions. - Not attending to ergonomics of machinery layouts forcing haphazard and random movements of men and materials leading to frequent on-set of high stresses. - Not showing much concern for maintaining satisfactory and good lighting arrangements in the work area forcing executives to work under heavy visual stress. - Absence of good quality breathing air in the work-place, absence of proper ventilation, high concentration levels of suspended particulate matter in the air, poor visibility in the work area due to heavy concentration of floating fine particles in the air. - High concentration of chemical fumes, vapours and smokes including toxic and poisonous vapours at the work place, • Always giving a slip to regulatory/statutory conformances. • Total absence of correlation between job execution details and customer application requirements or organisational commitment to external customers. • Exerting extra pressure or squeezing the workforce for extra production volumes without reference to many other associated standard requirements. • Absence of even obvious controls on different processes including some critical processes or process steps.	activities and maintains a good but dynamic balance between skill identification and provision. • Meticulous attention is paid to comply with all the required statutory guidelines. Required infrastructure is provided. • No hidden activity or objective is seen anywhere in the premises. As such, none would hide a data or an operation. • Details of job execution are directly corelatable with customers' application requirements and with organisational commitments. • Job execution and job design is prepared in such a way that none of the stakeholders' interests are at stake at any point of time.

5.	Developing an attitude of unconcerned approach towards process economy and/or effectiveness, output utility and performance levels – Putting extra strain on customers' economy.	➢ People are seriously concerned about process economy and global competitiveness of their activity output. All manufacturing activities ensure that material consumption is kept at most minimum levels per unit of satisfactory output. ➢ Manufacturing life cycle is established in such a way that it sets a standard for others in the field.
6.	Heavy stretching of non-maintenance service utility life-cycle of process equipments and machineries causing unexpected and/or sudden failure of processing equipments leading to onset of a series of blame-games.	➢ Equipment maintenance is attended in such a way that there will be no scope for stretching the cycle.
7.	Not serious about many of the ancillary and support services resulting in frequent breakdown in manufacturing life cycle. Attending to those services only in crisis situations.	➢ Activity layout and manufacturing life cycle is designed in such a way that all the critical support services are carefully identified and their specifications are well laid-out enabling people to properly plan all activities. ➢ Carefully identifying and putting in place necessary controls on procurement of ancillary services to ensure that activities are not hurt at any stage for want of a service support.

8.	Not appreciating the significance of a good internal communication mechanism. Causing many a hick-ups during activity execution.	➢ Carefully designing a good internal communication mechanism on lines with what is explained in published literature (Mruthyunjaya, 2002) to ensure that at no point of time activity life cycle is adversely affected for want of any data or information.

Conscience Keeping Operation Transparency

Transparency refers to situations where people engaged in carrying out various activities can unhesitatingly throw-open their activities for others to witness or verify. However, this component of *Corporate Governance* requirement should not be interpreted to mean that organisations should always keep their operations and documents or records open to anybody and everybody in the society. That is never the scope of this requirement. It is also a known fact that in reality, business corporates do come across many situations where they would be required to show their documents and records for verification by different people for different purpose. It is a basic requirement in corporate life, more so in today's vibrant social context. The purpose decides the type of verification and the scope of purpose decides the types of documents or records to be verified. It is in this context that the meaning and scope of this component of corporate governance should be understood as ever preparedness to show records or documents when required and nothing beyond.

Knowledge of standard operation management systems tells us that ever-preparedness can become a practical reality only when people meticulously follow the laid-out procedures and set norms during job-execution without resorting to any form of operation short-cuts, deviations or by-passes, which are typical of dishonest approaches, and in those situations where they will have nothing to hide from others. True transparency situations can come to physical existence only when procedural details of activities being executed are based precisely on the unadulterated knowledge that governs the said activity and not otherwise. When the driving force behind an activity happens to be the virgin knowledge, dishonesty will have no place and transparency reins the scenario. In other words, activity integrity prevails on all those situations which are free from dishonest approach or action. As such, wherever activity integrity prevails, transparency automatically co-exists. Naturally, neither of these two would have independent or isolated existence. These two *Governance* requirements are intricately interrelated with each other. Transparency demands activity integrity and activity integrity automatically leads to total transparency. Hence, these two governance parameters go in conjunction with each other.

The situation now sets a clear route for organisations to go transparent and to remain ever-transparent. They should never forget that they cannot make their operations totally transparent, if their activities lack true integrity or honesty in approach and actions. Wherever transparency becomes a questionable issue, integrity also remains a doubtful issue. Therefore, establishing total integrity of all actions and activities and freeing them from all types, forms and kinds of dishonesty, whether apparent and latent, is a basic pre-requisite for establishing complete transparency.

We have seen earlier under operation integrity that the first and foremost requirement for establishing total integrity of operations calls for complete elimination of the various types of hassles that one would normally come across in many organisations. We have also seen that such hassles prevail in organisations which would not have gone through the all the three stages of interface-evolution to evolve finally into integrated interface stage. When organisations evolve into one of integrated-interface stage, all the routine hassles automatically disappear and the operation environment gets itself completely transformed into one where activity non-transparency just cannot find place because transparency promoters rule the situations. (Table 2.12).

Table 2.12. Key Factors that Ensure total Transparency

Sr. No.	Transparency Promoters
1.	People's Ability to carefully identify Statutory Requirements
2.	Good Knowledge Back-up of People.
3.	Good Infrastructure Support (Freedom from operation constraints).

4. Competence and necessary execution Skills (good working knowledge of operating technology).
5. Total absence of Internal Frictions and Rivalry (Unrestricted sharing of facilities and free-flow of data and information).
6. Co-ordinated approach with collective commitment to corporate goals (liberal sharing of expertise and experience).
7. Effective Knowledge Deployment (Absence of Knowledge Voids).
8. Fairness in appreciation and recognitions (high comfort levels of workforce).
9. High degree of Involved Participation (Emotional and Intellectual Participations).
10. Strong Will Power not to fall prey to Allurements.
11. High degree of personal morale and ethos (invincible fortress against all forms and types of unethical or non-wholesome practices that would go against social values and corporate values).

Organisations should first carefully analyse all their activities and dissect their details to identify if any of their activities or activity steps is infested with an element of dishonesty without reference to its nature or magnitude. The moment an element of dishonesty is noticed they have to go to its root and eliminate the cause for the same at source and free the activity from dishonesty. Once the element of dishonesty is eliminated at its root, people would unhesitatingly demonstrate and throw open all their activities for inspection and verification by concerned authorities or agencies. They would similarly have no hesitation to straight put-up all the records that would be generated during the course of activity execution. When people have nothing to hide from others, why should there be any non-transparency?

Whenever an activity integrity takes a dip or a nose dive, people will have many things to hide from others, whether the general public or specific stakeholders including their own colleagues and co-workers. Naturally, they will resort to fabricating many records and evidences only for purpose of showing them to statutory agencies or system auditors. When organisations take to fabrication of records, they would be left with no alternative but to keep generating different types of records for different purposes. And in this process, many times organisations do get caught red-handed due to varying degrees of misalignment and non-correlation between different records being generated at different activity centres.

The adjective *Conscience Keeping*, used above, now stands fully justified because it is only the degree of transparency that could be displayed would speak of organisations' intentions and objectives behind their activities. When the intentions are clear and the objectives are noble, none can stop them from remaining transparent to the core. Wherever and whenever a deviation occurs, it would keep pricking people's conscience and they would immediately jump to action and bring the deviating situation back to normal. In this sense, transparency always guards peoples' conscience.

While operation transparency could be verified by different ways, two methods have gained more popularity. Obviously, the first of them is a physical verification of activity execution and their outcome to confirm whether or not those activities are being carried out as per laid down procedures, schemes and norms and whether or not those activities are yielding expected results. However, there is one limitation in this scheme. It is not always practical for many reasons and reality constraints that one can physically verify an activity for its full life-cycle. This limitation has given rise to another method. This is to carefully identify and verify all the records that get generated during the course of activity execution. Some system auditors follow a slightly modified mechanism to verify transparency. They also go through the records but with backward integration concept. They first like to confirm that organisational activities have truly yielded expected results and that their output beneficiary is fully satisfied with the output he/she gets from the organisation. With this data, they may like to move backwards to identify all the interested stakeholders and identify their interests in the activity and activity steps throughout its generation life-cycle and find out how well their interests are addressed both individually and collectively. The only limitation that camouflages the mechanism of records verification is that some auditors find it difficult to identify situations where records have only been fabricated. While all these methods are meant for others to verify and confirm, nothing can substitute true integrity and true honesty of organisations! The discussions given under test of integrity or integrity check points lay a clear blue print for designing a good governance system that would effectively integrate both operation integrity and transparency for business organisations.

Decision Pattern

During the course of carrying out their business transactions, corporates do take many decisions. Some of them could be directly related with job execution mechanism and its sequence and some could be related with activity effectiveness and efficiency and some other decisions could be to modulate the impact of their activity output. Some could be related with business strategies and marketing operations, etc., etc. Many times, certain decisions may have to be taken to initiate a series of decision making processes at different work centres in the activity chain. There would be many situations where the operation context decides the type of decision taken by corporates. Some decisions could have an immediate impact on contemplated target beneficiaries and some could have delayed and/or cumulative impacts. Impacts of some decisions could be far stretched and wide spread to cover a greater cross section of the society and some will have narrow target spectrum. Some decisions could bring expected results and some may not. In addition, active shop-floors create many situations where a decision cannot afford to wait for long to follow a stereotyped, elaborate decision making process but would call for immediate actions resulting from immediate decisions. Decision making process in a business corporate is, therefore, a fairly complex phenomenon.

When we explore this subject from the view points of *Corporate Governance*, what becomes relevant for us is the true, verifiable intention or the genuineness of the thought that works behind a decision making process. Figure 2.7 gives a schematic presentation of some of the key factors that could ensure that corporate decisions always remain good and acceptable without reference to the nature of the decision.

Spontaneous Decisions

Let us first examine the types of decisions that are taken in situations which cannot afford to wait for long but call for immediate action resulting from an immediate or almost on the spot decision. Such decisions could be described as spontaneous decisions. If we carefully examine all those situations of active shop-floors that demand spontaneous decisions, we do realise the following:

- These situations normally belong to an emergency category.
- The emergency could be of two types.

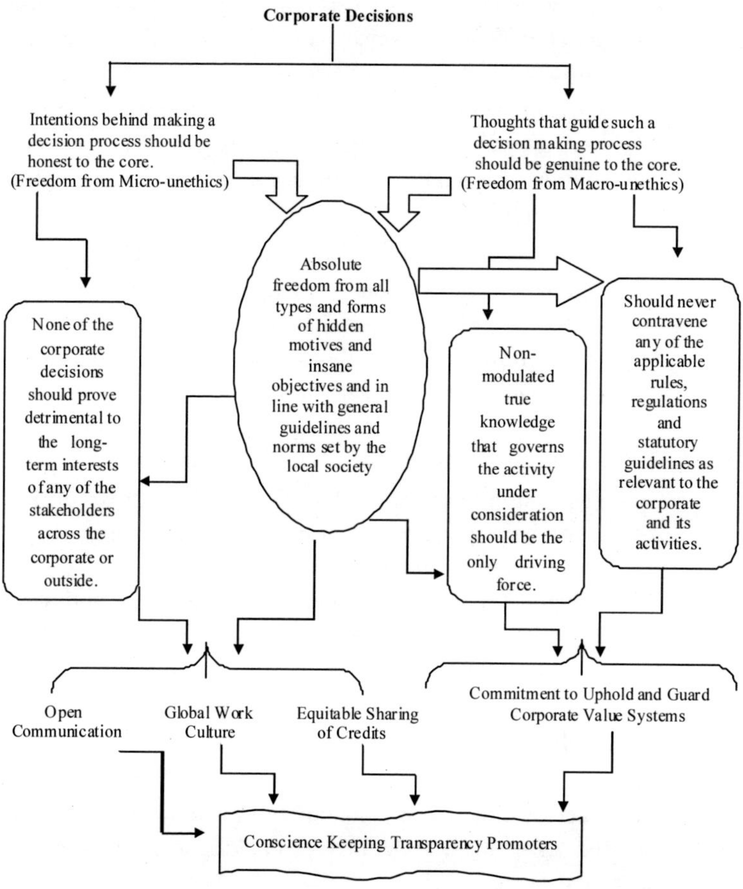

Fig. 2.7. Factors that make Good Corporate Decisions

1. The first of them refers to those situations which are generally understood by everybody as a true emergency situation arising from say an accident, a fire, an explosion, a pressure explosion, etc.
    - o These situations carry a high potential to cause severe injuries to people if not immediately arrested and averted and/or attended to quench and/or normalise the situation.

- o These situations also carry a high potential to cause heavy damages to organisational assets, resources and cause great economic losses.
- o Their impact profile could vary from an isolated activity centre, to an activity wing or activity division as a whole or in certain unique situations could extend to the entire organisation.

  Their damage potential also varies accordingly.
- o Discussions given in chapter five clearly tell us that those situations call for well designed, well organised and well managed and appropriately co-ordinated 'decision- action' management mechanism for satisfactorily handling the situations and to minimise injuries to people and also to minimise damages to assets of the organisation.
- o These discussions also tell us that decisions taken during those emergency situations, though appear to be spontaneous in nature at the face of it, are indeed well thought out, well laid out, well considered and well explored ones and are based on well understood scientific principles (knowledge) that govern the situations.

  Otherwise the results of actions from those decisions could be disastrous and least acceptable.

2. The other category refers to those situations which one would come across more often in manufacturing environments. In a limited sense, these situations also belong to the emergency category.

   These emergency situations, if not decided and attended immediately could lead to one or more of the following:

   - Generation of sub-standard products.
     - Under utilisation of precious resources.
   - Generation of non-standard products.
     - Complete waste of process inputs. Loss of Resources
   - Loss of machinery time, damages to assets and machineries.
   - Loss of precious manpower.

If we carefully study these situations, we do realise that shop-floor emergencies generally come-up due to one or more of the following reasons:

- Failure of processing equipments and machineries.
    - Not properly attending to maintenance works.
    - Not carefully fixing the time interval between two successive maintenance operations.
    - Using sub-standard/poor-quality components and parts for replacement during maintenance works.
- Engaging unskilled workforce for the job.
    - Wrong recipe.
    - Wrong setting of controls.
    - Wrong sequence and/or wrong methods for execution.
- Failure of an ancillary or a support service line/facility.
- Failure of process input supply quality.
- Failure of control mechanisms, etc.

While it may not be difficult to correct any of these situations as soon as the same is noticed, it may not always be easy to readily identify or locate the type of mistake that has taken place and has caused the occurrence of emergency situation.

These are the types of shop-floor emergencies or situations which call for immediate decisions and actions. Generally, such decisions which could be rightly described as discretionary decision powers rest with only a selected few senior executives. Occasionally and with rare exceptions even some highly experienced member of the workforce carries such responsibilities. It may not be a surprise that on many an occasion, even a so-called senior executive may like to either consult or may like to have a second opinion from a highly experienced worker at the shop-floor. We should not forget to notice that such decisions are not taken by anybody and everybody in the shop-floor but only by a selected few.

Who are those people that would be entitled to take such immediate decisions? What criteria would the organisation apply to identify them? It is needless to say that they are generally very senior executives and they carry with them rich experience of active shop-floors and they would be exposed to widely varying types of situations that could lead to different types of shop-floor emergencies. They would be highly knowledgeable and also carry with them experience of handling similar situations. As such, whenever they would be required to take an immediate decision to avert an unwelcome incident, they would weigh between many alternatives available at their disposal and finally identify an action which could ensure minimum material loss.

This is precisely what even the highly experienced member of the workforce (gold-mines of experience) also would do. The key purpose that would be served in those situations is the conservation of materials and/or resources. Therefore, they would not contravene any of the standard requirements to be explored before taking decisions.

Decisions taken by anybody else in those situations could prove to become spurious as they might carry a high degree of personal biases, opinions, impressions and convictions, etc.

What Contributes to Decision Making?

It is a common observation that it is only the investment managers who would generally be involved in decision making in any business corporate. They do so either on their own or in consultation with some shop-floor managers. When both these groups of managers are involved, decision making process will be explored from different perspectives. While one of the groups examines the issue from its impact potential on the entire organisational workforce, work environment, various compliances' requirements, operation effectiveness and efficiency parameters, input resources constraints, if any, operation sustainability, etc. the other group explores the same issue from financial commitments, financial performances, overall profitability angles, and business prospects.

One could, therefore, say that corporate decisions would be normally based on people's discretionary decision power, which, in turn, would be based on people's highest level of intelligence backed with most appropriate knowledge power governing the said process or phenomenon. Discretion, in turn, demands that before arriving at any decision, one has to thoroughly evaluate its impact on the following areas namely:

i. Any decision that would not call for heavy commitment of finances for implementation would carry a better chance to get accepted by a larger cross section of stakeholders.

ii. Any decision that does not carry a high potential to hurt a greater cross section of the workforce and the local society would carry a better chance to get accepted by a larger cross section of stakeholders.

iii. Any decision that would give a major boost to organisational overall competitive performance would carry a better chance to get accepted by a larger cross section of stakeholders.

iv. Any decision that would further brighten the prospects of business growth and prosperity in the globally competitive competition world would carry a better chance to get accepted by a larger cross section of stakeholders.

In other words it goes without saying that corporate decisions cannot afford to find acceptability if they lack total back-up of information, data analysis or observations weighed for their relative merits, limitations and consequences. In the absence of fulfilment of these criteria, it would just amount to a decision taken in habitual haste without verifying the pros and cons of an action and one may have to regret for the decision later. If such things should not happen, decision making group has to first improve on its.

Rationalisation and Reasoning Powers: Acquired through enhanced overall Knowledge Power, both in depth and in spectral width, and supported with rich experience and expertise.

The fact based rationalisation and reasoning power backed-up with appropriate knowledge and experience would ensure that the activity leader has a complete knowledge of pros and cons of all actions and their output together with a good knowledge of associated and involved resource stipulations and constraints as well as potential threats and opportunities and also the magnitudes of risks involved in translating a thought or an idea to an action plan supplemented with a knowledge of organisational priorities. This state actually represents true discretionary decision power. Corporate decision making process or mechanism should be designed in such a way that it is based on scientific principles, sound logics and appropriate data and information back-up. The mechanism should be such that it would never give room for people's taking spontaneous decisions. Otherwise, it is likely that organisational precious resources could go waste and the decision could prove to be spurious.

Well Configured Decision Mechanism

A good decision making mechanism, should, therefore, meet the following criteria:

- ➢ The first and foremost requirement is that the decision should be fair to all the concerned people/stakeholders.
- ➢ Concept of fairness
  - It should be fair to investors – Their investment should not go idle but should bring good returns.
    - o At the same time, their investment should be made in activities that uphold and guard good social values and respect the law of the land.
  - It should be fair to workforce – Their hard work and efforts should be fruitfully utilised for generating extra wealth by fair and respectable means.
    - o Decision implementation should not pose any threat to their professional growth and betterment prospects and also the general welfare.
  - It should be fair to financiers – Their finance investment should be put to profitable proposals preferably with nil or minimum gestation period.
  - It should be fair to customers – Corporate decisions should strengthen their relationship with the corporate.
  - It should be fair to suppliers – Corporate decisions should bring them more competitive comforts.
  - It should be fair to competitors – Corporate decisions should not dig into their comfort zone.
  - It should be fair to the society – Corporate decisions should bring better social comforts and welfare of the people.
  - It should be fair to the environment – Corporate activities should not add to environmental burden.

- There should be a well identified purpose which calls for a decision.
  - The decision should lead to identify and/or design a mechanism or scheme/means that could steadily lead the organisation/people towards achieving the identified purpose.

  This requirement therefore presupposes that the purpose should exhibit the following features:

  → The purpose should be unambiguous and free from uncertainties.

    - It should be readily explainable and easily understandable and conveyable to all people involved in the process of achievement.
    - There should be no scope for ifs and buts.

  → The purpose should be clearly definable.

    - Target beneficiaries and beneficiary profile should be clearly identifiable and definable.
    - Target beneficiaries should not be confined to pre-identified and pre-conceived or pre-contemplated select groups. Otherwise it may get highly prejudiced and biased. On the contrary, it should belong to a broader cross section of the society.

- Actions resulting from decisions should invoke ready response from target beneficiaries with special reference to acceptability or not.
- Decision implementation mechanism should be based on fully developed knowledge that is on par with most of the contemporary technologies and not on only part developed knowledge.
  - It should be in line with emerging and new technologies.
  - It should not adopt any of the resource-depleting technologies but should be based on resource-conserving technology.
  - It should not involve any type of harmful by-products.
- The purpose should not be based on any kind of unethical (non-wholesome) conceptions or conjectures.

  - It should not hurt anybody's sentiments, conscience beliefs (religious beliefs and personal convictions) of all involved and/or affected people either directly or indirectly.
  - It should not aim at playing with target beneficiary's sentiments.
  - It should not pose any threat to people's health and safety aspects.
  - Should not carry any kind of hidden or latent harm potential (including new types and kinds of safety threats), immediate or long-term, against any of the stakeholders' at any stage and at all stages of the process involved right from input procurement to field application and disposal after full utility-service-life-cycle.

➢ Implementation of a decision particularly those that carry a good potential to affect manufacturing and other shop-floor activities, including all types of field executions and activities, should aim at achieving a positive improvement in process reliability, output ruggedness and productivity and process economy.

  - Some of the other benefits these decisions should aim at achieving are:
    - o Reduction in process-life-cycle-time or product generation-life-cycle-time.
    - o Enhancement in competitiveness through elimination of and/or trimming of cost additive factors.
    - o Increase in product life-cycle.
    - o Improvement in output performance levels resulting in positively enhanced customer comfort levels.
    - o Enhancement in activity effectiveness and efficiency levels.
    - o Decrease in generation of non-performing or poor-performing outputs.
    - o Decrease in generation of reworks and process wastes during product's productive (utility)–life-cycle.
    - o Decrease in output generation cost and a positive increase in competitiveness and resource conservation.

   - o Decrease in field maintenance and in maintenance of product life-cycle cost.
   - o Should not adversely affect working environment with regard to workforce safety aspects, equipment safety aspects and environment safety aspects.
- Each one of these types of decisions would add an extra value to investors' interest in the corporate and its activities.

➢ Nature of decisions should be such that, when translated to actions, they should not give rise to onset of any kind of micro or macro-unethical activities like leading to any type of favouritism to any of the employee or any form of discrimination based on opinions and impressions but should be based only on true facts.

- On the contrary, these decisions should be such that they work towards eliminating all forms and types of unacceptable (unethical) practices from shop-floors.

➢ Should contribute to additional benefits and comforts of people in the society.

➢ Should aim at ensuring high value return to customers.

- Enhancement of customer comforts through one or more of the following:
   - o Elimination of latent and apparent defects in products.
   - o Extra cumulative competitive benefits.
   - o Wider utility spectrum.
   - o Sustained, trouble-free, long-time productive life,
   - o High quality performance of products and services supplied.
   - o Freedom from waste by-product generation.

➢ The decision should guard investor's interest well.

- It should promote business prospects.
- Should invoke participative management from concerned stakeholders in decision making.
- Should not lead to practice of any kind of discrimination while implementing the decision.

- Implementation of the decision should not cause any form of adverse impact on the environment.
- Purpose behind a decision should be in the nature of time-targeted response to a query from an interested stakeholder.

➢ The purpose should be quantifiable.
- People should not dope in darkness regarding their achievement.
- Resources necessary for achievement should be clearly identifiable and definable.
- Results should be co-relatable with resources input and justifiable for purposes of weighing on a competitive performances merit scale.

➢ Progress of implementation should be measurable on a suitable scale.

➢ It should be verifiable and confirmable.
- Should be verifiable on a time scale for progress of achievement.
    - Verification should lead to alter or amend the scheme/ design as may become necessary to reorient organisational efforts towards achievement.
- Verifiable and confirmable for the following:
    - The achievement and/or means of achievement should not defeat corporate policies, visions and missions, goals and objectives.
    - Does not contravene any of the statutory requirements.
    - Does not lead to creation of competition with another product or service of the organisation.
    - Achievement mechanism does not deviate from the path set by the true knowledge that governs the process.
    - None of the activities or activity steps involved in achievement should prove to be unethical.
    - Methodologies should provide for ready participation of a wide cross section of the organisational workforce.

- o Achievement does not lead to concealment of any of the earlier unethical activities or outputs.
- Does not lead to generation of a product or service which carries a good potential for use in anti-social activities and to commit heinous crime against mankind.
- Does not lead to violation of any of the prevailing professional norms or social norms, whether regional, national or international.

➢ All the stakeholders will have a heavy stake in corporate affairs. There can be hardly any corporate decision which cannot affect one or the other category of stakeholders. As such, whenever certain decisions are taken, corporates do carry a high responsibility to carefully guard and protect stakeholders' interests and to ensure that their interests will not be jeopardised or put to stake.

- Nature of interest which different categories of stakeholders will have in corporate decisions is briefly presented in Table 2.13.

  We can see from this table that the impact of corporate decisions embraces the entire cross section of the society and also the surroundings. As such, it is not easy for any corporate to satisfy each and every individual category of stakeholders on all counts and at all times. There would be many situations where interests of different categories of stakeholders would in juxtaposition with each others'. Therefore, what is desirable is that corporates go cautious while taking any decision by ensuring maintenance of a good balance between different types of stakeholders' interests.

Health and Safety Aspects

Though this is considered as an independent aspect under corporate governance by many, it is indeed not a totally independent aspect. On the contrary, this aspect is integral to guarding of employees' interests. If basic needs of health and safety aspects of work environment are not satisfactorily addressed how can corporates guard the general requirements of employees' interests?

Table 2.13 Stakeholders' Interest in Corporate Decisions (strategic movements)

Sl. No.	Stakeholder Category	Where their Interest Lies
1	Business Investors/Shareholders	Strategies that affect returns on their investment. Expansions and diversifications which carry high profitability-risk on their investment. Business takeovers that carry the risk of digging into high profitability on their investment. Expansions and investments in a hitherto unknown market area that carry the risk of poor profitability. Closure of well established business activities on grounds of principles that they do not fit into their core group or core strength.
2	Financiers /Investment Banks	Strategies that carry high potential to stretch profitability gestation period. Strategies that put their investment security at stake. Strategies that might result in reduced returns on their investments. Strategies that provide for their enhanced investment participation.
3	Customers	Strategies that result in increase in their purchase price. Strategies that open-up their application profile. Strategies that might minimise their product limitations. Strategies that might ease their tensions regarding maintenance issues associated with products supplied to them. Strategies that curtail their interest in corporate products and services. Strategies that add to their competitive benefits. Strategies that minimise their competitive advantages.
4	Suppliers	Strategies that affect returns on their supplies. Strategies that provide for enhancement in their supply-scope and profile. Strategies that result in either curtailing their supplies or shutting them out. Strategies that might add to the strength of their competitors. Strategies that might force them to cut profit margins on their supplies.
5	Employees	Strategies that affect returns on their hard work, time and energy investment. Strategies that affect their growth prospects. Strategies that open-up a wide horizon for their professional growth and prosperity. Strategies that pose true professional challenges by providing opportunities to prove their mettle. Strategies that pose severe threat to their normal, healthy and safe working conditions. Strategies and policies that might have an adverse impact on their compensation package or on their take-home salary. Strategies that may keep them away from the race in their fight for extra remuneration, appreciation and rewards for their hard work. Strategies that may break their unity.

6	Competitors	• Strategies that affect their competitive performance. • Strategies that affect their profitability. • Strategies that affect their business prospects. • Strategies that pose severe threats to their very survival.
7	Society	• Strategies that affect general welfare of the society. • Strategies that throw wide open opportunities for revenue generation for the local administration/government. • Strategies that adversely affect on employment potential for local people. • Strategies that result in a steady deterioration in the general health status of the population. • Strategies that result in shrinkage of monetary support to development and welfare activities of the local society. • Strategies that cause a heavy stress or burden on the social infrastructure.
8	Environment	• Strategies that result in total depletion of its precious, scarce natural resources. • Strategies that result in merciless exploitation of many of its precious natural resources. • Strategies and practices which lead to increasing pollution of land, water and air and add to the overall environmental burden. • Strategies that heavily pump underground water to add severe tension to the water table of the region. • Strategies that mercilessly contribute to polluting its serene natural atmosphere and add to steady changes in global atmospheric conditions that would, in turn, affect the entire bio-world, either directly or indirectly.

As discussed in published literature (Mruthyunjaya, 2011) and also explained briefly under social responsibilities, business establishments are generally abreast with different types and nature of health hazards. Discussions given under chapter five, *Support Systems* and also Table 5.1 give elaborate descriptions of the nature of risks that are generally associated with different types of industrial environment. As respectable members of the society and as an integral requirement to protecting their stakeholders' (employees') interests, corporates have to shoulder the responsibility to protect their workforce from all forms and types of work and work-environment related adverse impacts on their health and safety aspects. Corporates have to ensure that their workforce is never put to risk in and around the corporate premises.

In the background of descriptions given under *Support Systems*, corporates have to carefully study, understand and analyse their activities and activity environments to identify if any of those activities or activity steps or execution details are associated with any type of inherent and apparent risk element, without reference to the magnitude of risks. Such an analysis should, in turn, lead to designing and installing the required safety devices and other mechanisms to ensure that work and work environment always remain safe to work with and that people are never put to risk.

It is also well known that some industrial activities carry a hidden potential to cause a cumulative adverse health effects in the long run and over a period of time. As such, adverse impacts of some of these aspects will not be either seen or felt immediately. This situation induces both corporates and also the directly affected workforce to ignore them. But the nature of their cumulative damages could be severe including malfunctioning of many of the vital body metabolisms. Chemicals used in chemical processing industries and also some chemicals used in pharmaceutical industries are more prone to such long-term carry forward adverse impacts. Wherever chemicals that possess certain degree of risks like flammability, toxicity, corrosiveness, etc. are required to be used in the process, necessary safety devices should be provided to the workforce.

Intellectuals across the industrial world should carefully identify and notify all such known cumulative-risk-prone activities and activity environments. Both corporates and the workforce should collectively work towards installing required safety measures including imparting in people the right kind of execution skills backed-up with knowledge about the risks associated with their jobs and to equip them with necessary personal protection devices. Similarly, some of the neglected aspects of activity environments also carry the potential to cumulatively lead to major damages to certain environment or equipment components resulting in incidence of accidents, which in turn carry the potential to harm and injure people. Workmen should carefully identify all types of changes that might be taking place in safe working environments and environment components, however minor they may appear to be, and guard themselves again unwelcome incidents.

This is just the first phase of safety considerations. Corporate responsibility does not stop at mere protecting its workforce. Corporates generate products and services needed by the society. Many people use corporate products and services. They also should be safe throughout the active utility-life cycle of those products and services. It is for this purpose that corporates should go out of the way to educate customers in safe using or handling of their products. This part of customer education should be considered as serious as educating them on proper usage of products.

Machinery manufacturing industries should address most of the safety aspects through equipment/machinery design. Occasionally, handling of heavy equipments and machineries also poses safety issues. Wherever design safety would be inadequate to ensure total safety of customers and wherever customers either tend to or get an opportunity to meddle with built-in safety features, necessary warnings should be marked on the equipment at appropriate places so that customers are constantly reminded of the required safety precautions. In the case of electronic, electrical and electrochemical gadgets, etc. associated risks should be well identified and customers should be well informed of the same. Safety considerations are not confined only to equipments and machineries. They would become equally critical in the case of supply of chemicals and pharmaceuticals as well. Chemicals are generally abreast with a wide variety of safety issues right from inhalation to ingestion and/or accidental swallowing. Chemical vapours can cause irritation to eyes and noses. They can also cause suffocation. Some chemical vapours could also be toxic. Some chemicals are combustible as well. Some chemicals could carry cumulative or latent adverse effects. Therefore, the type of risks associated with them should be properly highlighted and customers should be suitably educated of the same. Customers should also be advised of the required safety gadgets. While pharmaceuticals may not carry all these types of risks which chemicals carry, they do carry risks of over dosage and risk of using beyond certain time duration beyond which the active bio-molecules would become less active or non-active. Further, pharmaceuticals carry one more type of risk namely using a particular pharmaceutical in a wrong situation or for a wrong application could prove very dangerous. This aspect of safety consideration will have to be clearly marked and customers should be warned of the same. Thus, wherever a safety aspect is involved whether within corporate premises or outside at customers' premises, the same should be carefully identified and suitably notified.

Compensation Package

This is one more area that is generally abreast with lots of favouritism and biased discrimination. Organisations generally find it difficult to come out of such a dubious distinction attached to this activity. Compensation package refers to that component of sharing corporate returns or generated wealth with the employees who spend the bulk of their time in carrying out corporate activities and in generating corporate wealth. It thus refers to parting with a small portion of what they have only contributed. Yet, this issue remains the *Bone of Contest* most of the times and in most of the business corporates because investment managers in business establishments and their representatives hardly recognise this basic truth that corporate wealth is actually generated only by its employees through their hard work and dedicated efforts.

An unusually strange concept that camouflages the *Phenomenon of Distribution of Corporate Wealth* is the fact that practically all the eight different categories of corporate stakeholders (Business Investors/ Shareholders, Financiers/Investment Banks, Customers, Suppliers, Employees, Competitors, Society and the Environment) tend to stake a big claim on this generated wealth. Each one of them tends to claim that it is only they who are basically responsible for wealth generation and therefore they should have a major share in the generated wealth. What should be the basic guidelines to distribute corporate wealth among all these rightful contenders is not the subject for our discussion here. We are concerned here with only that part of wealth distribution which is made to employees. There are many populist business schools of thought who advocate that a major chunk of corporate wealth should be distributed among employees only.

Compensation package generally comprises of two basic components. One of them is the routine annual component which does not call for any kind of extra consideration and the other one is the periodical recognition-cum-appreciation component. It is this second component which generally attracts discussions and dissentions. The element of dissention arises due to the fact that employees invariably feel that they have been discriminated because of prevalence of lots of favouritism and biases.

Corporate governance addresses this aspect of discrimination and favouritism while deciding about employees' compensation package. Any corporate that establishes good governance mechanism, has to fight this perennial menace that hovers around them. In order to fight this menace corporates have to evolve a strategy based on mutual trust and confidence. They have to first work towards building mutual trust and confidence. The first and foremost requirement in this direction is to recognise the fact that investment managers and their representatives, HR managers in this particular case, are also normal human beings and therefore they carry a high potential for practicing favouritism. The good base prepared by practice of activity integrity and operation transparency sets the rule for fighting this menace.

If the intentions behind the decision (appreciation) are clear and if they do not have anything to hide, then why not directly involve the employees in this process and share opinions of both the concerned groups? Good governance mechanism recognises the following key issues while deciding on compensation packages. Any other criteria will be unfair and will not be acceptable under good governance:

1. In the current competitive scenario, all intellectuals like to outperform others to ensure that they earn an extra mileage over others in competitive evaluations. As such, all intellectuals like to shoulder extra-responsibility so that they are able to push many of the processes through so that they are in a position to keep themselves at the centre of activities and achievements. Naturally they will be in the limelight and attract the attention of higher-ups who would be involved in evaluations and appreciations.
2. It may not be a surprise that many times, they create situations in such a way that their enthusiasm to do more work would get readily notified and higher-ups would love to provide suitable opportunities enabling them to fully explore their

unexplored performance potential that would have remained in hibernation (dormant/latent) for want of appropriate opportunities. This is certainly not an uncalled for situation for any performance-eager individual. In fact, every individual, irrespective of his/her socio-educational background should get an opportunity to fully explore whatever unexplored performance potential he/she has, to excel.

3. People do all these things not for mere love of work. Any such assumption would be totally wrong. As normal human beings living in this worldly environment, people do look for appropriate appreciation for their extra hard work and for their extra contributions.

4. Incidentally, all those who carry the responsibility for administering regular and/or periodical appreciation and rewarding of the organisational workforce, do go by such extra-ordinary performances of people. Considering people's performance as primary criteria for appreciation is a standard practice in all establishments.

   Appreciations and rewards act as good morale boosters and as boosters for innate internal drive of people to perform better and to excel especially if appraisal outcome is made known to people in advance and they are given an opportunity to countercheck and verify the same and compare their calculations with those people who have done it and find reasons for differences and get convinced of the same through fact based discussions.

5. Establishments should also recognise the fact that rewards and appreciations do act as performance catalysts to boost people's performance temperament. Naturally, they further promote peoples' performance efficiency because rewards and appreciations always work towards strengthening peoples' impulsive internal reasons for performing better.

6. Organisations should bear in mind that they have to go very cautious in this regard and ensure that people's tendency to perform better should not be kindled only by rewards and appreciations. It will have to remain as a natural instinct to perform better. While appreciation of extra-hard work is a

natural process, if the motive behind hard work happens to be exclusively appreciation magnitude and frequency, then it will be suicidal to those individuals as well as to organisations.

7. Another important aspect which organisations should never forget is the fact that, in the normal course, no intellectual would like to be assessed and evaluated by others. They always tend to believe that they have the necessary expertise in their activity field and therefore those who are busy in other activity areas do not have the requisite competency to assess them. The net result would be that these intellectuals always believe that there is high degree of biases and favouritism in the assessment mechanism. What is the way out? Allowing intellectuals to assess themselves is the only way out.
8. It is for this purpose that organisations should practice a transparent rewarding system. In this mechanism, organisations should list out the types of works under each activity head that would earn extra credit points for the performer. Organisation should also ensure that such a credit-earning mechanism would cover all types of works that are required to be carried out so that no single activity is allowed to suffer at the cost of other works. Activity break-through should get as much credit as an extra effectiveness shown in routine executions. Established work standards and norms should provide the cut-off base for earning extra credit points and should be known to everybody across the organisation. Such cut-off levels should be identified for both individual achievements as well for collective achievements. In fact, from organisational overall performance view points, collective achievements should always be given extra credit-rating. This would kindle the spirit of collective achievement over individual performance. Such a mechanism would provide equal opportunity to everybody to prove his/her mettle and merits both as an individual and as a group member. This is true transparent approach. In the absence of such an approach, it may not be a surprise that people tend to believe that they have been intentionally kept outside the competition race. They would straight dub it as a highly biased approach.

In this mechanism, every individual should enjoy an equal right to challenge the calculation or formula adopted for arriving at his appreciation quantum. Every aggrieved person should be given an opportunity to verify the calculation and to get convinced. When all these operations remain transparent to the core, people's tendency to weigh self above the rest also gradually disappears and the organisation will have a novel method for appreciating its workforce. People would remain highly satisfied.

9. Thus, there should be pre-defined and pre-notified compensation and appreciation policy for the organisation as a whole. The policy should embrace everybody from top to bottom, from the lowest level worker to the highest level worker (an intellectual worker), say CEO or MD. The policy should also specify in very clear words free from ambiguity the measures and formulations that would be followed by the company. The measures and formulations developed for the purpose should suitably be backed-up by well defined and rationalised logics for the same. The rationale itself should be open to refinement and modification as and when better logics get developed and get accepted.
10. The only constraint that organisations would face in this approach is their inability to identify equivalent cut-off levels for different activity areas. For this purpose, they have to directly involve people in identifying the cut-off levels under different activity heads taking care to ensure that an intellectual gets as much an opportunity as an ordinary skilled worker. Since opinions differ, this mechanism should be kept open for continuous improvement and refinement based on feedback from people.

Discrimination

This CG component belongs to that category which has always remained as a subject of *Bone of Contention* between managements of corporates and other stakeholders. Discrimination in simple words refers to biased preferences or practice of preferential treatment. Discrimination would generally be ascribed to preferences based on caste, creed, race, region, language, gender, religious faith, culture, etc.

Most of the aggrieved stakeholders would jump to conclusion that there is discrimination.

This is a well recognised area of common concern where the society has remained a silent spectator to many of the apparent and obvious but non-palatable issues taking place in many corporate activity areas. The phenomenon of discrimination is monstrously high in some corporates and much less in many others. One can hardly find a business corporate which is totally free from this malicious disease.

Discrimination and favouritism is a global phenomenon and is a common order in companies' routine administration and management all over the world. All societies have accepted the same as integral to corporate working pattern. Therefore, none of the societies have tried to either change or challenge some of these practices that clearly display discriminatory decisions and actions. The basic premise here is the belief that corporates know better as to 'what is good for them and what is not'. Only a few sociologists and social ethicists raise their voice against some of these practices. But for small corrections and changes, generally their cry falls on deaf ears.

In many business corporates, right from appointment of members to the *Executive Board or the Board of Directors,* all *Top Executives* are invariably identified and decided by only company's promoters or investment managers, if they happen to be from promoters' family. Exceptions would embrace only those areas which are mandated by law. In most of these situations, the only criterion for their identification and/or selection would be receipt of a recommendation, whether formal or informal, from some well known personal quarters/contacts or a recommendation from a popularly influential local luminary or a pressure group. Merit does not always remain the prime criteria. It is also a well understood but rarely expressed view that all those *top executives* or the members of the *Board*, would just function as mere mouth-pieces of business promoters i.e. *"Yes, Sir –* Category." These members or executives just serve to fulfil formal requirements and nothing beyond. Needless to say that this tendency liberally percolates and spreads to all nooks and corners of company's activity profile. Discrimination of different types, kinds and magnitudes has remained the order of company's management pattern all over the world.

There are different perspectives to be examined before declaring a particular practice as one of discriminatory type. There are both personal and sociological angles to this phenomenon. The personal angle essentially refers to the views, beliefs, opinions and considerations of business promoters and/or partners or the executives who is vested with sufficient authority to take decisions independently on matters related to company's affairs. When an individual invests on a business venture solely from his personal resources and runs the business, naturally, his/her personal views and considerations predominate over other considerations. As an individual, the investor has every right to his administrative practices and procedures to suit his comforts and convenience. He would keep for himself the full decision power as he continues to remain the sole beneficiary of his decisions and actions. Such a phenomenon is considered as belonging to the domain of 'personal-freedom' in all knowledge societies. As such, and as long as, business ventures remain within the family-portals, the local society simply does not bother about its administrative practices. Should a free society really bother about such individual activities or not is an issue which only knowledge societies can answer. A general view in this regard is that as long as those individual ventures would not have any adverse impact on the rest in the society and the activities of the individual investor remain useful or beneficial to the society, the society need not interfere in internal affairs of those individual/private ventures. A similar logic is extended to ventures of joint nature where two or more venture partners invest together and work for a common business cause. In such joint ventures, views of all partners form the basis for decisions and actions. Naturally, from *Governance* view points; this aspect of decisions does not constitute a major offence. It has also remained as a well accepted international practice.

Sociological viewpoints regarding business decisions exhibit similar trends across all societies. The key element of sociological viewpoints is generally described as 'Social Justice'. The element of social justice primarily refers to addressing the needs of the local community and the local society that houses the business ventures and also provides the necessary/critical infrastructural services and supports that are required to run the business. Key elements of 'social justice' normally hover around "*Provision of Employment to Local Residents or Natives of the Place or Region* and also *Ploughing Back a Significant*

Portion of Business Returns to the *Development of the Local Society."* Can such a thought be challenged by any intellect from anywhere across the world? Obviously No!

Similar concepts get multiplied and get manifested in larger scales in bigger business ventures. When joint ventures from different parts of the world come to existence, naturally, each one of the investing venture partners would like to have a say in decisions and affairs of the joint venture. Each one of them would like to control a specific aspect of business operations depending on his venture nature and magnitude. This is primarily from the view points of guarding their investment and the interests thereon. In such situations, the concept of 'social justice' gets suitably amended to accommodate the '*individual-social justice- elements'* of all the venture partners. If in a joint-venture, one of the controlling partners assigns a specific activity responsibility to a person to be brought or hired by him in preference to any other so called better suited local luminaries, one can just not declare the action as defeating the concept of social justice. Such decision powers would always be vested in them by virtue of a mutually agreed basic understanding that governs such joint ventures and are governed by the concept of international social justice where each of the participating national would have a share in 'practice of social justice'.

While local societies certainly have a right of share in the employment of companies, local societies certainly do not have a right to totally capture this area of corporate functioning. After all, business enterprises have to perform very proficiently and effectively for their own survival in a highly competitive global market environment. In order to meet their business goals and objectives, companies should have their own design for functioning and performing. Companies are answerable to their own business promoters and financiers and have also to comply with all legal stipulations of the land that are prescribed for their type of activities/works. And it is for this reason that no company can work exclusively to address a specific interest or demand of a local society. Concept of *'Social Justice'* should, therefore, be explored from true broader perspectives to address the needs of a larger cross section of the nation or a larger cross section of global society as the situation may demand. Work designs and methodologies have to be fine-tuned to address goals and objectives that would meet the requirements of larger cross sections of population. In such situations, the concept of discrimination shrinks to a limited area of activity and would become applicable to similar impact group or groups. Most unfortunately for all business enterprises across the world, the subject of *'Social Justice'* has always remained an ever disputed issue because different cross sections of intellectuals across the world entertain different views on this subject.

Therefore, when one explores business decisions and actions from these perspectives, one would realise that the concept of discrimination could be considered only with regard to certain decisions and actions and not for the entire activity spectrum of business corporates. If this happens, then, corporates will have no control over their performance and profitability levels in a globally competitive market environment. The way corporates remain answerable to the local society, they are equally answerable to all the other groups of stakeholders. They have to look for true merits wherever they are available. On all such situations, performance remains the only criteria and nothing else.

However, in public sector organisations or in business organisations where the venture capital is made-up of public contribution, the company virtually belongs to all those who have contributed to its formation and functioning. In such situations, since the configuration of virtual business promoters is wide and complex, no single promoter or executive would carry full right to personal decision regarding company's affairs. It is only under such contexts that one can apply the concept of discrimination, when an apparent and obvious differential treatment is meted out to two individuals who would, otherwise justifiably fit into a specific pre-identified business slot or an opening or an opportunity or for a reward or appreciation etc.

International Scenario

Over and above all these types of discriminations, we would come across an altogether different type of discrimination in international business scenario. Most unfortunately, many intellectuals across the international society do not consider these as discriminations. But on the contrary, they have built different economic or social theories to justify such unique forms of discriminations. These discriminations could be collectively described as exploitative discrimination.

Monetary-value discrimination is at the top of all of them. Similar materials and similar services from different parts of the world are valued differently in different countries. Source of materials and services decide their value. Similar materials and services from some countries of the world are grossly undervalued and from some other countries are grossly overvalued. This discrimination also typically embraces exploitation of precious natural resources of some regions under the cover of participation in socio-economic development or participation in international development activities. The next one is intellectual discrimination. Remuneration and compensation package for carrying out similar jobs depends on the country of origin of intellectuals handling those jobs and not on the nature of the job or job content. Offshore development and outsourcing of certain critical intellectual works and services also belong to this category. These discriminations are practiced under the cover of competition across international borders. Unfortunately again, societies across the world have readily accepted these forms of intellectual discriminations, rather exploitation of human labour or human values. Can intellectuals across the intellectual world consider *dumping of outdated and/or already well exploited technology in developing countries under the guise of techno-economic support for growth* as gross discrimination against humanity, society and nature? Certain forms of discriminations practiced by different professionals in different societies including some medical professionals' remains a heinous crime against mankind and the society.

Table 2.14 presents a brief description of discrimination profile. No attempt is, however, made here to present a comprehensive view of different types of discriminations that operate in business corporates across the world. These are only a few typical and more frequently encountered ones. While many giant public limited and public-sector organisations generally claim freedom from discriminatory practices, the reality, may not, always support their claims.

Employees, Customers and suppliers are the three specific groups who are sensitive to corporate decisions. These are the groups who would be most affected wherever discriminations rule the scenario. Employees feel that they were let down and their merits and contributions did not get due recognition. Customers feel discriminated

Table 2.14 Profile of Discriminatory Practices

<table>
<tr><th>Sl. No.</th><th>Contributory Element</th><th>Where it gets Manifested</th><th>How it gets Manifested</th></tr>
<tr><td>1</td><td>Caste</td><td rowspan="12">• Induction into the main stream of work-force.
• Work Assignment.
• Freedom of work.
• Degree of Accountability and Answerability.
• Execution Responsibility.
• Discretionary Decision Powers with Regard to Work Design and Execution.
• Compensation Package.
• Appreciation.
• Credit Sharing.
• Growth Prospects and Opportunities.</td><td rowspan="12">▪ Overall preference to people belonging to a specific category over others.
▪ Predominance of certain category or groups in different activity centres.
▪ Formation of groups belonging to a specific category to take a big share in company's affairs.
▪ Squeezing-out those people who do not fit into their own thought groups and those who entertain different thoughts and opinions regarding functioning and/or execution of a specific activity.
▪ Innovatively inventing ways and means not to entertain people who do not fit into any of the specific category of their choice.
▪ Managing to eliminate all those people who carry a high potential to intellectually supersede or overtake self.
▪ Managing to eliminate all those who are equally good or better in their professional calibre to ensure that they continue to have a final say in all matters and to ensure that nobody competes with them for a share in the credit.</td></tr>
<tr><td>2</td><td>Creed</td></tr>
<tr><td>3</td><td>Race</td></tr>
<tr><td>4</td><td>Region</td></tr>
<tr><td>5</td><td>Language</td></tr>
<tr><td>6</td><td>Gender</td></tr>
<tr><td>7</td><td>Religious Faith</td></tr>
<tr><td>8</td><td>Affiliation to different Faith Groups</td></tr>
<tr><td>9</td><td>Culture Groups</td></tr>
<tr><td>10</td><td>Intolerance to Dissention</td></tr>
<tr><td>11</td><td>Professional Rivalry</td></tr>
<tr><td>12</td><td>Supersession (overtaking) Complex</td></tr>
</table>

whenever they do not get certain supplies, in time, and at the same time someone else in the market gets them from the company. Such a feeling will be there without reference to as to when the other customer had placed his purchase order with the company. Similarly, on issues of product prices, trade discounts and credit periods, etc. they readily get tempted to believe that there is discrimination. Suppliers feel that there is discrimination especially if they do not get a purchase order from the company whereas other suppliers get them. This feeling would again be without reference to competitive performance of the other supplier.

This sort of a situation is, therefore, not new to any organisation. They have been living with such allegations for long. They have to strive hard to reverse this impression and to come clean. Business corporates should work-out an ever dynamic balance between interests and needs of all its stakeholders. It is equally desirable that the mechanism of arriving at a balance is to work-out the details in consultation and in concurrence with all stakeholders. Organisations should first notify people regarding their policies and procedures on all issues including pre-defining what they really mean by the pre-qualifying tag *Merit* in different situations. Efficiency, effectiveness, measurable contribution and clearly definable and verifiable competence should be the only criteria for staff appreciation. Product deliveries especially in times of short-supplies should be well organised and managed as per general guidelines outlined in Table 2.7. Similarly, purchase activities should be carried out as per general guidelines outlined in Table 2.9. Otherwise, it will be difficult to avoid allegations of being biased and discriminative.

Such a consensus mechanism should be suitably documented and well supported with clear definitions of guiding factors that decide the course of actions in any of the corporate activity area. The guidelines should also specify exceptions and exemptions to satisfactorily address specific needs and exigencies. Companies should work within the broader frameworks of those guidelines still retaining their right of discretionary decision power free from biases when conflicting contexts prevail. On all such situations, the companies should make their intentions and compelling factors known to concerned cross section of its stakeholders. If such transparent practices are meticulously followed, nobody can doubt its intentions and interests to charge them of practicing discrimination.

Participative Management & Freedom of Expression

This is one more activity area which is considered as an integral part of good governance. This component of corporate governance could be considered as an extension of two other concepts discussed earlier namely operation integrity and transparency. Wherever integrity and accompanying transparency prevail, freedom of expression cannot be curtailed or mortgaged. Operation integrity guards people's interests and transparency demonstrates the same. Then where is the question of not allowing interested people to express their views on different issues? Participative management in decision making process, therefore, acts as a good complementary component for the above two governance aspects.

This concept is based on the fact that no business corporate can work in total isolation and that no business corporate can come to existence without active participation of many in the society. This concept also recognises the fact that the society itself serves a major purpose for which a corporate comes to existence. As such, certain decisions taken by business corporates would always be of some interest and of some concern to many people both inside its own premises as well as outside in the society.

Who are all the people that get affected by corporate decisions? And what would be their area of specific interest in corporate decisions? If we examine this issue from holistic viewpoints, we realise that corporate decision-impact profile embraces a very wide spectrum across the entire cross section of the society. (Figure 2.8) Each one of the stakeholders shown in this figure and also given in Table 2.13 does have a specific interest in corporate decisions because there can be hardly any decision which will not impact any of the stakeholders shown in this table.

It is a common observation that decisions are invariably conveyed but not consulted beforehand except for an insignificant portion of

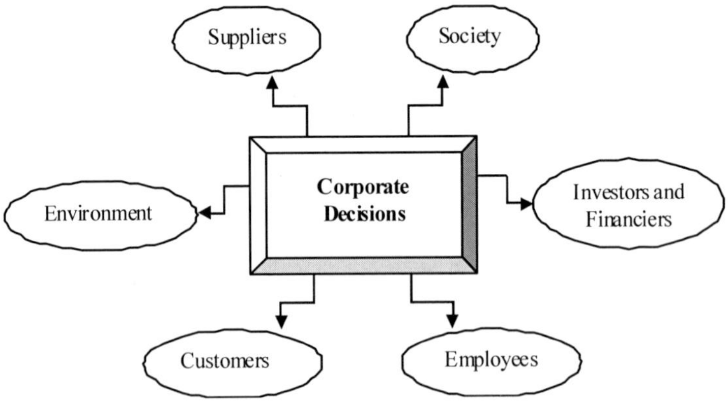

Fig. 2.8 Corporate Decision-impact Profile

decisions regarding identification of suitable equipments and other manufacturing and/or processing infrastructure with a small section of technocrats or shop-floor executives. Similarly, decisions regarding business expansions, diversifications, acquisitions and closures that are of vital interest to both shareholders and financiers are conceived and taken only by investment managers. Getting the decisions sanctified by the *Board of Directors* is a mere formality. What a sorry state of affairs! The only guiding factor here is that *Investment Managers* presume that they have full authority on all corporate matters and that they are fully knowledgeable. These investment managers also entertain a firm belief that they are the ultimate in all aspects and facets of knowledge that will have a bearing on business prospects and therefore any decision taken by them has to become acceptable to all concerned stakeholders.

Yet, an unfortunate truth for corporates is that it may not always be practical that many decisions taken by the managers who are administering the activities of a company or the decisions taken by a selected few shop-floor managers would keep a good cross section of impacted stakeholders happy and comfortable. While some would be more benefited by a particular decision, there could be many who are not at all benefitted by the same decision and as such would be more discomforted. All decisions carry the potential to keep at least some people less comfortable. Many times, it may so happen that in their over anxiety to grow and expand, some investment managers go aggressively and take a series of wrong decisions which cumulatively could sink the organisation and its finances. In fact, there are many live instances where investment managers themselves have systematically worked towards drowning the company. Everybody in the society including business investors, suppliers, customers, financiers and of course the helpless employees would silently watch the fall of the company. In some of those unique situations, investment managers virtually take shareholders for a free ride, employees, suppliers and customer will be taken for granted and financiers will be made to just blink.

Can corporates change this situation? Yes. They can. The only way is to take a decision in consultation with the appropriate cross section of potential stakeholders. Instead of analysing the impact and the degree of discomfort with an already taken decision, it is always good to involve the potential stakeholders in the process of decision making itself. Each stakeholder would be more concerned with his specific interest and wants to protect the same and would therefore love to participate in the decision making process. He would weigh the magnitude of its impact on his interest zone and would like to comment on the same. This could, however, become a practical reality when corporates give the freedom of expression to all those interested stakeholders. How many corporates practice this is a big question which only corporates can answer. Wherever corporates may like to answer this question positively, unless potential stakeholders confirm the same, it cannot be taken for granted as a fact. A careful study of corporate working would reveal that in most of the corporates, freedom of expression is always to be interpreted as mere *"Yes Sir"* and nothing beyond. That is just a positive affirmation and concurrence of whatever the management wants to decide and not otherwise. Any dissention especially if the same is expressed by an affected employee, the net result would be disastrous. It would lead to victimisation of the employee who has dissented. How many corporates would admit that they would not resort to victimisation of dissenting voices? It is not easy to find an honest answer to this question. But good corporate governance demands that people should have freedom to express their opinion on matters that would affect them.

Time Targeted Response Mechanism

As explained earlier, corporates do not have any existence in isolation. There would be many people to participate in corporate activities. As can be seen in Table 2.13, many stakeholders will be interested in corporate activities and performances. As further explained in this table, each category of stakeholders will have a specific interest in corporate activities and performances. Naturally, there would be many occasions when these stakeholders would like to know about certain aspects of corporate performance and/or programmes. Executives from different public administration offices may also like to know, from time to time, about certain compliance requirements and/or progress on the same. Intellectuals and general public from the society may like to know regarding corporate participation in certain social welfare activities and/or about their progress. Different groups of environmentalists from society may like to know about different aspects of environmental performances of corporate activities.

It is a well understood fact that stakeholders have a right to know about certain aspects of corporate functioning. Therefore, as a part of good governance, corporates should also practice giving timely responses to queries of interested stakeholders whether or not they are established customers or potential new customers or executives from different public administration offices or members of the society. Reasons for different stakeholders seeking information from corporates could be different depending on specific interest of that stakeholder. Their interest in specific information or data could be genuine and the purpose for which they seek the information could vary from one individual to another and from one occasion to another. Similarly, their interest in certain data could also vary from one social context to another.

As a responsible member of the society, corporates always remain duty-bound to respond to these queries. Response to some queries become mandatory, like for example a query from a law enforcement authority. Response to some queries become voluntary, like for example a query from a social welfare group. It is always a good practice to design a time-targeted response mechanism to queries received. There is, however, one limitation in this area. Under the guise of right to information, some miscreants could always ask for certain critical information about the organisation and misuse the same against larger interests of organisations. Both the elements of operation transparency and ready communication carry this risk. Corporates have a right to decide as to which data or information or which aspect and which component of a particular data or information can be shared with the rest in the society. Similarly, corporates may also like to guard themselves against sharing of fractional or part data about certain critical operations, requested at different times under different contexts and for different purposes by different individuals or social organisations, which collectively carry the risk of being compiled together and computed to arrive at strategic moves of the corporate. For this purpose, corporates should design a good mechanism which would ensure that all queries received by the corporate are suitably recorded and verified for the nature of query. The mechanism should also provide for someone in the line of authority to decide whether or not the query should be answered with requested data or information. The authority should also be free to examine the nature of query and to project whether any critical information is being sought in bits and pieces and then decide about the nature of response to be given. On all such occasions, corporates could certainly deny the data and could just send a polite reply expressing its inability to share the specific data.

There could also be situations when corporates need more time to respond to certain queries. Reasons for the same could be many. One should, however, not forget that the concept of 'timely response' need not always stand for immediate response. The element of time under governance aspects should provide for the time needed for generation of required data or information from concerned work centres. It should be practical and realistic. Also executives could be lost in attending to some other pressing business demand. Similarly, responses to certain queries may not be practical on certain occasions and situations for reasons known only to corporates. There could also be situations when queries keep pouring-in. The adjective *'Timely'* should be understood as referring to its effectiveness. A delayed or deferred communication might carry the risk of defeating the basic purpose for which a communication was sought and was generated from its source. What is important under this particular governance aspect is to clearly define a generally acceptable time factor associated with different types of queries. However, it is needless to say that there should be a mechanism to send an early communication regarding whether or not the corporate is in a position to answer a particular query with the requested data or information or whether it requires more time to generate a response. Organisations should not forget that communication is a powerful tool that can help them in translating many of the intangibles to tangible products, services and activities. It also helps them in understanding the gaps in their operations and services.

External queries generally originate from following three sources:

1. Customers including Prospective Customers.
    - Centred on generation of knowledge that could help them in making a purchase decision.
        - o Full information including product application scopes, utility life cycle and service constraints and limitations.

- Related to finding a solution for their problems, both already known and projected in anticipation.

2. Governmental Agencies.
   - Related to gaps in compliance requirements against various legal and statutory guidelines.
     - o Reminders and notices regarding mandatory compliances.
     - o Intimation regarding contemplated and/or formalised changes in compliance modes or requirements.
3. Sociologists and Environmentalists.
   - Proposals regarding contemplated social welfare events or development activities and requests for active corporate participation.
   - Intimation and/or warnings regarding projected or observed adverse effects of corporate activities on the general health and welfare of the public.
   - Intimation and/or proposals for aiming at better environmental performance

Naturally each of these queries deserves suitable response. A timely response to them would result in maintenance of cordial relations between business corporates and the society.

It is always a good practice to keep a ready reckoner of the type shown in Table 2.15 enabling to act suitably. Preparation of such reference matrix demands that a good collective brain-storming involving all the intellectuals of the company is carried out and documented in suitable format. Independent tabulated formats could be prepared as applicable to each activity centre and each category of query area and the person responsible for generating the response is kept informed of the same or preferably made custodian of the format. Nature and details of response can be reviewed periodically and updated.

Stakeholders' Interest Protection

This is yet another hotly debated area of corporate performance. Since business corporates come to existence through the active participation of many stakeholders from across the society, corporates are duty bound to protect the interests of each of their stakeholders. Conducting of all routine activities as well as expansions and diversifications should be managed in such a way that at no point of time genuine interests of any of the stakeholders are put at stake. There are many instances where investment managers take wrong decisions with regard to expansions and diversifications based on either wrong data or wrong projection of facts and force the corporates to suffer huge monetary losses. Many times, such wrong decisions could even lead corporates to sink. Such decisions eat into very vitals of investors' interests in business corporates. Another equally critical area of protecting stakeholders' interests also refers to guarding of employees' interests. Corporates should not forget that this is a very sensitive area that carries high potential for damaging work situation almost instantaneously. Knowledge force can desert the corporate en-mass to bring its activities to a grinding halt.

Table 2.15 Reference Matrix for Practicing Timely Response

Response Matrix									
Sl. No.	Source of query and date of receipt	Nature of query	Permit-ted/ accepta-ble time gap between query receipt and response	Activity centre or person responsible for generating response	Does the answer involve sharing of company's secrets or strategies or part thereof	Proposed response	Response details/ nature verified and approved by	Inter-mediate response needed if any	Response sent on
1									
2									
3									

Corporates should carefully identify areas of interest to different categories of stakeholders together with the type of protection that would satisfy the stakeholders under consideration. Each category of stakeholders would have a specific interest in corporate activities and would like that their interests should be well protected. If their interests are not satisfactorily addressed, then that category of stakeholder would become disinterested in corporate affairs and activities. Stakeholder's disinterest always works against long-term interests of corporates, in some form or the other. It is for this reason that corporates should carefully guard genuine interests of its stakeholders.

One typical area that may get readily ignored is unintentional creation of unhealthy and/or risky operation environment for their workforce. One more area that carries a good potential to get ignored or neglected is not addressing the long-term interests of those workmen who have actively participated in all activities of the corporate and have struggled throughout their active professional life period for the growth of the company. Very few organisations take this issue seriously. This is generally a dark area in most of the corporates. They shrink their moral responsibility and take shelter under law and manage.

As explained in published literature (Mruthyunjaya, 2013), shareholders of companies do invest in company's shares not for the sake of mere love for company's promoters' ambitions or its products and services, but basically with an eye on dividends and other monetary incentives. Investment in company's shares is actually an investment for their future and for their social security when needed. Business corporates do carry the basic responsibility to protect and guard their investments and also to ensure that certain minimum dividends and growth in their investment.

Environment is another mute stakeholder which generally becomes the first causality during most of the corporate experiments and development activities. It continues to get butchered till everything else gets settled for formally establishing eco-friendly operations and legal compliances or till some environmentalists raise a hue and cry over the issue or till law enforcement authorities come to know of those new development activities and catch them and order them to comply with certain compliance requirements. If such things happen, it carries a high potential to erode society's goodwill for the corporate.

Good corporate governance demands that corporates themselves identify the risk to which they would put their stakeholders through their activities and ensure that their interests are well protected at all points of time.

Following are some of the key aspects one can notice in some knowledge-organisations that have developed a good operation strategy to protect their stakeholders' interest.

- They quantify with fairly good accuracy and also define the interests of stakeholders with a high degree of clarity enabling them to periodically measure the degree of enhancement in stakeholders' comfort.
    - Unit of measure and the measurement scale is worked out in consultation with the concerned group of stakeholders.
    - Such a measure is doubly confirmed through organising periodical rating of corporate performance by different category of stakeholders.
    - Wherever stakeholders' performance rating is low, necessary corrective action will be initiated immediately.
    - Impact of those actions will be verified in subsequent stakeholder rating.
- Enhancement in stakeholders' comfort level is taken as an index to confirm that the organisation is satisfactorily addressing the aspect of protecting stakeholders' interests.
- Comfort level of intellectual cross section of stakeholders is measured in terms of the following parameters:
    - Satisfactory Compliance to all legal and statutory requirements.
    - Addressing social obligations.
    - Participation in social development activities.
- Comfort level of business investors is measured in terms of the following parameters:
    - Increase in return on corporate assets.
    - Increase in return on investment to shareholders.
        - Increase in frequency and magnitude of dividends.
        - Increased periodicity in declaration of bonus shares
    - Enhancement in share values and its frequency.
- Comfort level of employees is measured in terms of the following parameters:
    - Degree of transformation of workforce to true knowledge leaders in their respective activity areas.
        - Enhancement in knowledge wealth across the organisation.

  - Enhanced ability to take independent discretionary decisions.
  - Enhanced ability to design, guide and control the activity.
  - Enhanced collective approach and team performance attitude.
  - Enhanced skills in effective risk management.
  - Enhanced degree of cost-conscience, resource optimisation and process-effectiveness across the organisation.
  - Increased degree of freedom of information and sharing of execution expertise and infrastructural facilities.
  - Enhanced eagerness to root-out problems at source wherever they are noticed.
  - Enhanced degree of knowledge leveraging seen through following parameters:
    - o Enhanced activity effectiveness.
    - o Better infrastructure utilisation and achievement of enhanced productivity.
    - o Quick response to external changes and vibrant market environment.
    - o Frequent technological breakthrough.
    - o Reduced development time,
- Enhancement in people's innovation index.
- Degree of transformation of generative knowledge to intellectual capital of the organisation.
- Periodicity of launching of new and/or improved and also innovatively novel products that would enhance customers' competitive comforts.
- Degree of enhancement in employee satisfaction index.
  - Provision of innovation environment for exploring latent potential of people.
- Enhancement in their professional comforts.
  - Job correlation with educational background and experience
  - Comfort with the prevailing knowledge environment.

- Job challenge.
- Enhanced degree of commitment to job.
- Increased participation in enhancing operation comfort and health and safety features.
- Enhanced degree of eagerness to acquire additional knowledge and operation skills.
- Enhanced degree of eagerness to establish highly conducive knowledge-driven work culture.

• Enhancement in the degree of job satisfaction they derive.
  - Steady increase in motivation and intuitiveness index
  - Steady enhancement in performance temperament.
  - Prevalence of encouraging, learning environment for the workforce.
  - Display of highest degree of competitive cost conscience.
  - Sharing of skill-based execution responsibility and sharing of expertise.
  - Creating a knowledge driven ever-competitive work environment.
  - Absence of activity inappropriateness for want of appropriate data or information.
  - Absence of job hibernation in between during the process for want of necessary information or data.
  - Complete clarity regarding exact requirements of customers throughout the organisation.
  - Comfort with compensations, recognitions and rewards.
  - Impression regarding unhealthy competition and prevalence of differential and/or biased treatment.
  - Steady increase in average service-length of employees in the organisation.

➢ Comfort levels of customers is ensured through following measures:

  • Ensuring generation of most appropriate data on customer needs and requirements relevant to customer application environment, application stringency and preparing product delivery schedules to customers' satisfaction.

- Offering most competitive products to customers and increase in customer coverage-index.
- Periodically introducing innovatively novel products that would enhance customers' comforts.
- Establishing a mechanism to satisfactorily address customers' grievances.
- Taking customers' feedback seriously and working towards enhancing value-return to customers through:
    - Establishing good correlation between shop-floor activity and customer requirement across the organisation.
    - Elimination of product defects, both latent and apparent and other limitations to increase product ruggedness and to widen application range for products.
    - Enhancing product utility features.
    - Enhancing user-friendliness of the product.
    - Widening product application-life-cycle by providing customer demanded additional features and service components.
    - Enhancing product performance capabilities.
    - Redesigning and reconfiguring service components to enhance customers' comforts.
    - Initiating appropriate BPR based on customer product-positioning and competitive-rating.
- Establishing a mechanism to quickly respond to customers' continuously changing demands.
- Working on customers' feedback and developing new and improved products.
- Continuous updation of process technology to ensure that customers always get latest and emerging technology products.
- Continuous fine-tuning and refinement of process technology to identify and eliminate all cost additive factors to render the product most competitive.

- Comfort levels of suppliers is ensured through following measures:
    - Suppliers including potential suppliers are made fully knowledgeable about:
        - Methodology followed by the organisation to identify and select suppliers.
        - Calculations and formulations adopted for regular performance assessment of suppliers to decide on their continuation or otherwise.
        - Clear definition of reasons and specimen worksheets for placing purchase orders on a selected few suppliers in preference to other suppliers.
        - Working out realistic lead-times for different supplies in consultation with a good cross section of suppliers.
        - Provision of opportunity to challenge purchase executive's decision whenever suppliers suspect unethical understanding between purchase executives and some suppliers.
        - Provision of opportunity to scrutinise the details of various purchase orders placed by the company on different suppliers at regular intervals giving them an opportunity to improve on their performance levels.
        - Provision of opportunity to suppliers' technicians to challenge the reliability and suitability of verification procedures followed by the company.
        - Provision of opportunity to suppliers' technicians to demonstrate the shortfall in the practices of the company and to convince company's technicians to revise their verification methods.
        - Provision to give a confidential feedback to top management of the company expressing their grievances regarding harassment and discrimination or any other complaints.
            - Immediate analysis and evaluation of complaints by an independent high-power discipline-enforcement committee with provision for

witnessing the proceedings by aggrieved suppliers.

- Society's comfort level is ensured through following measures:
    - Allocation of expenditure for social development activities as a fixed percentage of income. Preparing annual budget for social development activities.
    - Aggressive participation in many social development and welfare activities.
    - Involving different social welfare activities in identifying welfare projects beneficial to a larger cross section of the society.
    - Ensuring most economic use of precious natural resources through adoption of resource-conserving technologies.
    - Ensuring that posterity is not denied or robbed off of its rightful entitlement to virgin nature and precious natural resources.
- Comfort level of the environment is ensured through following measures:
    - Adoption of eco-friendly green and clean technologies.
    - Phased-out discontinuation of use of resource-consuming and/or energy and resource guzzling technologies.
    - Taking appropriate measures to ensure that its activities do not leave any adverse or harmful impacts on the environment either immediate or in the long-run.
    - Adopting environment friendly practices to ensure that its activities do not emit or release polluting gases or discharge any harmful by-products or waste products to cause a loss in environment quality.
    - The company actively participates in educating the general public about environment protection measures by highlighting pollution through different human activities, the environmental burden being perpetrated by uncontrolled human greed by unnecessary material comforts and the need to contain the so called basic needs.

Expansions, Diversifications Acquisitions and Takeovers

Expansions, Diversifications Acquisitions and Takeovers are integral to any business. With a view to strengthening their performance base and/or to add extra muscle-power to their activity domain, business enterprises do take to these activities as a routine. Their jurisdictional area could vary from within the same premises, to national borders and international borders depending on the business situation. In their over anxiety to expand their operation domain, business enterprises go all out to woo many forces in the contemplated society. And in this process, they are likely to deviate from many of the well established norms of the society.

If business establishments have to ensure that they do not deviate from any of the standard business practices, their own policies and procedures, they should make sure that all expansions, diversifications, acquisitions and takeovers are also covered by a set of standard procedures to guide, govern and control all those activities. For this purpose, they should design a set of well formulated policies and guidelines together with well laid-out execution procedures. Policy guidelines should be administered by a high power committee (Credo Committee) specially constituted for the purpose.

These policy guidelines should specifically address the following issues:

- Would the new activity fall into organisation's goals and objectives?
- Does it carry any potential to adversely affect company's image?
- Can those activities either directly hurt the sentiments, faiths and beliefs of promoters, employees and investors or carry the potential to do so indirectly?
- Does it carry the potential, immediate or long term, to harm the workforce, local society or the surrounding environment?
- Status of technology development – Fully developed or only partly developed?
    - Resource depletion type or resource conserving type?
    - Environment pollution potential of product generation process, by-products?

- Can it pose new health and safety issues?
    - At different stages right from product generation, storage, transportation and usage?
- Does it pose new legal compliance issues?
- Is the new product application-life-cycle well validated and well established?
    - If not how would the new products' application-life-cycle be established?
    - Does the contemplated application pose new environmental/safety issues to customers?
- Does product generation life-cycle and utility-life-cycle fall in line with those of other products of the company?
    - If not what new strategy will be developed to make the product customer friendly?
    - Does it carry re-cyclability potential?
    - If not, how will be the customer helped in disposing-off the outlived product?
- Does it fall under company's core technology strength?
    - If not, what is the contemplated action to build requisite technology strength?
    - Does it call for development of new marketing strategies to promote the product?
    - Does it support a healthy but competitive marketing strategy?
    - If not how will the nobility of marketing practices be guarded?

All the contemplated expansions, diversifications, acquisitions and takeovers should pass through this clearance to make them good proposals that could fit well under good corporate governance mechanism.

Proposal should be prepared with the following data and details for policy guidelines' clearance:

➢ Identification and definition of the genuine reason that has induced the thought together with scope of the thought and its contemplated coverage profile.

- Short listing and/or identification of products or services contemplated for expansion, diversification, etc.
- Short listing of target organisations wherever joint ventures are contemplated for expansions and diversifications.
    - Analyses of their performance background and their share in the contemplated activity.
        - Target company's share in the market being served by them.
        - Market impression, credibility and opinion about the target company.
    - Status of development of technology for contemplated activities — whether fully developed, proven, well established or only partly developed technology.
        - Contemplated action to profitably and safely handle activity by-products, if any.
        - Known or hidden hazard potential of contemplated by-products and their safe handling and disposal methods.
        - Status of legal permits, licenses, compliances, etc.
    - Contemplated market segments together with detailed data regarding other competitors who are already in the field and are serving the same market segment.
        - Scope for entering other market segments and their potential.
    - Other most likely competitors who are vying to enter the same market segment together with their performance status.
    - An analysis of contemplated market potential together with data on demand-supply gaps, if any.
    - Apparent or latent potential of the contemplated activity to displace any of those existing organisations, whether small or big.
- Specific reasons for contemplated acquisitions and takeovers together with details of -

- Target organisations, their geographical locations and their financial performances.
- Detailed analysis of market segment/segments served by target organisations together with analysis of reasons for failure of target organisations to serve the market.
- Details of promoters of those business establishments and their background.
- Analysis of reason that has forced them to part with their ventures.
    - Analysis of current assets and liabilities of target companies including legal and other litigations if any.
- Impact of takeover on:
    - Company's present investors, financiers, suppliers, customers, etc.
    - Impact of liabilities of takeover organisations' on company's financial health and performance.
    - Target company's employees, suppliers, customers, financiers and investors.
    - Target society and its surroundings and environment.
- Status of technology practiced by target organisations together with scope of introducing technological innovations and advancements at the target location.
- Status of infrastructure and necessity for updation of the same.
- Employment potential for the local population and proximity of process-input and other services.

➢ Whether the products or services of the contemplated acquisitions and takeovers are in line with company's product policies.

- If not, what are the proposed changes in the product configuration for the target location?
    - Does it call for credo clearance to verify impact on sentiments of investors', employees and the society?
- What is the impact of changed product configuration on the target company's employees, customers, suppliers and the target society?

What is important for us while discussing the subject of corporate governance is that none these activities should deviate from any of the following requirements:

- ➢ Whenever an expansion activity is located in a place away from its normal operation premises/headquarters, the business should completely re-identify itself with the local society and should work for its overall development and well being of the people there without resorting to any type of exploitation, whether intellectual, economic, cultural or resources, etc.
- ➢ Wherever business transactions take place across international borders, a business enterprise has to be much more cautious. International business operations would come across different cultural, linguistic and religious backgrounds and multi-ethnic practices there could also be a wide variance in educational, social and cultural backgrounds of people that could give rise to differing views and opinions on common issues. Conducting business transactions from the new location may pose many problems on these issues.
    - o On all those situations, business activities should be designed and conducted in such a way that it respects local culture and local traditional practices and would adopt the same to the best possible extent.
    - o It should, however, always keep an eye open on slowly but steadily introducing internationally accepted standard operation norms and practices to ensure that there will be no conflict with the local ethnic culture and practices. By doing so, it would not impose its own local culture at the new premises to bring cultural conflict. Instead, it works towards following international norms to the comforts of many.
- ➢ Respect for the law of the land (the host country) should become a basic operation norm in all international business activities.
    - o There could be a variance in the statutory requirements of different nations. Business establishments should not take undue advantage of lenience of the local requirements

wherever they are not as stringent as that of the guest country.

  - On all such situations, the best practice to be adopted is to go for more stringent and more demanding requirements without reference to whether it is from the host country or from the guest country.
  - Law should always be treated only as a basic guideline for carrying out business transactions while actual practices could always stretch far beyond actual legal limits.

- All business transactions should be kept far above the influence horizon of undue inducements at any stage and at all stages of its coming into existence and all through its operations.
- Business organisations should not hire or engage any intermediary agencies for identifying and/or facilitating expansions, diversifications, acquisitions and takeovers.
  - Hiring an intermediary agency is always considered as unethical because they have a tendency to influence people in power in the host country or host region to favour the company.
- Whenever business transactions take place across international borders, operational accounts should be maintained as per norms laid down in international accounting practices.
  - Accounting practices should be maintained completely transparent and are allowed to be audited by independent auditors.
- None of these activities of expansion, diversification, acquisition or takeover should result in displacing another player in the field whether small or big. All of them should continue to have their share in the market.
  - Big business giants should not enter a market segment which is being fed by a few smaller units. Otherwise, these big units carry the potential to dig into smaller units' market domain and displace them over a period of time.
  - If such a thing happens, it would then be very unfair.

Corporate Citizenship

Business corporates are respectable members of the society. And as conscience members of the society, they carry a lot of responsibility towards the society. Concept of responsibility has its origin in the fact that corporates come to existence because of the society. They derive many benefits from the society starting from process inputs and services, workforce, public infrastructure, civic amenities and social security both for self and employees, etc. In fact, corporates again depend only on the society for finding outlet for their products and services. Thus, the society provides the full-life-line-cycle for all business corporates. Willing participation in different social development projects and welfare activities is a standard means of expressing gratitude towards society. Corporate social responsibility is an established forum to translate corporate citizenship concepts to actions. Discussions given in chapter four give some in-depth details of these issues.

Governance Models

Depending on the approach focus, two major governance models have come to vogue (Figure 2.9). Each of these models supports carrying out business processes and activities with different centres of focus. In addition, one more innovative concept model has also come to be recognised. In this model there is no specific, pre-identified centre of focus. On the contrary, this model keeps the entire stakeholder spectrum at the focal point. This governance model has emerged based on Gandhian principles of *Trusteeship Concept.*

In the first model, shareholders of a company are considered as the true owners of the company and they always remain at the centre of focus. With the result, company management and administration, including investment managers, MD and CEO, and all other activity heads and project group leaders become duty bound to conduct themselves in such a way that they always respect the non-negotiable, absolute rights of shareholders in company affairs and have to guard their interests in the company. One of the first requirements of this approach is that shareholders of the company should never be kept in darkness regarding any of the moves and decisions taken by the company. As such, investment managers would be required to develop and maintain close interactions with company's shareholders. Such interactions would help them in getting a true feedback from business investors regarding how they feel about conducting of routine activities namely administration practices, practices followed to interact with the general public, periodic updation on the status of compliance to various statutory requirements, plans regarding contemplated expansions and diversifications, etc. that carry a high potential to create a major impact on company's activities and their outcome. These interactions would also enable shareholders to examine all these issues from different perspectives and give appropriate direction to company's routine management.

Two key focal areas are:

- Protection and upholding the name and credibility of shareholders.
- Protection of shareholders' investment interests.

This model is primarily a market-oriented model as it focuses on effectively managing and managing in a dignified way, product development, distribution and marketing activities to ensure that the business activity always remains more profitable so that shareholders' primary interests (investment interests) are well protected. While there may not be any extra emphasis on the rest of the society, since the activities of the company are conducted in a dignified way and also profitably, this model indirectly works towards the welfare of the rest in the society.

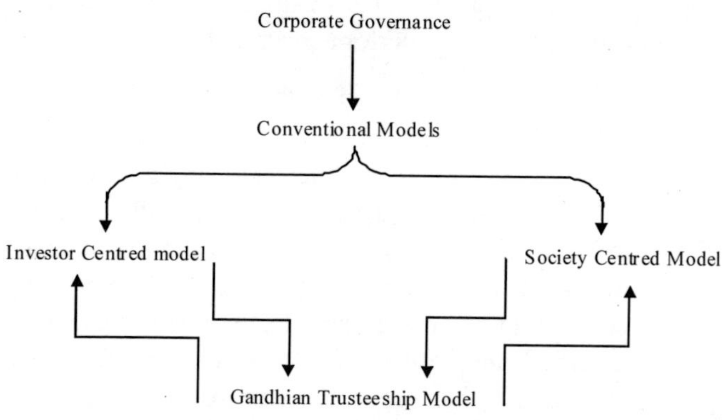

Fig. 2.9 Governance Models

The second model keeps all the other stakeholders collectively at the focal point. In this model, interests of workers, factory managers, suppliers, customers, and the local community are to be given topmost priority. Company management and administration should remain duty bound to protect the interests of this group of stakeholders of the company. All activities, whether routine or expansions and diversifications, should be formulated and conducted in such a way that they never undermine the interests of these stakeholders.

This model is primarily a network oriented model as its approach is one of upholding collective interests of a group of stakeholders. Since this model ensures that none of the associated stakeholders' interests are jeopardised during the course of conducting any of the activities of the company, it focuses on the welfare of a larger cross section of the society. Thus, in this model, business investors primarily serve as effective means of serving the society at large. Since welfare of a larger cross section of the society is the focus, this model also works towards maintaining certain profitability levels, which, in turn, indirectly, protects the interests of shareholders of the company.

The first model is also described as the *Capital Centred Model* and the second one as *Society Centred Model.* Both these models work on the basic premise that each executive irrespective of his activity area and activity profile has certain rights and carries certain execution responsibilities to fulfil the goal of the corporate. The rights confer on him the authority to decide on the right course of actions and right means of execution and the responsibility ensures that he remains accountable to his actions, performances and results.

These two governance models have given rise to two types of company board configuration:

1. In the market oriented model, company's activities would be overseen by an elected board of executive directors comprising of shareholders of the company. This board sets the rules of the game and holds for itself ultimate responsibility for conducting and managing all activities of the company in a dignified and profitable way. The board identifies investment managers or business managers for the company, MD and CEO, and authorises them to function under board's broad guidelines and directives.

2. The network oriented model works on a two tier board configuration:
   i. The first one would be the supervisory board with ultimate authority for company affairs. This board comprises of elected directors from shareholders of the company. This board also encourages and accommodates representatives of employees on its board.
   ii. The second one would be the executive board to be identified by the supervisory board. Executive board to be headed by a MD or CEO, comprises of company executives to support the supervisory board in conducting all routine and day-to-day activities of the company including identifying and appointing senior managers for different activity centres, fixing their compensation and also dispensing with their services in case they fail to bring expected results.

   The executive board remains duty bound and fully accountable to the supervisory board.

The third model is one of Indian approach to governance mechanism. This model fuses Gandhian trusteeship concept to its mechanism and brings the entire stakeholder spectrum to its focus. In this approach, each of the directors of the company board, whether an elected director or an appointed executive director including investment managers MD and CEO, functions as a trustee of the business investors and also as a trustee of a larger cross section of the society. Thus, he becomes duty bound to guard the interests of both the class of stakeholders, namely the stakeholder spectrum. The trusteeship concept demands that the directors and MD/CEO function in such a way that they always keep company's interests above everything else. Thus, in trusteeship model all issues will be explored and examined from global perspectives. Company's interests overweigh personal interests, likes and dislikes. In a true trusteeship practice, all activities of the company are conducted in a highly dignified and ethical way to ensure that all the stakeholders of the company can always keep their heads high. Some schools of thought entertain an apprehension regarding this model namely since this model explores the interests' domain of the entire stakeholder spectrum, concept of profitability may not get due importance and the result could be business investors (shareholders) may gradually lose interest in company affairs. Gandhian trusteeship model also works with both the other two conventional governance models.

Governance Management

The key objective behind establishing a good governance mechanism is to create an administrative and/or control-cum-support mechanism which can ensure satisfactory compliance to all the legal requirements and also adherence to all the other governance aspects discussed earlier. Since adherence and/or compliance to all the requirements of governance aspects are a collective responsibility, this mechanism does not call for an elaborate separate structure to administer and manage governance issues. Activity management and execution mechanism itself should be designed and conducted in such a way that actual practices automatically comply with all the requirements.

However, from responsibility distribution and accountability considerations the following scheme (Figure 2.10) could be considered.

In any organisation, the board carries the maximum responsibility for company's profitable performance and sustained growth and

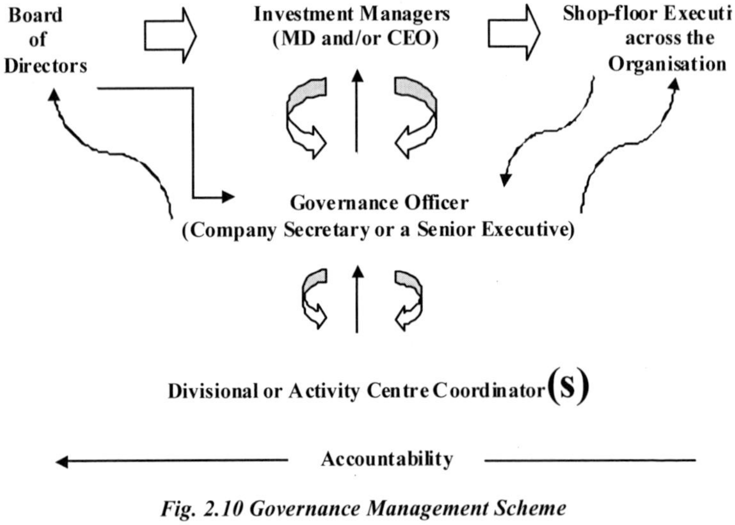

Fig. 2.10 Governance Management Scheme

perpetuation in the ever dynamic and ever vibrant global competition scenario. Naturally, responsibility of the board embraces designing and evolving of organisation's strategies for different activities and for different contexts, close monitoring of company's financial health on a continuous basis, regular performance evaluation and addressing of all potential risks; and ensuring accountability of the organisation to its shareholders and public authorities. Since the concept of corporate governance has its roots in the concept of accountability to government authorities and other public administrative and control agencies, general public, shareholders and the society, it is only the board of directors that carries highest responsibilities for satisfactorily addressing corporate governance requirements. With continuously changing social environment and also with increasing awareness about governance issues, duties and responsibilities of company directors have extended beyond mere loyalty to shareholders. Since the board members are directly responsible for company affairs, they also become directly accountable to the society from external control view points and therefore have to share much higher responsibility to ensure that the organisation would comply with all the standard and necessary performance requirements and would uphold established social ethos and value systems.

Board members are generally supported by investment managers/ business managers and their team in this regard. And in this sense, both responsibility and accountability for maintaining satisfactory governance mechanism in an organisation is suitably shared and distributed between business managers and shop-floor managers across the organisation (Table 2.16). We should, however, keep in mind that compliance to requirements is actually a shop-floor activity. This is primarily because it is only in the shop-floors that different job-execution activities take place and most of the compliance requirements are activity-execution-details based.

Similar to ethics management systems and other certifiable management systems, it is highly desirable that a suitable governance management structure is established. Organisations would be greatly benefited if the executive who shoulders the responsibility for designing and administering ethics management system for the company shoulders this responsibly also. Since legal compliance is a major component of governance and is mandatory in nature, a qualified company secretary

Table 2.16 Sharing of ResponsibilityAcross the Organisation

Sl. No.	Management Level	Responsible for
1	Board of Directors	Ensuring that the company complies with all the statutory guidelines and requirements.
		Ensuring that the company follows all the standard operation norms and guidelines as per National and/or International Standards and guidelines as applicable.
		Ensuring that the company follows standard norms and directives of the industry and other relevant professional bodies to build and project company's image in the society.
		Ensuring that the company follows standard guidelines and norms set by the society and approved by the board.
2	Business Managers	Ensuring that all the statutory norms and guidelines as applicable to the activities of the company are suitably identified.
		Ensuring that all the standard industrial practices and general norms and trends are suitably identified and carefully evaluated for their significance in the global business context and in the background of fast changing social-credibility scenario.
		Prioritising different sets of norms and guidelines to be complied with and apprising the board members of the same and obtaining their concurrence.
		Providing necessary infrastructural and skill-power support needed for ensuring those compliances.
		Establishing a satisfactory administrative and control mechanism/ structure.
		Ensuring that all activity executions satisfactorily comply with relevant approved norms and standard requirements to guard company's image in the society.
3	Shop-floor Managers	Carefully identifying and organising the required facilities and other supports for ensuring compliance to all standard requirements.
		Carefully identifying skill-power gaps, if any, and organising the same.
		Satisfactorily complying with all the standard performance requirements during activity execution.
4	Governance Officer	Identifying different legal requirements and other formal requirements with the help of company secretary or legal experts and classifying the same as per their applicability to different activity centres across the organisation.
		Designing, administering and maintaining a satisfactory governance system and ensuring that the company complies with all the standard norms and guidelines.
		Organising periodical verification of conformance to requirements and to confirm that systems is well maintained.
		Identifying gaps, if any, in performance compliance levels and ensuring that the same is made good immediately.

could also shoulder this responsibility as he would have good knowledge of a fairly wide spectrum of legal requirements and many other compliances. Governance coordinators, to be identified from different activity centres, could help people across the organisation in identifying the statutory requirements applicable to their specific activity area and in establishing compliance to those requirements.

Sequence of Operations

People should always remember that good corporate governance systems and good ethical management systems are complementary to each other and work in tandem. Hence, whenever one of them is satisfactorily established, the other one automatically becomes a practical reality. This realisation tells us that one should not get confused between good governance practices and good ethical practices. If organisations have successfully gone through the ten-step-process of establishing good ethical management systems, then establishing a good governance mechanism would almost become a foregone achievement. Published literature on business ethics (Mruthyunjaya, 2013) would come as a handy tool for establishing satisfactory governance mechanism.

Organisations could adopt the following sequence of operations for establishing a good governance management mechanism:

1. Make everybody understand and realise that practice of governance requirements would help organisation in establishing and retaining good credibility in the society.
2. Build the required temperament and commitment in people across the organisation.
3. Train people in the requirements of good corporate governance.
4. Closely interact with people and generate their response to the same and find out how comfortable they would be in practicing governance requirements.
5. Identify reasons for discomforts, if any, and eliminate them at source.
6. Give them necessary support.
7. Carefully identify all the applicable laws ensuring that such identification is comprehensive.
    - Understand all the activities and their execution mechanisms to identify impact potential of different process ingredients and activity execution details.

- Correlate the statutory requirements with activity centre-wise execution details.
- Identify infrastructural support needed by different activity centres for ensuring total compliance to requirements including specific skills as may be required for certain special compliances.
- Identify the gaps and organise to fill the gap and ensure proper compliance.
- Periodically verify compliance levels and ensue that deviations do not creep-in.

8. Analyse activity execution environment to identify activity centres where operation integrity and the accompanying transparency does not prevail. Find out reasons for the same and address the issue and help people in upholding operation integrity and to build transparency to their operations.
9. Similarly identify health and safety issues associated with activity execution, machineries and equipments used for the purpose, activity ingredients, etc. and address the same to the comforts and satisfaction of workforce.
10. Go through the details discussed earlier under each of the governance components and find reasons for why they cannot be practiced in the organisation.
11. Eliminate causes for difficulty, if any, at their roots and prepare a healthy execution environment where people can comfortably practice the requirements of governance.
12. Ensure that people practice all the requirements and do not take to deviations. Whenever deviations occur, find out whether it is just accidental or out of sheer helplessness. In both the situations find out the reason and provide a satisfactory solution to people and rebuild the confidence and execution comforts in them enabling them to go out of the way to prevent deviations from requirements.

If each and every individual activity centre in the organisation, meticulously follows and implements this operation sequence, establishing a good governance mechanism for the organisation could be accomplished with ease.

Legal Aspects

Significance of Law Abidance

We have already seen earlier that the brazenly unholy and globally ignoble malpractices that operate in many corporates and nucleate many corporate scams and scandals to give severe shocks to the society and big jolts to society's confidence in corporate activities, now and then, forced all societies to ensure that they enforce certain operation-discipline-based control measures on corporate activities. Ensuring overall welfare of the society is the key driving force behind enforcing such control measures on industries. Overall welfare of the society does not depend on the availability of different types of products alone. Welfare of the society embraces a very wide spectrum of requirements of the society right from good quality drinking water to pure breathing air, both of which have now become just a hypothetical subject for mere academic discussions. The bulk of our population do not get safe drinking water and pure breathing air. Air that we normally breathe is so much polluted that we hardly realise the same particularly because unpolluted air has become a very rare commodity in nature. This has resulted in a steady deterioration and lowering down of the overall health status and the general immunity levels of the population. As we know, this situation is the outcome of uncontrolled industrial activities which the society accommodated for a long time.

We have also seen earlier that based on the desirability of specific control measures on corporate activities, all societies have been prescribing, from time to time, different legal requirements and stipulations though the emphasis on controls over industrial activities varied from one society to another based on their social-economical-educational and cultural-background dependent perspectives of welfare. We have further seen that since all these statutory guidelines are designed to guard and protect the general welfare of the society and the populace, they are mandatory in nature and attract initiation of punitive measures in case of deviations and non-compliances.

Law Abidance is a major component of *Corporate Governance* as it stands for the conscience concern of corporates to general welfare of the society and for true corporate citizenship. Law abidance prepares the most appropriate background across the organisation and prepares a firm deck for a take-off for installing a good governance mechanism in any business establishment (Figure 3.1). We have further seen that by establishing a satisfactory compliance to all the applicable laws, many other components of governance find an easy way into governance mechanism. This is basically because legal requirements embrace such a wide spectrum of corporate activities and operations that there would be hardly any scope for any of the known malpractices to find an entry into corporate activity arena. However, establishing total compliance to all the legal requirements is not an easy task. It calls for a highly committed approach from business corporates. Usually, in the beginning, many business corporates find it difficult to start clean and stay clean on their operations with respect to legal compliances and would fumble and would be tempted to take recourse to fudging with compliance requirements. A good exposure to live realities of active shop-floors in business corporates tells us that remaining dishonest forever is also not easy for corporates. In fact, most of the business corporates do not like to remain dishonest forever. Dishonest approach in one of the activity areas nucleates and catalyses the practice of dishonesty in a host of other associated and/or aligned activity areas to forcefully initiate a series of malpractices spread across the organisation, many of which may not be to their own likings. Dishonest practices, in turn, force people to hide many critical information or data from others.

Ironically enough, it may not be a surprise that we occasionally come across small pockets of people including a few so-called educated executives associated with different business activities who view statutory compliances as a major impediment for their smooth and efficient performance, growth and prosperity in a highly competitive market environment. Very unfortunately for the business world, such black-sheeps would be there in all organisations. In some organisations even some senior executives would entertain such thoughts. Fortunately for business enterprises and the society, such pockets are confined only to narrow bandwidths of corporate activity spectrum and a few isolated individuals and not across the entire cross section of business establishments.

All social conscience citizens should strive hard to win over such small pockets full of biases against statutory requirements, and convince them of the fact that the reality is exactly reverse of what they tend to imagine and project. Members of these reserved pockets should be made to realise that they stand to gain many advantages and benefits by staying law abiding.

- ➢ The first and foremost benefit they derive is the fact that business activities would always remain healthy and effective.
- ➢ Sincere implementation of all the statutory requirements will boost the morale of the employees as they feel that they remain sincere to their social conscience and feel proud of their organisation.
    - o Employee pride in their organisation lays a strong foundation in the society for boosting the image of the company in the society as a socially conscience business enterprise in the region.
    - o Other organisations envy the situation.
    - o Not a small benefit for the organisation!
- ➢ Meticulous practice of statutory requirements imparts in people fairly good levels honesty, integrity and good business behaviour without any extra efforts. The honesty which reigns throughout the organisation helps further in carving a respectable status for the enterprise in the society.
- ➢ Law abidance induces the enterprise to recognise and respect the rights of business stakeholders which, in turn, ensures that the enterprise would never work against interests of any of the stakeholders'. On the contrary, business enterprise would always respect their views and strive to uphold the same.
    - o This would further strengthen the society's goodwill for the enterprise.

- o Intellectual elites across the society get attracted towards the enterprise and together they work towards achieving excellence.
- - Not a small gain for the enterprise!

- ➢ A fair and honest distribution of business profits between all the genuine stakeholders of the company and the management.
  - o All stakeholders feel comfortable with the organisation and its profit sharing practices without grouse against the management with the thought that they are pocketing a lion's share in company's profits.
- ➢ Activity integrity and honesty of business practices instils in people great confidence in the accounting and audit practices of the enterprise and share holders get a true picture of company's financial status, performances and other breakthrough activities through companies' annual balance sheets.
  - o People's comfort level with the organisation further catalyses organisations' confidence in their own operations and induces them to perform still better.
- ➢ Activity integrity helps genuinely interested stakeholders or appropriate government agencies to examine and investigate into different types of business transactions that carry a high potential to pose conflict of interests and a challenge to integrity of people.
  - o Outcome of such investigations further enhances comforts of stakeholders and society's confidence in organisation's activities.
- ➢ This practice of law abidance by the business enterprise automatically ensures that their business associates, like for example suppliers of materials and services also tend to become, and many a time forces them to become, law abiding.
  - o A great service to the society!
- ➢ Law abidance in all spheres of business activities automatically supports and works towards overall welfare and development of the society.
  - o Not a small gain for the society!

A close study of corporate life tells us that the reality of business life is that it may not always be true that corporates either prefer to stay dishonest or feel highly comforted to remain so. Dishonesty is not their motif. (Dishonesty is never the religion of anybody on earth. People become dishonest only by force of certain circumstances. Once those unwelcome forces are eliminated, people do like to become honest and remain honest. This is the law that governs human conscience!) Given an opportunity, many corporates like to go clean and stay clean and honest forever.

Total compliance to legal requirements could pose many hurdles in the beginning especially if they are not well prepared for the same. Some of the typical hurdles normally encountered by business corporates are given in Table 3.1. These hurdles are not much different from what we have already discussed under practice of integrity in the previous chapter. As seen earlier, practice of integrity and total abidance to legal requirements are complementary to each other and one cannot come to existence without the other. For a quick recollection of the types of forces that induce practice of dishonesty, let us examine Table 3.1.A close examination of this table tells us that there are only three major unwelcome forces that operate against organisations' staying clean. Once these negative forces are eliminated as suggested in the table, organisations would find it fairly easy to become law-abiding to stay clean forever.

Once organisations successfully get over all the hurdles listed in Table 3.1 and once people are convinced and develop a clear conviction about the true purpose and the guiding sociological and/or philosophical perspectives behind framing of those statutory guidelines and the overall benefits of ensuring compliance to those requirements, nothing would come in their way. People would love to comply with stipulated legal requirements. Conduct of all activities and executions become smooth. People do not resort to any of the operation short-cuts and would have nothing to hide from others. On the contrary, they would love to keep their operations open for scrutiny and cross verification enabling generation of suggestions for improvement. Thus, establishing satisfactory legal compliance status is extremely critical for institutionalising a good governance mechanism in any organisation.

Table 3.1 Hurdles for Staying Clean

Sl. No.	**The Negative Force** Nature of Hurdle for Practicing Total Statutory Compliances	Satisfactory Remedy ⇩ Some Useful Tips	Super-influential Catalyst that Ensures that Corporates Remain Unclean
1	Lack of required knowledge and execution skill. Lack of knowledge and skill manifest in the following ways: i. People's inability to correctly identify all the relevant applicable laws and ensuring its adequacy. ii. Inability to correctly interpret the requirements and their scope together with their intricacies, if any, as applied to specific operation environment of the enterprise and to translate the same to actions while executing jobs. iii. Inability to project true impacts of their commissions and omissions or malpractices. iv. Inability to identify the required infrastructural facilities and back-up. v. Inability to handle those equipments with the requisite care. vi. Inability to maintain those equipments in an ever satisfactory working condition.	i. Periodically give people booster doses of requisite knowledge through suitably designed training and/or knowledge-updation programmes, and as and when necessity for the same arises. ii. Provide necessary expert support and help to people in correct identification and understanding of legal requirements and also in ensuring adequacy of requirements identified by them. iii. Provide necessary guidance and help in translating those requirements to actual shop-floor practices and in identifying compliance gaps, if any, without reference to any specific activity centre. iv. Carefully identify prevalence of knowledge voids, if any, and fill those voids. Similarly, identify prevalence of knowledge pockets here and there and ensure satisfactory deployment of appropriate knowledge across the organisation. v. Train people suitably in correct handling of special equipments, if any, and in their proper care and maintenance as may be required.	➢ Ready vulnerability of enforcement officers to ignore certain non-compliance situations and supporting corporates to stay unclean and leveraging the situation to their personal gains ➢ Ready vulnerability of powerful market environment that induces and/or forces corporates to go unclean ➢ Multiplicatively proliferating corruptive executives, spread across the entire societies, who force corporates to go unclean and to remain unclean. ➢ Multiplicatively proliferating political bigwigs and socially influential public figures who force corporates to go unclean and remain so.
2	Lack of necessary infrastructural facilities and/or support.	i. Help people in carefully identifying necessary facilities and provide the same as may be required. ii. Help people in suitably sharing certain common facilities as may be required with a common approach to compliance achievement.	
3	Lack of required willpower to go clean and stay clean.	i. Help people and provide environment that would support and encourage in developing well coordinated, consensus and willingly committed collective approach to compliance requirements. ii. Help and encourage people in suitably sharing certain common facilities and expertise as may be required with a common commitment to ensure total compliance to all legal requirements across the organisation without reference to any specific activity centre.	

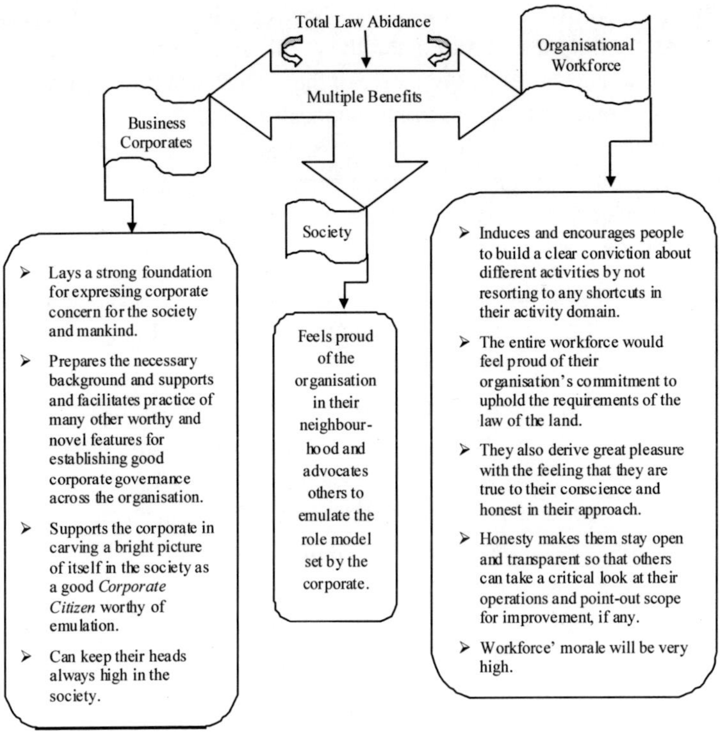

Fig. 3.1 Multiple Benefits of Law Abidance

However, a law could always have certain practical limitations both in terms of its coverage profile and application scope. Both these aspects will have to be decided by the local society depending on the nature of impact on the society by either a commission or an omission on the part of corporates. It is a well understood fact that a law alone cannot fully save the society from all types and kinds of unwelcome situations arising from corporate malpractices. It is in this area of ensuring complete freedom from misinterpretation and misrepresentation of a law that *Corporate Governance* plays an important role in corporate life by fusing holistic views and totality of approach while ensuring compliance to legal requirements.

Some Typical Spreadsheets

A few typical spreadsheets are given below to guide corporates in making a start in this direction, if they have not already done so. These formats are not designed to make them either comprehensive and/or exhaustive. They are only indicative of the sequence of thought process that could help organisations in systematically proceeding with ensuring compliance to applicable legal requirements. With the gaining of experience and confidence in their operations, people could redesign these formats better suited to their operation environments and/or convenience.

Business establishments should, however, always keep in mind that for ensuring satisfactory legal compliance, they have only to follow a few critical steps shown below:

- Correct identification of all the applicable statutory requirements as relevant to their activity nature, magnitude and scope.
- Correct understanding of the nature of compliance expected.
- Accurate translation of compliance expectations to actual shop-floor practices.
- Correct understanding of demonstrations or evidences to be generated for formal verification and confirmation as may be required.
- Generating and maintaining appropriate and/or prescribed records for the purpose.

Where to Make a Start

The following spreadsheets give some typical tips regarding how to proceed with legal compliance activity. As mentioned above these formats should only be treated as mere indicative guidelines and not as full compilation of all the legal requirements for an organisation. Completion of statutory requirements should be individually established.

However, from practical considerations of faster identification of requirements, it would be better if organisations would not leave the issue of identification of statutory requirements entirely to shop-floor executives themselves. This is not because of their non-competence to do the job but primarily because of the fact that they would generally be lost in their own busy schedules of product and/or service generation and distribution activities and may not be in a position to do full justice to the process of identification of legal requirements.

Since legal compliance is a major component of corporate governance and is mandatory in nature, it would always be advantageous to assign the responsibility of identifying and analysing the requirements under statutory guidelines to a person who has a good knowledge of corporate activities and their nature and scope as well as a good knowledge of different types of legal requirements. As suggested earlier under governance, it may be beneficial if a qualified company secretary could shoulder this responsibility, at least in the beginning till all the necessary statutory requirements are suitably identified, as he would have good knowledge of a fairly wide spectrum of legal requirements and many other statutory and/or professional requirements and their compliances. Any other senior executive who could carefully and confidently identify and analyse legal requirements and help shop-floor executives in translating the same to actual practice, could also take this responsibility. Governance coordinators could also be identified from different activity centres and they could help people across the organisation in identifying the statutory requirements as applicable to their specific activity areas and in establishing compliance to those requirements.

Satisfactory compliance to statutory requirements could be established by following a simple 'Seven Step' process as detailed below:

Step One

The starting point would invariably be proper understanding and identification of organisational configuration, definition and scope of activities, contemplated and/or being carried out and trade classification together with identification of the broad categories of the applicability of different regulatory requirements.

a. Understanding of organisational configuration

   i. Alignment with trade classification is very important for any organisation because trade classification is generally accepted in courts of law as "*As per Trade and Technology*" unless a major change takes place in interpretation of the phrase "*Trade and Technology*" based on the Company Act, 2013. Falling in line with such classification or categorisation is always beneficial for an organisation (Table 3.2).

ii. Whenever, organisations like to be identified and/or categorised under different groups, they would be required to prove and establish their claim.

iii. Company Act, 2013, categories companies to 'three major' groups as under:

1.	A Public Company:	Formed by a group of seven or more persons. Should have a paid-up capital of Rs Five lakh or more as may be prescribed from time to time.
2.	A Private Company:	Formed by a group of two or more persons. Has a paid-up share capital of a minimum of Rs One lakh and restricts the rights to transfer of its shares Has a maximum of 200 members. A maximum of 100 members for business association or partnership firms without formal incorporation under Companies Act.
3.	One Person Company:	Formed by one person. Business venture of an individual with limited liability.

a. A government company is one where fifty per cent or more of paid-up share capital is owned by central government or a state government or jointly by the central government and state government.

b. Holding company refers to a company of which such other companies are subsidiary companies.

c. A subsidiary company cannot hold shares of its holding company.

d. No subsidiary company or a partnership company or a business association can be formed exclusively for the purpose of acquisitions.

Table 3.2 Identification of Applicable Laws

<table>
<tr><th>Sl. No.</th><th>Nature of Activity and Trade Classification of Activity Category</th><th>Organisational Configuration</th><th>Applicable Laws</th><th>Correlation with Activity Nature and Law</th></tr>
<tr><td colspan="5">All these are Only Indicative and not Comprehensive.
A host of many other laws could be applicable depending on specific activity nature and other impacting parameters.
Each category of commercial establishments should carefully identify applicable laws and ensure that their identification is Comprehensive.</td></tr>
<tr><td>1</td><td>Trading Activities</td><td rowspan="6">Proprietary Concern
Partnership Firm
Joint Ventures
Company</td><td rowspan="6">Local Civic Administration Rules
Sales tax act and Rules
Income tax Act and Rules
Professional Tax Act and Rules
Companies Act
Indian Corporate Law
Accounts Management and Finance Control Act and Rules
Shops and Commercial Establishment Act and Rules
Labour Act and Rules
Factories Act
Negotiable Instruments Act
Industrial Disputes Act
Merger and Acquisitions Regulation Laws
SEBI Regulation Laws (Prohibition of Insider Trading)
Environmental Protection Acts and Rules
Electricity Act and Rules
Motor Vehicles Acts and Rules
Indian Explosives Act
Public Liability Insurance Act
The Petroleum Act
The Plantation Labour Act
Building and Other Construction Workers Act,
Wild Life Protection Act</td><td></td></tr>
<tr><td>2</td><td>Consultancy</td><td></td></tr>
<tr><td>3</td><td>Professional Bodies</td><td></td></tr>
<tr><td>4</td><td>Factories -
Manufacturing
Assembly
Captive Industries</td><td></td></tr>
<tr><td>5</td><td>Farming and Plantation</td><td></td></tr>
<tr><td>6</td><td>Service Providers –
Transport
Communication
Engineering Services
Repairs and Maintenance
Foods and Beverages
Research and Test Laboratories
Healthcare Services
Warehouse
Entertainment
Education Services
Inspection, Assessment and Certifying Activities
Freight and Forwarding
Housing and building Construction</td><td></td></tr>
<tr><td>7</td><td>Any other classification recognised in trade and technology</td><td></td><td>Other applicable laws and regulations</td><td></td></tr>
</table>

iv. Depending on the nature of organisational activities many laws would become applicable. While identifying the category, one should not forget that as per the Companies Act, 2013, there are certain specific guidelines for formation of a business enterprise or a company.

b. Understanding of organisatinal activities and their execution intricacies

This is precisely an analysis step to understand the prevailing work nature and work environment with specific reference to actual nature and composition and/or configuration of different process inputs, equipment layouts, facility layout, materials and methods movement, available infrastructure, established execution methods, precautions to be taken during handling and activity execution, etc.

Each one of the above components of an activity execution process and its process environment depends on the primary nature of activities of the organisation. Like for example, the work environment in a heavy duty equipment manufacturing industry will be different from the work environment of a pharmacological industry or from the work environment of an analytical and test service laboratory. Each industry will have its own unique work environment. In fact two different types of industries will have similar work environment. There are different schools of thought who would like to group different types of industries under different heads. The following is one such grouping. Since the basic objective of this activity step is just to understand the nature of organisational activities to identify broad categories of applicable statutory guidelines and also activity specific statutory guidelines, categorisation or grouping by itself does not carry any sanctity. It is just a matter of conviction and convenience. However, the best possible correlation with the broad category would help in quickly identifying statutory requirements.

- Engineering Industries — Machine building both heavy duty and light duty machines and equipments, Engineering Workshops and Assembly Shops, OEMs, Accessories and Modular Units, Machine Tools, Miscellaneous Equipments and Machinery Manufacturing Industries, Tractors and Turbines Industries, etc.

- Mines, Minerals, Metallurgical and Foundry Industries – Steel industries, Aluminium Industries, Zinc Industries, Copper Industries, Heavy Duty and Light Duty Casting Industries, Diamond and Pearl Industries, Granite Industries, Coal Mining, Gold and Precious Metals Mining, etc.
- Electrical Industries – Power Industries, Light Duty and Heavy Duty Control Equipments, Generators and Distributors, Components and Accessories, Assembly Units, Solar Energy Drives and Generators, etc.
- Electronic Industries – Computer and Communication Industries, Electronic Office Equipments, Mobile and Telecom Industries, etc.
- Entertainment Industries – Film Industries, Television and Broadcasting Industries, Recreation Products and Leisure Goods, Entertainment Instruments and Equipments Industries, Musical Instruments Industries, Entertainment Solar Devices, etc.
- Agricultural Industries – Commercial Farming, Farming of Herbs and Medicinal Plants, Plant Nurseries, Horticulture, Forestry, Food and Processed Food Products, Sugar and Paper Products Industries, Coffee/Tea Industries, Chocolate Industries, Coir Industries, Cotton and Textile and Weaving Industries (Garment Industries, Fashion-ware Industries,) Jute Industries, Tobacco Industries, Fermentation and Beverages Industries, Bakery and Biscuit Industries, Vegetable and Fruit Processing Industries, Timber and Timber Products Processing Industries, Wooden Toys Industries, Furniture Industries, Rubber and Rubber Products Industries, Silk Industries, Bio-enzyme Industries, Herbal, Cosmetic and Medicinal Extraction Industries, etc.
    - o Some people also like to group a selected few items of this category to classify them as *Genetic Industries* to convey that they are primarily engaged in re-production and multiplication of certain natural plants, birds and

animal species for commercial purposes like for example Cattle Rearing, Cattle Breeding, Poultry Industries, Fishing and Aqua Farming Industries, Dairy and Dairy Products Industries, etc.

Multiplication is just only the first less significant part of these activities. The real commercial value addition would come from processing these into edible products which is an ever flourishing industry.

- Biological, bio-chemical and bio-engineering industries.
- Pharmacological Industries – Drugs and Drug Intermediates Industries, etc.
- Healthcare and Cosmetics Industries – Medical Equipments, etc.
- Service Industries – Hotel Industry, Tourism Industries, Recreation Services, Printing and Advertising Industries, Jewellery Industries, IT Industries, Solar Gadget Industries, Leather and Leather Products Industries, etc.
- Pathological/Virological Laboratories.
- Analytical Services and Instrumentation Laboratories.

  } Medical Diagnostic Laboratories

- Chemical Industries – Fine Chemicals, Heavy Chemicals, Commodity Chemicals and Special Chemicals, Petrochemicals and Oil and Natural Gas Industries (Exploration and Production, Paint Industries, Fertilizer Industries, Plastic Industries, Soaps and Detergents Industries, Cement Industries, Insurance Industries, Banking and Financial Services, Investment and Assets Management Services, Mutual Fund Industries, etc..
- Construction Industries – Building Construction and Real Estate Holding and Development Industries, Bridges, Roads, Dams, Canals, etc.
- Transport Industries – Surface Transport (land and sea), Air and Space Transport, Aviation Industries, Automobile Industries, Shipping Industries, Railway Industries, etc.
- Nuclear power stations.

In fact within each one of these category groups there will be almost innumerable numbers of sub groups based on application or utility category or based on manufacturing group category or component family group category, etc.

This analysis could be carried out with the help of a ready activity location map that gives a two-axis disposition or geographical distribution of all activities across the organisation with specific reference to boundaries of the premises and important landmarks within the organisation. Such an analysis would help people in easily identifying work stations that need to be attended to fuse the concepts of statutory compliances to prevailing execution layouts and operation sequences.

c. Understanding the types of Regulatory Requirements

Once a business venture or the concept of an enterprise is conceived by an individual or groups of individuals, one of the first thoughts that would strike people's mind is to explore the basic regulatory or statutory requirements that one may have to comply with for starting and running of the enterprise. It may not be a surprise that if one starts carefully exploring the entire gamut of legal requirements, one may even get lost in the plethora of rules and regulations and in the multiplicity of acts and guidelines. Fortunately for business corporates, while there could be innumerably large numbers of acts and rules that have been promulgated to embrace every conceivable area of corporate activity that could have an impact on the society or the environment, for any specific business corporate, applicable legal requirements may not be too large to make them beyond their reach.

Company act tops the list of acts that one would like to explore for its applicability to the contemplated activities. Tables 3.3a to 3.3q give a skeletal cross-sectional view of the requirements under companies act. If one carefully examines these tables, one would realise that a high degree of compliance to these requirements and a few others under companies act would ensure that good corporate governance rules the scenario. This act is followed by environment protection acts and rules. Both these acts are of universal nature because of their applicability to all types of companies irrespective of the nature of their activities.

Most of the other acts are activity specific and therefore an entrepreneur would explore them at later stages. Further, these other acts arc not universally applicable to all companies. Their applicability depends only on the nature of materials being used or handled or the mechanisms used for carrying out product or service generation activities, handling and storage of incoming materials or outgoing materials.

There are a few other acts which are not profession specific but are almost universal in nature. Yet, all of them may not become applicable to all sorts of business activities. Applicability of these acts and rules depends only on the activity magnitude, activity coverage profile and scope and the way they are executed. Some of the acts and rules of this category are: Indian Contract Act, The Industries (Development and Regulation) Act, Trade Unions Act, The Competition Act, The Arbitration and Conciliation Act, The Foreign Exchange Management Act (FEMA), Foreign Trade (Development and Regulation) Act and The EXIM Policy, Laws relating to Intellectual Property Rights and Laws relating to Labour Welfare, etc.

Wherever organisations are already carrying out their activities, this step may not be very relevant as organisations would have already gone through this stage. This step could just be used to doubly ensure that all relevant and applicable laws have been identified.

Step Two

After identifying broad categories of acts that would become applicable to their activity domain, nature and scope, organisations should next proceed with identification of details of statutory requirements under each of the act or law together with activity specific laws as may become applicable to their activity nature and scope of operations (Table 3.3 – 3.14). We should, however, not forget that each one of the acts, by itself, is very elaborate, exhaustive and embraces a very wide spectrum of issues relevant to the aspect being referred. As such, it is not practical to summarise all the key aspects covered under any of the acts here as it would then mean total reproduction of different acts. It is neither desirable nor practical. Even a listing of all the available laws at one place is not practical. Only some of the more frequently encountered acts and some typically selected few aspects under these acts are given here for information. In some cases only the name of a law is mentioned but not any of the applicable element from the law. Organisations should examine all the applicable elements and then proceed with summarising actual requirement. Some of the details given in some of these tabulated formats are direct extracts from the act (the Gazette of India notification on Company Act, Factory Act, Environment Act and Rules, etc.). In some cases, the method of expression may not match the exact words/expressions used in the act. Some words are changed here and there. In some places the expectation of the act has been expressed differently to match the language used elsewhere in the text. In a few other situations different words or different phrases are used just to emphasise the spirit of compliance expectation. Organisations should, therefore, carefully study the original act or law and ensure accuracy of their understanding of the requirement and *Comprehensivity* of identification for their use and act accordingly.

Table 3.3a. A Few Requirements under Company Act Formation

Some Basic Requirements under Company Act Formation

- Formation of a company is permitted for carrying out any activity permitted by the law of the land.
  - A company is a "corporation" and an independent entity created by law. In this sense, a company is a "legal" person. A company thus has legal rights and obligations similar to any other individual in the society.
  - Memorandum of association and articles of association, together constitute the constitution of the company.
  - A company could be Limited by Shares, Limited by Guarantee or Unlimited
  - Since a company happens to be a separate person as per law, it will have its own assets, liabilities and commitments as well as its own earnings and expenses.
    - Therefore, shareholders of a company are not liable for the debts and liabilities of the company and cannot be sued by the company's creditors.
    - Shareholders can sue the company if they have a genuine reason for the same. Similarly, the company can also sue its shareholders when it becomes necessary.

  - A Public Company – seven or more persons.
  - A Private Company – two or more persons.
  - One Person Company – one person.
- A listed company refers to a company whose securities (shares, scrips, stocks, bonds, debentures, or other securities of marketable nature, etc.) are listed in any of the recognised stock-exchange (recognised by the central government).
- Subscription money, share capital should be brought before commencement of business or a business borrowing by a newly formed company.
- Following are some of the issues that should be carefully addressed in the memorandum of association:
  - Full and correct name of the proposed company including the word "Limited" at the end as may be applicable.
  - Registering a company name which already exists in ROC's records will be an offence.
  - Name of the company should not be framed/coined in such way that it readily gives an impression that it is affiliated to central government or state government or govt. departments or public sector corporate constituted by the government.
  - Liability of members of the company should be specifically stated.
  - The state in which company's registered office will be located.
  - Share capital of the company and the shares held by each of the signatories to the memorandum should be shown.
  - Memorandum or articles can be altered/changed by company's general body through a resolution or by the BOD.
- The memorandum of association should contain key objectives for which the company is proposed to be incorporated together with other relevant ancillary objectives which could further promote key objectives.
- Memorandum of the company should be filed in appropriate forms specified in Tables, A, B, C, D and E in Schedule I of the act as may be applicable.
- Articles of the company should contain regulations for management of the company.
- Articles of a company should be in appropriate forms specified in Tables, F, G, H, I and J in Schedule I as may be applicable.

Table 3.3c. A Few Statutory Requirements under Company Act Management Responsibility – Board of Directors

Some Basic Requirements under Company Act: Board of Directors
Board of Directors • Every company should have a Board of Directors consisting of individuals as Directors. • Companies should have a minimum of three Directors for a public company, two Directors for a private company and one director for a one person company and a maximum 15 numbers of Directors in any company.

  - More directors can be appointed by passing a special resolution to that effect in the general body.
  - Independent directors do not add to this count.
  - When a special resolution is passed, there will be no need to obtain prior permission of the central government.
  - All listed companies and other government companies having either a total paid-up share capital of over one hundred crores or having a turnover of over three hundred crores should have at least one woman director on their board.
  - Signatories to the memorandum should act as directors of the company till regular directors are appointed in the general body.
  - At least one of the directors of companies should have resided in India for not less than 182 days in the immediate previous year.
  - A director can assume office only after filing his consent with ROC within 15 days of being appointed as a director.
- All listed public companies should have at least one-third of the total number of directors as independent directors.
  - An independent director should not be a managing director or a whole-time director or a nominee director.
- Directors of the board for all listed companies and some other prescribed class of companies should be nominated by a special committee constituted for the purpose.
- Listed companies could have one director elected from small shareholders.
- A director should have a director identification number issued by the central government.
  - Registrar of companies should be informed of the director identification number of all the directors within 15 days of their appointment as directors of the company.
  - Failure to inform ROC will attract punishment.
  - No director should have more than one director identification number.
- BOD can appoint an alternate director in place of a regular director to function in his place during his absence of not less than three months (being away from India).
  - Alternate director cannot be appointed in place of an independent director unless the person is fully qualified to be appointed as an independent director.
- A director cannot serve, including as alternate director, on the boards of more than 20 different companies of which there should not be more than 10 public companies including associate, holding or subsidiary companies of a public company.
  - The general body of the company can fix still lower limits for its directors.

Duties of Directors

- With a view to ensuring active involvement in company's affairs and activities and useful participation of directors, it is necessary that directors attend and participate in the deliberations of board meetings.
- Directors should act in accordance with the articles of the company to promote the basic objectives of the company and in the best interests of the company, employees, shareholders, the community and the environment.
- Should always discharge his duties with utmost care, great skills and with due diligence and independent judgement in the interests of the company.
- Should not derive any benefits either for self or for relatives of self any kind of advantage or benefits from the company failing which will become liable for penalty to the extent of gains derived.
- Directors contravening the stipulations of the company act will become liable for punishment that could be between Rs One lakh to five lakhs.
- All directors should declare their concern and interests in any company or companies, firms or other association of individuals that could influence his decisions and actions in the company where he is being appointed as a director. Such declaration should be made at the very first board meeting and in every financial year or whenever there is a change in disclosures made earlier.
- Should not get involved in or create situations of conflict of interests between those of the company and the self.
- A director cannot assign his office or duties thereof to anybody else.
- Contravention of the act will attract punishment varying between Rs One lakh to Five lakhs.
- No director, other than the managing director or the whole time director, is eligible for availing a loan from the company.

Vacation of Office

- The office of a director will become vacant whenever he gets disqualified due to any of the reasons specified in the act.
  - Unsound mind.
  - Undischarged insolvent.
  - Pending application for insolvency.
  - Convicted by a court for an offence with six months' imprisonment, and five years have not elapsed after expiry of the sentence.
  - Disqualification by a court of law or Tribunal.
  - Not paid share amount for more than six months.
  - A director of company which has not filed annual financial statement or returns for three successive years.
  - Holds directorship of more than 20 different companies.
- Does not attend the board meeting consecutively for the preceding twelve months with or without a formal permission from the board.
- Contravenes the requirements of the act by either entering into a contract or arrangement where he is either directly or indirectly interested or fails to

inform the board of his interests in any of the running contracts or arrangements.

- Whenever he takes-up an employment in the company or in any of its subsidiaries or associates.
- A director can resign on-his-own but should suitably inform the registrar of companies giving details of reasons for resignation within thirty days of resigning.
- A company can remove through a resolution, a director (who is not appointed by the Tribunal as a director of the company) after the expiry of his office by giving him an opportunity to be heard.
- Whether or not a director continues to be an active member of the board, and whether or not he has attended board meetings, and whether or not he was involved in board decisions and actions, and whether or not he continues to have any interest in the affairs of the company, he would always have to shoulder responsibility for all the misdeeds and frauds that have taken place during his tenure as a director and becomes liable for punishment, irrespective of when such frauds and misdeeds get identified.
- A director continuing to function as a director even after being formally disqualified will be liable for punishment of up to one year or a fine varying between Rs One lakh up to five lakhs or both.

Board Meetings

- The first board meeting (Board of Directors' meeting) to be held within 30 days' of incorporation and thereafter a minimum of four meeting in a year.
  - Minimum of clear seven days' notice for calling a board meeting.
  - All directors should disclose to the board in its first meeting and in the first board meeting on all subsequent financial years or whenever there is a change in the details of their earlier disclosures regarding their concern or interest in other companies or firms or associations including the shares held in those companies.
  - Directors, who either directly or indirectly, are concerned and interested in a contemplated contract or an arrangement should disclose about their interest to the board where the issue is being discussed.
    - o Whenever a director develops an interest to finalisation of a contract or arrangement should inform at the immediate next board meeting regarding his interest.
  - Liability of Rs 25,000.00 penalty for the person responsible for giving notice of board meeting.
  - Gap between two successive board meetings should not exceed a maximum of 120 days.
  - A director can participate in board meeting either directly in person or through video conferencing or through any other formally approved audio-visual means.
  - In case of emergency meeting with shorter notices, at least one independent director should be physically present in the meeting.

    - o In the absence of an independent director from the meeting, at least the decisions taken in such urgent meetings should be ratified by an independent director.
  - In case of an equality of votes, the Chairperson of the Board, if any, shall have a second or casting vote.
- In the case of one person company/small companies two board meetings in a year, at least one in each half calendar year with a minimum gap of 90 days between them would be OK.
- One-third of total numbers of directors on the board or two directors whichever is higher should be present to form the quorum for board meetings.
    - o Vacancy of directorship of the board will not count for quorum.
    - o However, since a director can also participate in board meeting through video-conferencing, participation of director through video-conferencing or any other audio-visual means would also count for quorum for board meetings.
  - A continuing director can add to quorum figure for a resolution of BOD calling for a general meeting of the company and not for any other purpose.
  - Whenever the number of participating interested directors is either equal to two-thirds the total strength or is more than non-interested directors, a minimum of two non-interested directors will form the quorum for BOD meetings.
- A resolution can be passed by the board has to pass through a pre-circulation to all the directors together all relevant support documents/papers.
- Decisions taken by a board will not become invalid due to disqualification of a participating director.

Vigilance

- Every listed company or such class or classes of companies, as may be prescribed, should establish a vigilance mechanism for directors and employees to report genuine concerns in such manner as may be prescribed.

The vigilance mechanism should provide for adequate safeguards against victimisation of persons who use such mechanism and make provision for direct access to the chairperson of the Audit Committee in appropriate or exceptional cases subject to the condition that the details of establishment of such mechanism is disclosed by the company on its website, if any, and in the Board's report.

Powers of the board

- The Board of Directors of a company are entitled to exercise all such powers, and to do all such acts and things which they are authorised by the company.
- However, while exercising such powers or doing such act or thing, the Board should not contravene the requirements of companies act, or the

memorandum or articles, or any statutory regulations, including regulations made by the company in general meeting.

- Regulations made by the company in general meeting will not invalidate any prior act of the Board which would have been valid if that regulation had not been made.
- The Board of Directors of a company should exercise the following powers on behalf of the company by means of resolutions passed at meetings of the Board:
    - to make calls on shareholders in respect of money unpaid on their shares;
    - to authorise buy-back of securities Under Section 68;
    - to issue securities, including debentures, whether in or outside India;
    - to borrow monies;
    - to invest the funds of the company;
    - to grant loans or give guarantee or provide security in respect of loans;
    - to approve financial statement and the board's report;
    - to diversify the business of the company;
    - to approve amalgamation, merger or reconstruction;
    - to take over a company or acquire a controlling or substantial stake in another company;

Restrictions on the Powers of the Board

- The board of directors of a company can exercise the following powers only with the consent of the company by a special resolution:
    - To sell, lease or otherwise dispose of the whole or substantially the whole of the undertaking of the company or where the company owns more than one undertaking, of the whole or substantially the whole of any of such undertakings.
    - To invest otherwise in trust securities the amount of compensation received by it as a result of any merger or amalgamation;
    - To borrow money, where the money to be borrowed, together with the money already borrowed by the company will exceed aggregate of its paid-up share capital and free reserves, apart from temporary loans obtained from the company's bankers in the ordinary course of business: Provided that the acceptance by a banking company, in the ordinary course of its business, of deposits of money from the public, repayable on demand or otherwise, and withdrawable by cheque, draft, order or otherwise, will not be considered to be a borrowing of monies by the banking company within the meaning of this clause.
    - To remit, or give time for the repayment of, any debt due from a director.

Table 3.3d. A Few Statutory Requirements under Company Act Management Responsibility – Independent Directors

Some Basic Requirements under Company Act: Independent Directors

Mandatory Requirement

- All listed public companies should have at least one third of the total numbers of directors on its board as independent directors. For other classes of public companies, the number of independent directors could change depending on the directives of the central government.
- CSR committees of all companies should have at least one independent director.
- Company's audit ccommittee should consist of a minimum of three directors with independent directors forming a majority.
- All listed companies and other prescribed companies should constitute a *Nomination and Remuneration Committee* for identifying suitable people for being appointed as directors or for senior management positions in the company and should consist of three or more non-executive directors out of which not less than one-half should be independent directors.
- Whenever board meetings are required to be called at shorter notices for transacting urgent business issues, at least one of the independent directors should be present at such meetings.
- Further, whenever none of the independent directors will be able to attend an urgently convened board meeting, the decisions taken at the meeting will become final only when the same is ratified by at least one independent director.

Who are Independent Directors

- An independent director in a company context is one who is
  - Not a managing director or a whole-time director nor a nominee director but still a director on the board of the company.
  - A respectable person in the society with a high degree of personal integrity and carries with him a high degree intellectual calibre, a high degree of professional talent, expertise and a rich exposure to a wide spectrum of professional and/or industrial activities.
  - Neither himself nor any of his relatives was a promoter of the company or any of its subsidiaries and associates as partners or proprietors and was not involved in company promotion when it was launched.
  - Not related to either the promoters of the company and its subsidiaries or any of its directors.
  - Not holding or had held a key managerial position in the company or its subsidiaries in the immediately preceding three financial years.
  - Not an employee nor was one in the company or its subsidiaries in the immediately preceding three financial years.

- Not had any type of monetary relationship with the promoters of the company or its subsidiaries or its directors in the preceding two financial years or during the current financial year.
- None of his relatives had any type of monetary relationship with the promoters of the company or its subsidiaries or its directors amounting Rs 50 lakhs or 2 Per cent of company's gross turnover or gross income.
- Not holding company's stocks or would receive stocks of the company during his tenure as an independent director.
- Entitled only for the fixed remuneration for attending the meetings together with reimbursement of expense incurred in connection with attending the meetings. Any other profit-related commission that may be permitted by the members of the company.
- Would not accept any remunerative assignment from the company either directly or indirectly for a minimum period of three years after his retirement from directorship of the company.

Why Independent Directors.

- Generally companies' boards comprise of directors from promoters' family, business investors, representatives of financial institutions, or representatives of certain governmental agencies, etc. As a natural consequence, it is very likely that certain decisions to be taken by the board might be influenced by different biases ranging from investment biases to professional biases.
- On the other hand, independent directors who would not have any specific personal interest in company's affairs could view all issues from globally holistic perspectives which would be highly beneficial to the company in the long run.
- Naturally, independent directors are expected to:
  - Fuse the concept of a totally unbiased independent judgement to all decisions of the board especially when exploring and evaluating critical issues like strategic policy decisions, assessing company's performance in the context of globally competitive hi-tech oriented market scenario, dynamic strategies and innovative mechanisms being developed and adopted while managing risks, induction of senior and key personnel to the main stream and in evolving highly desirable codes of conduct and good ethical practices for everybody in the company.
  - Objectively evaluate the performance of the board and the company management.
  - Critically evaluate the performance of company's management in meeting the set targets.
  - Monitor performance progress and re-orient the goals wherever necessary.
  - Build the required confidence in the honest approach towards financial transactions and finance management activities of the company.

- Doubly ensure that internal finance controls and risk management mechanisms are satisfactory and robust enough to be relied on.
- Safeguard the interests of all class of stakeholders especially the minority shareholders who are not represented on the board.
- Bring a dynamically good balance between the conflicting interests of different classes of stakeholders.
- Help in identifying suitable people and hiring people for senior management levels and also to fix remuneration for executive directors and other key senior management executives in the company.
- Correctly assess and review the performance effectiveness of executive directors and other key senior personnel for deciding about their continuance or otherwise. And in case their services are not found to be useful to the organisation, to recommend their removal from company's services.
- Moderate and arbitrate in arriving at a dynamic balance between the interests of management and shareholders whenever situations of serious conflicts arise.

Appointment

- Company's board should select their independent directors from a data bank maintained by professional bodies, institutes, associations or notified by certain government agencies on their websites.
- Companies should exercise due diligence while selecting independent directors, taking care to ensure a good balance of intellectual calibre, professional skills and expertise and knowledge across the board that would help the board in discharging its functions and duties more effectively.
- Appointment of independent directors should be independent of company management.
- Board of Directors of the company should certify that in their opinion, the person proposed to be appointed as an independent director has all the necessary qualifications to become an independent director.
- No alternate director can be appointed in place an independent director unless he is also independently qualified an eligible for being appointed as an independent director.
- The general body of the company should approve appointment of independent directors.
- Appointment of independent directors should be formalised by issuing the appointment letter giving full details of:
  - Terms of appointment.
  - Board-level committees to be represented.
  - Confidential responsibilities to be discharged as a part of his duty together with consequential liabilities for failure to either discharge the duties diligently or failure to keep-up the confidentiality of the assignment.
  - Expected code of business conduct and ethics.
  - Type of activities directors are not expected to get engaged in the company.

  - Expectations of the Board from independent directors being appointed, and others as may be relevant.
- An independent director should submit a certificate of declaration to the board that at the time of his being appointed as an independent director, he enjoys full independence as prescribed in the act and has no direct interest in the activities of the company or any of its associates and subsidiaries.

Resignation and Removal

- An independent director can resign from his office by giving a notice in writing to the company. Resigning director should also forward a copy of his resignation to registrar of companies within thirty days of resignation.
- The company also should inform the ROC about the same as per requirements.
- Directors' report should refer to resignation of a director.
- Director's resignation will come to effect from the date the resignation is received by the company or from the date specified in the resignation whichever is later.
- However, the basic liability principle, namely, a director will always continue to remain liable for punishments for all the mistakes, mischiefs and/or frauds that have taken place during his tenure as director of the company with or without his knowledge.
- Director's vacancy should be filled within a maximum of one hundred and eighty days from the date of resignation of an outgoing director except in situations where the company would still continue to fulfil the requirement of minimum numbers of independent directors even when the vacant place is not filled-up.

Tenure of Office

- The tenure of office of independent directors will be restricted to two consecutive terms of five years duration each with a cooling-off period of three years in between before being reappointed as a director for the third term.
  - In order to qualify themselves for reappointment, these directors should not have had any direct or indirect affiliation or association with the company or its subsidiaries and associates during the cooling-off period.
- An independent director can be reappointed by passing a special resolution to that effect and further recorded in board's report.
- An independent director cannot hold the office for more than two consecutive terms of five years' duration each.
- A company can consider an independent director for a suitable appointment in the company only after passing off of three years' of his retirement, that is, only after three years' of his retirement from directorship, he could take—up a job in the company.

Re-appointment:

- Any independent director could be considered for re-appointment provided his performance during his tenure is satisfactory.

- Board should independently evaluate the performance satisfaction level of an independent director.

Expected Professional Code of Conduct

- An independent director should:
  - Uphold ethical standards of integrity and probity.
  - Act objectively and constructively while exercising his duties.
  - Exercise his responsibilities in a *bona fide* manner in the interest of the company.
  - Devote sufficient time and attention to his professional obligations for informed and balanced decision making.
  - Not allow any extraneous considerations that will vitiate his exercise of objective, independent judgment in the paramount interest of the company as a whole, while concurring in or dissenting from the collective judgment of the Board in its decision making.
  - Not abuse his position to the detriment of the company or its shareholders or for the purpose of gaining direct or indirect personal advantage or advantage for any associated person.
  - Refrain from any action that would lead to loss of his independence.
  - Assist the company in implementing the best corporate governance practices.
  - Wherever and whenever circumstances arise which make an independent director lose his independence, the independent director must immediately inform the Board accordingly.

Duties of Independent Directors

- Independent directors should:
  - Undertake appropriate induction and regularly update and refresh their skills, knowledge and familiarity with the company.
  - Seek appropriate clarification or amplification of information and, where necessary, take and follow appropriate professional advice and opinion of outside experts at the expense of the company.
  - Strive to attend all meetings of the Board of Directors and of the Board committees of which he is a member.
  - Participate constructively and actively in the committees of the Board in which they are chairpersons or members.
  - Strive to attend the general body meetings of the company.
  - Where they are seriously concerned about certain issues regarding running of the company or a proposed action, they should ensure that these issues are addressed by the Board satisfactorily.
  - Further, wherever those issues are not resolved to their satisfaction level they must insist that their concerns are recorded in the minutes of the Board meeting.
  - Keep themselves well informed about the company and the external environment in which it operates.

- Not to unfairly obstruct the smooth and proper functioning of an otherwise good performing Board or committee of the Board.
- Pay sufficient attention and ensure that adequate deliberations are held before approving related party transactions and assure themselves that the same are in the best interests of the company.
- Ascertain and ensure that the company has an adequate and functional vigilance mechanism.
- Further ensure that the interests of a person who uses such mechanism are not prejudicially affected on account of such use.
- Report concerns about unethical behaviour, actual or suspected fraud or violation of the company's code of conduct or ethics policy.
- Acting within his authority, assist in protecting the legitimate interests of the company, shareholders and its employees.
- Not disclose confidential information, including commercial secrets, technologies, advertising and sales promotion plans, unpublished price sensitive information, unless such disclosure is expressly approved by the Board or required by law.

Separate Meetings

- The independent directors of the company should hold at least one meeting in a year, without the attendance of non-independent directors and members of company's management.
- All the independent directors of the company should strive to attend such meetings.
- The meeting should review the performance of non-independent directors and the Board as a whole.
- The meeting should also review the performance of the Chairperson of the company, taking into account the views of executive directors and non-executive directors.
- The meeting should assess the quality, quantity and timeliness of flow of information between the company management and the Board which is necessary for the Board to effectively and reasonably well perform their duties.

Evaluation of Independent Directors

- The performance evaluation of independent directors should be done by the entire Board of Directors of the company excluding the director being evaluated.
- On the basis of performance evaluation report prepared by the full board minus the independent director being assessed, the board should decide whether or not to extend and continue the term of appointment of the independent director.

Liabilities

- All independent directors of companies have to perform certain specified duties and have to shoulder certain responsibilities.

- If independent directors do not meticulously discharge their legitimate/duty bound responsibilities with the degree of expected diligence, they attract punitive measures including compensatory fines.

However, they will be held liable, only in respect of such acts of omissions or commissions by a company which had occurred with independent director's knowledge, attributable through Board processes, and with his consent or connivance or where he had not acted diligently.

Table 3.3e. A Few Requirements under Company Act Management Responsibility – Board Committees

Some Basic Requirements under Company Act: Board Committees
• All listed and prescribed classes of companies should compulsorily establish following four sub-committees of the board. - Audit Committee - Stakeholder Relationship Committee - Nomination and Remuneration Committee - Corporate Social Responsibility Committee

Table 3.3f. A Few Requirements under Company Act Management Responsibility – Audit Committee

Some Basic Requirements under Company Act: Audit Committee

- The Board of Directors of all listed companies and also some prescribed class of companies have to institute an independent internal high power audit committee to examine and review all types of financial statements prepared by the company for their meaning and impact on company's performance and to ensure initiation of immediate action to bring the situation back under control as may become necessary. This is to ensure that the financial operations of the company does not receive any shocks or jolts and the investment made by different investors and the innocent public remains safe.
- The Audit Committee should consist of a minimum of three directors with independent directors forming a majority.
- The majority strength of audit committee should be made-up of independent directors.
- While it is highly desirable that all the members of this audit committee should have good exposure or expertise and/or experience of correctly reading the various figures of financial statements of the company and are in a position to suitably interpret their meaning and scope and are capable of correctly projecting their impact and implication on the performance of the

company, at least the Chairman of Audit Committee and its majority members should necessarily carry such an expertise with them.

- Among other responsibilities as may be assigned by the Board, Budit Committee should shoulder the following responsibilities:
  - Identifying and recommending the appointment of an auditor or audit company for the company.
  - Fixing the remuneration and terms of appointment of auditors for the company.
  - Ensuring independence of auditors.
  - Reviewing and monitoring the performance and effectiveness of the audit process.
  - Examining and understanding the implications of the financial statement prepared by auditors together with details of the audit report with modifications, if any, of transactions of the company with related parties.
  - Scrutinising inter-corporate loans and/or investments.
  - Valuating the undertakings or assets of the company as may become necessary.
  - Evaluating internal financial controls and risk management mechanisms.
  - Monitoring the end use of funds raised through public offers and related matters, if any.
- Audit Committee has full powers to:
  - Call for comments and observations of auditors about internal control systems and their effectiveness.
  - Review the financial statement before submission of the same to the board.
  - Discuss these matters or any other finance management related issues with company auditors and the management as may become necessary.
- Audit committee also carries full authority to:
  - Inquire, verify the records and investigate into any of the accounts related matters.
    - Inquiry should be conducted in such a way that auditors as well as company's management should get an opportunity to be heard,
  - Look into any specific issue referred to it by the board.
  - Seek external professional advice as may become necessary for correctly understanding the operations and their implications on company's financial performances.
- Whenever the Board does not Accept Audit Committees reports or recommendations, the same should be recorded in board's report together with reasons for not accepting the same.

Table 3.3g. A Few Requirements under Company Act Management Responsibility – Stakeholders Relationship Committee

Some Basic Requirements under Company Act: Stakeholders Relationship Committee
• Companies having more than one thousand numbers shareholders, debenture-holders, deposit-holders and any other security holders at any point of time during a financial year, should constitute a Stakeholders Relationship Committee consisting of a chairperson who should be a non-executive director and such other members as may be decided by Company's Board. • This Committee should design, develop and evolve a mechanism capable of effectively redressing all types of grievances of investors. • This committee should carefully examine all types of grievances of security holders of the company and resolve them to security holders' comfort. • With a view to ensuring both timely intervention and effective redressal of all grievances and to carefully protect the interests of investors, the committee can configure an independent set-up with a nonexecutive chairman to oversee the proceedings and timely actions. • The Chairperson of the Committee or his authorised representative should attend the general meeting of the company to answer unanswered or unresolved grievances, if any. • In case of contravention of these requirements, the company will become liable for a punishment of between Rs One lakh and five lakhs.   - And every officer associated with the default will be punishable with a fine of between Rs Twenty five thousand and up to one lakh or both except in situations where non-consideration of stakeholders' grievances does not contravene the requirement. **Protection of Minority Shareholders' Interest** • The promoter and shareholders having control of a company which has unutilised money raised from public through prospectus and which proposes to change its objects should provide an exit option to the dissenting shareholders in accordance with regulations to be specified by SEBI. • Where any benefit accrues to promoter, director, manager, KMP, or their relatives, either directly or indirectly as a result of non-disclosure or insufficient disclosure in the explanatory statement annexed to the notice of general meeting then such persons shall hold such benefit in trust for the company and will become liable to compensate the company to the extent of the benefit received by him.

Table 3.3h. A Few Requirements under Company Act Management Responsibility – Nomination and Remuneration Committee

Some Basic Requirements under Company Act: Nomination and Remuneration Committee

- All listed companies and such other class or classes of companies, as may be prescribed should constitute the Nomination and Remuneration Committee consisting of three or more non-executive directors out of which not less than one-half should be independent directors.
  - Chairperson of the company could also be appointed as a member of this committee (whether executive or non-executive) but he cannot chair the committee.
- The Nomination and Remuneration Committee has to shoulder the responsibility to identify people suitably qualified to become directors and those who could be appointed in senior management cadre in the company as per criteria laid down for the purpose.
  - The committee should recommend their appointment and also removal if it becomes necessary.
  - The committee should evaluate the performance of directors of the company.
- The Committee should evolve and formulate the criteria for determining necessary qualifications, positive attributes that a director should possess.
- The Committee should evolve and formulate the criteria for ensuring independence of a director serving on the board.
- The Committee should also evolve and formulate policy for fixing the remuneration for the directors, key managerial personnel and other employees of the company.
- The details of the policy so worked out should be disclosed to the board and should become part of the board's report.
  - While formulating the policy for fixing remuneration for directors and other senior employees of the company, the Committee should never forget that the remuneration levels and their composition should be good enough to attract, retain and motivate highly qualified and efficient directors and other senior employees of the company in such a way that they always put-in their best quality input for running the company very effectively and very successfully.
    - The Committee should also know that in the ever vibrant and ever dynamic socio-economic and competition scenario, remuneration package has a close relationship with people's performance levels, because it is this parameter that holds the key to catalyse the effectiveness process and to hold the motivation levels of even inherently very efficient people.

- Composition of remuneration should therefore be worked out in such a way that there is one fixed component to match the levels of assignment and a performance linked variable component.
- The variable component could be both short-term objective achievement linked as well as long-term objective achievement linked incentive.
- Such a work-up is very critical to attract and retain efficient people at key managerial positions and also at senior management levels.

Table 3.3i. A Few Requirements under Company Act Management Responsibility – Corporate Social Responsibility

Some Basic Requirements under Company Act: Corporate Social Responsibility - CSR

Who should Participate in CSR

- Any company that meets the following criteria has to mandatorily implement CSR activities as per recommendation provided in the act.
  - Whose net worth is rupees five hundred crores or more in a financial year.
  - Whose gross turnover in a financial year is one thousand crores or more.
  - Whose net profit in a financial year is five crores or more.
    1. This qualifying amount refers to net profit before taxation and as per books of accounts maintained by the company.
    2. For purposes of calculating net profits, companies cannot include the profits earned by their foreign branches even if the business outside India is being carried under the same name. They have to confine only to net profits earned within the country from their Indian branches.
    3. Naturally, the net profits of previous three financial years also refer to net profits earned in the country by pooling together the profits of all the branches in the country.

How much to Spend on CSR

- All companies meeting any of the above criteria have to mandatorily reserve two per cent of average net profit of preceding three financial years.
- Funds reserved under this category have to be spent only on CSR activities specified in the act.
- Companies should build proper justification for not spending the said amount on CSR activities whenever the company does not spend such allocated amounts on CSR activities within the financial year.
  - Such justification developed, if any, should be recorded in the proceedings of the board meeting,
- Unspent money from CSR funds' allocation should not be routed back to main business funds of the company, but should be transferred back to CSR corpus.

How to Control and Monitor

- For purposes of dedicatedly administering, guiding, controlling and managing CSR activities, companies should appoint a special committee to be designated as CSR committee.
    - The CSR Committee should comprise of at least one independent director and two other directors of the company.
    - Wherever an unlisted public company or a private company is involved which is not required to have an independent director on its board or a private company which has only two directors on its board, it is not mandatory that those companies should appoint a third director or an additional independent director only to configure a CSR committee.
    - An independent director is required to be identified for the CSR committee if the company's board already has such directors on its board.
- CSR committee should establish a transparent monitoring mechanism to oversee the implementation and effectiveness of CSR activities of the company.
- The committee should frame and formulate a CSR policy for the company and recommend the same for approval by the board of directors of the company.
    - The policy should specifically highlight the types of CSR projects which the company plans to undertake.
    - The policy should also specify the modalities to be followed by the company for implementing the CSR project and the mechanism to be followed for monitoring the progress of the project.
    - CSR policy should specifically make a categorical statement that the unspent surplus money from CSR projects will not be ploughed back to company's finances but will be transferred back to CSR corpus.
    - CSR committee could recommend to the board of directors to incorporate the details of company's approved CSR policy and projects on its website for information of the general public.
- CSR committee should recommend to the board of directors the list of projects that could be taken up during the year. It should also recommend the amounts to be spent on each of the projects.
- Committee should identify CSR projects relevant to the local community and/or local area and recommend projects to be initiated in the region.

What Constitutes CSR Domain

- Ministry of Corporate Affairs, Govt. of India has issued a notification on 20th Feb, 2014, identifying the following ten broad categories of activities as qualifying for CSR activities effective from 1st April, 2014.
    i. Eradicating hunger, poverty and malnutrition; promoting preventive health care and sanitation and making available safe drinking water.
    ii. Promoting education, including special education and employment enhancing vocational skills especially among children, women, elderly, and the differently abled and livelihood enhancement projects.

iii. Promoting gender equality, empowering women, setting homes and hostels for women and orphans; setting up old age homes, day care centres and such other facilities for senior citizens and measures for reducing inequalities faced by socially and economically backward groups.
iv. Ensuring environmental sustainability, ecological balance, protection of flora and fauna, animal welfare, agro-forestry, conservation of natural resources, and maintaining quality of soil, air and water.
v. Protection of national heritage, art and culture including restoration of buildings and sites of historical importance and works of art, setting up public libraries, promotion and development of traditional arts and handicrafts.
vi. Measures for the benefit of armed forces veterans, war widows and their dependents.
vii. Training to promote rural sports, nationally recognised sports, paralympic sports and Olympic sports.
viii. Contribution to Prime Minister's National Relief Fund or any other funds set up by the Central Govt. For socio-economic development and relief and welfare of the scheduled castes, the scheduled tribes, other backward classes, minorities and women.
ix. Contributions or funds provided to technology incubators located within academic institutions which are approved by the Central Government.
x. Rural development projects.

Eligibility Criteria

- Only those CSR projects that are taken-up in India are eligible for qualification under CSR and not any form of CSR activity carried outside India.
- Further, it is only that specific category of CSR projects which are exclusively identified for the purpose or on-going pre-identified CSR projects that are eligible for qualification under CSR activity.
- If the basic nature of a business activity is such that it automatically embraces certain CSR activity area in the normal course of its business conduct, then those activities do not qualify for CSR activity.
  - On all such situations, those companies will have to separately identify certain independent CSR activities.
- None of the CSR projects should be designed exclusively for the benefit of participating companies' employees or their family members.
  - This stipulation under qualifying CSR activity criteria should be carefully interpreted.
  - While a higher education or vocational skill implantation training programme is conducted and/or organised by the participating company and children of a few employees of the company also take advantage of the same along with many other general public in the town or village, then one would not be morally justified to disqualify such a CSR activity. After all, employees and their families also have to live in the same society as many others live. CSR will have to be viewed from broader perspectives.

  - Similarly, if a CSR project for providing solar energy or free drinking water supply to all the houses in a township/village or a small habitat in the region is launched, and if some employees and their families also live that township or village, then what should happen? A village or a township is meant for anybody to live. Employees of the company cannot be barred.

    Naturally, CSR projects taken-up in such habitats where a few employees and their family members also get benefited along with many other in the region, then those CSR projects will have to fully qualify.
  - The spirit of the act is that contemplated CSR projects should not aim only at the welfare and overall development of participating companies' employees and their family members or should not focus exclusively on the welfare of companies ' employees and their families.
  - One has only work out a consensus figures for the quantum of benefits shared by companies' employees and their families.
  - While individual opinion of system auditors could vary in this regard, any figure of up to say about 20 percent (employees and their families) of the total target beneficiary population should be considered as a qualifying figure.
- Contribution to any of the political parties in any form and magnitude will not qualify for CSR activity irrespective of whether a specific contribution is being collected under the name of a social welfare project or a general welfare project which would otherwise fully qualify for CSR activity when independently identified and executed.

CSR Corpus

- From the administrative considerations, all companies who are mandatorily spending on CSR activities should create an independent corpus for CSR.
- Seed money for the corpus is the funds allocated for CSR.
  - Companies should transfer average 2 per cent minimum of previous three years profits before tax to CSR Corpus.
  - For qualifying companies, while the minimum amount is fixed at 2 per cent of net profits before taxation, companies are always free to spend more on CSR activities and there is no bar on the same.
  - Any other income that could arise out of CSR activities.
  - Any unspent money on CSR activities namely surplus arising out of CSR activities.

Outsourcing CSR Activities

- Wherever participating companies' activities and commitments do not permit for ready and direct participation in conducting of CSR activities or in providing the necessary supervision, the same could be organised through a separately established society, trust or a non-profit company.
- However, on all such situations, the role of trust or society will be limited exclusively to satisfactory implementation of the CSR project and not in identification of CSR projects.

- Identification of CSR projects, its activity scope and profile will have to be defined by the participating company itself.
- Further, the required monitoring has also to be done by the participating company itself.
  - The monitoring mechanism should be designed in such a way that the implementing company does not take to any deviations or changes in the activities or in their scope.
  - Monitoring mechanism should also be in a position to immediately identify if there is any mismanagement of the funds allocated for CSR projects or if any diversions of CSR funds to other activities taking place.
- Participating companies could also off load their CSR activities to other already well established not-for-profit organisations which carry a minimum of three years of good performance track records in handling similar CSR projects.
- There is one more option open to participating companies. – Two or more participating companies can join hands together to pool their CSR funds and launch mutually agreed and collectively identified common CSR projects in a big way. A major advantage of such pooled operation would be widely enlarged activity profile and provision of a platform of multiple monitoring of CSR project progress and performance. The target beneficiary profile would also be enlarged proportionately.
  - On all such collaborative CSR ventures, each of the individual CSR committees should be in a position to prepare progress reports on their projects to their respective boards.

CSR Reporting

(Notification of the Ministry of Corporate Affairs, Govt. of India, 27th Feb., 2014)

- Effective from 1st April, 2014, all annual reports of companies should also carry an annual report on CSR.
- Foreign companies which do not hold their AGMs in India should append a report on CSR in their annual Balance-sheets.
- **Format for CSR Report:**
  (Specification provided by the department)
  Key aspects to be covered in the CSR annual report are:
  i. A brief outline of company's CSR policies and practices.
  ii. A skeletal overview of various CSR projects envisaged and/or contemplated to be taken up during the year.
  iii. A reference to company's website that gives details of company's CSR policies and projects.
  iv. Composition of the CSR committee.
  v. Average net profits of the company for previous three years which has been transferred to company's CSR corpus.
  vi. Details of expenses incurred on various CSR projects during the year together with details of unspent money, if any, along with necessary

details of constraints that did not permit complete utilisation of allocated CSR amount on projects during the year.

vii. Brief details of mechanism followed to spend the allocated CSR amount on different projects during the year:
   a. Serial number of the project.
   b. CSR project title.
   c. Broad sector to which the identified CSR project belongs.
   d. Contemplated target beneficiary location (Details like state, district, taluk/tehsil where the project is undertaken).
   e. Contemplated/budgeted expenses on the project for the year
   f. Amount spent on the project during the year under review giving details of subheadings like direct project cost and overheads, etc.
   g. Cumulative expenditure incurred on the project so far.
   h. If the project implementation is outsourced, then the amount spent by the implementation agency, name and other details of CSR implementing agency together with any other relevant information about the agency that may be desirable.

viii. Reasons for not spending the allocated total CSR amount during the year.

ix. A confirmatory statement from CSR committee to the effect that implementation and monitoring of CSR projects is in line with companies declared CSR policies and objectives.

x. The CSR report should be signed by companies MD or CEO or a director and chairman of CSR committee.

Table 3.3j. A Few Requirements under Company Act Management Responsibility – General Meetings

Some Basic Requirements under Company Act: General Meetings of Members

General Meeting

- Quorum for general meeting - Presence of members in person only should be counted.
  - Quorum for a private company is 2 members personally present.
  - Quorum for a public company: 5 members for up to a total of 1000 members; 15 members for a total numbers of members between 1000 and 5000 and 15 members for a total of more than 5000 members.
- Through special resolutions, general meeting can:
  - Override memorandum, articles, etc. of the company.
  - Appoint a managing director for the company and fix his remuneration.
  - Change the terms of contract referred in prospectus by a special resolution.
  - Alter the authorised share capital in a limited company.

  - Capitalise company's profits or reserves for issuing fully-paid up bonus-shares.
  - Authorise purchase of its own shares or other specified securities.
  - Issue of debentures with an option to convert such debentures into shares, wholly or partly.
  - Authorise company to accept deposits from members subject to clearance from RBI.
- A general meeting of a company may be called by giving not less than clear twenty-one days' notice either in writing or through electronic mode.
  - Shorter notice meetings can be arranged if the consent in writing or by electronic mode is obtained from not less than ninety-five per cent of the members entitled to vote at such meetings.

Annual General Meeting

- In addition to any other meetings, all companies should hold one annual general meeting of its members.
  - Gap between two successive AGMs should not be more than 15 months. In such situations the first AGM should be held within nine months of closing of first financial year and the other one within six months of closing of the next financial year.
  - If the first AGM is held within nine months of closing of first financial year, it is not necessary to hold AGM in the year of incorporation of a company.
  - ROC can permit companies to extend AGMs by up to three months for subsequent AGMs but not first AGM.
- In case of defaults in holding AGMs, tribunal can organise AGM of the company.
- AGM should be held within a maximum of nine months of closure of annual accounts by giving a clear notice of twenty-one days, either in writing or electronic form.
  - Liability to pay penalty for defaults in conducting AGM up to one lac rupees with an additional penalty of Rs 5000.00 for each day of default during which default continues.
  - First AGM should appoint auditors/audit firms for the company.
  - AGM should be held only between 9.00 am and 6.00 pm and only on working days at the registered office of the company or at some other place within the city, town or village in which the registered office of the company is situated.
  - AGM should not be held on a declared National Holiday.
  - Short notice meetings can be organised only with the consent of a minimum of 95 Percent of members entitled to vote at the meeting.
  - Meeting notice, which should be given to all the directors, auditors, all members of the company and legal representatives of deceased members, should specify the place, date, day and time of meeting and also business to be transacted during the meeting.

  - General meeting notice should carry a statement regarding the interests and concern of all directors, KMPs in relation to the issues to be discussed and decided upon.
  - Any business to be transacted in the annual general meeting, other than the consideration of financial statements and the reports of the Board of Directors and auditors, the declaration of any dividend, the appointment of directors in place of those retiring, the appointment of, and the fixing of the remuneration of, the auditors, should be considered as special business transaction.
  - Whenever any item of business to be transacted refers to a document which is to be considered at the meeting, the time and place where such document can be inspected should be specified.
  - A company cannot prohibit a member from exercising his voting except when he is at default of payment against shares registered in his name.
  - Except when a poll is demanded or electronic voting is organised, a resolution put to vote in the general meeting can be decided on a show of hands.
  - If a requisite majority of shareholders give their assent to a resolution through postal ballot, the resolution should be deemed to have been duly passed in the general meeting.
- Companies should prepare correct and accurate minutes of all general meetings, board meetings and the meetings of board committees and should record all resolutions passed in the meeting or through postal ballots.
  - The minutes should be duly signed and kept in the books kept for the purpose within thirty days of the meeting at company's registered office and should be kept open for inspection during business hours.
    - Members have a right to demand for a copy of the minutes of the meeting.
  - All appointments made at any of the meetings aforesaid should be included in the minutes of the meeting.
  - In the case of a meeting of the Board of Directors or of a committee of the Board, the minutes should also contain the names of the directors present at the meeting, and in the case of each resolution passed at the meeting, the names of the directors, if any, dissenting from, or not concurring with the resolution.
  - The Chairman should exercise absolute discretion in regard to the inclusion or non-inclusion of any matter in the minutes if the same appears to be defamatory of any person or detrimental to the interests of the company or irrelevant or immaterial to the proceedings.
- All listed public companies should file a report of AGM with ROC within thirty days of holding AGM.

Table 3.3k. A Few Requirements under Company Act Management Responsibility – General

Some Basic Requirements under Company Act: A Few General Requirements

General

- Prescribed companies should have only a MD or a CEO or a factory manager and not all of them at the same time.
  - Only in the absence of MD or CEO, a company manager or a full time director or the company secretary or the chief financial officer can formally oversee the activities of the company.
- Appointment of a company secretary who will be a key managerial person is a basic requirement.
  - Secretarial standards should be maintained by the companies – Refers primarily to policy guidelines that should be followed for different aspects of secretarial practices.
  - Companies should carry out secretarial audits.
  - Secretarial audit report should form a part of board's report.
  - Company's annual returns should be certified by a director and the company secretary.
- All companies should file with the registrar of companies a copy of the annual return, within sixty days from the date on which the annual general meeting is held.
- Prior approval of National Company Law Tribunal (NCLT) should be obtained for effecting changes in share distribution-configuration that would result in changes in shareholders' voting percentage.
  - Not to issue any share, other than sweat equity share, at discounted prices.
  - Redemption of preference shares within 20 years' of issue except in cases of annual part redemption for approved infrastructure projects.
  - Filing of redemption notice within 30 days in prescribed form with registrar of companies for redeemable preference shares.
- Dividends on shares cannot be made in kind like bonus shares or in any other form of gifts to shareholders. It should be paid in cash only within 30 days of its declaration.
- Whenever dividends remain unpaid or unclaimed and the amount is transferred to IEPF (Investor Education and Protection Fund) corresponding shares on which the dividend was not paid should also be transferred to IEPF.
- All charges (interest or lien creation on assets) should be registered with registrar of companies within 30 days of effecting charges.
- In case of amalgamations, agreement, compromises, etc., company auditors should certify that accounting practices of companies under consideration are in conformity with Accounting Standards prescribed under Section 133 of the Company Law.
  - Filing of this certificate with the tribunal.

  - Notification of such processes together with all the relevant documents to be sent to SEBI, RBI, IT authorities, registrar of companies, stock exchanges, official liquidator, competition commission of India, and other sector regulators and authorities who are likely to be affected by such amalgamations enabling them to raise their objections, if any, in this regard within three days of receipt of notification and corresponding documents in their office, failing which the amalgamation process to be deemed as having no objection from these authorities.
  - Prior approval of RBI should be obtained for cross-border merger of companies.
  - Filing with the registrar of companies, a certificate from company secretary or chartered accountant or cost accountant certifying that the amalgamation processes are in accordance with the guidelines set by the National Company Law Appellate Tribunal.

Company Seal

- The Board should provide for the safe custody of the company seal.
- The seal of the company should not be affixed to any instrument except by the authority of a resolution of the Board or of a committee of the Board authorised by it for that purpose.
  - At least two directors and the secretary or any other person appointed by the Board for this purpose should be present while affixing company's seal on any instrument.
  - Those two directors and the secretary or other authorised person should sign every instrument to which the seal of the company is affixed in their presence.

Passing a Resolution

- No resolution can be passed by the board or by a committee of the board unless the same has been circulated in draft together with all the necessary support papers or documents to all directors or members of the committee as may be applicable at their address registered with the company in India or by post or courier or through approved electronic media and approved by a majority of directors who are entitled to vote on the resolution.
- Whenever not less than one-third of the total number of directors desire that the draft resolution should be discussed and then decided at board meeting, the chairperson should place the draft for discussion and decision at board meeting.

Chairing a Meeting

- Directors of a company board should elect a chairperson to conduct all its meetings and should also decide on the period for the person should hold the office.
  - If no such chairperson is formally elected, or at any of the scheduled meetings the chairperson would not be present within five minutes of the

scheduled time for holding the meeting, the directors present should elect one of their members to chair the meeting.

Delegation of Authority/Sharing of Responsibility

- Without contravening any of the requirements of the act, the board can delegate any of its powers to a committee formed for the purpose of examining the issue in greater depths and details.
  - Members for such committees could be decided by the board as it thinks fit.
  - Such committees should work within the framework set by the board and exercise the powers delegated to it for executing the assignment as per directives of the board.
  - Such committees can meet as frequently as it thinks necessary and similarly, it can adjourn as thinks fit.
- Whenever an issue cannot be resolved by a majority of directors sitting on the particular committee and the votes get equally divided on either side of an opinion, the chairperson can exercise a second or casting vote and decide on the matter.

Validity of a Decision/Resolution

- None of the decisions or resolutions passed by a board or by any of its committees become invalid even if any the directors or a member of a committee gets disqualified subsequently.
- Without contravening any of the requirements of the act, a resolution can be passed by the board or by a committee of the board, if the resolution gets circulated to all the directors or members as may be applicable and gets approved and duly signed by all the members entitled to vote as if the meeting had been actually convened and held.

Prevention of oppression and Mismanagement

- Class action suits can be filed by one or more members or class thereof or one or more creditors/class thereof.
  - Class action application should be filed with NCLT for orders to prevent the affairs of the company being conducted in a manner prejudicial to interests of the company.
  - Applicants can also claim damages/compensation for fraudulent/unlawful/wrongful acts from or against the company/directors/auditors/experts/advisors etc.

Loans and Advances

- Companies should not give loans or advances to any of the directors, except for whole time director (WTD) or managing director or give guarantee or provide any security in connection with such loans to any director or related persons.
  - However, loans and advances can be granted to WTD or MD, if such loans fall within the terms and conditions of service that is extended to all

employees of the company or if the same is specifically permitted through a special resolution approved by shareholders.

Deposits

- Companies cannot invite and accept fixed deposits from the general public, a facility which they were enjoying for long.
  - Wherever, long-term fixed deposits are held, they cannot be renewed but returned to deposit holders with whatever interests due on those deposits.

Table 3.31. A Few Requirements under Company Act Management Responsibility – Annual Returns

Some Basic Requirements under Company Act: Annual Returns

- All companies should prepare an annual return in the prescribed form giving true facts and figures as on the date of closing of financial year.
- Annual return of companies should carry the following details:
  - Company's registered office, principal business activities, particulars of its holding, subsidiaries and associate companies.
  - Details of shares, debentures and other securities and shareholding pattern.
  - Company's indebtedness.
  - Details of members and debenture-holders along with changes therein since the close of the previous financial year.
  - Details of promoters, directors, key managerial personnel along with changes therein since the close of the previous financial year.
  - Details of meetings of members or a class thereof, Board and its various committees together with attendance details.
  - Remuneration of directors and key managerial personnel.
  - Penalty or punishment imposed on the company, its directors or officers, if any, and details of compounding of offences and appeals made against such penalty or punishment.
  - Matters relating to certification of compliances, disclosures as may be prescribed.
  - Details, as may be prescribed, in respect of shares held by or on behalf of the Foreign Institutional Investors indicating their names, addresses, countries of incorporation, registration and percentage of shareholding held by them; and any such other matters as may be prescribed, and signed by a director and the company secretary, or where there is no company secretary, by a practicing company secretary.
  - In the case of one person company or a small company which does not maintain a secretary, annual returns can be signed by the director.
  - In the case of listed companies or companies whose paid-up capital or turnover gets prescribed, annual return should be certified by a practicing

company secretary to the effect that annual return reflects true facts and that the company has complied with all the provisions of the act.
- Report of the board should carry an extract of the annual return prepared by the company.
- All companies should file their annual returns with ROC within sixty days from the date of AGM.
- Wherever AGM is not held for some reason or the other, reasons for the same should be filed as prescribed in the act.
- Failure to file annual returns before the expiry of the date fixed for this purpose, the company becomes liable for a fine ranging from Rs Fifty thousand to five lakhs.
    - Further each officer of the company involved with default will become punishable with imprisonment up to six months or with a fine varying from Rs Fifty thousand to five lakhs or both.
- Practicing company secretary who makes a false certification with regard to company's annual returns, becomes liable for punishment ranging from Rs Fifty thousand to five lakhs.

Table 3.3m. A Few Requirements under Company Act Management Responsibility – Secretarial Standards

Some Basic Requirements under Company Act: Secretarial Standards

What are Secretarial Standards

- They are a set of work discipline defined by SSB to help corporates in conscientiously guarding their integrity and honesty while discharging their responsibilities and to bring uniformity of approach across the corporate world.
- All companies should strictly adhere to the secretarial standards evolved by, Secretarial Standards Board' (SSB) of the 'Institute of Company Secretaries of India' (ICSI) and should follow the guidelines set out in these standards while executing different aspects of secretarial activities.
- Following are some of the activity areas for which SSB standard guidelines are available:
    - Conducting meetings of the Board of Directors.
    - Conducting general meetings of company's members.
    - Preparing and maintaining the minutes of board meetings, committee meetings and general meetings.
    - Procedures to be followed for passing of resolutions by circulation.
    - Broad outlines of the body (contents) of Board's Report.
    - Registers and records to be maintained by company secretariat.
    - Handling issues related with dividends.
    - Practices to be followed for transmission of shares and debentures.
    - Procedures to be followed in situations of forfeiture of shares.
    - Procedures to be followed for affixing of common seal.

Standard Guidelines on Meetings of the Board of Directors

- Among other things, the standard guidelines embrace following aspects of meetings of board of directors in particular:
  - Notice, form/contents and means of notice for convening a meeting, frequency of meetings, quorum for meetings throughout its duration to ensure that decisions/resolutions do not become void, attendance registers, resolutions, recording and preservation of minutes, disclosures in annual reports, etc.
  - Typical lists of items to be considered at different meetings including drawing directors' specific attention to significant issues to be discussed.
  - Leave of absence of directors from board meetings.
  - Ascertaining the 'will of the majority of directors' on different issues/resolutions through circulation.
  - Ensuring authenticity of decisions/resolutions passed by circulation through placing the same before the next meeting of the board and making it part of the minutes of that meeting.
  - Approval of quarterly, half-yearly and annual financial results in the board meeting and not through circular.
  - Circulation of draft minutes of meeting within a week's time from the date of board meeting.
  - Circulation of committee meetings to board members along with board agenda during its next meeting.
  - Highlighting the background that triggered a proposal for a decision/resolution and the rationale behind such proposals in the minutes of the meeting.
  - Recording the views of directors who either dissented from the majority of the opinion or abstained from voting on a decision
  - Generation of a base for evidencing a director's conduct when a board decision comes under challenge subsequently.
  - Permanent preservation of minutes of all board meetings.

Standard Guidelines on General Meetings

- Among other things, the standard guidelines embrace following aspects of general meetings in particular:
  - Procedures and practices to be followed for convening and conducting of general meetings like notice, form/contents and means of notice, requirements of quorum, voting, proxies, conduct of poll, withdrawal/rescinding/modification of resolutions, adjournment of meetings, preservation of minutes, distribution of gifts, presence and duties of company secretary/auditors, etc.
  - Chairman's responsibility in ensuring that all eligible members get equal opportunity to express their views on different aspects of company's activities and performances and get satisfactory answers to their queries, explaining the scope and purpose of resolutions proposed for voting.

- Disclosures to be made in the annual reports of companies.
- Presence of all directors at all meetings of shareholders to answer queries from shareholders.
- Presence of practicing company secretary who has issued compliance certificate and company auditors to answer members' queries in the AGM.
- Wide circulation and/or publicising of poll results in appropriate media in the case of listed companies.
- Specific discussions on issues that might have an impact on share prices of the company.
- Inclusion of details of all general meetings in the annual report.

Standard Guidelines on Minutes of Meetings

- All companies should maintain separate books for recording the minutes of meeting of the following meetings:
  - Meetings of Board of Directors and committees thereon.
  - Meetings of members.
  - Meetings of debenture holders.
  - Meetings of creditors.
  - Any other meetings as demanded by the act and matters related thereto.
- The standard provides guidelines for maintaining, recording, signing, dating, inspecting and preserving the minutes to ensure that the minutes depict true and faithful reproduction of proceedings of the meetings free from aberrations and assumptions with a view to enabling absentee directors to know as to what had been precisely transacted in the meeting, and about accessibility of minutes for future reference, etc.
- Some of the details of standards guideline also include the format (like number and type of the meeting, company, day, date, venue, time of commencement and time of conclusion of the meeting, names of officers in attendance and invitees for specific items, if any, if a director had participated only for a part of the meeting then those agenda items in which he had participated during discussions and decisions or if a director had participated in a meeting through video conferencing or through tele-conferencing then those agenda items in which he participated, names of directors who dissented from a decision or expressed a different opinion on a resolution, background and rationale behind proposals, company secretary present at the meeting, etc.), for preparing the minutes of meetings.
- Minutes should specifically mention the presence of Chairman of the Audit Committee, auditors and the practicing company secretary who has issued compliance certificate, court appointed observers or scutinisers, if any, at AGM.
- Minutes should also give summary of chairman's opening remarks, clarifications provided in the meeting, resolutions passed through postal ballots together with scrutiniser appointed to oversee postal ballot, reference to cross references of documents that were referred for taking a decision and chairman's signature or concerned director on those reference documents, etc.

- Circulation of draft minutes among all members of the Board or the Committee, as the case may be within stipulated time for comments, if any.
- Placing of minutes of all committees in the subsequent board meeting.
- Permanent storage of minutes of all meetings.
- Storage of office copies of notices, notes on agenda, etc. for specified period and subsequent destruction under the authority of the board.
- Custodian of minutes' books.

Standard Guidelines on Passing of Resolutions by Circulation

- As per the standard guidelines, the following are some of the procedures that a company has to follow for passing a resolution through circulation:
  - Circulation of draft of proposed resolution together with supporting documents/papers to all directors including interested directors and directors who are usually staying abroad through approved modes like hand circulation or by post or by facsimile, or by e-mail or by any other approved electronic mode.
  - Circular to carry a note detailing elements of the proposal, its pros and cons and method of expressing assent or dissent on the same.
  - Passing of resolution on the day when majority of directors express their approval or on the day of receipt of approved resolution at company's office in case a director forgets to date his approval. .
  - Recording the resolution in the minutes of the next meeting and the dissents, if any.
  - Guidelines also provide a brief list of illustrative items which cannot be passed through circulation.

Standard Guidelines on Board's Report

- Standard guidelines broadly set the framework of contents/body for preparing the annual report of the Board of Directors of a company.
- Company's balance sheet should carry board's report as an annexture.
- Among other things, board's report should specifically refer to the following issues/aspects:
  - The state of affairs of the company, systems to ensure compliance of all laws applicable to the company, details with respect to conservation of energy, technology absorption and foreign exchange earnings and outgo as per statutory guidelines, factors leading to sickness and the steps proposed to be taken, if any, changes in the composition of board, amount transferred to IEPF, composition of audit committee, payment of managerial remuneration in excess of limit, disqualification or vacation of office of director, disclosures pursuant to the listing agreement of stock exchanges, RBI, National Housing Bank directions and employee stock option and employee stock purchase schemes, information on accounts, amount, if any, proposed to carry to any reserves, material changes and commitments, if any, affecting the financial position of the company, reasons for failure to implement any proposal relating to preferential

allotment or to redeem debentures or preference shares on due date(s), amount, if any, recommended by way of dividend per share, details of issue of sweat equity shares, status of buy-back process key changes during the year of the specified items, explanations regarding every qualification, observation or adverse remark by the auditor in his audit report or by an external independent practicing company secretary in his secretarial audit report, etc.

- Board's report should be considered and approved at a duly convened meeting of the Board and signed by the chairman or by a minimum of two directors including MD, if there is one.
- Board's report is the collective responsibility of the entire board irrespective of dissentions if any on any of the issues covered in the report.

Standard Guidelines on Registers and Records

- As per standard guidelines all companies should maintain, among other documents, the following registers and records in particular:
    - Register of investments in securities not held in the name of the company. Register of buy-back of securities, register of charges, register and index of members, register and index of debenture holders, foreign register of members or debenture holders, register of renewed and duplicate certificates, register of contracts in which directors are interested, register of directors, managing director, manager and secretary, register of directors' shareholdings, register of inter corporate loans and investments, register of deposits, register of allotment, register of payment of dividend, register of directors' attendance, register of postal ballot, register of proxies, register of inspection, register of investments (other than securities not held in the name of the company), register of documents executed under common seal, register of records and documents destroyed, register of investors' complaints, register of transfer of shares, register of transmission of shares, register of transfer of debentures, register of transmission of debentures, register of employee stock options, register of sweat equity shares, register in respect of sebi (substantial acquisition of shares and takeovers) regulations, register in respect of sebi (prohibition of insider trading) regulations, books of accounts, annual return.

Standard Guidelines on Dividends

- Among other things, the standard guidelines embrace following aspects of dividends in particular:
    - Dividends to be declared only out of free reserves and surplus in the profit and loss account of the Company but not out of Securities Premium Account or the Capital Redemption Reserve Account or Revaluation Reserve or Amalgamation Reserve or out of profit on reissue of for feited shares or out of profit earned prior to the incorporation of the company.

- Interim Dividend to be based only on the Interim financial statements for the period under consideration after taking into account depreciation for the full year and arrears of depreciation, appropriations and transfers to statutory reserves, taxation, etc.
- Irrevocability of dividends declared whether interim or final.
- Transfer of unpaid/unclaimed dividends to iepf together with interests thereon.
- Preserving dividend register for eight years.
- Balance sheet, annual report and annual return of the company to reflect unpaid dividends.
- Annual report and annual return to reflect amounts transferred to iepf.

Standard Guidelines on Transmission of Shares and Debentures

- The following are some of the basic guidelines set out in the standards for handling issues related with transmission of shares:
  - Transmission of shares, whether singly held or jointly held, to nominee's name within stipulated time.
  - Transmission of shares, whether singly held or jointly held, to legal heir or beneficiary identified in a will name within stipulated time.
  - Permanent storage of records of all transmissions by company secretary or a person authorised by the board.

Secretarial Standard on Forfeiture of Shares

- As per standard guidelines, companies have to broadly follow the following steps:
  - Provision should be made in Articles of the company for forfeiture of shares from defaulting members.
  - Board approval to precede such actions.
  - Share forfeiture should be done only after a call on shares and interests thereon served through registered post acknowledgement due giving details like call amount, accrued interest and the date before which amount should be paid failing which forfeiture will be resorted to, etc., remains unpaid beyond the stipulated period.
  - Individual intimation to defaulting members regarding share forfeiture.
  - Entry of share forfeiture in members' register.
  - Reference to share forfeiture in directors' report to shareholders.
  - Board to decide on either reissue or destruction of forfeited shares.
  - Whenever reissue is resorted to, entry of new holder's name in the register.

Standard Guidelines on Affixing of Common Seal

- Secretarial standards provide a unique status for company seal. In order to protect this uniquely esteemed status of the company seal, standards have provided the following guidelines for affixing company seal on any instrument and document:

- Common seal refers to the metallic seal of a company which can be affixed only with the approval of the Board of directors of the company.
- Common seal should be adopted through a resolution of the board. Impression of the seal should become part of the minutes of the meeting which adopts the seal.
- The authorised person in whose physical presence the seal is affixed should sign every instrument to which seal of the company is so affixed.
- Custodian of common seal (a director, company secretary or any other authorised person) to be specified by the board.
- Business transactions carried out outside India can use an official seal which will be a facsimile of the common seal.
- Name of the territory where it is used and state in which the registered office of the company is situated should be engraved on the official seal.
- Person authorised to affix the official seal should sign and write on deed or other instrument, the date and place where it is affixed.
- Records of documents and instruments on which official seal is affixed at the office where the official seal is kept.

Table 3.3n. A Few Requirements under Company Act Management Responsibility – Secretarial Audit

Some Basic Requirements under Company Act: Secretarial Audit

Mandatory Requirement

- Every listed company or other class of companies as may be prescribed should enclose to its board's report a copy of secretarial audit carried out by an independent practicing company secretary (PCS) and hence becomes a part of company's annual report/balance sheet to be presented to the members of the company at AGM.
- Secretarial audit is a systematic verification of all the practices and records generated and maintained thereon by company's secretariat to ensure that the company maintains good compliance status of the legal requirements and other requirements as per secretarial standards and guidelines issued by SSB.
  - Therefore, a good compliance status to secretarial practices is also understood as standing for:
    - o Good corporate governance (though not exclusively confined only to areas embraced by secretarial standards).
    - o Self regulation by corporates by strict adherence to requirements of secretarial standards and through those practices suitably protecting the interests of stakeholders.
    - o Self regulation by corporates by strict adherence to requirements of secretarial results in transparent, ethical and responsible governance of the company.

- Since secretarial audit report prepared by an independent external practicing company secretary (PCS) becomes an integral part of annual report of board of directors or company's annual report, the board has to mandatorily offer satisfactory explanations to each and every qualification, observation or adverse remarks made by a PCS, together with those observations and comments made by company's auditors, it helps company boards in establishing a powerful compliance mechanism.
- The scope of secretarial audits embraces verification of compliances to all the applicable laws, rules and regulations of the Company Act, Secretarial Standards, Accounting Standards, SEBI Regulations (Substantial Acquisition of Shares and Takeovers, Prohibition of Insider Trading, Issue of Capital and Disclosure Requirements, Employee Stock Option Scheme and Employee Stock Purchase Scheme - Guidelines, Issue and Listing of Debt Securities, Delisting of Equity Shares, Buyback of Securities), FEMA Regulations, Banking/Insurance/Telecom/Electricity Law (Sectoral Compliances), Compliance of Labour Laws, wherever mandated and other applicable laws including local laws.
- Penalty for non-compliance: Company/any officer or PCS, who is in default, will become liable for punishment with fine ranging from Rs 1,00,000 to Rs 5,00,000.

Reporting of Fraud

- While conducting the secretarial audit of a company, if a PCS comes across situations that could lead to make him believe that an offence involving a fraud against the company has been committed by officers or the employees of the company, then it becomes his bounden duty to report the same to the central government, failing which, he himself becomes liable to punishment with a fine of ranging from Rs 1,00,000 to Rs 25,00,000.

Penalty for Fraud

- Anyone who makes an intentional false presentation (omission or commission or concealment) of facts or hides a material truth in any return, report, certificate, financial statement, prospectus or other documents as may be required under different provisions of company's act, will become liable for punishment.
  - Punishment for frauds is imprisonment ranging between six months up to ten years together with a fine of amount equal to the amount involved in fraud and could go up to thrice the amount involved in the fraud.
  - Wherever the fraud involves public interest, imprisonment will be a minimum of three years
  - Whenever the fraud is committed with connivance of others with the objectives of either deceiving or for some gainful benefit and adversely affects the interests of the company or its shareholders, creditors, will become liable for punishment.

Table 3.3o. A Few Requirements under Company Act Management Responsibility – Finance and Accounts Controls

Some Basic Requirements under Company Act: Finance and Accounts Controls

Mandatory Components

- All companies should follow a uniform financial year from: 1st April to 31st March.
  - Wherever a foreign associate company operates, permission from National Company Law Tribunal should be obtained to follow different financial year till financial year uniformity is achieved.
  - Financial year uniformity should be achieved by all companies latest by 2015.
- All companies should follow a 'Component-Approach' towards working out depreciation on their assets.
  - In this approach, the most significant component of a composite equipment or machinery should be taken for calculating depreciation of the equipment. Depreciation calculations should be in accordance with details specified in Schedule II, Part 'C' of the Act.
- All companies should mandatorily establish a reliable system of internal audits and reporting on internal financial controls.
  - Internal auditor should be appointed by the company should be chartered accountant or a cost accountant.
  - Company board may identify and appoint any other equally competent professional as internal auditor for the company.
  - Audit frequency and details of audit mechanism is not yet notified. Till a formal notification is issued, companies could follow the standard practices of other management systems.
    - o It is a good practice to carry out a quarterly audit of each of the accounts and finance activity functions.
    - o For purposes of internal audit-control of finance activities, each of the different categories of income and expenses heads could be considered as equivalent to one individual activity centre and could be covered under one audit cycle ensuring that data generated and/or compiled under each and every individual income and expenses head would be audited at least once in an audit cycle of one quarter.
- All companies should compulsorily establish a suitable system of reporting on internal financial controls and its operative effectiveness.
  - Directors' reports should specifically refer to adequacy and effectiveness of well established and well implemented/practiced internal financial controls.
  - Audit reports should also specifically refer to the effectiveness and adequacy of internal financial controls that operate in the company.

- Internal financial controls should embrace, among other things, the following:
  i. Development of business policies and procedures and their implementation namely translation of company policies and policy procedures to actual conducting of business activities should be framed and formulated in such a way that they would always guard and uphold the following:
     (a) Basic objectives and goals of the company.
     (b) None of the execution practices and procedures namely 'Conduct of Business Processes' would contravene the requirements of the Company Act.
     (c) They would never defeat or go against the spirit of any of the applicable statutory requirements.
     (d) Business practices would never cause any form of damage to company's assets and would always protect the same.
     (e) Business practices are designed in such a way that genuine interests of all the stakeholders of the company are well protected and well guarded.
     (f) Business practices are designed such that they carefully guard and protect all activities against entry of frauds and errors into their operation domain and the mechanism established and practiced to prevent practice of frauds and errors is very powerful and very effective.
     (g) In addition to establishing an effective preventive mechanism, company also practices a well formulated and well implemented mechanism to immediately detect the practice of frauds and errors wherever they find an entry into the operation system.
     (h) Business practices are designed to ensure total accuracy of all records of data and financial information generated by company's accounts division.
     (i) Business practices are designed to support timely preparation of highly reliable financial statements for the company.
  ii. This, in other words, means that necessary controls have been designed and put to place to ensure that:
     a. Executives do not have any scope to put company's finances to wrongful deeds to leverage any undue or unfair advantages through unfair means.
     b. Company's finances are very judiciously utilised for productive activities as per design.

• All internal audits should be carried out in accordance with the requirements of *Audit Standards* prescribed by the central government.
  - Till a formal notification regarding issuance of Audit Standards for companies is issued companies might profitably follow the procedures recommended by the Institute of Chartered Accountants of India (ICAI).

- An independent authority named National Financial Reporting Authority (NFRA) is constituted to design, evolve, formulate and lay-down the details of accounting and auditing standards, policies and practices together with a suitable mechanism for compliance enforcement and monitoring of practices followed by companies with a view to overseeing the quality of services rendered by concerned professionals.
- Once this authority becomes functional, accounting and auditing practices followed by companies will be fully controlled and monitored by this authority. And a good-governance-practice-era will emerge!)

• Chief financial officer of a company has a statutory status in a company and has to shoulder certain key responsibilities.
  - CFO carries the right of a KMP (Key Managerial Personnel – MD or CEO, company secretary, whole time director, CFO or any other person as may be prescribed) and has to discharge his duties.
  - Books of accounts can be maintained in electronic format as per procedures prescribed for the purpose subject to the same being made accessible to concerned authorities across the country.
  - CFO would become liable for punishment if:
    i. Books of accounts are not maintained as per prescribed requirements.
    ii. Non-preparation of timely and completely reliable financial statements.
    iii. Failure to file with the registrar of companies, well in time, the financial statements of the company.
    iv. Financial frauds and errors practiced in the company.

Consolidated Financial Statement

• It is a mandatory requirement for all companies whether or not listed under SEBI regulations and whether or not they are private limited. companies and whether or not they are intermediate holding companies, for presenting a global picture of financial performance of companies to the general public who normally go by annual financial performance statements of companies.
  - Preparation of a Consolidated Financial Statement (CSF) of all the companies/business establishments working either under one common umbrella or as apparently separate business entities but actually a part of a common group or a main group, either directly or indirectly, in different capacities and forms like associate companies, subsidiary companies, captive units, joint ventures, etc. is a basic requirement.
    o A separate statement containing the salient features of the financial statements of subsidiaries should be prepared and attached to the main consolidated financial statement to be presented to the general body of the company.
    o Any business venture in whose activities and performance the main company or the parent company has a direct or indirect interest and therefore will have a say in its policies and practices or is in a position to control either the composition of its directors or in the appointment

of its directors or holds a major share, including preference shares, is a company under its umbrella of the main company.

- o Any business venture, where in the main company or its directors may not have a majority of share but only about 20 per cent of the shares, but could exercise significant influence on the policies and practices of the venture, is a company under its umbrella of the main company.
- o There is one other unique category of business ventures working under the umbrella of the main company. These are generally family owned and/or family run companies which have taken birth only for certain specific and unique purposes of shying away from compliance to many of the formal requirements of the society and for working out reallocation and/or redistribution of profits and losses, expenses, tax liabilities, payment of compensation to workmen, etc., etc. to their advantage.

  In these ventures the formal configuration of the board will be different and share holding pattern will be different. Different members of the family circle or family group will be shareholders of different ventures and nothing will be in common with the main company, on records. Policies and practice requirements for these ventures will be decided elsewhere. Independent board of directors will be a mere formality and will function as mere mouth pieces of people controlling from elsewhere. But the ventures present themselves as independent entities/establishments.
- o It may not be a surprise that if many such hypothetical companies exist only on a piece of paper whereas the same set of people carry out the work but prepare activity records under different names and different heads.
- o Such situations prevail even in many public sectors – private sector joint ventures also. Many activities will be off the records and interlinking their activities with the main venture may not be easy or practical.
- o How to handle such situations? As emphasised in published literature on business ethics and value systems, it is the same human element that works everywhere (Mruthyunjaya, 2013) and people have a tendency to present themselves as highly dignified and highly respectable figures in the public whereas their practice of nobility and saneness in privacy would always remain a questionable issue. It is only the integrity of people that could save such situations!

- Preparation of annual financial statements of individual companies should be in the same common format as is used for preparing the consolidated financial statement for the group as a whole.
- Financial statements of companies should also carry a *Cash-flow* statement.
- Companies can no more transfer funds from profits to reserves before declaration of dividends.

  - Companies can declare dividends out of their current profits even if they carry accumulated business losses from earlier years.
  - Companies could declare interim dividends subject to a ceiling limit of average of preceding three years' dividends.
- Provision for preparation of restatement of annual financial statements.
  - Any statutory regulatory authority like SEBI, IT authorities, a department of the central government, etc. can order preparation of restatements and reconsolidation of facts and figures to represent reality for a period for which they feel the necessity.
  - Similarly, any other concerned and interested stake holder who has a firm conviction about misrepresentation of facts and figures and/or fraudulent playing with facts and figures rendering the financial statement not-reliable, can also initiate such restatement process by approaching a court of law or the National Company Law Tribunal, though in such events preparation of restatements would be restricted only to preceding three financial years.
  - If the board of directors of the company feel that the financial statement is not fully in conformity with the requirements of the act with respect to any of the aspects, voluntary restatement would be allowed subject to obtaining prior approval from the National Company Law Tribunal and copied to ROC. Such restatements would be allowed only once in a financial year.
- Companies would become liable for tax based on restatement.

IFRS - A Desirable Discipline

Adopting International Financial Reporting Standards (IFRS) is a good governance practice for a company as it opens-up its accounting practices (Books of Accounts) to any interested person across the world to check and confirm that the company has a good system of accounting practices.

  - IFRS is a common system of accounting practice across the world.
  - It is readily comparable, verifiable and understandable and could be uniformly interpreted by people across the world for purposes of evaluation and/or comparison of financial performances of a company.
  - The basic guidelines and the principles that should be used while preparing financial statements for the benefit of external users like potential investors, lenders and other creditors, who use that information to make decisions about buying, selling or holding equity or debt instruments and providing or settling loans or other forms of credit, etc., are given in the IFRS Framework which dwells into depths of objectives of financial reporting, the qualitative characteristics of useful financial information, the definition, recognition and measurement of the elements from which financial statements are constructed , the reporting entity, and concepts of capital and capital maintenance, etc.
    - o These financial decisions are well supported by financial statements prepared based on IFRS framework as they speak of the stewardship

of the company's management by presenting a true picture of how effectively and efficiently different resources have been leveraged to company's financial progress.

- Financial statements prepared as per IFRS, are a structured presentation of the financial status and financial performance of a company.
- Key objective behind such financial statements is to provide reliable information regarding the financial performance of the company during the period covered in the statement.
- It also gives a true picture of financial flow and financial status of the company at any given point of time during the period.
- These statements could, therefore, be used for a variety of application by interested users as these financial results speak of company's ability to cut-across-the-international-competition-edge and the commitment and stewardship qualities of the management.
  - The application to which different users put these financial statements are primarily the economic decisions of varying nature which could either further strengthen or weaken the financial base of the company.
  - With a view to fulfilling this objective, the financial statement should provide reliable data on company's: (a) assets; (b) liabilities; (c) equity; (d) income and expenses, including gains and losses; (e) contributions by and distributions to owners in their capacity as owners; and (f) cash flows.
  - This information together with other comments and/or support data from auditors should help people in projecting with a high degree of accuracy, the company's prospects and performances in the foreseeable future.

Key Components of IFRS

i. Fair Presentation

This element emphasises the fact that all companies should make a highly relevant and faithful presentation of facts and figures pertaining to financial transactions and other financial events including assets, liabilities, income and expenses set out in the IFRS Framework.

- Fairness aspects of assets should refer exclusively to true realisable, market value of an asset and not just a hypothetical non-realisable book value.

ii. Going Concern

A fundamental assumption behind attempts to understand a financial statement is that the company intends to continue forever and strives through all odds to put itself at the top except in situations where the management decides to liquidate the unit or to go out of business.

iii. Materiality and Aggregation

Every material class of similar items should be presented separately. Items that are of a dissimilar nature or function shall be presented separately unless they are immaterial.

iv. Reporting Frequency

At least one complete set of annual financial statements should be prepared. Wherever, interim finance reporting is done, the same should be IFRS compliant.

v. Comparative Information

As per IFRS guidelines, it is necessary to give corresponding information of preceding period for all amounts reported in the current financial statement. Such comparative information will help in understanding of company's relative performance on a time scale.

vi. Consistency of Presentation

Criteria for classification and grouping of each and every item and their analyses presented in the financial statement should always be consistent for ensuring uniformity of accounting practices and in helping consistent application of the statement by users.

vii. Elements for Measuring Financial Position

Assets (resources under company's control), Liabilities (obligation arising from a past event), Equities (residual interest in assets), Revenues (increase in economic benefits during the accounting period) and Expenses (decrease in economic benefits during the accounting period) are the key elements that should be considered for measuring company's financial performance. These parameters collectively speak of company's financial strengths and weaknesses.

viii. Cash Flows

Operating cash flows (principal revenue-producing activities of the company), Investing cash flows (acquisition and disposal of long-term assets and other investments) and Financing cash flows (activities that cause changes in the size and composition of the contributed equity and borrowings of the company) collectively help in predicting future ability of the company to generate cash inflows.

Table 3.3p. A Few Requirements under Company Act Management Responsibility – Company Audit

Some Basic Requirements under Company Act Audit Scope and Responsibility
Appointment of Auditors • The Board of Directors of all types of companies whether listed or unlisted or specified should appoint the first auditor/auditors for the company within thirty days from the date of registration of the company. • Alternatively, the board of directors can recommend the names of auditors to be appointed for the company and the members of the company can appoint

the first auditor at the Extraordinary General Body Meeting which should be held within ninety days of notification of EGM.

- All companies should appoint an individual or a firm as an auditor at the first AGM.
- If the office of auditor falls vacant due to reasons of resignation, within the first year.
- Beyond first AGM, it is only the members of the company who have the right to appoint auditor/auditors for the company and not the board.
  - However identification and recommendation for appointment of auditors for the consideration of the general body has to be made only by the board of directors.
- All such appointments should take place only after obtaining a written consent from the auditors.
- After the conclusion of the AGM, the company should issue a letter of appointment or a certification of continuance of office, as may be applicable.
- The company should inform the central government (ROC) within fifteen days of AGM about appointment of the auditor.
- In situations where the office of auditors becomes vacant for reasons of resignation or for any other reason, members of the company should appoint another auditor within three months' of the office falling vacant.
- The board of directors can, however, appoint an auditor within thirty days of the office becoming vacant.
- In the case of government companies or other companies owned or controlled, directly or indirectly, by the central government or by any or partly by central government and partly by state governments, state government it is only the Comptroller and Auditor-General of India (CAG) who can appoint the auditor for the company and not the general body.
  - CAG has to identify and appoint an auditor for the company within 180 days from 1st of April.
  - This stipulation is applicable for both first appointments as well as for subsequent appointments.
  - However, at the time of formation of the company, either the extraordinary general body or the CAG can appoint the first auditor within 60 days from the date of registration.
    - If the CAG does not appoint the auditor within 60 days of registration of the company, then the board of directors can also appoint an auditor within next thirty days.
    - If the board also fails to appoint the auditor then auditor should be appointed by the members in an Extraordinary General Meeting (EGM) within next 60 days.
- Whenever the office auditor's falls vacant for reasons of resignation or some other reason, the board or the CAG should appoint an auditor within thirty days of the office falling vacant.

- However, if the office of auditor, appointed by CAG, falls vacant for reasons of resignation, company's Board of Directors should fill the vacancy within thirty days.
- And such appointments should be approved by the general body within three months of board's recommendation and such auditors will hold office till conclusion of the next AGM.
- In case of companies whose accounts are subject to CAG's audit, casual vacancy of auditor should be filled by CAG only within thirty days.
  - o If CAG does not fill auditor's vacancy, company's board should fill the vacancy within next thirty days.

- Whenever, either the board appoints an auditor, the appointment will have to be ratified and confirmed by the general body within three months.
- Wherever a company is required to constitute an Audit Committee, all appointments, including the filling of a casual vacancy of an auditor should be made after taking into account the recommendations of audit committee.
- Whenever the AGM does not specifically appoint or re-appoint an auditor and remains silent on the issue, the existing auditor will continue to be the auditor of the company.

Tenure of Office

- Tenure of the first auditor, appointed by either board or the first EGM, will last till the conclusion of the first AGM of the company.
- Tenure of office of auditors appointed by the First General Body will be five years and will last till the conclusion of the sixth AGM from the first AGM that appointed the auditors.
- However, reappointment of auditors should be ratified by the members of the company at each of the subsequent AGMs.
- There seems to be no bar for non-listed companies on reappointment of auditors for periods beyond the first tenure of five years.
- However, in the case of listed and specified companies, auditors cannot be reappointed for periods beyond a maximum of two consecutive terms of five years each namely a total of maximum of ten years at a time.
  - Individual auditors to be mandatorily rotated every fifth year and audit companies every tenth year.
- Beyond two consecutive terms, there should be a minimum cooling-off period of five years. That is, the same auditor/auditors can be reconsidered for appointment as auditors for the company after a gap of minimum of five years in-between two consecutive terms and the next term.
- Audit companies having common partner or partners with the outgoing audit company cannot be considered for fresh appoint as auditors of the company till the expiry of the five year gap or the so-called cooling-off period.

Termination of Office

- Change of auditor before expiry of five year term would be allowed only with passing of a special resolution to this effect in the AGM and with a special permission from the central government.

- A special notice should be issued to members for this purpose and copied to concerned auditor.
- This process of change of auditors before five years' should provide for the concerned auditor being heard.
- Whenever the auditor resigns on his own, he is required to submit a statement of reasons and facts to the registrar of companies and CAG as may be applicable within thirty days of formal submission of resignation.
- Failure on the part of the resigning auditor to inform either ROC or CAG, will attract fine ranging from Rs 50,000.00 to Rs 5,00, 000.00.
- In special situations where the tribunal is satisfied that the auditor of a company has, whether directly or indirectly, acted in a fraudulent manner or abetted or colluded in any fraud by, or in relation to, the company or its directors or officers, it may direct the company to change its auditors.
    - o Whenever the tribunal passes an order against an auditor, the said auditor or audit firm cannot be appointed as auditor for any company for a minimum period of five years from the date of tribunal's order.

Eligibility

- Only a chartered accountant can be appointed as auditor for the company.
- In the case of auditing firms, only the partners, who are chartered accountants are authorised to act and sign on behalf of the firm.

Non-eligibility

- Employees of the company or chartered accountants in full-time service or relatives or partners who hold securities of the company or have a direct interest in the company or in any of its subsidiaries or associates cannot be appointed as auditors of the company.
- However, relatives of employees who hold securities of face value of up to a maximum of rupees one thousand can be appointed as auditor.
- People who are indebted to the company or to any of its subsidiaries or associates.
- A guarantor to a third person who is indebted to the company or its subsidiaries.
- A person having direct business relationship with the company or any of its subsidiaries.
- A person who is related to the director of the company or a KMP in the company.
- A person or a partner of a audit firm which holds the appointment as auditors for more than twenty different companies.
- A person who has been convicted by a court for an offence involving fraud and where ten years have not elapsed after conviction. A person whose subsidiary or sister concerns or associate companies are engaged in offering those services which an auditor cannot practice after being appointed as auditor of the company.

Remuneration for Auditors

- The general body of the company should fix the remuneration for company's auditors.
- Company's Board of Directors could fix the remuneration for the first auditor appointed by the board.
- Auditor's remuneration will include only the audit fee and other incidental expenses incurred by the auditor in connection with conducting the audit and do not include any remuneration paid for other service charges rendered by him at the request of the company.

Formal Restrictions

- Company auditors (or their associates or any other auditor companies in whose activities the auditor of the company has a direct or indirect interest or has a say or can influence their decisions and actions) cannot render any of the following or any other non-audit services to the auditee company or its associates, subsidiaries, etc., either directly or indirectly:
    i. Any type of non-audit service whether incidental or activity specific oriented.
    ii. Directly participating, guiding or helping in organising accounting and book-keeping activity of the company.
    iii. Directly participating, guiding or helping in organising internal audits of the company.
    iv. Directly participating, guiding or helping in organising design and implementation of financial processes management and/or data and information management services or related service packages.
    v. Actuarial services.
    vi. Advising and/or guiding or participating in investment management, investment banking services, outsourced financial services, management services, etc., etc.
    vii. Guiding, advising or helping company directors in managing their personal financial portfolios or other management services.

Rights of Auditors

- Unrestricted right to access to all the books of accounts and all types of expenses vouchers of the company and at all times.
- To check from the officers of the company any information and explanations that might add to building better clarity to certain types of incomes and expenditure.
- To carry out elaborate enquiries into matters of serious audit concern.

Duties

- Preparation of different types of financial statements that may be required to be presented to the members of the company.
    - Report on accounts maintained by the company.
    - Annual Reports.

- Cash-flow Statements.
- Balance sheets.
- Profit and Loss account.

- If, in the opinion of the auditor, any of the officers of the company has committed an offence in the nature of fraud against the company, auditor should inform the central government about the same immediately.

Participation in AGM

- Auditors or in their absence, formally permitted by the company, their representatives who are also qualified auditors, should attend the AGM.
- Observations and comments made by auditor which may have any adverse effect on the functioning of the company, and referred by him in his audit report, should be read before the general body of the company in the meeting and should be kept open for inspection by interested members.
- Auditors have the right to express their views on points of concern referred by them in audit reports.
- All notices and communications sent to members of the general body regarding meeting should be forwarded to auditors.

Audit Reports

- Auditor report should specifically highlight, among other things, the following in particular:
  - ➢ Failure on the part of the auditee company to provide any data, information, explanation or satisfactory clarifications against certain audit observations or denial of access to certain data generation and/or processing operations, etc. that could have an impact or a cascading effect on the final financial statement and its preparation.
  - ➢ Methodology and details of accounting practices and management and maintenance of accounts and book-keeping together with its reliability and accuracy.
  - ➢ Observations and comments on financial transactions and other finance related issues of the auditee company that would either directly have an adverse impact on company's performance and functioning of the company or carry a high potential to leave an adverse impact on its functioning.
  - ➢ Observations and comments on auditee company's internal finance controls and audit controls and their effectiveness in ensuring satisfactory finance management practices.
  - ➢ Any other critical issue that might come-up during audits and could carry a high potential to adversely impact on company's finance performance and functioning, delays in making deposits in Investor Education and Protection Fund.
  - ➢ Auditors should also comment on the various pending litigations and legal and/or other pending contests or contemplated contests and their potential to create dent on company's financial status or financial performance and functioning.

- Auditors should also comment on the various on-going projects and long-term projects and/or contracts that might carry a latent potential to dig into company's profits and could thus have a cascading effect on company's financial performances.
- Whether the required data and information has been received from branch offices of the company.
- If the branch offices of the company has been separately audited by different auditors, in that situation, do the details given in those audit reports tally with the details of books of accounts maintained by the company and whether the financial statements prepared for branch offices are as per accounting standards, etc.
- Whether any of the directors of the company has been disqualified from being appointed as a director.
- Auditors should also comment on whether the company is regularly and systematically make necessary deposits in *Investor Education and Investor Protection Funds.*

Disqualification and Penalty

- An auditor will be liable for penalty if he fails to:
  - Inform the registrar of companies about his resignation and reasons for resigning or an auditor appointed by the Comptroller and Auditor-General of India, should inform the registrar of companies about his resignation and reasons for resigning within thirty days of resignation.
    - Will become liable for payment of penalty varying between a minimum of Rs 50,000/- up to a maximum of Rs 500,000/-.

  An auditor appointed by the Comptroller and Auditor-General of India, should inform the registrar of companies about his resignation and reasons for resigning within thirty days of resignation.
- An auditor will be disqualified if he fails to :
  - Follow the stipulated requirement that he should not render certain specified services to the company, as per details referred earlier.
  - Prepare completely reliable and totally accurate financial statements of the company and other reports that would result in deceiving the company, either knowingly or wilfully.
    - Will become liable for imprisonment of minimum of one day to a maximum of one year in addition a fine of minimum of Rs 100,000/- up to a maximum of Rs 2500,000/-.
    - Will be liable for refunding the remuneration paid by the company.
    - Will be liable to pay for damages arising out of misleading or incorrect information.
    - In case wrong statements are prepared without knowledge or any intention, auditor would become liable for payment of a fine of a minimum of Rs 25,000/- and up to a maximum of Rs 500,000/-.
    - Will be liable for refunding the remuneration paid by the company.

- Will be liable to pay for damages arising out of misleading or incorrect information.
- In case of audit companies are involved in committing such mistakes, it would be considered as fraud committed and civil suit or criminal suit could be initiated against the firm as per law.

➢ Inform the concerned government department and/or official as may be required, regarding frauds being committed or had been committed in the past by company's employees or officers.
  - Will become liable for payment of penalty varying between a minimum of Rs 100,000/- up to a maximum of Rs 2500,000/-

- Employees or officers involved in committing frauds will be liable for a minimum of one day imprisonment and up to a maximum of one year's imprisonment in addition to fine varying between a minimum of Rs 10,000/- up to a maximum of Rs 1,00,000/-.

Table 3.3q. A Few Requirements under Company Act Management Responsibility-Investor Protection

Some Basic Requirements under Company Act-Investor Protection

Prevention of Oppression and Mismanagement

- Any member of a company can directly approach the Tribunal for relief whenever he feels that the affairs of the company have been or are being conducted in a way which is oppressive or prejudicial to the interests of the public or members or the company.
- Members can also approach the Tribunal whenever they feel that the material changes being carried out in the company are against the interests of creditors including debenture holders or any class of shareholders of the company.
- Whenever an officer/office of the central government opines that the affairs of the company are being conducted in a manner which is prejudicial to public interest, it can approach the Tribunal to set right the matter.

⇩

➢ The Tribunal can order the following

- The regulation of conduct of affairs of the company in future.
- The purchase of shares or interests of any members of the company by other members or by the company.
- Restrictions on the transfer or allotment of the shares of the company.
- The termination, setting aside or modification, of any agreement between the company and the managing director, any other director or manager.

- The termination, setting aside or modification of any agreement between the company and any person.
- That no agreement should be terminated, set aside or modified except after due notice and after obtaining the consent of the aggrieved party.
- Setting aside of any transfer, delivery of goods, payment, execution or other act relating to property made or done by or against the company within three months before the date of relief application, which would, if made or done by or against an individual, result in his insolvency or a fraudulent action.
- Removal of the managing director, manager or any of the directors of the company.
- Recovery of undue gains made by any managing director, manager or director during the period of his appointment and transfers the recovered amount to Investor Education and Protection Fund or repayment to victims.
- Appointing right persons as directors of the company and authorising them to report to the tribunal on such issues.
- Restraining the company from committing acts which defeat the spirit of articles or memorandum of the company.
- Declaring a resolution altering the memorandum or articles of the company as void if the resolution was passed by suppression of material facts or obtained by misstatement to the members or depositors.
    - Restraining the company and its directors from acting on such resolutions.
- Restraining the company from doing an act which is contrary to the provisions of Companies Act or any other law in force.
- Restraining the company from taking action contrary to any resolution passed by the members.
- Claiming damages or compensation or demand any other suitable action from or against the company or its directors for any fraudulent, unlawful or wrongful act or omission or conduct.
- Claiming damages or compensation or demand any other suitable action against the auditor or audit firm of the company for any improper or misleading statement of particulars made in his audit report or for any fraudulent, unlawful or wrongful act or conduct.
- Claiming damages or compensation or demand any other suitable action against any expert or advisor or consultant or any other person for any incorrect or misleading statement made to the company or for any fraudulent, unlawful or wrongful act or conduct.

- Orders of the tribunal are binding on the company and its members, depositors, auditor, audit firm or expert or consultant or advisor or any other person associated with the company.
- Companies that fail to comply with tribunal's orders, will become liable for punishment ranging from Rs five lakhs to twenty five lakhs and every

officer who is in default will become liable for imprisonment of up-to three years and a fine of twenty five thousand rupees to one lakh rupees.
- Certified copy of Tribunal's order should be sent ROC within thirty days of the order.

Investor Protection Measures
- Provision of class action suit.
- Exit option for dissenting shareholders.
- Internal audits, rotation of auditors and independent directors on company's board.
- Establishment of vigil mechanism to safeguard stakeholders' interests.
- Restriction on forward dealing in securities by key managerial personnel.
- Prohibition of insider trading of securities.
- Establishment of serious fraud investigation office – Investigation to be carried out on receipt of report from ROC, receipt of resolution of a company, public interest litigation, request from state or central government offices.

Investor Education and Protection Fund
- The central and state governments may contribute to the fund.
- The amount in the Unpaid Dividend Account of companies transferred to the Fund.
- This fund should be utilised for refund in respect of unclaimed dividends, matured deposits, matured debentures, the application money due for refund and interest thereon.
- Promotion of investors' education, awareness and protection.
- Distribution of any disgorged amount among eligible and identifiable applicants for shares or debentures, shareholders, debenture-holders or depositors who have suffered losses due to wrong actions by any person, in accordance with the orders made by the Court which had ordered disgorgement.
- Reimbursement of legal expenses incurred in pursuing class action suits by members, debenture-holders or depositors as may be sanctioned by the Tribunal and any other purpose incidental thereto.
- Organises nationwide investor education and awareness programmes including seminars and symposia.
- Handles reconciliation of accounts of investors.

Table 3.4. A Few Requirements under Different Acts/Laws

Some Basic Requirements under Competition Act

Basic Objectives
- Ensuring that commercial establishments do not enter into agreements which are *Anti-Competitive* in nature.
  - Business agreements between commercial establishments should be such that they should not prevent generation of competition in the market through:

- o Creating all sorts of barriers to new entrants into their market domain.
    - ◆ Creating market situations, including through purchasing customer-goodwill, in such a way, that already existing players in the field (competitors) find an automatic exit from the market.
    - ◆ Creating a *fear psychosis* in the market in such a way that customers refrain from opting for other competitive products or services (through spreading the message that other competitive products and services are highly uneconomical in the long run because of their poor performance quality and high cost of maintenance, non-ready availability of spares or replacements, etc.).
    - ◆ Creating a *welcome wave* where in customers eagerly look forward to install the new product or service of the enterprise under consideration through aggressive spread of the message that nothing can beat these products and services in the market.

    } Foreclosure of competition even before entry of a new player into the market

- o Creating a situation where the competition finds a natural death.

- Following are some of the things that are not permitted under competition law:
  - o Joint determination (by organisations) of selling or purchase prices of process inputs or process outputs, product price and price range, trade discounts and discount structure, forcing dealers on their selling price and product range, unilateral participation in tender biddings without reference to competitors, supplying price calculation formula for different dealers and different regions, not giving publicity to their product price range, refraining from supplying products to certain customers or not to purchase process inputs from certain suppliers, fixing of production volumes and schedules, declarations regarding competitors offer knowledge, regarding understanding on prices agreed between different competitors while participating in tender bid, discussion with competitors their price structure, production plans and product distribution pattern, agreeing with competitors on prices or pricing policies, discussing with competitors their own purchase prices, cost price structure sales volumes and trading practices, imposing restrictions on competitors using similar quality tags or labels or fixing their own independent prices,

- Ensuring that organisational dominance in the market (high volume production, good storage and distribution capacity, good financial status of the organisation to support liberal payment terms, service provision, etc.) should not result in abusing their monetary-muscle power.
  - Imposing unfair and/or discriminatory conditions on purchases or sales volumes and also on sales and purchase prices.
  - Controlling production volumes and product release to markets to modulate market situation.
  - Controlling product development and innovations to their self advantage without reference to customers' needs, desires and dire necessity.
  - Entering a new market and directly gaining control over the situation based on their dominance elsewhere in other regions.
  - Enforcing certain conditions on all types of commercial contracts regarding product sale and purchase as well as market development and distribution that do not have any direct bearing on the main subject of contract.
  - Following are some of the things that are not permitted under competition law:
    - o Discrimination between different customers with reference to product price, supply terms and conditions, delivery terms and schedules, trade discounts and incentives, variable discounts linked to sale volumes, offering higher discounts than competitors, discriminatory credit facilities, refusal to supply products, sudden stopping of service provision to selected market segment or customers, operating on variable price structure directly linked to input price changes, imposing unfair conditions on customers who have contractual relationships with other suppliers.
- Ensuring that there is a good control on combinations, acquisitions, mergers etc. so that there is a good socio-economic balance in the society in terms of useful product/service demand and supply, utility features and price, etc.
  - This stipulation also demands that people or organisations do not resort to gain full control on some organisations through acquiring of major part of shares so that they get much higher voting rights on some activities, expansions, diversifications of target organisations.
  - Through such higher voting rights these people or organisations try to control mergers, amalgamations, acquisitions of the other organisation over which they have gained a major control. Thereby they ensure that their market continues to remain safe for them. Such activities should also be suitably controlled.
  - Competition law demands that amalgamations, mergers, acquisition, etc. should be such that their combined sales turnover should be well within Rs 4,500/- crores per annum for individuals and Rs 18,000/- crores for groups of organisations.

- Ensuring that the market liberally supports prevalence of a healthy competition between different commercial establishments in terms of good product supply and distribution of all competitive products and that customer are in a position to derive full benefits of market environment.
- Such highly conducive market environment should encourage development and innovation of technology and breakthrough in process technology and process economy and in service quality and utility service features.
- Ensuring that different organisations do not enter into such kinds of amalgamation, merger, acquisition agreements which would result in one or more of the following:
    - Fixing prices of their products and services in such a way that together they are able to earn higher profits through establishing collective product generation and distribution monopoly.
    - Gaining total monopoly on product supply or service provisions so that they are in a position to manipulate prices and supply terms to their collective advantage especially while participating in big value purchase tenders.
    - Establishing product supply and service provisions on an ongoing arrangement basis depending on the market situation in different market segments such that collectively they still monopolise the situation in all potential market segments.
    - They are, together, in a position to ensure that they could force certain pattern of purchase decisions on customers so that customers purchase, by force of circumstances, some products from one of the organisations and some from the other organisation so that together both the organisations are in a position to enjoy steady outlet for their products and services.
    - Following are some of the things that are not permitted under competition law:
        - o Acquisition of a potential new entrant into the field thereby eliminating the possibility of a competition coming-up, acquisition of a firm ahead of an intending competitor to cut competitor's opportunities, acquisition of an existing enterprise that is likely to become a potential competitor, acquisitions with the sole objective of preventing the other unit from entering other geographical regions with similar products, acquisitions for gaining combined supermacy over a market, acquisition of a critical process input supplier company or a critical input manufacturing company to ensure that the competitor does not get sufficient quantities of his process input thereby curtailing his product strength, etc.
- Organisations ensure that product dealers deal with exclusively products of the organisation and do not deal with any product of competitors and further that the dealer sells company's products only at prices fixed by the company without being impacted by flexible market situations.

Table 3.5. A Few Requirements under Different Acts/Laws

Some Basic Requirements under Environment Protection Act

General

- Obtaining Consent from State Pollution Control Board to establish and operate industrial operations – Before start of activities.
- Preparation of preliminary environment statement and assess impact of contemplated activities on the environment.
- Submission of annual environment statement in Form V.

AIR

- Installation, maintenance and monitoring of air pollution control equipments.
- Regular monitoring of pollutant discharge/emissions to air and ensuring that emissions do not cross prescribed limits.
- Maintenance of ambient air quality as per prescribed limits and maintaining records of the same.
- Ensuring absence of noise pollution.

WATER

- Obtaining permission/licence from SPCB for consumption of water from approved sources for industrial and domestic purposes.
- Installing meters to measure and monitor water consumption quantity for each individual category of purpose – Industrial and non-industrial.
- Payment of water cess and submission of monthly returns.
- Monitoring and maintaining effluent discharge quality and quantity. Periodical collection of effluent samples for SPCB analyses.
- Immediate intimation to SPCB whenever pollutant discharge quantities exceed limits.

BATTERIES CONTROL

- Maintenance records of purchase and disposal. Disposal to be made only to approved agents.
- Half yearly submission of returns in form VIII to SPCB.

ODS CONTROL

- Obtaining of permission from deputy secretary Ministry of Environment and Forests for purchase, storage and disposal of ODS materials.
- Adherence to regulations on sale, purchase and holding of ODS and filing of reports to Deputy Secretary Ministry of Environment and Forests.
- Maintenance of records for usage of ODS.
- Declaration of period of use of ODS before purchase.

HAZARDOUS CHEMICALS – Manufacturing, Storage and Imports Control

- Obtaining permission to import, manufacture and store hazardous chemicals before starting the activity.

- Obtaining approval of site engaged in hazardous processes.
- Obtaining permission for storing, handling, treatment and disposal of hazardous materials and for disposing hazardous wastes (Form 01).
- Organising external safety audit every third year and submission of safety-audit report to SPCB.
- Sharing with SPCB data and information about hazardous chemicals being used in the premises.
- Preparation of on-site and off-site emergency plans and conducting six monthly on-site emergency mock drills.
- Disclosure of materials and/or processes that carry a potential to create emergency situations to concerned district emergency authority.
- Preparation of material safety data sheets (MSDS) for each hazardous chemicals and their display.
- Appropriate labelling of all containers containing hazardous chemicals.
- Decontamination facilities for containers of hazardous chemicals.
- Establishing safe operation mechanisms and safe handling of hazardous chemicals as per established and well accepted international and industry norms and recommended practices and steps to prevent incidence of accidents involving hazardous chemicals.
- Preparation and submission of yearly environmental statements.
- Authorisation and renewal of facility operator for handling and management of hazardous wastes.
- Authorisation of facility operator and disposal for hazardous materials.
- Intimating concerned SPCB regarding accidents involving hazardous chemicals.
- Six monthly medical examinations of people engaged in handling hazardous chemicals, appropriate provision of medical facilities and medical help and support facilities, occupational health centres (OHC), ambulance, and maintenance of regular health check records for workers.

MANAGEMENT OF HAZARDOUS WASTES

- Obtaining authorisation for holding, handling, disposal and treatment if any, from concerned SPCB.
- Submission of information to concerned SPCB about different types and nature of hazardous wastes being generated and being handled in the premises.
- Establishing proper system of handling, storing with appropriate identification and/or labelling of and disposing of hazardous waste.
- Ensuring proper containment (secondary containers) of hazardous wastes stored in containers to prevent causing of pollution and accidents.
- Proper identification and storing of certain categories of hazardous wastes in secured containers.
- Maintaining of records of hazardous waste generation, stock of wastes in the yard and disposed quantities (Form No. 3) and updation of records to reflect each consignment.

- Submission of annual return to concerned SPCB (Form 04).
- Suitably intimating SPCB (Form No. 5) on each incidence of accident involving hazardous wastes.
- Disposal of hazardous wastes only to approved agents who should transport the same in vehicles approved for the purpose and in containers approved for the purpose.
- Containers used for transporting hazardous wastes to carry appropriate labels (Form No. 8).
- Disposal process to generate necessary statements in designated coloured sheets (Form. No. 9).
- Hazardous waste material transporter to carry trum cards with necessary information about the nature of the material being transported together with destination (Form No. 10).
- Disposal of non-ferrous metallic (Hazardous) wastes and used oil to approved recyclers or re-refiners.
- Adherence to 90 days limit for storing any generated hazardous waste.
- Submission of annual returns (Form No. 13) to SPCB.
- Designing schemes for achieving reduction in hazardous waste generation under intimation to SPCB during each renewal process.
- Suitably intimating SPCB about these activities.
- Immediate intimation to concerned director of industrial health and safety regarding incidences of poisoning and/or diseases caused due to hazardous substances being handled in the factory premises.
- Wherever hazardous waste disposal facility is established, obtaining approval for the same including obtaining approval for facility operator from SPCB. Submission of environment impact assessment statement and details of site where hazardous waste would be disposed to SPCB.
- Obtaining renewal for facility operation before expiry (Form No. 1).

Table 3.6. A Few Requirements under Different Acts/Laws

Some Basic Requirements under Factories Act

General

- Obtaining approval, registration and licence – Before start.
- Obtaining stability certificate for the premises once in five years.
- Intimation of occupation before physical occupation of the premises for carrying out industrial activities.
- Yearly renewal of licence.
- Good maintenance of premises and submission of records to director of industrial health and safety.
- Obtaining permission from concerned health officer for connecting drainage lines from factory premises to public sewerage systems.

Safety Aspects

- Regular monitoring and proper maintenance of work place ventilation, temperature, lighting, provision of safe drinking water, WC.
- Regular monitoring of drive mechanisms like belts, chains, gears, etc.
- Declaration of safety policy and submission of copies to local health and safety inspector and director of health and safety.
- Sharing of health and safety related aspects of corporate activities with the general public.
- Appropriate safety provision for factory workers.
  - Listing of all activity centres that carry an element of operation risk and identification of requirements for Fencing of machineries, running motors, motorised mechanisms, etc.
  - Identification and listing of all types of process wastes and waste by-products that carry an element of risk.
    - Organising careful collection and storage of different types of risky and hazardous wastes with necessary precautions to ensure 'No-mix-up' of different types of wastes.
    - Disposing off risky and hazardous wastes suitably through approved agencies and maintaining necessary records of risky-waste generation and disposal.
  - Tight fitting clothes, protective clothes, safety belts.
  - Appropriate PPEs, screens and goggles, head gears, gum boots, face masks, ear plugs, etc.
  - Annual safety inspection of hoists, chains, ropes, other lifting equipments.
  - Protcction against dangerous fumes, fire, lightening, etc. provision of adequate numbers of fire fighting equipments and other facilities including portable fire extinguishers.
  - Storage of compressed gas cylinders, storage of flammable liquids, under suitable shelters and in secured places.
  - Readily accessible, appropriately illuminated exits not farther than 30 meters from any corner of active shop-floors with ever unobstructed free runway.
  - Provision of a minimum of not less than 100 centimetres width stairs with not more than 12 centimetres height per flight wherever staircases are provided for internal movement.
  - Provision of eye-showers, wash rooms, shelters, dining rooms, rest rooms, etc.
  - Safety of working in isolation and inside confined chambers and/or containers.
  - Effective exhausts for fumes, vapours and dusts, etc.
  - Establishment of safe working practices of LOCKIN-LOCKOUT systems.
  - Adequate First aid boxes and portable fire extinguishers, rest rooms, etc.
  - Safety audits and submission of audit reports to SPCB within prescribed time limits, safety committees, etc.

- Maintenance of minimum greenery in the premises with intimation to concerned factory inspectors and also concerned director of industrial health and safety.
- Maintenance of records of accidents and intimation to concerned director of industrial health and safety.
- Formal submission of incidents to concerned inspectors of factories.
- Immediate intimation of dangerous occurrences (serious injuries or death) to concerned inspector of factories and concerned director of industrial health and safety.
- Maintenance of a register of accidents and dangerous occurrences and annual submission of summary statement (Form No. 30) to concerned inspector of factories.
- Maintenance of inspection books.

Table 3.7 Identification of Statutory Requirements under Different Acts/Laws

Some Basic Requirements under Indian Explosives Act

- No company can manufacture, import, export, transport, possess, sell or use any explosive material unless the same has been declared as an authorised explosive, by an order issued by the Chief Controller and published by the Central Government in the Official Gazette and approved by the Chief Controller of Explosives.
  - Manufacture and use of explosives in small quantities by established laboratories can be taken up exclusively for research and development and/or test purpose in a dedicated place specifically designated for development of such materials and specially approved/permitted for the purpose by the chief controller of explosives.
  - In case of existing plants or conventional type of explosives, the Chief controller may permit trial manufacture directly in the already approved manufacturing plant without manufacturing the same in laboratory scales.
- Application for getting licence for manufacture of an explosive material should be submitted to the Chief Controller of Explosives with the following details (separately for each product):
  - Detailed process starting from the raw materials, to the finished product describing the plant and equipment, quantities of materials handled, operating conditions and parameters, nature of controls and safety devices provided in the proposed method of treating effluents and waste Explosives.
  - Nature and composition of the explosives proposed to be manufactured or imported or sold.
  - Limiting percentage of each ingredient of explosives.
  - Specification of various raw materials including substitutes, if any, used in the process of manufacture.

- Physical and chemical characteristics of final product.
- Name and percentage of marking agent to be added in plastic explosives for detection by vapour detection technique.
- Safety management plan as stated in sub-rule to be followed by the company in case of high explosives or blasting accessories.
- Any other particulars as may be required by the licensing authority.

- Authority for granting licence to manufacture, import, hold and sale of explosives of different types (class and categories) rests with the chief controller of explosives, controller of explosives authorised by the chief controller and district magistrate depending on the explosive type and quantity.
- All categories of explosive materials should be packaged for inland transport purposes must follow the specifications detailed under Part -1, Schedule II of the act. Similarly, packaging methods for import and export of explosive materials should follow the specifications detailed under Part – 2, Schedule II.
- All explosive substances should carry a four digit identification number (UN number) assigned to the article or substance under the United Nations system for transport and storage of dangerous goods as stated in the Model Regulation on the Transport of Dangerous Goods published vide ST/SG/ AC.10/1/Rev 12 in ISBN 92 -1-13974-5.
- Transport of all explosive materials should follow the guidelines set by the United Nations Model Regulations on the Transport of Dangerous Goods published vide ST/SG/AC 10/1 Rev. 12 in ISBN 92-1-13974-5.
- Schedule VII of the act should be referred for detailed specifications of the manufacturing and storing premises, specifications of site, layout, construction and safety distance, traverses, explosive limits, etc. and also for construction details of A, B and C types of magazines and also for construction of magazine for fireworks manufacture and store house.
- Schedule VI of the act should be referred for elaborate descriptions of necessary safety provisions for transport vehicles to be used for bulk delivery (part 2), transport of explosives through water (part 3) and transport by rail (part 4).
- Packing of explosives should be done as per specification given in schedule II of the act.
- Companies involved in manufacture, handling and storage should maintain the safety distance as specified under schedule VIII of the Indian Explosives Act which specifies the quantities and safe distances for different categories of explosives (Category X, Category Y, Category Z and Category ZZ), between process buildings, public transport routes like railway, road, etc., residential buildings, offices, factories, etc.
- Manufacture, handling, storage and transport of any of the four categories of fireworks (listed in the act) are covered under this act and people dealing with fireworks should follow the requirements specified under the act.

- Companies interested in developing a new explosive material and getting the same included in the official list of explosives, should apply for the same to the Chief Controller of Explosives and follow the sequence of operations as specified in the act.
- Temporary shops for possession and sale of fireworks during festivals should meet the following conditions:
  - During festivals, the District Magistrate can issue temporary licenses for possession and sale of fireworks in a temporary shop.
  - The fireworks should be kept in a shed made of non-flammable material, which is closed and secured so as to prevent unauthorised persons having access thereto.
  - The sheds for possession and sale of fireworks should be at a distance of at least three meters from each other and fifty meters from any protected work.
  - The sheds should not face each other.
  - No oil burning lamps, gas lamps or naked lights should be used in the shed or within the safety distance of the sheds. Electrical lights, if used, should be fixed to the wall or ceiling and should not be suspended by flexible wire.
  - Switches for each shop should be fixed rigidly to the wall and a master switch should be provided for each row of sheds.
  - Display of fireworks should not be allowed within fifty meters of any shed.
  - In one cluster not more than fifty shops should be installed.
- All persons/companies licensed to manufacture, possess, sale, use or transport of explosives should maintain records as specified in Part 5 of Schedule V and should produce such records on demand to any authority specified in rule 128.
- Stock books in prescribed forms should be page numbered and certified by an officer authorised for the purpose and should be retained for period of three years or as directed by the authority.
- Quarterly returns of explosives (other than fireworks) manufactured, received, sold or transferred or used or destroyed or imported or exported should be filed with the Controller of explosives as well as District Magistrate in the form prescribed in Part 5 of Schedule V so as to reach the above authority within tenth day of every succeeding quarter.
- Six monthly testing of pressure vessels for suitability from approved external inspectors and intimation to concerned director of industrial health and safety.

Obtaining approval and stamping of containers from chief inspector of explosives.

Adherence to minimum specified wall thickness for fabricated containers and approval by chief inspector of explosives.

Secured holding of empty containers used for filling petroleum products. Provision of empty receptacles.

Proper control against leakage and seepage and/or escape of petroleum products by any other means.

Ensuring non-hiring of people below 18 years of age in the licensed premises

Adherence to strict prohibition of smoking, fire, lights within the defined proximity of petroleum tanks.

Table 3.8. Identification of Statutory Requirements under Different Acts/Laws

Some Basic Requirements under Public Liability Insurance Act

Embraces Accidents related to and/or associated with handling of hazardous substances in factories and other establishments

- Any company responsible for causing an accident, either directly or indirectly, where a hazardous substance is involved becomes liable for paying necessary relief or compensation to the victim.
  - Under the act, the word *Accident* embraces all types of incidents arising from a fortuitous or sudden or unintended occurrence while handling any hazardous substance resulting in continuous or intermittent or repeated exposure leading to death or injury to, any person or damage to any property.
  - The word injury includes permanent disability, total or permanent partial disability or sickness resulting from an accident.
  - The expression *Handling* means the manufacture, processing, treatment, package, storage, transportation by vehicle, use, collection, destruction, conversion, offering for sale, transfer or the like of such hazardous substance.
  - Further, the act clearly specifies that the scope of words *accident or injury* is not limited only to the workmen of the company. Its coverage extends far beyond company's premises and company employees. Anybody else in the neighborhood or a property beyond company premises can also suffer injury from accidents and the company becomes liable to pay compensation.
- Under the act, a claimant for compensation is not required to plead and establish that the death, injury or damage in respect of which the claim has been made was due to any wrongful act, neglect or default of any person from the company or outside.
- Before commencing the activities involving hazardous substances, the company should take-out insurance policies to cover all liabilities against reliefs to be paid in an accident situation.
- Such public liability insurance policies should remain in force throughout the period during which such handling of hazardous substances takes place.
- These public liability insurance policies should be for amounts not below that of the paid-up capital of the company up to Rs Fifty crores.

- In addition to regular payment of policy premium, companies should also remit an equivalent amount towards a *Relief Fund* established under the act.
- Whenever an accident involving a hazardous substance takes place, the concerned district collector should verify and give necessary publicity to the incident.
- An affected person or his legal representative or an authorised agent can file an application for compensation with the concerned district collector, who would decide on the same based on a personal hearing of the case and award the compensation from the relief fund which, in turn, should be reimbursed by the insurer.
- Under the act relief can be claimed only within five years of occurrence of the incident.
- Central government can authorise a person to visit, inspect and search and seize a company premises for concealed activities, if any, involving handling of hazardous substances or for taking any action including organising of immediate disposal of hazardous substances to prevent the occurrence of an accident. All expenses incurred in this connection can be recovered from the company.
- Central government can organise restraints, through courts of law, on companies handling hazardous substances.
- Contravention of the act will attract punishment of 18 months' to six years' of imprisonment or a penalty of not less than Rs One lakh.
- Organising public liability insurance policies in case of certain listed hazardous chemicals that carry potential to cause damage to the general public and public property under intimation to concerned district collector.
- Ministry of Environment and Forests Notification, New Delhi, the 24th March, 1992, gives fairly elaborate list of chemicals with qualifying quantities for application of Public Liability Insurance Act.
  - About 180 chemicals have been listed under three groups of toxic substances, highly reactive substances, and explosive substances. In addition one more group of flammable substances is also given.
- Quantum of compensation to be paid to victims of accidents:
  - Reimbursement of medical expenses – up to Rs 12,500.00 in each case.
  - Fatal accidents - Rs 25,000 per person in addition to reimbursement of medical expenses, if any, incurred on the victim up to Rs 12,500.00.
  - Permanent total or permanent partial disability or other injury or sickness - reimbursement of medical expenses up to Rs 12,500.00.
  - Cash relief on the basis of percentage of disablement as certified by an authorised physician. The relief for total permanent disability will be Rs 25,000.
  - Loss of wages due to temporary partial disability - monthly relief of Rs 1000.00 per month for three months subject to victims' hopitalisation of not less than three days.
  - Damage to property - up to Rs 6,000 depending on the actual damage.

Table 3.9 A Selected Few Labour Laws

Some Labour Laws of Concern to Corporates

Sl. No.	Key Area	Some Typical Acts/Rules	Applicable Element	Compliance Required

General

- No activity can be carried without the involvement of the intellectual human element. As such, human labour is popularly described as the intellectual capital for any organisation. However, unlike all other forms of an organisational capital, intellectual capital keeps ever appreciating with time and unlike all other forms of industrial capital, this capital remains ever mobile. Further, this capital is extremely sensitive to a large number of socio-economic-intellectual-parameters and uniquely responds to different facets of each one of these impacting parameters. And therefore, it needs to be handled with utmost care to harness its ever unlimited potential.
- The ever sensitive human conscience has been constantly interacting with this sensitive element and has been innovatively evolving, from time to time, different mechanisms to handle this sensitive element. These mechanisms have given rise to onset of a large number of labour laws.
- Some of the laws related to labour welfare and labour relations are named below. Business corporates should identify laws applicable to their activity nature and check the details as relevant to them in terms of applicable elements and the expected compliance requirements.

Sl. No.	Key Area	Some Typical Acts/Rules	Applicable Element	Compliance Required
1.	Industrial Relations and Other Activities	The Trade Unions Act, The Industrial Employment Act and Rules. The Industrial Disputes Act.		
2.	Wages of Industrial Workers and Other Related Activities	The Payment of Wages Act, The Payment of Wages Rules, The Minimum Wages Act and Rules, etc. The Working Journalist (Fixation of Rates of Wages) Act, Working Journalist (Conditions of service) and Miscellaneous Provisions Rules, The Payment of Bonus Act, The Payment of Bonus Act and Rules.		
3.	Industrial Activity Specific or Activity Nature Dependent Laws	The Factories Act. The Dock Workers (Regulation of Employment) Act, The Dock Workers (Safety, Health & Welfare) Act. The Plantation Labour Act. The Merchant Shipping Act. The Motor Transport Workers Act.		

		The Beedi & Cigar Workers (Conditions of Employment) Act, The Beedi Workers Welfare Fund Act, The Beedi Workers Welfare Cess Act. The Contract Labour (Regulation & Abolition) Act, The Sales Promotion Employees (Conditions of Service) Act and Rules. The Inter-State Migrant Workmen (Regulation of Employment and Conditions of Service) Act. The Shops and Establishments Act, The Working Journalists and other Newspaper Employees' (Conditions of Service and Misc. Provisions) Act and Rules. The Mines Act, The Mica Mines Labour Welfare Fund Act, The Limestone & Dolomite Mines Labour Welfare Fund Act, The Iron Ore Mines, Manganese Ore Mines & Chrome Ore Mines Labour Welfare Fund Act, The Iron Ore Mines, Manganese Ore Mines & Chrome Ore Mines Labour Welfare Cess Act, The Coal Mines (Conservation and Development) Act, etc. The Cinema Workers and Cinema Theatre Workers (Regulation of Employment) Act and Rules, The Cine Workers' Welfare Fund Act, The Cine Workers Welfare Cess Act. The Building & Other Construction Workers (Regulation of Employment & Conditions of Service) Act, etc. The employment of Manual Scavengers and Construction of Dry latrines Prohibition Act.		
4.	Empowerment of Women	The Maternity Benefit Act, The Equal Remuneration Act,		
5.	Empowering Deprived and Disadvantaged Section of the society.	The Bonded Labour System (Abolition) Act. The Child Labour (Prohibition & Regulation) Act.		
6.	Social Security of Industrial Workmen	The Workmen's Compensation Act, The Employees' State Insurance Act, The Employees' Provident		

		Fund & Miscellaneous Provisions Act, The Payment of Gratuity Act.		
7.	Appreciating the Intellectual Capital.	The Employment Exchanges (Compulsory Notification of Vacancies) Act and Rules, The Apprentices Act		
8	Other Acts and Laws	The Fatal Accidents Act, The War Injuries Ordinance Act and The War Injuries (Compensation Insurance) Act, The Weekly Holiday Act, The National and Festival Holidays Act, The Personal Injuries (Emergency) Provisions Act, The Personal Injuries (Compensation Insurance) Act, The Public Liability Insurance Act,		
9	Any Other Applicable Law			

Step Three

After identifying broad categories of acts' that would become applicable to their activity nature and scope, organisations should next proceed with identification of activity centre-wise applicability of legal requirements and prepare ready reference correlation matrix (Tables 3.10 – 3.12). Such a reference reckoner would help people in ensuring that no activity centre would go non-compliant.

Table 3.10. Details of Legal Requirements (1)

Validating Statutory Requirements									
SL No.	Activity Centre and Exact Activity	Appli cable Act	Section or Division of the Act	Applicable Rule and Sub-rule	Clause and sub-clause, if any.	Activity Area where Applicable	Correlation, between activity and legal stipulation including Special correlation, if any. (Why a particular law is applicable here)	Exemption sought, if any, under a particular rule or sub-rule and laid-out guidelines	Justification for seeking Exemption or for Ascribing a Different Rule and Sub-rule
1									
2									
3									

Table 3.11 Details of Legal Requirements (2)

Applicability Potential								
Sl. No.	Activity Centre and Exact Activity or Work Station	Which aspect of an activity or activity input carries a direct correlation with a law						Why Applicable Is a direct correlation with law available
		Input material and Services	Execution Process and Methodo-logy	Process Output	Handling	Storage	Transport-ation	
1								
2								
3								

* Knowledge of why a particular law or rule becomes applicable to a particular activity centre would always strengthen people's conviction for remaining law abiding.

Table 3.10 and table 3.11 should be supplemented with additional tabulated data as given table 3.12.

Table 3.12 Details of Legal Requirements (3)

Potential for attracting applicability of Safety Regulations											
Sl. No.	Which aspect of a process or its input carries a safety concern									Impact Field, Range and Potential	Applica-ble Safety Regula-tion
	Activity centre	Material nature like toxicity, pun gency, causing skin irrita-tion on contact, etc.	Emitting suffo-cating fumes and vapours	Flam ma bility	Becoming readily airborne or forming-explosive mixture with other input materials	Special contro-lled job execu-tion environ-ment	Restricted ventilation or light in work area,	Moto-rised move ments of materials and equip-ments,	Storage and handling methods practiced		
1											
2											
3											

Step Four

Obviously the next step would be to identify and understand the nature of expected compliance against each of the requirement at each of the relevant work station. This understanding should also result in identification of the types of records to be generated for the purpose of evidencing compliance achievement and also the frequency of verification and confirmation of compliance status (Table 3.13). Such audit verifications would help organisations in ensuring continuing compliance status.

Table 3.13 Details of Legal Requirements (4)

Confirmation of Compliance Status							
Sl. No.	Activity Centre and Exact Activity	Compliance Details				Frequency of Verification and Confirmation	
						Internal	External (Formal and prescribed)
		Nature of Expected Compliance as per legal stipulation	Details of Contemplated Compliance Mechanism	Adequacy of Contemplated mechanism for compliance purpose	Records to be generated for evidencing compliance		
1							
2							
3							

Step Five

The above four steps, when properly carried out, would prepare the necessary background for ensuring good statutory compliance. However, the organisation would still not be ready for a take-off. One more preparatory step is called for. This is identification of certain prelims as applicable to their activities. This activity may not be relevant to running organisations as they would have already gone through this exercise earlier. Prelims actually refer to identification of various registrations, permits, consents, licences, approval, inspections, certifications, etc. which are mandatory in nature for many industrial activities. Some of them would be of one time nature and some are not. Many of them may have to be renewed periodically depending on the prescribed periodicity. Renewal frequency could be high for some permits and could be less frequent for some others. Wherever renewal frequency would be high, it is always advisable that renewal process is initiated before the expiry of current permits. Strictly speaking, carrying out an activity without a valid licence or valid permit is an illegal activity and attracts punitive measures. Both manufacturing and non-manufacturing organisations would have some common registrations, licences, approvals, etc. But, generally, manufacturing organisations are governed by a larger number of regulatory controls. The key reason for this is the multiplicity of their activities and also the fact that manufacturing organisations carry much higher potential to adversely

Table 3.14 Identification of Prelims

(Registrations, permits, consents, licences, approval, inspections, certifications, etc.)

Sl. No.	Applicable Act	Rule or Clause	Require-ment	Periodicity of Renewal or Formal Submis-sions	Approving or Permitting Authority or the Office Where Formal Submissions are to be Made	Status of Permits, Approvals or Licences, etc.
1	Company Act					
2	Accounts Control and Finance Management Rules					
3	SEBI Rules					
4	Factory Act					
5	Environment Protection Act					
6	Indian Electricity Rules					
7	Indian Explosives Act					
8	The Petroleum Act					
6	Central Motor Vehicles Act					
7	Other Applicable Acts and Rules					

affect the safety of people and the environment by their omissions and commissions. With a view to facilitating good control on compliance to such mandatory requirements, it is always advisable that organisations keep a ready reference matrix of these requirements (Table 3.14).

Step Six

With this homework, organisations would now be almost ready for a take-off. However, with a view to ensuring that they do not get stuck in-between after they make a start, they should ensure their competence to satisfactorily comply with all the statutory requirements.

This verification process calls for two specific actions:

i. Identifying special facilities in terms of equipments or instruments required, if any, for achieving compliance to applicable requirements in any of the work centres.
   - ➢ Expert help could be taken for this purpose wherever called for, for doubly ensuring that people do not face limitations while executing their jobs.
     - Equipping those work centres with the identified facilities and accessory infrastructure facilities.

ii. Identifying special skills needed, if any, for achieving compliance to applicable requirements in any of the work centres. Expert help could be taken for this purpose wherever called for.
     - Imparting required skills in people through necessary supports and training to help them in acquiring required skills that would enable them to properly and confidently handle those equipments.

Step Seven

Ensuring that people develop necessary conviction with a clear understanding of requirements and the required confidence to achieve satisfactory compliance to all the statutory requirements as applicable to their specific activity centres. It is always advisable that wherever people need support, the same should be provided to strengthen their confidence levels. Once people get started and keep going with compliance activities, the same could be periodically checked through suitably designed audits and shortfalls noticed, if any, should be immediately made good through appropriate corrective actions as may be required.

Thus, by following these activity steps, organisations could achieve satisfactory statutory compliance status and support good corporate governance.

Social Responsibility

The Change Wave

Although the subject of *corporate social responsibility* has remained very active in the corporate world for a long time, this concept had always remained ever flexible and ever open to innovative imagination of corporate executives. Many corporates vociferously claim that they have been actively participating in these programmes. However, but for a few stray instances, here and there, the true impact of these corporate activities is hardly felt by the society especially in the background of what is projected by the corporate world in the media and what is seen in highly glorified, rather magnified, corporate balance-sheets. CSR project-forums have essentially remained as a media to serve the key purpose of projecting company's image in the public, particularly in the local society, and for other publicity works rather than as an expression of corporates' true concern and commitment to social development and welfare.

The basic reasons for prevalence of this situation are the following:

- Absence of a systematic and streamlined approach to this subject due to absence of any set guidelines.
- Business corporates were totally free to decide on the key issues like:
  - How much to spend on CSR activities?
  - When to spend?
  - Why to spend?
  - How to spend?

Answers to these mind boggling questions of business executives hovered essentially only on one basic issue namely "What would the corporate get in Return?

Naturally, the answer used to be very vague and uncertain if not always in the negative.

The net result used to be that this activity was invariably considered as an optional one at the discretion of business enterprises.

Such an approach with no specific direction or orientation had the limitation of total dependence on the whims and fancies of a few individuals. Any activity these individuals would entertain under the influence of some local luminaries would become a CSR project. Naturally, the commitment to end results and achievements will not be high. Further, whenever these corporates come under the heavy influence of some other political bigwig, the focus would shift and some other CSR project would be identified. End result of such CSR projects was never auditable and whatever the corporates would write in their annual reports would become acceptable to investors and the general public. Further, a good number of corporates used the so-called CSR forum to buy and strengthen the goodwill of their own employees. It was not a surprise that on a good number of occasions, social welfare projects would be so identified that the bulk of the benefits from those projects would be derived by their own workers and their families.

Fortunately for the society, the situation has now changed. The concept of competition has now changed drastically across the globe. Today, the description competition also embraces the concept of the global image as a highly responsible and respectable member of the global society. This concept therefore demands that business corporates spend a good amount of their productive time and resources for promoting and ensuring welfare of the society in general and the location where they operate in particular.

The world business council defines Corporate Social Responsibility as sustained commitment to behave themselves in such a way that they steadily contribute to economic development of the society at large and in improving the quality of life of their own employees and their families and the local society in particular.

The latest updation of the companies act has brought a sea change in corporate approach to CSR projects by bringing full clarity to all the above issues of business executives. A highly organised, suitably streamlined and appropriately managed approach to this issue has been spelt out in the act.

Reciprocity Concept

The act now recognises the basic truth that *discharging corporate social responsibility* is not a favour a business corporate does to the society but on the contrary it is actually a basic duty of all corporates due to the fact that no corporate can either come to existence or continue to survive without the support and participation of the society and without drawing heavily from the society and the surrounding environment for practically everything right from critical infrastructural support for their operations, material and manpower input to their processes and for providing an opening for their output. Such total dependence of corporates on the society and the surrounding environment, literally, knows no bounds. Therefore, it becomes the bounden duty of all corporates to reciprocate and express their gratitude towards society and the environment in some form or the other. The act does not directly refer to fairness of corporate operations as the core element of corporate social responsibility. However, published literature (Mruthyunjaya, 2011) clearly highlight that it is indeed so. The literature also tells us that the concept of fairness when carefully dissected, all the elements of corporate governance emerge automatically. Different aspects or elements of *operation-fairness* have been distributed between *corporate governance* and *corporate social responsibility* in the act.

Participation in CSR projects is no more a voluntary activity for business corporates to be carried out at their discretion, rather, at the whims and fancies of some executives or to be initiated at the instance of some local luminaries. Active participation in CSR projects has now become mandatory for all business enterprises who meet the minimum criteria. Similarly, the act also spells out unambiguously the minimum amount to be spent by business establishments on CSR projects and brings total clarity to this issue, which in the absence of such a prescription would have continued to remain at the discretion of business executives. The only freedom business executives now have is to cross the minimum and spend more at their discretion and commitment to the local society. Another important aspect all companies should bear in mind is that participation in CSR projects is not a onetime activity. It is an ever perennial process. This perennial nature of participation opens-up a big 'Pandora of Novel Opportunities' to corporates to work towards sustained welfare activities which in the long run could bring about a phenomenal change in the target society. Business corporates can conceive novel CSR projects which need to be nurtured and nourished for a long time in the beginning before the target beneficiaries could derive full benefits from those projects and where they can continue to derive benefits forever.

Mandatory Nature

The company act has now directly linked both these aspects to:

(i) Business investment,

(ii) Turnover and

(iii) Net profits earned by a corporate in a financial year.

Each of these parameters could now independently drive a company to actively take to CSR projects. Naturally, the immediate first question that arises is whether all business enterprises are bound by this requirement and whether there are any exemptions. At this moment, the act has been very considerate to all small and medium size business establishments.

Positive participation in CSR activities has not been made mandatory for all those small and medium size companies whose:

- Net worth is below rupees five hundred crores in a financial year.
- Gross turnover in a financial year is below one thousand crores
- Net profit before taxation from business transactions carried out within the country in a financial year is below five crores.

However, this concession does not bar small and medium size companies from voluntary participation in CSR activities and projects at their discretion. On the contrary, if some of them like to set a precedent to the rest in the society, it would be welcome and would be well appreciated. If small and medium size business establishments desire to display their exemplary conscience-commitment gratitude to the society and work towards welfare of the society which provides them the required socio-environmental support for their operations and survival, why should they not? The society would always wholeheartedly welcome such novel gestures!

CSR Funds Allocation

If business enterprises meet any of the three criteria referred above, as per the act, those companies should compulsorily reserve for CSR activities, a minimum of two percent of their average net profit of preceding three financial years. The act has imposed one more restriction on the companies namely the allocated funds should be spent during the same financial year for which the allocation has been made. Further, under no circumstances, the funds so reserved for CSR activities could be diverted to meet any other exigencies or emergencies of the company. CSR funds can never be used for any other purpose or ploughed back to company's main operating funds. This aspect is auditable.

Recognition of Constraints

However, in reality, on certain situations, business organisations may not be able to spend the entire reserved and/or allocated funds for CSR activities during the year under reference for many genuinely valid and justifiable reasons beyond their control.

Some of the more commonly encountered reasons for non-utilisation of reserved CSR funds could be one or more of the following:

- Time constraints arising from delays in identification of suitable CSR projects with specific reference to the contemplated target location.
- Time constraints arising from delays in identification of most appropriate target location in the region.
- Time constraints arising from delays in identifying the right beneficiary cross section of the target location.
- Time constraints arising from delays in suitably quantifying the expected results from those CSR projects and correlating the same with actual needs of the target beneficiary cross section.

- Time constraints arising from delays in enthusing the target beneficiaries wherever their participation is called for in making a CSR project a success.
- Time constraints arising from delays in identifying and organising suitable local resources and establishing proper co-ordination between those resources.
- Time constraints arising from delays in identification of reliable and credit-worthy external agencies that could execute the project on behalf of the company and achieve expected results.
- Time constraints arising from execution delays due to some unforeseen situations erupting at execution-agency place that came in the way of project execution.
- Time constraints arising from delays due to lack of commitment of the staff of the execution agency.
- Time constraints arising from delays due to some unforeseen natural phenomenon.
- Time constraints arising from delays in flow of funds from other companies whenever wide-scope CSR projects are jointly ventured with other companies with a view to ensuring that a larger cross section of the target society is benefitted from those CSR projects.
- Time constraints arising from delays in completion of an intermediate stage in a multi-stage, long-term CSR project.

CSR Corpus

On all such situations, where business enterprises cannot fully spend the allocated CSR funds during the same financial year, then, business enterprises have to suitably record and document their reasons for not spending the earmarked amount on contemplated CSR projects and should make it a part of their board meetings. Such reports should also become a part of company's annual report and should be presented to the general members of the company during AGMs. Reporting of such situations together with reasons to be justified by the board of directors ensures that their inability becomes questionable by a large cross section of general members, which in turn, ensures that companies do not look for flimsy excuses but make an earnest attempt to address the requirements of the act.

Further, to address such unforeseen situations, all companies should open a separate *CSR Corpus Account.* The seed money for the corpus is the funds allocated for CSR. Unspent money, if any, should be transferred to the corpus. The amount in corpus fund should again be mandatorily directed back to same or similar CSR projects to be initiated at a later stage or for other CSR projects as may become necessary but not for any other exigencies or expenses of the company. For qualifying companies, while the minimum amount is fixed at 2 per cent of net profits before taxation, companies are always free to spend more on CSR activities and there is no bar on the same.

The concept of CSR corpus can serve many noble causes of perennial nature. Whenever a company or a group of companies collectively decide to launch a novel CSR project like for example, establishing a chain of educational institutions for the benefit of the downtrodden, weaker sections or women folk of the region, they could use the concept of CSR corpus. All the companies could deposit their budgeted CSR funds into the corpus and through the funds from the corpus educational institutions could be run. The act, this point of time, does not bar companies to dedicate and/or invest their entire CSR funds into just one good social cause either individually or collectively.

While different schools could entertain different thoughts on this subject, it is always good for corporates to identify one or two such noble causes and leave a long lasting impact on the local society. Such projects, particularly the ones like providing good education to weaker sections of the society or empowering women through both good education and imparting specialised skills in them, by itself triggers many other chain processes which would either individually or collectively induce a major change in the attitude and approach of weaker sections to different issues or aspects of life to change their life style. A good education superimposed with imparting of vocational skills would lead to elimination of extreme poverty of the region because people get educated and acquire necessary skills to improve on their earning capacity. This is certainly not a small contribution to eradication of extreme hunger and poverty of the region!

Profile of CSR Projects

CSR projects have been conceived by many industries for a long time as representing those types of projects which carry a high potential to do good to the society. It is this concept which had induced many industrial corporates in the past to take to social development projects. However, other equally prosperous business houses who were not directly involved in any kind of industrial activity did not evince as much interest in CSR projects as industrial houses did. One of the key reasons for this is the realisation of the intellectuals across the society that industries depend very heavily on the society for running their activities and for their growth and prosperity and therefore industries should do something good to the society. This realisation resulted in development of social conscience over a period of time and brought pressure on industries to participate in social development activities. Most of the industrial corporates did not lose this opportunity to leverage the situation to create a long-lasting good impression in the public through these CSR activities. This concept induced corporates to embrace a wide spectrum of social activities.

Notable among them are:

- Development of social infrastructure like roads, sanitary systems development and improvement, water management programmes like water storage facilities, water distribution facilities, maintenance of natural water bodies, provision of safe drinking water in rural areas, street lighting and rural electrification, etc.
- Cultural development programmes like projects and programmes or events that would give a platform to support, encourage and harness potential skills of people in fine-arts, sports and physical culture.
- Social welfare programmes like health camps, health centres, creating, developing and supporting educational and vocational training facilities, supporting and encouraging pursuance of higher education and specialised skill trainings, appreciating and honouring meritorious students through awards, scholarships, etc.
- Social forestry and enrichment of green coverage, etc.

Thus, one can see that industrial corporates did not fall back too much behind in this area of active participation in CSR activities.

Accountability

However, the only limitation these CSR activities carried for long, earlier, till promulgation of the latest company's act, was the fact that none of the industrial or business corporates were either accountable for their activities or their CSR activity outcome or answerable to the society or any other governmental agencies in this regard. Regardless of what companies used to claim in their balance sheets as the amount spent on CSR activities or whether they had actually spent the amount on CSR projects, there was no formal verification and confirmation mechanism.

The situation has now changed and all business enterprises have been made accountable for CSR activities. As explained above, the concept of accountability has been fused to their operations through certain mandatory stipulations in this regard and ensuring compliance of stipulatory directives through audits.

CSR domain is now open to audit by three independent categories of auditors. Of these the first two types of audits, namely, the audit from a practicing company secretary and the audit from a registered chartered accountant are mandatory in nature as per the act.

1. **Practicing Company Secretary**—Would audit this area from the view points of:
   - Secretarial practices with specific reference to operations of CSR.
   - CSR-activity-dedicated board of directors'-committee,
   - Committee configuration.
   - Committee meetings and proceedings.
   - Maintenance of secretarial records related CSR activities.
   - Allocation of funds for CSR projects and reporting on the same at appropriate forums.
   - Annual reports on CSR.
2. **Company Auditor**—Would audit CSR area from the view points of:
   - CSR funds management and maintenance of accounts.

- Expenses control.
- Budgeting and funds distribution.

3. **Governance Auditor** - Would examine this activity domain from globally holistic viewpoints, namely:
   - Company's CSR policy and policy commitment.
   - Policy publicity and dissemination to appropriate levels.
   - CSR committee configuration and its functioning.
   - Criteria applied to select a CSR project.
   - Rationale behind allocation and/or distribution of funds between different CSR projects.
   - Criteria applied and the mechanism followed to identify an external implementation agency wherever a CSR project-implementation is off-loaded.
   - Mechanism used to monitor the progress of CSR project implementation achieved by the agency.
   - Relevance of the identified CSR project to prevailing socio-economic context of the target location.
   - Relevance of the project and its outcome to target beneficiaries.
   - Methods used to measure and quantify the benefits from CSR projects to target beneficiaries.
   - Effectiveness of the mechanism devised to monitor and report progress on CSR projects in appropriate forums.
   - Funds utilisation and handling of non-utilised carried forward funds, etc.

Thus, business corporates have now been rendered more accountable with regard to discharging their basic duty towards society.

Prescribed CSR Projects

The major change that has been introduced is that over and above the stipulations on funds to be earmarked for CSR projects and administration and management of the same, the notification of the Ministry of Corporate Affairs, Govt. of India dated 20th Feb, 2014, also defines the broad social impact area for identifying CSR projects. While business enterprises should continue to actively participate in CSR projects, they do not have much freedom in selection of their CSR projects.

The following ten broad categories of activities have been listed in the above referred notification as qualifying for CSR activities effective from 1st April, 2014.

Addressing Basic Issues of the Society

i. Eradicating hunger, poverty and malnutrition; promoting preventive health care and sanitation and making available safe drinking water.

ii. Promoting gender equality, empowering women, setting homes and hostels for women and orphans, day care centres for children of working women, etc.

iii. Setting up old age homes, and such other facilities for senior citizens and measures for reducing inequalities faced by socially and economically backward groups.

iv. Promoting education, including special education and employment, enhancing vocational skills especially among children, women, elderly, and the differently abled and livelihood enhancement projects.

v. Reducing child mortality and improving maternal health; combating human immunodeficiency virus, acquired immune deficiency, syndrome, malaria and other diseases.

Environmental Issues

vi. Ensuring environmental sustainability, ecological balance, protection of flora and fauna, animal welfare, agro-forestry, conservation of natural resources, and maintaining quality of soil, air and water.

vii. Protection of national heritage, art and culture including restoration of buildings and sites of historical importance and works of art, setting up public libraries, promotion and development of traditional arts and handicrafts.

Social Upliftment Programmes

viii. Measures for the benefit of armed forces veterans, war widows and their dependents.

ix. Training to promote rural sports, nationally recognised sports, Paralympics sports and Olympic sports.

x. Rural development and Social business projects.

xi. Contributions or funds provided to technology incubators located within academic institutions which are approved by the Central Government.

Benevolent Activities

xii. Contribution to Prime Minister's National Relief Fund or any other funds set up by the Central Govt or State Govt. for socio-economic development and relief and welfare of the scheduled castes, the scheduled tribes, other backward classes, minorities and women.

Outsourcing and Collective Venture

Many times activities and commitments of participating companies' do not permit for ready and direct participation in conducting of CSR activities or in providing the necessary supervision, the same could be organised through a separately established society, trust or a non-profit company. It may also so happen that the business enterprises may not be able to provide the necessary execution infra-structure and monitoring mechanism on its own for many reasons including for reasons of inadequacy of necessary in-house skill power. This would, however, not allow companies to seek exemption for mandatory participation in CSR activities.

On all such situations, the act provides for identifying a satisfactory external implementation agency who could be assigned the total responsibility to see that the project becomes a success in bringing the expected benefits to the target beneficiaries. However, companies cannot assign the responsibility of identifying useful CSR projects also to external agencies. Companies have to shoulder this responsibility themselves.

Companies, CSR committees to be more precise, could always consult external experts, sociologists, environmentalists, social development organisations, local intellectuals and the local people in identifying most useful and appropriate CSR project to be launched and supported. In fact, this is always a welcome approach because this approach fuses a much wider angle and much deeper considerations to the identification process especially in the context of the fact that any CSR project should always maintain a good and dynamic balance between true needs of the contemplated target beneficiaries and the fast changing socio-economic background prevailing in the target society. Only then the funds spent on those CSR projects would go well utilised.

The role of companies does not just stop at mere identification of an external agency for execution, but extends to designing and implementing a monitoring mechanism which would ensure that the project implementing company or agency does not take to any deviations or changes in the activities or in their scope. Monitoring mechanism should be designed in such a way that it is in a position to immediately identify if there is any mismanagement of the funds allocated for CSR projects or if any diversions of CSR funds to other activities taking place. One of the basic requirements in selecting an external agency for implementation of a CSR project is that the agency should already be a well established not-for-profit organisation and should have a standing experience of a minimum of three years in satisfactorily handling CSR projects.

There is one more option open to participating companies.—Two or more participating companies can join their hands together to pool their CSR funds and launch mutually agreed and collectively identified common CSR projects in a big way. A major advantage of such pooled operation would be widely enlarged activity profile and provision of a platform of multiple monitoring of CSR project progress and performance. The target beneficiary profile would also be enlarged proportionately.

On all such collaborative CSR ventures, each of the individual CSR committees should be in a position to prepare progress reports on their projects to their respective boards.

Administering CSR Projects

In the normal routine, business enterprises would be very busy with their own manufacturing and/or service generation activities. Their routine may not allow them to spare the required time and give adequate attention to CSR activities. It is a well understood fact that no project, whether a CSR project or a manufacturing project, can progress well unless the requisite disciplinary intellectual input in terms of supervision, control and guidance is provided. It is for this reason that the act has recommended an independent mechanism to monitor and control the progress of CSR projects. In the absence such a monitoring and control mechanism, the funds spent on CSR projects would either go waste or at least may not be properly utilised and consequently they may not bring expected benefits to the target society or the region.

In order to ensure that CSR projects are properly managed, organised and administered, business establishments should establish an independent control mechanism which should be guided by a CSR policy of the company. One of the first control mechanisms recommended in the act is the constitution of an independent and dedicated CSR committee of the board of directors of the company. The committee should comprise of at least one independent director and two other directors of the company. Such CSR committees should be assigned the task of developing and evolving a transparent mechanism to oversee the implementation and effectiveness of CSR activities of the company. Transparency of this administering, controlling and monitoring mechanism is necessary because the entire CSR activity is auditable. As explained above, CSR domain could be audited by three categories of auditors.

The CSR committee should specifically shoulder the following responsibilities:

i. Developing a suitable CSR policy for the company which could be notified for the knowledge of the general public through company's website and other publicity literature.

   a. Bringing a company's CSR policy to the knowledge of the general public is always beneficial as it provides a forum for intellectual interactions across the society and generation of useful feedback on different aspects of the project right from its identification to its outcome.

   b. It also provides a forum for open participation from intellectuals across the society and opens-up the means to identify the most appropriate CSR.

   c. It also provides a forum for remote sensing as well as remote monitoring from intellectuals across the society and to generate true feedback on both the utility and relevance of proposed CSR projects and also a true feedback on the actual progress of the project and useful suggestions for reorientation and fine-tuning of activities as may be required from time to time depending on the general sociological changes taking place in the target society.

ii. The policy should clearly express company's commitment to the welfare of the society and the nature and types of CSR projects it proposes to embrace.

   a. Company's CSR policy should make a categorical statement that CSR funds will never be diverted towards meeting any other expenses of the company and would always be transferred to corpus whenever the same or part of the same remains unspent for some reason or the other during the specified financial year.

   b. The policy should also broadly define and/or spell out the modalities that the company would follow while implementing CSR projects and monitoring the progress of the same.

   c. Monitoring mechanism so designed by the committee should also address the aspect of measuring and quantifying the net benefits from the project.

   d. The mechanism should further define means of correlating the benefits with the pre-contemplated target beneficiaries.

iii. Getting the CSR policy of the company approved by the board of directors of company.

iv. Identifying the most appropriate CSR projects and recommending the same for approval by the board.

   a. CSR projects identified for the company should be such that they are in the nature of highly relevant to the local population and the local surroundings.

   b. While there is no specific bar on target locations for CSR projects to be launched, keeping in mind the reciprocity-concept, the act recommends that it is highly advisable that CSR projects are initiated in the immediate region where the corporate is located.

c. This is to ensure that the local society would actually feel the impact of the business corporate being present in their midst apart from the general impact on employability potential for local people.

   v. Preparation of a list of CSR projects to be taken-up during the year together with suitable plans, budget proposals and execution mechanisms for each of the CSR projects.

   vi. Preparation of an annual report highlighting the composition of the CSR committee, summary of its meetings and their outcome, various CSRT projects identified and recommended to the board for approval and adoption, expenses contemplated and spent on different CSR project, reasons for delay in project execution, projects of continuing and long-time nature, unspent allocated money to be transferred to CSR corpus, highlights of achievements during the year, etc.

Eligibility Criteria

Since funds allocation for CSR activity is a mandatory requirement, business enterprises should clearly follow the set guidelines to ensure that the projects they launch do get qualified for the purpose. The first and foremost criteria, as per the act is that only those CSR projects that are taken-up in India are eligible for qualification under CSR and not any form of CSR activity carried outside the country. Further, it is only that specific category of CSR projects which are exclusively identified for the purpose and referred in the act or on-going pre-identified CSR projects that are eligible for qualification under CSR activity.

The act brings further clarification to this concept. If the basic nature of a business activity by itself is such that it automatically embraces certain CSR activity area in the normal course of its business conduct, then those activities do not qualify for CSR activity. On all such situations, those companies will have to separately identify certain independent CSR activities and implement the same.

The law also makes it clear that none of the CSR projects should be designed exclusively for the benefit of participating companies' employees or their family members. The basic premise for such a stipulation is the fact that addressing certain minimum welfare activities of their employees is a basic responsibility of business enterprises and therefore by taking-up such welfare activities the enterprises they do not do any favour to the society and therefore such activities cannot stand for display of any extraordinary sense of commitment to the general welfare of the society. Business enterprises should guard their CSR projects against such limitations.

However, this stipulation for qualifying CSR activity criteria should be carefully interpreted. While a higher education or vocational skill implantation training programme is conducted and/or organised by the participating company and children of a few employees of the company also take advantage of the same along with many other general public in the town or village, then one would not be morally justified to disqualify such a CSR activity. After all, employees and their families also have to live in the same society as many others live. In this context, CSR projects will have to be viewed from broader social perspectives.

Similarly, if a CSR project with a fairly wide application profile like providing solar energy or free drinking water supply to all the houses in a township/village or a small habitat in the region is launched, and if some employees and their families also live that township or village, then what should happen? A village or a township is meant for anybody to live. Employees of the company cannot be barred. Naturally, CSR projects taken-up in such habitats where a few employees and their family members also get benefited along with many other in the region, then those CSR projects will have to fully qualify.

The spirit of the act should therefore be understood as standing for all those CSR projects whose target beneficiary profile covers a broad spectrum of the contemplated population but is not restricted or confined only to the welfare and overall development of a limited cross section of participating companies' employees and their family members.

As a good management practice, business enterprises should work out a consensus figure that can be validated by any non-challengeable mechanism regarding the quantum of benefits shared by companies' employees and their families and the rest in the target society. While individual opinion of system auditors could vary in this regard, any figure of up to say about 20 per cent (employees and their families) of the total target beneficiary population should be considered as a qualifying figure.

A note of caution! Contribution to any of the political parties in any form and magnitude will not qualify for CSR activity irrespective of whether or not a specific contribution is being collected in the name of a social welfare project or a general welfare project which would otherwise fully qualify for CSR activity when independently identified and executed.

CSR Reporting

The notification of the Ministry of Corporate Affairs, Govt. of India, dated 27th Feb, 2014, has also made it mandatory that effective from 1st April, 2014, all annual reports of companies should also carry an annual report on CSR. Those foreign companies which do not hold their AGMs in India should append a report on CSR in their annual Balance-sheets.

The annual CSR report should carry, among other things, the following key aspects, namely,

- A brief outline of company's CSR policies and practices as finalised by CSR committee and approved by the company's board of directors and publicised through company's website and other publicity literature. A reference to company's website that gives details of company's CSR policies and projects should also be made here.
- A skeletal overview of various CSR projects envisaged and/or contemplated to be taken up during the year highlighting the rationale behind identifying a particular project and elaborating on the projected/expected benefits to the target beneficiaries.
- Brief details of relevance of the identified project to the target beneficiary and location and the rationale behind the same.
- Composition of the CSR committee highlighting the number of independent directors on the committee.
- Funds that has been transferred to company's CSR corpus in relation to average net profits of the company for previous three years.

- Details of proposed budget and actual expenses incurred on various CSR projects during the year together with details of unspent money, if any, along with necessary details of constraints that did not permit complete utilisation of allocated CSR amount on projects during the year.
- A tabulated presentation of brief details of the mechanism followed to spend the allocated CSR amount on different projects during the year. Tabular format should give the following details:
  a. Serial number of the project.
  b. CSR project title and details of sector to which the project belongs.
  c. Broad sector to which the identified CSR project belongs.
  d. Contemplated target beneficiary location (details like state, district, taluk/tehsil where the project is undertaken).
  e. Contemplated/budgeted expenses on the project for the year
  f. Amount spent on the project during the year under review giving details of sub-headings like direct project cost and overheads, etc. together with details of method of spending namely whether direct or through an external implementing agency.
  g. Wherever projects are continuing in nature, cumulative amounts spent on the project and the cumulative quantified benefits derived from the project. Wherever the net benefit is still in the offing for want of completion of the project, net cumulative progress of the project and the magnitude of pending works.
  h. Cumulative expenditure incurred on the project so far.
  i. If the project implementation is outsourced, then the amount spent by the implementation agency.

     Name and other details of CSR implementing agency together with any other relevant information about the agency that may be desirable.
- Reasons for not spending the allocated total CSR amount during the year.

- A confirmatory statement from CSR committee to the effect that implementation and monitoring of CSR projects is in line with companies declared CSR policies and objectives.
- The CSR report should be signed by companies MD or CEO or a director and chairman of CSR committee.

Support Systems

Satisfactory practice of *Corporate Governance* and addressing the requirements of *Corporate Social Responsibility* demands good support from two other critical activity areas namely *Accident Management* and *Emergency Preparedness*. Both these activities are as much critical to success of *Corporate Governance* and *Corporate Social Responsibility* as any other activity that could be normally visualised under these activity heads. This is basically because if those activities are not suitably supported by good accident management mechanisms and equally good emergency preparedness plans in place, then many of those activities might even lose their base or significance on certain occasions. An accident is always an unwelcome event because it carries a very high potential to cause great harms to people and properties. It can cause injuries to people or result in pushing people to suffer from severe health problems including causing death in some cases. Similarly, accidents can cause widely varying magnitudes of damage to equipments and machineries and other assets of the business corporate. Ensuing discussions will tell us that accidents are invariably caused by people because of their certain omissions and certain commissions by not following certain basic safety norms and set procedures for the purpose of executing a job.

If corporate premises or industrial premises is full of hazards and risks for people in and around and people continue to suffer, silently, do claims of corporate social responsibility or good governance carry any meaning? Never! Accidents never take place with any forewarning. They generally follow Murphy's law namely they always take place when people are least expecting them and more so when they are least prepared to face them and/or are lost elsewhere in some other busy schedules. If accident situations are not well managed and quickly controlled, there would be disasters in organisations. Damage coverage during corporate accidents, may not, always, be confined only to those people who would physically be present at the corporate premises at the time of accident, but can also embrace people outside the premises as well. In addition, many accidents carry a very high potential to pollute the environment which, in turn, would adversely affect not only people but also all other members of the global bio-sphere. We all know that environmental damage is irreversible and the bio-world has to continue to suffer forever. It is for this reason that corporates should be properly equipped to ensure that accidents do not take place in the first place and if for any unknown reason accident does take place, damage to people and the bio-world will be controlled at most minimum levels.

From the ensuing discussions one should not construe that they are designed with a focus on only for manufacturing organisations. That is not the prime objective. Manufacturing environments have been taken for typical explanations and for design of tabular formats and pointed suggestions because unlike other types of industrial and business establishments, they provide more live situations to justify the necessity for establishing effective support systems. Similarly, manufacturing environments generally carry much higher potential to create emergency situations than most of the other industrial and/or business establishments. Good support systems would always be highly beneficial for all types of business corporates in formulating and practicing good governance mechanisms. Wherever some of the discussions or tabular formats appear to be not applicable for their specific types of operation environments, the same could be replaced with suitably modified formats keeping in mind the sequence of thoughts and concepts that are given here.

The two support systems referred above form critical components of organisational management systems (Figure 5.1). In their absence, *Corporate Social Responsibility* concept does not serve much purpose in addressing basic responsibilities of corporates towards society. Yet, very unfortunately, most of the industrial corporates and business organisations do not view them as absolutely essential and never ignorable components of their operations. That is precisely the reason

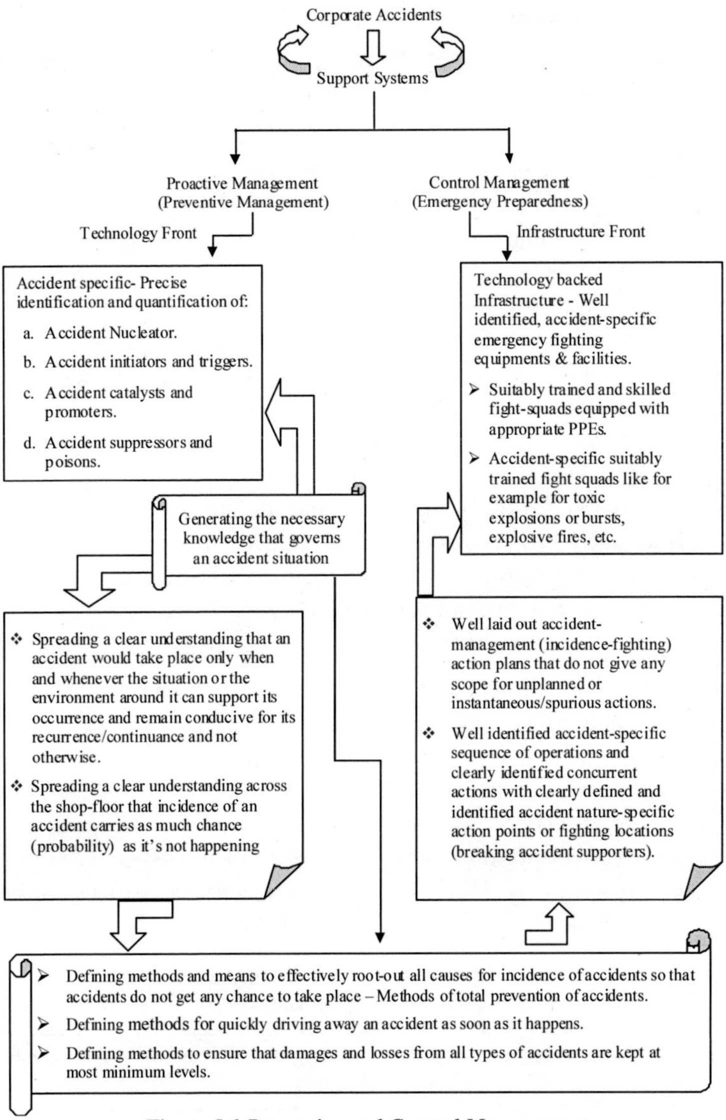

Figure 5.1 Pro-active and Control Management Components of Business Corporates

for why many industries and business corporates are, generally, least prepared and least equipped to face true emergencies.

Nature of Corporate Accidents

Let us first start with understanding the nature of different types of corporate accidents.

Corporate Accidents generally refer to those uncalled for unfortunate incidents that leave a severe, adverse impact on a large section of organisational workforce or the general public or both. These accidents carry a high potential to readily come to the knowledge of the general public and to create a long lasting unwelcome impression in the society, rather a black scar on the memory of the general public. Such accidents come to limelight to draw the attention of all intellectuals and many others across the world primarily because of their high magnitude of damage to human life and corporate assets and/or public property. All industrial activities are generally abreast with some form of accident potential though this fact is not readily recognised as such. Damage magnitudes and occurrence frequencies of industrial accidents vary from one industry to another depending on the nature of activity being carried out by them. Similarly the nature of damage to human life also varies from one industry to another.

While all types of accidents could take place in all kinds of industries, when viewed from their occurrence frequency, damage magnitude and harm potential perspectives, it becomes apparently clear that some industries typically and/or inherently carry much greater accident potential and are more readily prone to accidents whereas some other industries do not carry such inherently high accident potential. Accidents associated with different types of industries generally exhibit the pattern shown in Table 5.1, though accident nature may not be confined only to the pattern shown in this table.

Table 5.1 Nature of Accidents Normally Associated with different Types of Industries

Sl. No.	Industry Type	Nature of Accidents and their Harm Potential
1.	All types of Engineering Industries including Heavy Engineering Industries and Engineering Workshops	Potential for causing physical injuries is generally high in engineering industries. Some of the more frequently encountered types of injuries are cuts from sharp metallic edges, crushes when caught between moving equipments or

		machineries, slippages and falls arising from spillages of oils and lubricants, heavy impacts and deep cuts from accidental fall of heavy components on the foot or other parts of the body, etc. Fatality is also a possibility when sharp edged objects flying at high speeds from equipments in high-speed rotary motion hit certain critical parts of the body.
2.	Electrical Industries and Assembly Shops	Electrical shocks and burn injuries are the two direct accident hazards generally associated with all types of electrical industries. This accident potential is not confined only to industrial activities but also embraces all types of routine activities involving energised lines. More frequently encountered types of accidents are fires from short-circuits and associated burn injuries and direct electrical shocks of varying magnitudes including fatality due to ultimate electrocution. Indirect accident potential associated with these activities are loss of balance causing fall injuries from sudden shocks when working at heights on energised electrical lines. Fatal falls could also take place.
3.	Biological Laboratories and Bio-Engineering (BT) Industries	High potential for causing metabolic damages due to contamination (accidental inhalation, ingestion or entry through open injuries) of bio-active molecules with high harming potential.
4.	Electronic Industries including Electronic Gadget Assembly Units	Metabolic damages and functional impairment are the two more frequent types of accidents associated with these activities due to exposure to varying magnitudes of radiation frequency with high damage potential.
5.	Pathological and Virology Laboratories	High risk of contamination with disease causing deadly viruses is the greatest accident potential associated with these activities. High potential for infection

		from pathogenic micro-organisms (Virus, bacteria, fungi, etc.). Mild to severe health hazard potential due to infection through inhalation of airborne pathogenic micro-organisms or due to accidental ingestion or entry through open cuts and injuries.
6.	Chemical and Processing Industries	High potential for burn and toxic injuries of varying magnitudes due to presence of flammable and toxic chemical vapours including from those flammable and toxic chemicals that can readily become air-borne and become diffusible to spread their accident potential far away from source. High potential for high pressure explosion and fire accidents. High risk of multiple injuries of varying magnitudes from a combination of chemical burns, toxic exposure and pressure bursts or pressure explosions. High risk potential wherever (only) input chemicals carry high accident potential. High risk potential wherever (only) output chemical products carry high accident potential. High risk potential during activity execution wherever (only) intermediate reaction products carry high accident potential even though their inputs or final outputs may not carry such risk potentials. Source of fire accidents – Neglected spillages and leakages of flammable, combustible and inflammable chemicals; pyrophoric type of auto-ignitive chemicals that can trigger fire and induce fire accidents. Explosions and pressure bursts – High explosion risk potential causing multiple injuries and chemical burns or toxic exposures wherever highly exothermic reactions or high energy releasing type

		of gaseous reactions are carried out in partly closed reactors and/or reactors with controlled openings. Toxic exposures – High potential for accidental inhalation and/or ingestion of toxic chemicals and their vapours from toxic leaks, spillages and pressure bursts that carry the potential to impair certain natural metabolic processes on long exposures or heavy ingestions. Chemical induced type of accidents – Corrosion induced weakening leading to braking away or crumbling of load bearing metallic structures, elevated platforms and workstations, supports and scaffoldings causing fall injuries and/or to trigger multiple chemical accidents or failure of critical control devices fitted on service lines carrying different types of chemical fluids under pressure to cause pressure bursts and accompanied injuries.
7.	Pharmaceutical Industries	High potential for chemical/drug induced metabolic damages
8.	Petrochemical Industries	High potential for fire accidents, exposure to carcinogenic vapours and pressure explosions
9.	Nuclear Power Stations	High radiation damage potential causing varying degrees of metabolic-dysfunctions.
10	Transport industry (surface, land, sea, air and space transport)	High potential for causing physical and burn injuries with high fatality potential.

A Base for Design

In order to design good accident management mechanism, organisations have to pass through a critical dissection exercise namely a detailed analysis of safety environment across the organisation. This exercise should reveal and highlight the following two aspects:

- Organisational built-in ability to prevent occurrence of accidents and to quickly arrest recurrence of accidents.
    - Built-in-ability to effectively prevent occurrence of accidents, in turn, depends primarily on the following three basic elements:
        - Right type of infrastructure.
        - Right type of skills in people:
            - To design appropriate activity execution layout.
            - To create right kind of activity performance environment.
            - To conduct activities in the right way such that accidents do not get an opportunity to make their presence felt in any of the activity areas but are always kept at bay.
        - Requisite knowledge backup to carry out the above.
- In situations where accidents do take place for some reason or the other, beyond the knowledge or control of executives, organisational built-in ability to satisfactorily handle events resulting from non-anticipated accident situations when things go completely out of control.
    - People's mental make-up not to get over-powered with thoughts of becoming helpless.
    - People's mental make-up not to become *Panicky.*
        - A condition where people just fail to initiate the right course of action as their reasoning power eludes them.
    - Built-in courage in people not to just surrender to the situation.
    - An attitude of firm determination to fight those adverse situations in such a way that those unacceptable situations are readily reversed and brought to normalcy at the earliest.
    - A clear conviction and confidence in their capability and skills to effectively fight the situation and to quickly capture control over the situation and to arrest accompanying damages and losses at most minimum.

- o People's mental preparedness to quickly recompose their knowledge-driven thought processes in the right direction and to initiate the right type of co-ordinated actions and/ or movements that can effectively prevent situations moving from bad to worse.

Scenario that could Rule an Accident Situation

Whether or not people just surrender to *Out-of-Control Situations,* many unacceptable incidents do take place in an accident situation. The magnitude and severity of damages and losses, however, depends on how soon the situation would be brought under control. The word accident is generally understood and interpreted to represent a situation where there is a loss of life or loss of a body organ or damage to an organ beyond recovery/rectification or damage to equipment beyond repairs or a huge material loss. This is a wrong notion. The description accident, in a true sense of the term, stands for a situation that witnesses an unforeseen or unacceptable event without reference to either nature or magnitude of harm or injury caused to people or damage caused to materials or machineries. Even the slightest injury of ignorable or negligible magnitude caused to a person or a negligible damage to machineries or materials in a work environment should be treated as an accident and handled accordingly. If people develop an attitude of assigning either the magnitude or the nature to a situation for qualifying the same to be described as an accident, then no work premises could be transformed into an absolutely safe place to work. Accident management should always fuse this concept to its activity fold and holistically explore the governing technology and its translation to live reality in active shop-floors.

Root Cause

Accidents generally have their roots in one or more of the following three reasons:

- ➢ Improper or incomplete understanding of the technology being handled and its practice methodologies adopted.
  - • This is the first major cause of accidents in all organisations. People do not know the intricacies of technology translation and process criticalities.

  - In the absence of this knowledge, people design their own transformation routes including taking to many operation short-cuts.
  - This situation could also lead to identification of wrong processing equipments or fixing of wrong limits for process variations or for process controls.

- When technology translation methods are not correctly understood, operation criticalities lose their significance. With the result, people do not know the following:
  - o What
    - What to do to ensure processes smoothness.
    - And what to do if things go out of control.
  - o Why
    - Why a particular activity has to be carried out in a particular way only.
    - And why not in any other way and what happens if a specific scheme is not followed.
  - o When
    - When would a control parameter become critical.
    - And when would it acquire a dangerous situation.
  - o Where
    - Where should one act to control the situation.
    - And where should one not meddle.
  - o Who
    - Who is the most competent person to handle a critical situation.
  - o How
    - How to ensure normalcy of a situation that has gone out of control.
    - How to readjust, during an emergency situation, process criticalities and their controls as well as further activity sequences, etc.
  - o When such a situation rules an active shop-floor buzzing with many activities, the result could be anybody's guess.
- Non-committed or half-hearted approach to activity execution.

Catalysts for Accidents

- o Failure to correctly project and maintain process criticalities and controls.
- o Lack of skill to maintain those required conditions.
- o Lack of skill to identify and implement effective and adequate corrective or diffusive measures when things go out of control.
- o Not taking preventive and diffusive measures serious.
- o Taking things for granted and assuming that things would work on their own.
- o Taking things easy and playing with chance elements.
- o Not taking preventive and positive diffusive measures.
- o Driving people to other works and ignoring the care necessary for process execution.
- o Not ensuring availability of dedicated teams while setting process criticalities and controls.

Each one of these is a grievous crime that could trigger an accident and stands for gross negligence of duty and hence grossly unethical on the part of corporates! Accidents generally take place as a result of grossly negligent attitude of people arising from regular monotonous routine checks, verifications and confirmation process of non-eventful schedules. This is where shop-floor executives have to shoulder extra responsibility and become truly accountable for maintaining accident-safe operation environment. These executives should ensure that the monotony-fatigue does not set-in to induce an attitude of negligence in people.

This is probably the most tedious task in the entire chain. Ineffective execution of this task becomes unethical on the part of shop-floor executives!

Any infrastructure installed to create an accident-free operation environment could always fail to function satisfactorily if not diligently well-maintained in an ever-fit condition and could become a cause for an accident. While people attending to such routine checks and maintenance activities could remain attentive for some time, maintaining a sensitive, attentive-temperament evergreen and ever fresh and never dying is certainly not an easy task. Shop-floor executives have to ingeniously work towards maintaining this temperament in people. Accidents take place only when people take things easy even for small time durations and when people are lost in attending to other busy schedules.

Thus, in a broad sense, corporates have to step in and shoulder this responsibility to ensure that:

- All concerned shop-floor executives diligently discharge their duty-bound responsibility towards safety-management through ensuring that the organisational workforce would always remain on their toes and would never give accidents a chance!

Thus, we can conclude that the gross responsibility for preventing accidents comprises of two key components:

- The macro-safety-management namely providing the necessary knowledge and the support infrastructure.
  - Rests totally at the corporate level.
- The micro-safety-management namely ensuring that the right knowledge acts as the key driving force behind all executions including configuring the necessary infrastructure to leverage the same for maintaining an accident-free work environment.
  - Rests partly at corporate level for identification and imparting the right kind of knowledge in people and partly at shop-floor execution level for translating the knowledge and skill to practical reality.

Accident Types

Unacceptable incidents belong to following two basic categories:

1. *Accidents (Injury Causing Incidents)*

   a. Personnel Accidents.

   More commonly encountered types of injuries/wounds to people in corporate/industrial environment generally belong to one or more of the following categories. These are only indicative, typical and qualitative descriptions and not comprehensive and quantitative.

Physical Environment:

- Heavy impacts/hits that throw away people with force causing fall injuries of varying magnitudes, from stationary or mobile infrastructures like for example elevators mounted on fork-lifts, motorised mobile infrastructures, machines and other mechanisms in motion like for example lifts, overhead cranes, hoists, elevators, jacks, moving fork-lifts, heavily loaded intra-corporate material movement mechanisms, etc.
- Fall injuries from varying heights from temporarily erected, non-stable scaffoldings/elevators/supports, etc., not fully-secured or improperly secured elevators or elevated platforms, slippages from heights due to loss of balance resulting from sudden vibrations of support structures, diversion of attention while working at elevated heights which do not have suitably designed fall-safe guards, electric shocks of varying magnitudes, etc., fall injury on slippery floors while in swift motion in a heavily congested and poorly maintained work place, etc.
    - Temporary loss in utility of body parts is not uncommon in an industrial environment.
    - Permanent loss of body parts or fatality due to fall from great heights cannot be ruled out.
- Crushing impacts/injuries due to fingers, hands and other parts of the body, unintentionally coming in-between a fixed structure/wall and a mobile mechanism, or caught between two mobile mechanisms or when people get caught under a falling weight or falling load, etc.
- Cuts and cut injuries and wounds including tearing of body tissues and parts (fingers, hands, toes, etc.) from sharp edges in shop-floors, from sharp tools or other accessories/components having sharp edges from processing equipments or support systems, fingers or hands coming in contact with sharp cutting/machining tools in motion, or other sharp objects in motion including from flying heavy and/or sharp objects from unsecured

or improperly secured and unguarded machines in operation/motion, etc.

- Combination of one or more of all the above types of injuries in some cases leading to situations demanding far greater health concern or even fatality in some rare cases.
- Loss of vision when struck by lightning bright sparks while working without proper eye protectors/shields/ guards especially while working in enclosed chambers.
- Loss of visible body parts and/or damage beyond rectification/recovery.
- Loss of life or heavy damage to body organs resulting in near incapacitation of people.
- Electrical shocks of varying severity causing injury/ damage to people
  - Temporary and/or permanent loss of sensation of hands, fingers or other parts of the body.
  - Compounded impacts resulting from electric-shock-triggered situations that lead to any or all the above types of injuries to people.
  - Fatality in some rare situations.

Fatality in any of the above accidents depends on the severity and magnitude of injury caused to people.

Chemical Environment:

All the above types of injuries can take place in a chemical environment with added complications due to chemical contamination at open wounds and injuries.

Petrochemicals are also basically chemicals only and as such accident potential would be somewhat similar to what is noticed with other chemicals, though not in all aspects discussed below. However, petrochemicals are uniquely characteristic in one aspect namely they offer a wide range of individual chemicals that are typically highly inflammable and therefore offer great fire and explosion accident potential.

- Chemical burns from physical contact with corrosive chemicals whether solid, liquid or gas, – Injuries of varying magnitudes and concern.

- Weakening of fabricated elevators, elevated work stations, support platforms, elevated work stations, scaffoldings, etc. due to highly corrosive chemical atmosphere resulting in sudden breakdown/crumbling of elevated support structures causing fall injuries from varying heights.
  - Temporary and/or permanent loss of body parts or fatality due to fall from great heights cannot be ruled out.
- Chemical leakages, sprinkles, spurts and splashes, etc. causing slippery surface leading to falls and accompanying injuries including chemical injuries of varying degrees of concern from direct droppings of corrosive/toxic chemicals or splashes on the body.
- Suffocation and/or forced inhalation of toxic or poisonous fumes, vapours, gases, etc. due to sudden ejections or emissions from leaky joints, weakened service lines/by-passes/pressure outlets, etc. while working in confined enclosures, or due to sudden entrapment with no built-in provision for quick escape.
  - Entrapment in confined areas filled with toxic/pungent/suffocating vapours or gases resulting in excessive inhalation/ingestion of chemicals leading to temporary loss of sensation or varying degrees of damage to natural body metabolic activity.
  - Entrapment in confined area with limited or no fresh-air supply but copious supply of chemical vapours leading to suffocation.
- Toxic exposure from pressure bursting of stored containers leading to temporary or permanent loss of some sensation.
  - Fatality in case of forced inhalation of highly toxic and poisonous vapours or entrapment for longer duration without being immediately rescued cannot be ruled out.
  - Fatality and/or serious health situation arising from inadvertent ingestion and/or entry of poisonous chemicals from open wounds/injuries cannot be ruled out.
- High pressure impacts from flying objects (metal/glass pieces from processing equipments or accessories, service lines, etc.) during pressure bursts.

    - In rare/exceptional cases where human body is hit by sharp and piercing objects flying at great speeds from high pressure bursts could result in fatality.

- Fire burns resulting in varying degrees of burn injuries during chemical fires calling for varying periods of hospitalisation from short-term to long-term.
    - Chemical and processing industries particularly petrochemical and petrochemical products processing industries are invariably camouflaged with ever-live-fire-blankets due to the fact that most of their inputs would be highly inflammable and could burst into flames even at the slightest opportunity.
    - Fatality resulting from severe burns cannot be ruled out.
- Damage to natural body metabolism due to sudden/excessive exposure to certain toxic and harmful chemical vapours.
- Damage of sensory tissues/sensory organs from excessive and prolonged exposure to certain chemicals.

Biological/Pharmaceutical Environment:

Accidents involved in this category of industrial environment would be slightly different in its impact nature and magnitude. Biological environment carries a high potential to cause severe damage to body metabolism of varying magnitude. Pharmaceutical environment is somewhat similar to chemical environment and accident magnitude will be low. Both these environments could pose high risks when they find an entry to body during accidents. They also carry high potential to pollute environment around with associated risks.

Radiological Accidents:

Accidents of this category are generally seen in nuclear power stations. They can also happen with equipments used for radiological treatment. Radiations of certain wavelengths always cause severe threats during exposure due to damage to natural body-metabolism.

b. Environmental Accidents.

These accidents basically belong to three categories.

- o Pollution of air due to emission of toxic/poisonous and other gaseous or particulate chemicals.
  - Ejection of toxic/poisonous chemicals into the air during pressure bursts or leakages.
  - Contamination of air from chemical powders or particulate solid chemicals that would readily become air-borne.
  - Contamination of air from chemical dusts in chemical storing and/or processing areas.

The severity and impact coverage profile arising from forced inhalation of contaminated air depends on the nature and quantum of the ejected chemical and the human population in the affected area.

- Light and readily diffusible gaseous chemicals spread over a long area to affect many people in the region including those in a far away location in some cases.
- Dense gaseous and particulate chemicals have a tendency to settle in a narrower area depending on the magnitude and duration of ejection.
  - o Impact coverage range and profile depends on other environmental factors.
  - o Fine particulate corrosive chemicals have a tendency to diffuse to faraway places and settle on nearby metallic structures and corrode them to cause induced but delayed accidents elsewhere.
  - o Fine particulate carbonaceous and other particulate chemicals have a tendency to diffuse to faraway places and settle on historic and other creative monuments of high architectural value/significance to spoil their aesthetic look or to create ugly scenes.
- Ejection/release of gaseous chemicals with high GWP and high ODP.

  GWP: Magnitude of warmth generated by different chemicals is expressed in terms of a numerical figure called *Global-Warming-Potential, GWP.* GWP is a ratio of the warmth generated (thermal energy or heat energy conserved) by a chemical under reference to the warmth generated by carbon dioxide which is taken as one unit. GWP of some fluoro-organic chemicals varies from a few hundreds to a few thousands and goes up to as high as about 20,000 when compared to carbon dioxide).

ODP: Ability of different chemicals to decrease ozone layer thickness in the stratosphere is generally called *Ozone Depletion Potential, ODP*. ODP is just a number (ratio) that represents the relative ozone depleting ability of a chemical under reference with specific reference to ozone depleting ability of mono-chloro-mono-fluoro-carbon compound whose ODP is considered as one unit, cause far greater damage, though not immediately felt, to global environment to affect global population.

- o Most unfortunately these impacts are slow in nature and not readily seen. And as such, these impacts are not taken serious during accidents.

- Ejections of highly acidic and/or corrosive and diffusible chemicals including those that readily become air-borne to diffuse in different directions depending on air direction and slowly settle down.
  - o Acidic ejections cause acid rains, which, in turn, spoil natural vegetation, flora and fauna of the region.
  - o Acid rain (or acidic chemicals settling down on natural aqua bodies) is also very dangerous for aqua-life and can kill some sensitive members of aqua-life and cause severe damage to others.
  - o Acidic rain (or acidic chemicals settling down) would spoil both the flora and fauna of the region.
  - o This impact also belongs to the category of slow in nature and not readily seen. And as such, is not taken serious during accidents.

o Pollution of water due to discharge of toxic/poisonous chemical effluents or fluids containing chemicals.

- Contamination of water from seepages and leakages of toxic chemicals stored in containers reaching natural water bodies.
  - o Highly chemical contaminated water can cause severe damages to aqua life including killing many members of the same.

  - o Highly chemical contaminated natural water body would pose severe risk to animal life and can spoil flora and fauna around its surroundings.
- Contamination of underground water from seepages and percolation of toxic chemicals.
- Contamination of underground water from seepages and washouts of stored solid chemicals or chemical containing solid wastes dumped in the backyard.
  - o Contamination of land due to open dumping of chemicals or chemical containing wastes.
- Open discharge of chemical wash liquids, toxic effluents, solvents directly onto the land.
- Contamination of land from seepage/leakage of stored toxic chemicals.
- Contamination of land from percolation of toxic washouts from stored chemical containing solid wastes.

c. Precious Materials and Natural Resources' Accidents.

During accidents large quantities of stored precious raw materials or goods in process and finished goods can get spoiled and become useless. Non-productive use of all forms and kinds of natural resources is a great national loss.

d. Infrastructure' Accidents.

This is another outcome of accidents. In some accident situations many of the organisational infrastructures would be involved and could suffer severe damages including their crumbling down.

e. Capital Assets' Accidents.

Loss of organisational assets is the ultimate outcome of accidents. The magnitude and severity of accidents decide the magnitude of loss caused to capital assets.

2. *Creation of Emergency Situations*

Emergency situations, (A situation resulting from total loss of control on processes being carried out and where the situation offers a risky environment for people or a natural curse/calamity that carries high risk potential or high danger potential), could embrace all the above five sub-groups under accident category.

The type of organisational preparedness decides how effectively an organisation could fight an emergency situation and could bring it under complete control to minimise all forms of losses and damages taking place.

What Needs to be Done

During accidents, people may get severely hurt and could suffer serious injuries, precious natural resources may be lost and/or could go waste, infrastructure may suffer damages of varying magnitudes, damage and/or loss of capital assets cannot be completely ruled out. And the entire situation could also lead to severely damaging the environment. None of these situations would be acceptable to the society as each one of them represents loss of national wealth of its own category. Organisations should, therefore, not allow panicky-conditions to prevail for long during accident situations. That would become a practical reality only when people are well prepared for facing all types of *unacceptable situations*. Such preparations should result in well laid out action plans (Figure 5.1) that could achieve one or more of the following key objectives:

- Prevent loss of all types of wealth forms.
- Where prevention is not practical for different reasons ruling accident situations, mitigate (minimise) the loss.
- Restrict the loss profile (coverage range and magnitude) to limited and confined activity zones.
- Bring the situation back to normalcy at the earliest to clear the air of tension.

A Hidden Potential

While the accidents shown in Table 5.1 belong to the category of global concern about corporate working, industrial corporates also carry a high latent potential to occurrences of one other category of accidents that usually skip the attention of the general public. This other category would mostly remain outside the domain of public knowledge though they could also be as critical as the other one due to the fact that cumulatively and/or collectively they carry an equally high potential to cause harm to people and also damage to corporate and/or other public assets. By nature, these accidents cause minor injuries to people and/or minor loss of properties at any specific point of time. As such, they get ignored and do not draw the attention of many. In fact, most of the times, even those who are directly affected by those injuries tend to ignore them without realising the nature and magnitude of their cumulative and long-term harmful adverse effects, if any, especially during repetitive incidents.

These accidents generally embrace wider cross sections of corporate workforce for many reasons like changes in affiliation to different activity centres at different times within the corporate activity domain for reasons of situation demanded skill re-distribution (intra-corporate migrations), skill updation, technology modification and updation, entry of new people to the workforce, etc. The exact nature of this category of accident, frequency of their occurrence and the magnitude of their damage/harm potential, etc. depend on the type of industry, prevailing operation environment and infrastructure, skill levels of people, etc. Each industry will carry its own specific accident and cumulative damage potential.

Damage to people and the environment and also loss of property would be incremental and additive in nature which, over a period of time, could either add up to a high figure or could trigger a major accident if ignored. These minor accidents with repetitions could also carry high potential to result in permanent damage to certain organs leading to total loss of certain virgin metabolic features of people rendering them permanently handicapped and/or incapacitated with specific reference to those basic metabolic features. Similarly, such cumulative impacts could also result in permanent damage to the virgin eco-system.

Building Ability to Prevent Accidents

This exercise should start with building a strong knowledge base (Technology Front) which means achieving the following:

- Developing a clear understanding of the reasons that nucleate (sowing the seed), initiate (germination) and trigger (growth and propagation) occurrence of accidents.

How to achieve such an understanding? This would become a practical reality for the organisation only when it proceeds in the following sequence of understanding process:

- Explore and analyse all accident situations purely from scientific viewpoints namely fusing the concept of *Scientific Temper* to analysis process.
  - Therefore, the first and foremost requirement to proceed in this direction is to apply the view points that all accidents are the outcome of a specific process or phenomenon, natural or induced, taking place at the time of incidence of an accident.
  - When we view an accident as a process or a phenomenon, the seventh principle of *Knowledge Management* (Mruthyunjaya, 2011) triggers our thought process by drawing our immediate attention to one of the fundamental principles that highlights what initiates and triggers occurrence of a process or a phenomenon.
    - The seventh principle of knowledge management tells us that "Any event, whether desirable or non-desirable, would take place only when and whenever the situation or the environment around it can support its occurrence and remain conducive for its recurrence and not otherwise".
    - An immediate inference from this basic principle regarding an accident is that an accident would take place only when and whenever the situation or the environment around it is conducive for its occurrence and continues to support its continuance or sustenance.
      - o There should be a participating member.
      - o The environment surrounding the member or prevailing around should encourage and support incidence of an accident.
      - o Wherever the accident belongs to continuing nature the surrounding environment should continue to support its continuance.
      - o Or, whenever an accident recurs/repeats again, a similar environment or surroundings that had supported the occurrence of the accident earlier should once again come to existence.

- This understanding would, in turn, guide us to proceed in the following sequence to understand the reasons for an accident:

  Nucleation

  There should be a seed. This is a basic requirement. We should never forget that without a seed there can be no germination and sprouting.

  Thus, for example, for a fire accident to take place there should be a fuel or a combustible material that can catch fire and burn. There can be no fire without a fuel! The fuel provides the seed for a fire. Here, a fuel is the nucleus.

  This example answers the first derived inference from the seventh principle of knowledge management stated above namely *"Presence of a Participating Member"*.

  We all know that a fire accident can take place not necessarily only in chemical store house or only in a petrochemical industry where we all believe that plenty of potential fuels are available. A fire accident can take place inside an office premises as well where we all know for sure that there will be no conventional fuel. In fact, all combustible materials are potential fuels present in different forms. A fuel could be present in any of the three different physical forms namely a solid, a liquid or a gas. But its physical presence in the vicinity is a basic requirement.

  Similarly, for a fall injury to take place, there should be a reasonably heavy unsecured material located or available at an elevated place from where it can fall when pushed due to vibratory forces or dragged down or there should be a mechanism which can throw a person off his feet or push him with such great force that the person loses his normal balance and falls down.

  For a chemical burn to take place, the availability of a corrosive chemical is a basic requirement.

  Or for a piercing injury to take place a sharp edged material should be flying in the air at high speeds.

  Or for a temporary loss in some sensation or metabolic activity due to high toxicity, the presence of a highly toxic chemical or a bio-active synthetic drug (again a chemical) should be available for inhalation or for ingestion or swallowing is a primary requirement.

These are typical examples that make the point clear namely availability of a nucleus is a basic requirement.

These descriptions further clarify the first derived inference cited above. What is required is just "*Physical Presence of a Participating Member.*" There is no conditional pre-qualifying adjective that specifies any particular form in which the participating member should be present. Incidentally, absence of a pre-conditional/pre-qualifying adjective further tells us that the description *Participating Member* is not confined to one single member. There could be more than one participating members for an accident to take place. The situation or the nature of accident decides the numbers of members needed for an accident to take place. In addition to a fuel, all fire accidents demand another member to actively participate. The second member in this case is oxygen. Normal fire is actually a chemical reaction process. It is actually an oxidation process where oxygen, generally derived from the ambient air, reacts with another material (fuel) to generate an oxide of the chemical that gets burnt. In the absence of requisite quantity of oxygen, even a fire cannot come to existence let alone a fire-accident taking place.

For a crushing impact type of fall injury to take place during an accident two primary requirements exist:

- Physical availability of a non-secured (non-fastened, without protective guards or barricades or containers, etc.) and a heavily weighing material, either as such or placed in a container.
- Its physical location at an elevated height.

  In the absence of height advantage crushing impact type of fall injury cannot take place because it is common sense knowledge that a stationary object located on the floor can never cause such fall accidents. Similarly, more the height more will be the damage/risk potential.

In these types of accidents, there will be another invisible member participating in the accident. This is the gravitational force that adds the requisite momentum to cause the said injury. While different views are expressed to explain the situation, the fact that the magnitude of damage/injury depends exclusively on the actual height from where the weight under consideration falls remains an undisputed reality. Some people tend to describe the height element as part of "conducive environment required for the phenomenon to take place." But unless the gravitational force induced force of momentum acts, damage cannot be caused.

The element of environment that can induce an accident to take place needs to be understood differently. Let us consider an example of a heavy weight falling from a height. Let us suppose that a secured/fastened weight (secured through bolt-nut fastening is placed on an elevated fabricated platform. Let us further suppose that the said activity shop-floor also houses a work station which is located exactly below this fabricated platform and carries out an activity which periodically ejects a highly corrosive moist vapour during the process. This vapour straight reaches the fabricated platform to provide transient corrosive sheath around the same. Let us further suppose that the platform also houses a motorised mechanism for carrying out some mechanised material movement. This is the environment which certainly does not have anything to do with the type of accident that we are considering. What happens over a period of time? A chemist knows the answer. Following sequence of activities take place without being noticed:

- The first and foremost action is the on-set of corrosion of the fabricated platform.
- Corrosion process sets-in at the weakest point of the platform; say a weak weld joint or a joint that had been subjected to heavy stress during fabrication.
- Corrosion of the fabricated joint steadily progresses.
- On a fine day, under the additional steady impact of vibratory forces arising from the motorised mechanism, the entire area gives way and crumbles down due to weight placed on it and causes an accident.

- o Alternately, where the heavy weight alone is fastened with a bolt-nut combination, under the influence of steady vibration, the nut gradually loses its grip to become a weak fastening.
- o Further, corrosive vapours steadily eat away the threads and the nut slips out and the situation moves to "an unsecured load on an elevated platform."

This is typical of environment impact on an accident. Environmental elements do not directly participate in but would indirectly facilitate or support incidence of an accident.

- o Corrosion of fabricated platform or the bolt is just incidental to accident but not integral to it.
- o There is one other aspect of environment to be understood here. Housing of an activity centre that typically ejects corrosive vapour exactly below the fabricated platform is an aspect of process-layout design. Corrosive nature is characteristic of the vapour. As long this particular activity station is located in that specific activity shop-floor corrosive environment continues to prevail and the accident continues to get opportunity to take place though corrosion phenomenon by itself is not integral to the accident.

A flaming combustion demands the presence or availability of flaming fuel namely volatile combustible gases. Other forms of fuels namely a liquid fuels or solid fuels also can give rise to a flaming fire. But the requirement here would be that the solid or the liquid should first undergo low-temperature combustion when flammable volatile gases are released and these gases in turn could burn to give rise to flames.

In some fire accidents, flames burst explosively to multiply the magnitude of fire incident and the attendant difficulty in quenching such explosive fires. For such a phenomenon to take place, liberation of combustible/flammable volatile gases should take place in huge volumes in a short time and in a limited space. At the same time, availability of oxygen to support heavy combustion should be limited. In such situations, the huge volumes of combustible gases build sufficient pressure in a small space within the flame volume and burst open to throw/push/spill the heated volatile gases, under high pressure, far away from flaming area where plenty of oxygen would be available and the flame spreads far away from its fuel source.

Initiation and Triggering

This understanding tells us that mere physical presence of a nucleus (a seed) or a situation that carries a high potential to cause an accident alone cannot ensure incidence of an accident. For an accident to take place there should also be an initiation or triggering process which can ensure that the process of an accident takes a kick start.

Thus, for example, for a fire accident to take place, in addition to the physical presence of a readily combustible volatile fuel, a source of a fire or flame, however small it may be like a spark, splash of a flame, presence of heated glowing surface or particle, etc. should also be physically present. Otherwise, how can huge volumes of highly inflammable volatile liquids, or readily flammable gases, etc. be stored safely?

Accident Catalysts and Promoters

Violent chemical reactions provide typical examples for catalysed and/or promoted accidents. Depending on the nature of reaction involved in the incidence of an accident, the catalyst could be either a specific physical entity or a non-physical entity. These catalysts do not directly participate in the phenomenon of accident but they carry varying degrees of potential to hasten the process. Let us examine the following typical example of thermo-chemical situation that carries a high potential to cause a high-pressure-explosion accident. The interaction between two chemicals called formaldehyde and phenol is exothermic in nature and liberates heat. If the same reaction is carried out in large volumes where removal of generated heat does not take place effectively, then accumulated heat further energises the two reactant molecules and forces them react more vigorously to liberate more heat. In a short time the entire reactant mass enters into reaction and the liberated heat will be of such high magnitude that it converts the total mass to vapours and a high pressure builds in a limited volume and depending on the pressure developed inside, the entire reaction vessel could explode to cause severe chemical burn injuries to people. Here the liberated heat acts both as catalyst and as promoter for the accident to take place.

The magnitude of damage caused in this typical high-pressure explosion accident depends on one other critical invisible parameter which actually serves as a catalyst/promoter in this particular situation. The invisible member here is the *Time Element*. Let us examine the phenomenon a little further to understand the role of time element.

- This is a thermo-chemical reaction.
- The liberated heat further heats-up the reaction mixture.
- With the supply of additional thermal energy, more and more molecules of interacting chemicals get thermally excited and their collision frequency increases. With the result, the number of molecules interacting with each other will increase many fold.
- Increased interaction will liberate further thermal energy which again further activates more molecules and pushes them to the reaction front.
- And the process continues with multiplied intensity. The result is that in a short time interval the amount of thermal energy liberated will be much more than its dissipation capacity. The net result is the entire reaction mass gets heated beyond tolerable limits and the pressure building takes place beyond the tolerance limits of the cooking vessel or the view-glass panes and other accessory fittings and causes them to burst to cause pressure-explosion.
- Thus, the time element actually accelerates the reaction and enhances reaction speed such that people have very little scope to bring the reaction back to normalcy but just witness the explosion.

Time factor here, thus, provides an environment that ensures that the explosion does take place.

In fact, those who remember the nuclear explosions of Fukushima would readily recollect that all the nuclear reactors did not explode simultaneously but with good time gap between explosions of each of the reactors. This is because the time factor that they got was sufficient enough to raise their pressures to explosion levels. But at the same the entire global community of nuclear scientists just witnessed those explosions as they knew that they could do nothing to avert explosions and resulting radiological hazards.

Accident Suppressors and Poisons

A clear understanding of the role of a nucleus, initiator or a trigger and also the catalysts and promoters for an accident would automatically tell us what should be an accident suppressor or a poison. A simple explanation would be that any parameter/factor that eliminates any one of the above three critical requirements for an accident to take place is an accident suppressor or an accident poison.

Dissection Outcome

Thus, with a careful dissection of each and every individual accident and also a potential accident to identify each of the above critical parameters that constitute the *Technology Front* or the *Knowledge Base*, one would now be ready to proceed with working out a detailed mechanism for designing an appropriate *Proactive* or *Preventive Management* to ensure that accidents do not take place. Incidentally, it goes without calling for further discussions that *Preventive Management* and *Control Management (Emergency Preparedness)* are one and same with a slight difference in the perspectives from which they are explored.

This concept can be better understood by examining a live example of an accident. Let us consider a multinuclear accident like for example a fire accident. We know that for a fire to come to existence a minimum of two nuclei namely a fuel and oxygen have to meet together at the interaction phase. In reality, a fire situation may involve more than one fuel. Any other combustible material in the fire scenario would provide that additional fuel source. We also know from the above discussion that identification of nucleus is the starting point in designing an effective preventive mechanism because unless we design a mechanism to quickly isolate the fuel source or sources from the fire scene, quenching of fire would not be easy and effective. There would always be a chance for fire to restart at the immediate next available opportunity particularly because an accident scenario would always provide plenty of hot surfaces for the fuel to once again catch fire. Hot surfaces always provide the necessary catalyst surface where the two interacting molecules of fuel and oxygen meet together to once again catch fire.

Therefore, when we explore a fire phenomenon from the other angle, namely from view points of quenching a fire that has already come to existence, what becomes obvious to us is to ensure that the fire is put on total starvation so that there will be no supply of fuel molecules at the interaction phase and fuel-oxygen interaction that gives rise to a fire stops immediately. In this particular situation, the other interacting molecule namely the oxygen is always supplied from ambient air. It is also a known fact that establishing total control over ambient air is not easy and hence it may not be easy to simultaneously prevent traverse of both interacting molecules towards interaction phase. But at the same time we know that both these two independent nuclei are required for a fire to come to existence. As such, it would always be advantageous to fight a fire situation from both the fronts namely cutting-off fuel molecules as well as oxygen molecules from reaching the interaction phase. It is precisely for this reason that in a fire situation, one has to work towards establishing control over both the routes on a top priority basis. Obviously, any other approach would be less effective in quenching the fire.

Thus, establishing a sound *Knowledge Base* and acting suitably on those details would pave way for designing appropriate accident preventive mechanisms as well as in identifying effective routes for successfully fighting an accident situation. We have already seen from the earlier discussions that for establishing a knowledge base for operations, our thought processes would first be triggered by the seventh principle of knowledge management. We should, however, not forget here that this is just a starting point. Further journey will be smoothened out only when we correctly understand, carefully interpret and diligently practice the requirements of all the ten knowledge management principles (Mruthyunjaya, 2011) to a situation under consideration, and successfully traverse through the path set by knowledge management principles; we could doubly ensure that the knowledge base is suitably anchored and appropriately strengthened.

Knowledge management principles would together tell us the following:

- All activities should be planned for execution only after fully understanding the knowledge that governs them and not with part understanding.
- Knowledge generated and/or acquired for intended purposes should be complete in all respects, doubly checked and ensured for its sufficiency and adequacy for intended purposes; If need be, it should be suitably supplemented with additional knowledge to ensure that the planned activities always yield desired results.
- Knowledge generated and/or acquired for the purpose of planning and execution of activities should be updated and supplemented as and when additional knowledge becomes available and whenever the results demand or the situation necessitates the same.
- Acquiring knowledge is an ever-green, ever-revolutionary and eternal voyage. One should never stop pursuing.
- Any technology can yield its best only when put to work under a specific but unique operation environment. Hence, understanding the uniqueness of ingredients of operation environment and evaluating criticality of processing environment and controls there on is a pre-requisite to manage activity effectiveness.
- The time taken to locate, identify and correct a mistake committed during execution of any activity is much more than the time needed to commit a mistake in haste that is typical of unplanned actions.

If the stipulations of these principles are correctly transformed to an activity environment, then no accident can take place. Yet, the reality of corporate or industrial life is that accidents do take place. This is where the eighth principle of Knowledge Management specifically draws our attention to one of the basic truths of life namely "*At any given point of time, both the occurrence (happening) of a desirable event and non-occurrence of an undesirable or unwelcome event carry an equal chance or an equal opportunity.*" It is this chance element that answers as to why accidents do take place.

When viewed from a different perspective, this principle of chance element always keeps drawing our attention to following facts, rather warns us to remain on our toes for ever:

- ➢ There could always be a gap in our understanding of the governing principles behind a particular process or phenomenon.
  - o Development trajectory traversed by knowledge clearly tells us that it is hard to believe that at any given point of time, knowledge regarding a phenomenon is fully developed and has acquired a status that could be described as *Complete and Total (Perfection Status).*
    - Scientific developments and breakthroughs achieved periodically keep telling us that there were many latent facets of knowledge that were not known earlier and are being explored and expounded now including in those areas where we had a belief that we knew everything.
- ➢ There could always be a gap in our translating the principles to practice.
  - o We have failed to maintain the criticalities of operation environment demanded by the process.
  - o Or, the control equipments or facilities being used are not in a position to maintain the required criticalities of operation environment.

The first of these warnings highlights following two critical aspects of corporate working:

1. The first and foremost is that business corporates should never undermine the importance and significance of technology/knowledge management that would embrace both macro-management and micro-management.

a. Macro-management focuses only on ensuring profitability and maintaining brand equity and quick exploitation of the available technology in an ever dynamic market.

b. Micro-management of technology specifically addresses generation of right quality output at most competitive prices and establishing optimum productivity. This focus generally induces people to explore facilities and infrastructure configuration and associated support services only from enhanced productivity view points and builds a tendency to ignore other aspects including associated risk potentials.

  - The complimentary component of safety management calls for careful identification of key issues related to accident prevention (Tables 5.2 and 5.3).
  - Micro-management also calls for a careful dissection of activities to identify both apparent and latent risk potentials (Tables 5.4, 5.5 and 5.6).
  - The next stage of micro-management is obviously the identification of methods to eliminate or minimise those associated risks and to ensure safe operations.
  - It is a well known fact that accidents do take place due to many unknown reasons. The nature and magnitude of accident situations decide whether they can be successfully controlled and managed internally or external help should be taken.

2. The second one is that skill management is another equally critical activity that can never be ignored particularly skill updation aspects in tune with technological developments and ever changing execution environment, if their activities have to remain ever productive and ever safe. (Refer to table 5.12 for key issues of skill management related to accident prevention).

Hazard Management

This activity area embraces two specific activity spheres:

- Management of operation hazards
- Management of hazardous wastes.

Operation Hazards

The description *management of operation hazards* is also known as *Risk Management* and one should not get confused when these descriptions are interchangeably used in different contexts or on different situations or by different people. All activity shop-floors are generally abreast with some form or the other of operation hazards. The least critical category being the routine stress/fatigue induced hazards related to an office type of work environment. As explained earlier under accident types, most of the industrial activities carry different types of accident risk potential of varying magnitudes depending on their work nature and work culture. Further, as emphasised at many places in these discussions, it is always a good practice to prepare a ready reckoner or a reference matrix (Tables 5.2 – 5.4) that gives a bird's eye-view of accident potential spread across the organisation. Such ready matrices would help organisations in periodically reviewing, updating and fine-tuning of support systems and also emergency preparedness programmes based on experience gained and/or additional knowledge generated.

Table 5.2 Hazard/Accident Reference Matrix

Hazard Potential Across the Enterprise					
Sl. No.	Source of Hazard	Likely Incident	Incident Frequency		
			High	Medium	Low
1	Electrical Service Lines and Accessories - Short Circuits - Overloading - Loose and Open Connections	Electrical Shocks and Fires.			✓
		Electrical shocks of varying magnitudes.		✓	
		Fatal electric shocks.			✓
		Burns of differing degrees.			
		Mild to medium degree			✓
		High degree		✓	

2	Fire - Leakage of Inflammable gases and stored inflammable fuel tanks and other stored flammable liquids. - Storage of combustible stationery materials. - Electric sparks or Weld-sparks in close proximity to combustible materials.	Fires of varying severity		✓	✓ ✓
3	Explosions and Pressure Bursts: - High pressure/high temperature reaction vessels. - Compressed air/gas cylinders. - Fuel and other flammable liquids storage tanks. - Pressure bursts of compressed air,/water and other service lines. - Loss of control on violent chemical reactions leading to generation of excessive pressures and/or temperatures	High pressure impact injuries of differing magnitudes. Severe magnitude Low magnitude Fatal impacts		✓	✓ ✓ ✓
4	Miscellaneous types	Mechanical injuries. (Machineries and Equipments with motorised mechanisms) Minor injuries Fatal injuries Chemical injuries. Biological and virological damages. Minor damages. Fatal damages	✓	✓ ✓	✓ ✓
5	Miscellaneous men and material movement equipments: Lifts, raisers, elevators, hoists, overhead cranes, scaffoldings, portable ladders, chain pulleys, trolleys, etc.	Physical injuries arising from drops, falls, impacts, jerks, etc. due to breakages and/or failures, slips, etc. due to poor maintenance. Minor injuries Fatal injuries		✓	✓

Hazardous Waste Management

A good design of corporate governance demands that there should also be a good system of waste management, though the general belief

Table 5.3 Typical Accident Potential Matrix Across the Enterprise

Accident Potential across the Enterprise												
Potential Sites or locations that can generate Emergency Situations						Impact Magnitude or severity			Emergency Preparation and Measures			
									Emergency Squad			
Sl. No.	Accident Category	Accident Nature		Activity Shop-Floor	Activity Centre	High	Medium	Low	Within the same Shop-floor	From other Shop-floors	External Sources	Mitigation Infrastructure
1	Personnel Accidents	Physical Injuries	Fall from Heights			✓						
			Cuts & Cut Injuries					✓				
			Heavy Impacts & Hits				✓					
			Crushing Impacts			✓						
			Fatality					✓				
		Chemical Injuries	Chemical Burns					✓				
			Toxic Exposure				✓					
			Chemical Explosion				✓					
			Suffocation (Resricted Breathing Air Circulation or Working in Confined Space)					✓				
		Fatality						✓				
		Biological Injuries Or Metabolic Injuries	Permanent damage to Natural Metabolism				✓					
			Permanent loss of Specific Sensation			✓						
			Incapacitation & Permanent Damage to Organs				✓					
			Chronic Viral Infection					✓				
			Fatality					✓				

2	Electri-cal Acci-dents	Burns and				✓					
		Shocks				✓					
		Others					✓				
		Fatality					✓				
3	Fire Acci-dents	Electrical connection and Short-circuits					✓				
		Inflammable Materials - Chemicals			✓						
		Inflammable Materials – Stored Combustible Gas Cylinders			✓						
		Inflammable materials – High speed Diesel			✓						
		Inflammable Materials-Other Fuels				✓					
		Fatality					✓				
4	Envi-ronmen-tal Acci-dents	Air Pollution			✓						
		Water Contamination			✓						
		Land Contamination			✓						
5	Dam-age to Infras-tructure during Fire & Explo-sion Acci-dents	Installed Warehouse Facilities - Stored Flammable Gas Cylinders			✓						
		Installed Warehouse Facilities - Stored Flammable Liquid Fuel Tanks				✓					
		Infrastructure within the Activity Shop-floors – Chemical Reactors					✓				
		Organisational total Infrastructure Depending on Fire and Explosion Spread Profile – Other Combustible and Explodable Materials Held at Different Activity Locations					✓				

6	Damage to Capital Assets during Fire & Explosion Accidents					✓					

Table 5.4 Typical External Sources Causing Accidents

None of the following belong to the category of direct participant in a process but they always support execution of a process. Whenever any of these services fail, they carry a high potential to cause a series of unfortunate incidents within the corporate premises depending on the nature of activities or processes being carried out. Particularly continuing types of chemical processes carry much higher accident potential. If the power supply or coolant-water supply fails during a typical exothermic-chemical reaction of the type discussed earlier, the magnitude of accident and its impact could be anybody's guess.

Sr. No.	Potential Source	Cause	Triggers emergency Elsewhere			Emergency Prepared-ness
			Catalyses some activity being carried out elsewhere	Location	Most likely out-come or Result	
1	Gas Line	Rupture/bursting				
2	Electric Power Supply Line	Failure				
3	Water Supply Lines	Blockage/bursting/rupture				

that prevails in industrial environments is that corporates have to address *"Waste Management Issues"* only if they opt for ISO 14000 certification and not otherwise. What a pity! People equate a good management practice to a system certification process. Even the standard factory act demands a good waste management practice particularly management of hazardous wastes. Most unfortunately, business organisations shy away from this subject as they do not view this subject as an integral component of their activities. While it is an admitted fact that no business establishment likes to generate a waste product or waste their precious input or in-process materials, the harsh truth of the fact is that practically all manufacturing organisations, irrespective of their activity nature, and with rare exception, generate wastes in some form or the other. The only difference from one organisation to another could be their physical quantities, form, type and nature which depend on the

Table 5.5 Accident Management Index Across the Shop-floor

Activity Designation as Understood/Known across the Organisation												
Activity Location Index/Map reference as can be Readily Recognised												
Sl. No.	Shop-floor (Activity Area)	Activity Centre	Nature of Potential Accident	Constituent Members of an Accident (Technology Base)	Actions under Pro-active or Preventive Management	Strategic Actions under Control Management or Emergency Preparedness	Strategic Infra-structure Front					
							Auto Diffusers /Quenchers/By-passes	Emergency Fighting Equipments	Equipment Location	Alarms/ Warning Signals	People/ Activity Centres to be Signalled	Dedicated Teams
1				Identified Nucleators								
				Known Initiators and Triggers								
				Known Catalyst/s and Promoters								
				Known Suppressors and Poisons								
2												
3												

basic nature of corporate activities, process design and the type of input materials used by them. Waste management should always aim at conserving precious natural resources by putting them to useful applications. A responsible person in-charge of scrap yard management should be able to handle these activities.

Business establishments, who have not yet installed a streamlined waste management programme, should take a conscious walk through their scarp-yard where all sorts of materials would be just dumped or thrown here and there to give either a ghastly look, if they are viewing it for the first time and particularly if all the generated wastes are dumped at one common place or at least as a big eye-sore to their operation efficiency. Business establishments hardly realise that an effective waste management mechanism would, in turn, carries a high potential to conserve a lot of precious materials and other resources. Wastes do not carry any specific description. It could be a machinery component, an accessory, finished product, an intermediate product or a process input material. Anything that an executive finds *not-useful* would be declared as waste and just discarded and dumped in the scrap yard.

Waste management mechanism refers to a well designed system of collection, transportation, storage and disposal of different types of wastes generated in-house. The fact that it is a streamlined/organised collection and storage operation, itself ensures that it does not provide for free movement of anybody and everybody into the scrap-yard to throw whatever they feel like but introduces a sort of a control over waste generation and handling processes.

A well configured waste management design incorporates following features:

- A formal declaration of the type of waste, its nature and quality and also the quantity being sent to the yard from the source (an activity centre or section or wing, etc.) of waste generation.
- The formal declaration should also give information like reason for waste generation like process upset, power failure, inability to reuse or reprocess the material either as it is or after some modification of process details to generate a useful output. Such a declaration should be approved by an appropriate authority of the activity-in-charge.
- This declaration or record, in turn, should lead to generation of another record at the yard that gives the following details:
    - Waste generation source.
    - Identified reason for waste generation.
    - Quantity.
    - Nature of waste sent to the yard, whether hazardous or non-hazardous.
    - Recommended method for storage and disposal.
        - Special care or precaution, if any, required to be taken during handling, storage and disposal of hazardous wastes.

  - Recommended PPE to be used, if any, in case of hazardous wastes.
- Date of receipt together with details like storage method adopted, special precautions taken if any during handling or storage or while disposing it-off.

- Naturally, at all points of time scrap-yard management should maintain classified data (Waste Balance Sheet) on both non-hazardous and hazardous types of wastes received by the yard, their respective quantities, nature and storage method, stored location with appropriate designation marks for quick identification, partitioned isolation with locking facility as may be required, etc.
- Yard management should also maintain a list of approved and/or licensed agencies who could be assigned the job of clearing different types of wastes from the yard.
- Similarly, whenever a formal disposal of a specific category waste takes place, a record to that effect should be generated giving details like type of waste cleared, clearing agency together with details of license, destination where final disposal takes place, approval/license details of destination or actual disposal centre, date of disposal, approval and authorisation details, etc.

While all types of process wastes and other types of wastes need not be hazardous in nature, some wastes could always be hazardous by virtue of their form or nature. Thus, for example, while cut pieces of metallic wastes need not be hazardous, wastes with sharp edges would always become hazardous. Wastes from drilling/milling/turning/grinding, etc. operations could readily become hazardous. Toxic/poisonous chemical wastes and containers of such chemicals and their wash liquids are always hazardous. Statutory guidelines prescribe precautions to be taken for handling, storing and disposing-off of different types of hazardous wastes and types of records to be generated. As per these guidelines, disposal of hazardous wastes should always be done through agencies approved for the purpose by appropriate governmental agencies and transported to approved disposal centres only through transporters approved for the purpose.

Waste Generation

Wastes are generated at many places or work centres in a manufacturing unit. Some of the more frequently encountered waste generation centres are the following:

- Incoming material receipt station.
  - o Wastes generation during unloading and from containers.
  - o Fine particulate dusts from powdery materials could readily become air-borne to severely pollute the normal breathing air by raising SPM levels (Suspended Particulate Matter) far above permitted limits to render it a hazardous operation. This would be more critical for dusts from toxic and poisonous chemicals.

    We should not forget here that even if the air-borne dust or particulate matter is not directly toxic, it could become dangerous when either the exposure duration is high or when SPM levels cross dangerous mark. Extra precaution should therefore be taken while working in confined areas.
  - o Residues from containers.
  - o Non-recyclable or re-usable containers.
  - o Packing materials (crates, pallets, boxes, cartons, etc., carrying sharp edged metallic protruders, nails, corrugated pins, metal straps, etc.).
- Internal storage, handling and transfer centres /material conveying mechanism.
  - o Spillages and overflows.
  - o Residues and incomplete transfer from transfer equipments.
  - o Material spoilage during prolonged storage due to exceeding expiry dates, loss of activity or useful cycle life, physical and/or rodent, other macro and/or micro-organisms' infestation, etc.
- Material processing centres.
  - o Material waste during process-upsets, pre-stabilisation stages due to failure of control mechanisms, machineries, ancillary service feed/supply lines, power failure, changeovers, etc.

- o Process rejects/wastes generated due to process sequence/ execution mechanism design.
- Intermediate processed goods handling/storage/transport centres as applicable.
  - o All types of wastes that are similar to the ones generated at goods storage centres.
- Finished goods handling/storage/transport centres as applicable.
  - o All types of wastes that are similar to the ones generated at material storage centres.
  - o Finished goods consumed for test and approval purposes.

Goods waste management mechanism demands that enterprises should carry out a careful analysis and assessment of waste-generation at each and every individual work centre throughout the organisation. A typical approach to carry out such assessment is shown schematically in the following diagram (Figure 5.2). All activity centres should carry out such an exercise very meticulously and carefully identify their process wastes. The basic objective here is to doubly ensure that no form of waste, however small may be its physical quantity, would be left out in the process.

Such evaluations should be quantitative and should also indicate associated hazard nature of generated waste. A typical evaluation format could be as shown in Table 5.6. Preparation and maintenance of such records is a statutory requirement in case of hazardous wastes.

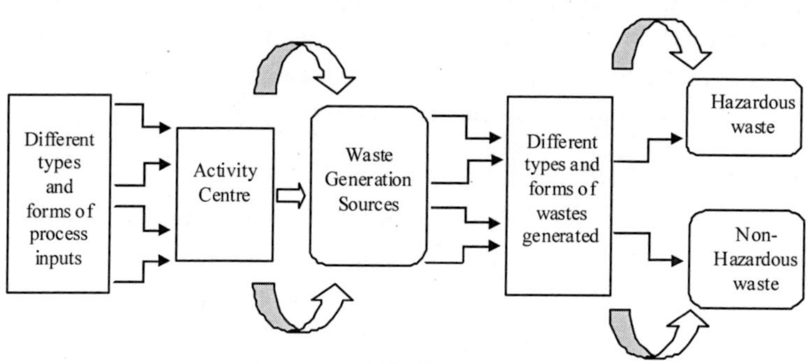

Fig. 5 .2 Typical Scheme for Waste identification

Table 5.6 Waste-Generation Assessment Format

<table>
<tr><th colspan="12">Waste-Generation Across the Enterprise</th></tr>
<tr><th rowspan="3">Sl. No.</th><th rowspan="3">Work Centre</th><th colspan="3">Waste Generated</th><th rowspan="3">Collection and transfer methods practiced</th><th rowspan="3">Storage in Secured Con-tainers, labels, barrica-des, fences, etc</th><th colspan="5">Method of disposal</th></tr>
<tr><th rowspan="2">Quantity</th><th colspan="2">Nature</th><th rowspan="2">Recyclable/ reusable for similar application or for alternate application</th><th rowspan="2">Agency Details</th><th rowspan="2">Details of license</th><th rowspan="2">Disposal approved by</th><th rowspan="2">Date of dis-posal</th></tr>
<tr><th>Hazard ous</th><th>Non-hazar dous</th></tr>
<tr><td>1</td><td></td><td></td><td></td><td></td><td></td><td></td><td></td><td></td><td></td><td></td><td></td></tr>
<tr><td>2</td><td></td><td></td><td></td><td></td><td></td><td></td><td></td><td></td><td></td><td></td><td></td></tr>
<tr><td>3</td><td></td><td></td><td></td><td></td><td></td><td></td><td></td><td></td><td></td><td></td><td></td></tr>
</table>

As per statutory guidelines, the requirement is that different types and forms of hazardous wastes should be handled and stored in a specific way, preferably in separate containers including making necessary arrangement for secondary containers as may be required and kept in isolated and secured place in a designated/dedicated location.

Once this exercise is done, all activity centres should carefully study details/mechanism of waste generation and trace the root cause for the same at source. With this analysis, they can identify ways and means of minimising waste generation at its very source and put them to practice. The key objective being 'minimising waste generation wherever the same cannot be completely avoided through modifying equipment or process design'. This objective should be followed by thorough exploration to identify means and mechanisms to reuse the generated waste either for similar end-use application that can accept modified stringency of requirement or for another well identified application.

Safety Management

This is one other management support mechanism that speaks high of corporate governance. Safety management, as the name indicates, is an activity that gets into details of identifying inherent unsafe situations associated with different activities being carried out by the organisation followed by identifying appropriate safety measures and installing the same at concerned work centres to ensure that safety of organisational workforce is never at stake. Safety management is a statutory requirement under factory act. All industrial establishments have to install such a mechanism and evidence its effective working. For this purpose, a safety structure or a safety committee will have to be constituted. Safety committee should be headed by a senior executive of the organisation and should be assisted suitably by others involved in the process. The committee should comprise of representatives from all concerned activity wings that carry a good potential to create unsafe work conditions. One of them should function as secretary to the committee and should suitably coordinate and organise safety-committee meetings at predefined time intervals to discuss in depth all the agenda matters prepared for the purpose. Agenda for discussion should include among other things, reports of safety audits, unwelcome incidences and their cause analysis together with remedial measures established for preventing recurrence of such incidences.

One of the prime assignments, members of this committee should handle, is preparation of exhaustive *Job Safety Analysis* for all activity centres of their respective activity divisions. A typical *Job Safety Analysis* format is given in Table 5.7. This exercise involves a good understanding of the technology that governs processes and also the process environment together with skill needs for satisfactory execution of the job. This exercise should be followed by careful analysis of available skills and identification of additional skills needed at the centre to safely execute the job. The committee should also recommend desired safety requirements for the activity division and follow-up with the division to evolve satisfactory measure to enhance operation safety of the centre. Such improved or additionally installed safety measures should be audited for their effectiveness.

EHS Management

This is a comprehensive complimentary component of organisational safety management system. EHS system explores all activities from combined perspectives of environment safety as well as operators' health and safety angles. Each and every job being executed in the corporate premises is examined holistically from EHS considerations. That is, each and every individual component or member of equipments or machineries, operations and operation sequences used for job processing, job support facilities or infrastructure components

Table 5.7 Typical Job-Safety-Analysis Format

Activity Division : Shop-floor										
Work Centre										
Sl. No.	Work Station and Actual Exe-cution step	Hazard or Unsafe Situation		Incidence History or Fre-quency	Most Likely Cause for Creating Unsafe Situation			Identi fied Preven tive Measu res	Effective ness of Preventive Measures	Audit Obser vation
		Apparent - Clearly Observ able	Latent - Not Obvi-ous to the Naked Eye but Potentially Exists		Equipm ent Failure	Design Limita tion	Handling or Execution Lapses and Mistakes			
1										
2										
3										

and also all other components that constitute job-execution environment are carefully dissected to identify, both apparent and latent potential to cause adverse impacts, if any, on either the environment around or the people around.

EHS system design and administration calls for identifying a well qualified senior executive having good overall knowledge of all jobs being executed in the premises to function as chief EHS coordinator. The chief EHS coordinator should be vested with full/adequate authority on all matters regarding EHS design and practice enforcement. If the chief EHS coordinator also has a good working exposure to different types of industrial environments, it would be highly beneficial for system management because he can readily visualise the types of risks people are exposed to during job execution. He can also project the type of risk environment people can create for themselves as well for their co-workers. Depending on the organisational activity nature and complexity and also widely spaced distribution of different activity centres at different places away from each other, chief EHS coordinator could be suitably assisted by departmental EHS coordinators.

Job Safety Analysis is the starting point for designing EHS system. With this data as the take-off point, EHS systems should next further dissect the hazard element shown under column three in Table 5.7 independently from three viewpoints namely, environmental considerations, operators' health considerations and operators' overall safety considerations. Outcome of such a dissection should give rise to preparation of EHS matrix for the organisation (Table 5.8) and enable EHS coordinators to identify appropriate safety-protection measures in consultation with system designers and process executives. A comprehensive documentation of EHS analysis and administration mechanism followed to ensure satisfactory practice of appropriate safety-protection measures together with necessary work instructions for each of the safety executions and supporting records' formats constitutes EHS Manual for the organisation. Satisfactory administration of EHS system calls for periodical reviews of satisfaction-level of EHS effectiveness at regular intervals. Reviews should explore opportunities for continuous improvement in EHS design and enforcement mechanism.

Such reviews should be suitably scheduled at appropriate intervals and should be carried out by people who are directly responsible for safe execution of jobs. EHS (review) committee should comprise of both job administrators as well as job executors (workers)

Table 5.8 Typical EHS Matrix for the Organisation

EHS Issues Across the Organisation											
Sl. No.	Activity Shop-floor and Activity Station	Nature of Activity	Areas of Concern								
			Aspects of Environmental Concern			Aspects of Health Concern			Aspects of Safety Concern		
			High	Medi-um	Low	High	Medi-um	Low	High	Medi-um	Low
1					✓			✓			✓
2				✓		✓			✓		
3			✓			✓			✓		
4					✓		✓				✓
5			✓				✓			✓	

Knowledge Management for Safety

The subject of technology management is generally viewed from the considerations of achieving higher productivity; increased operation efficiency; sustainability in an ever vibrant and ever dynamic global environment and to top-it-up, capped with ensuring maintenance of competition edge over others in the field. There is no second opinion on these considerations. However, when we explore this subject from its complementary-component-viewpoints of good governance namely, the safety environment that needs to be created and maintained while translating the technology to live shop-floor practices; it becomes clear that we should simultaneously examine each and every individual activity step from safety considerations (Tables 5.3 – 5.5) with respect to all the five constituent components of safety-aspect shown in Figure 5.3. Each and every activity shop-floor in an industrial corporate where many activities would be simultaneously being carried out should go through this sort of an exercise and prepare safety-evaluation charts for their operations.

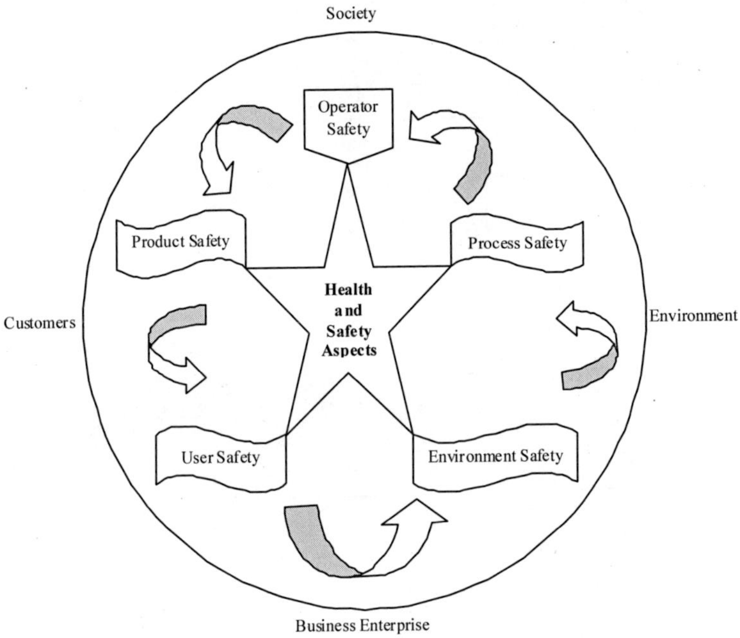

Figure 5.3 Full Circle of Safety-Cycle

The secret of success in safety management essentially hovers around a thorough understanding of a work situation that inherently carries a high risk element either due to basic design of work environment configuration or due to practice methodology (Figures 5.5 – 5.6 and Tables 5.9 – 5.10).

Safety management also calls for generation of many new and additional facets of operation knowledge and technology knowledge that could be suitably translated to transform the prevailing work environment to safer work environment. The true strength of such a mechanism essentially comprises of two complementary knowledge spheres:

- Knowledge of Safety Performance Requirements.

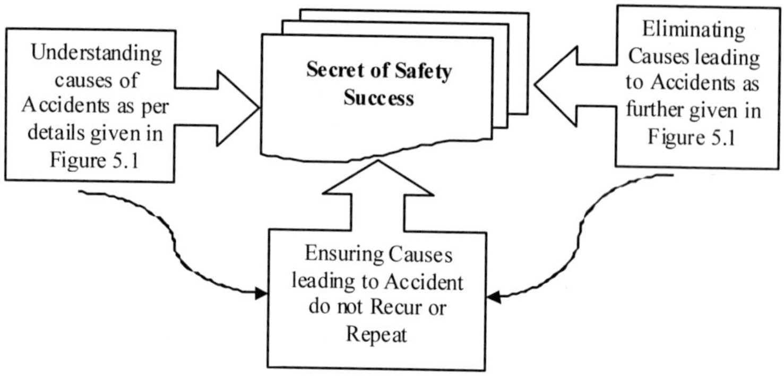

Fig. 5.4 Safety Success Parameters

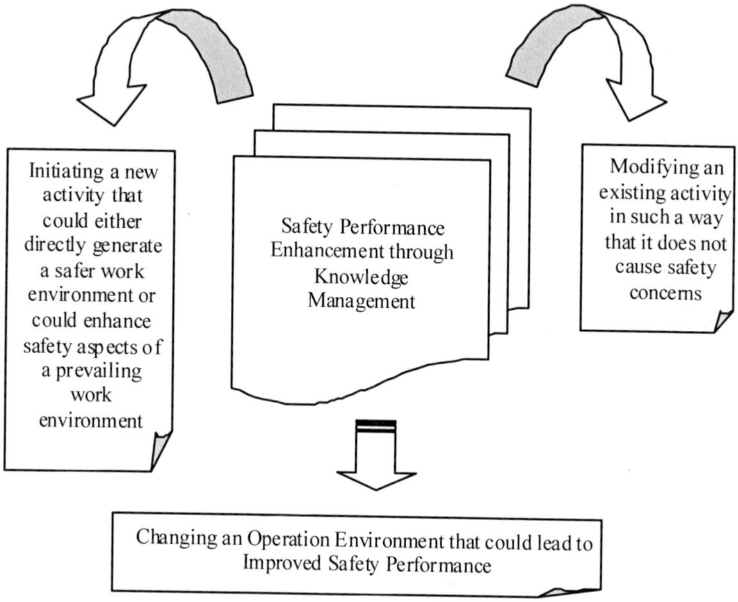

Fig. 5.5. Knowledge Management for Enhanced Safety Performance

- Right type of technology translation methods and their sequences to be followed.
  - o Different alternatives for safe execution.

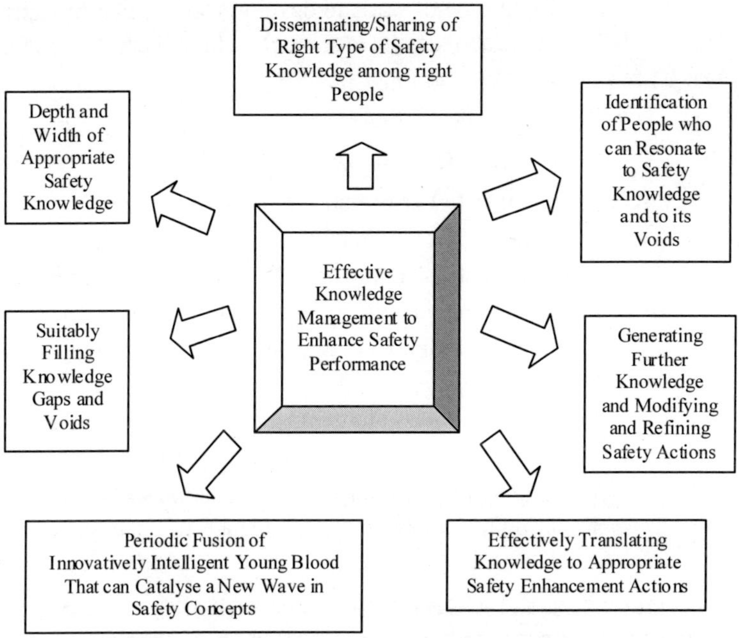

Fig. 5.6 Effective Knowledge Management to Enhance Safety Performance

- Right type of processing equipments and facilities to be used for technology translation purpose, their criticalities, limitations and maintenance.
- Right type of execution skills to be used for technology translation purpose including the type of manoeuvrability skills to be used for handling certain critical situations during the execution process.
    - o Right type of skills to recognise and identify indications leading to equipment and facility breakdown.
    - o Right type of skills to recognise and identify deviations in practice methodology that could eventually lead to incidence of unfortunate incidents.
    - o Right type of skills to establish reliability of processing equipments and facilities and process inputs.

- o Right type of skills to develop clarity regarding any of the above failures or combinations thereof through:
    - What to Look for
    - Where to Look for
    - How to Look for

➢ Knowledge of Safe Performance Failure Situations.

- Thorough understanding of execution skill limitations and/or limitations in personnel approach to perfection.
- Thorough understanding of limitations of processing and control equipments and facilities and their fatigue limits.
- Thorough understanding of correlation between input variations and their impact on safety performance.
- Thorough understanding of actions, action sequences and action points for reversing incidence of an unfortunate incident and to bring the process back to normalcy.

Table 5.9 Some Key Aspects of Concern for Preventing Accidents

Knowledge Facets to be Explored
• An unbiased dissection of all activities including their inputs, execution methodologies, handling of process outputs and their application environment to identify apparent and latent risk potential with specific reference to each of the five sub-components of safety aspect. - Careful identification of characteristic features of inputs to a process with specific reference to their apparent or latent accident potential either alone or in combination with other ingredients to the process or under the influence of operating/processing environment. - Careful identification of deviations from required specifications of inputs that could, in turn, create an unsafe situation whenever deviations cross certain safely-tolerance limits. - Identifying-activity-specific safety precautions including incorporating necessary safety automation. - Identifying activity-specific knowledge gaps in practices across the organisation and projecting associated and/or impending risks if gaps in knowledge practices are not suitably filled. - Identifying effective methods to fill knowledge voids and making good all identified knowledge gaps. - Identifying activity-specific mistakes committed by unskilled people and the accident potential those mistakes carry.

- Preparing activity-centre-wise or activity-nature-wise risk matrix across the organisation to educate people and to ensure their active participation in meticulously enforcing required safety measures.
- Quantifying, where practical, the magnitude of associated risk in each of the sub-component areas and projecting the damage on a relative time-scale.
    - Working out 3D image projection of damages caused to environment wherever environmental safety is at stake.
    - Making a quantitative assessment of cumulative and/or long-term adverse effects on individual safety component.
    - Exploring simulated 3D models to confirm projections.
- Identifying effective measures to counter all those identified factors that could adversely affect each one of the five safety elements.
    - Assessing effectiveness and reliability of countering measures.
    - Identifying and updating those counter measures in line with technology-advancement.
- Clarity of purpose or reasons for which fresh knowledge is being sought and precise nature or aspect of knowledge that is required to be generated and/or supplemented to ensure operation safety.
    - Which aspect of safety is under consideration here?
- Identification of competent and dedicated people who could initiate and organise collection of required knowledge that would have a direct bearing on safety elements of an operation.
- Methods followed to ensure that those people posses required competency and have been provided with necessary facilities and also the required intellectual freedom and infrastructure for generating the required knowledge.
- Methods followed to confirm the righteousness/appropriateness, suitability and adequacy of information being collected for the purpose for which a particular knowledge is being generated.
- Is new knowledge generation a standard activity in the organisation or is it just an activity taken-up only to address the needs of a specific unfortunate-incident?
- Methods followed to identify activity centres that are required to use fresh/additional knowledge and the application purpose for the same enabling those centres in transforming their activities and activity environment to become safer. Methods followed to ensure that fresh/additional knowledge is used for the right purpose and in the right way and is free from flaws to ensure that generation of fresh/additional knowledge serves the purpose of doubly ensuring that transforming an activity centre safer than what it was earlier.
- Methods followed to effectively share the knowledge across the entire activity shop-floor or the entire organisation as may be desirable and in particular with all those who are required to put the same to practice.
- Methods used to ensure that necessary and adequate knowledge percolates down and spreads across all needy levels and appropriate knowledge practices prevail throughout the organisation and total safety regime ushers in.

- Methods followed to ensure that the entire work premises remain safe for ever from the considerations of all the five individual components of safety aspect.

Table 5.10 Typical Safety Planning

Sl. No.	Key Elements of Safe Operations
1.	Preparation of detailed activity flow charts showing operation sequences and activity phasing to ensure that an unsafe work environment does not get a chance to come to existence.
2.	Preparation of detailed material flow charts covering all materials including accessories, spares, services and packing materials, (and their inherent or latent safety features together with required safety measures, if any needed).
3.	Superimposing material flow charts onto process flow charts showing clearly which material or service (activity) enters the main stream and at which stage of operation so that safety element is never at stake.
4.	Indicating appropriately wherever materials move parallel or activities take place concurrently ensuring that safety aspect is never ignored at any of the activity stage.
5.	Carefully examining requirements/specifications of all inputs, raw materials, services and intermediates and ensuring that they are well within safety limits.
6.	Evaluating each parameter for its impact on process safety effectiveness/efficiency and on product safety features and then fixing specifications and tolerances for each input individually.
7.	Evaluating service or utility elements the same way as a raw material is evaluated for its suitability for safe operations
8.	Evaluating criticality of processing environment and controls to doubly ensure that safety aspect is never jeopardised.
9.	Examining and evaluating each process parameter for likely variations in its safety tolerances.
10	Assessing quantitatively the influence of variations of each of the process parameter on overall safety features.
11.	Fixing maintainable tolerances and rejection levels for each activity output to ensure that safety aspects are never compromised.
12.	Analysing critically the significance of each of the output parameter with particular reference to end user safety requirements.
13.	Identification of most appropriate process controls, listing out the types, levels and frequency of verifications that are required to be carried out at different operation stages and at different activity centres to establish conformance to safe-control requirements.
14.	Fixing check levels and verification methods to ensure that people do not neglect safety requirements.

15. Identification of necessary corrective actions wherever needed and enabling appropriate activity centres to install the same to ensure that unsafe situations do not recur.
16. Examining the types of additional controls that can be introduced to ensure better operation environment that ensure total safety.
17. Evaluating quantitatively and establishing the types of additional safety performance control features or their enhanced control levels that would help in widening safe-application range.
18. Identification of methods for improving safety performance levels through better design.

Table 5.11. External Support in case of Emergencies

Sl. No.	Help		Medical Support			Fire Brigade	Transport Facilities	Social Service Organisations
			Ambulance	Doctors	Hospitals			Nature of Help Available
1	Co-ordinators							
2	Contact Numbers							
3	Facility Available							
	Neighbouring Industries							
	In the Town							
4	Organisa-tional Infrastructure and Backup	First Aid						
		Facility Location						
		Medical Team						
		Facility Location						
		Hospitali-sation						
		Facility Location						
		Status						
		Co-ordinators						

Execution Skill for Safety

We have explained at many places in these discussions that all accidents, whether major or minor, could ultimately be traced to some individual or the other as a result of a commission or an omission. Whether a commission or an omission, both have their origin in people. It is only an individual who can commit a mistake either unintentionally or unknowingly.

Let us now briefly explore a few activity-related issues from the viewpoints of safety considerations.

Each individual with a high potential for inventions, innovations, and improvisations, is an institution by himself due to differing academic, professional, socio-economical and cultural backgrounds. As such, there would be a natural variance in their participation and performance levels. Integrating these individual institutions with great invisible potential into an invincible corporate force would pave way for perennial success of safety management through steady performance enhancement. Performance enhancement could be achieved through appropriate knowledge deployment that would ensure both intellectual involvement and also emotional involvement (collectively both these two spheres stand for the skill power and the will power of the workforce). When both these spheres are satisfactorily addressed people would build a common concern for corporate safety and they always work towards systematically enhancing safety performance. Once appropriate skill power is built and necessary decision power gets vested in people, creating a safe work environment may not pose any difficulty because people themselves would identify and acquire the right technology and manage the right type of infrastructure needed including identifying and planning necessary changes and improvements as may be needed to ensure maintenance of ever safe-work-environment.

Periodical training in basic technology and its development would help in preventing technology obsolescence causing safety concerns. It will also help in maintaining a dynamic balance of skills in a true operation environment where skilled and experienced people keep deserting the enterprise for many reasons, personal or professional, and the new incumbents may not straight away fit into the main activity stream because of their differing exposures. Continuous training also helps in building good multi-skills in people which is necessary to maintain safe-work-environment. Knowledge of people drives them to become enterprising. However, the level of their entrepreneurship depends on the depth of knowledge they have acquired. An energised Employee will bear the *Labour of Safety Conception* and *Delivers Safe Performance*! Unsafe operation (activity) boundaries prevail wherever there is lack of activation energy. Globally pervasive knowledge only can provide energy necessary to transform unsafe activity domains with boundaries to boundary-less safe activity domain.

However, before proceeding further in exploring activity-related-skill-oriented issues one should keep in mind two critical phases of execution skill. One of them is competence. Competence, should be understood as representing a suitable combination of three basic elements namely knowledge, process/activity manoeuvrability and experience. The other one is what is normally described as skill. Skill is always an acquired feature, acquired through exposure to relevant technology together with an understanding of the governing principles behind its operation and practical realities. Skill can therefore be built through appropriately designed training programmes. The training should comprise of both basic theory and the necessary practice.

- ➢ Can something go wrong in this activity step whether due to a wrong action committed by people or due to failure of an operation mechanism or due to unidentified changes in input materials or services or execution environment, etc.
  - o If something goes really wrong, can it trigger an accident either immediately or with a time gap or in a different activity centre where the job undergoes further processing or elsewhere when put to application.
    - Which element of human commission or omission is involved in this action?
  - o Could there be shortage of execution-skill among people carrying out this activity leading to incidence of mistake, which, in turn, could lead to an accident?
    - What are the different types of mistakes people could commit due to lack of appropriate skill? (Refer to Table 5.12 for a few typical features of works carried out by unskilled people.)

        - What types of execution skills are required of people to carry-out activities safely? (Table 5.13).
    - Are processing machineries and/or control equipments designed and fabricated and/or manufactured to be rugged enough to withstand other external variations and continue to provide required safety?
        - Can process inputs deviate too much from tolerances?
            - Why the normal/natural variations of process inputs under real-life situations not considered while designing or manufacturing of process equipments for sustained safe performance?
        - Can process control parameters stipulated by process-design, deviate too much from tolerances to cause an unsafe situation?
            - Can process control equipments/instruments/ devices fail during operation and lead to unsafe situation?
    - What can happen under each one of these situations?
- Is there any latent or hidden aspect associated with either the inputs or processing environment that can trigger incidence of an unhappy situation due to its inherent risk potential?
    - Can the latently inherent risk potential blow-up under some changed circumstances?
    - What needs to be done to prevent incidence of unhappy events due to blowing-up of latently inherent risks?
- Is the inherent risk potential recognised earlier and appropriate preventive/safety mechanisms established?
- Was the inherent risk potential not known earlier because necessary base knowledge or data had not been either collected or generated earlier?

Table 5.12 Accident Risks Associated with Unskilled Workforce

Risks due to Lack of Adequate Knowledge

Sl. No.	Risk Nature
1.	• Can ensure shop-full of risks
2.	• People are not aware of what care should be taken to carry out activities without causing risk for either self or for others in the shop-floor.

	Risk Nature
3.	• Even when informed, they do not fully understand and do not know how to carry out a safe execution.
4.	• They do not have access to right information about safety aspects of operations and they cannot improve on their safety performance.
5.	• Right kind of analytical data is not generated and no one knows what went wrong during a particular accident and unsafe environment continues to prevail.
6.	• People are not aware of significance of certain control criticalities and hence they do not take safety precautions/ preparations serious.
7.	• People are not aware of methods of reversing a risky situation to one of normalcy.

Risks due to Lack of Adequate Execution Skill

Sl. No.	Risk Nature
1.	• People cannot handle operations independently and cannot recognise changes in process details - Unsafe work environment.
2.	• People cannot create and ensure a safe work environment in their work-station as they cannot safely handle their processing equipments, accessories and associated infrastructure. Unsafe work-station.
3.	• People set process-controls only by practice or observation and cannot control variations when noticed – Unsafe work-station.

Risks due to Non-committed Approach

Sl. No.	Risk Nature
1.	• Safety aspects of execution are not taken serious. People do not care for minor and non-serious types of accidents taking place frequently.
2.	• People do not care to understand the criticalities of safe process control limits. People attend to safety preparations only when supervised and specifically pointed out or enforced.
3.	• People do not collect necessary safety information before starting an activity and they do not identify and/or organise right kind of safe-execution facilities.
4.	• People do not check satisfactory working conditions of safety devices before starting an activity. When things go wrong, they highlight some operation limitations.

5.	•	They just project their imagination, impression and opinion and start working. When things go wrong, they highlight some other unknown mistake.
6.	•	Similarly they do not bother to check suitability of other inputs to process but would ever be prepared to blame input supply source.
7.	•	People show poor response whenever others point-out mistakes in their operations that carry a high potential to lead to unwelcome situations.
8.	•	People get easily distracted towards other activities and have a tendency to neglect safety precautions of their own activity centres.

Risks of Design Origin

Sl. No.		Risk Nature
1.	•	Inadequate/incorrect identification of safety data related to the processes being designed.
2.	•	Improper identification of process equipments and process inputs and service accessories for translating the design to safe, live shop-floor practices.
3.	•	Improper evaluation of continuing safe performance of process facilities and associated infrastructure in the prevailing shop-floor practice environment.
4.	•	Improper evaluation of process complexity that could lead to inadvertent creation of unsafe work environment.
5.	•	Inadequate identification of process variables that could lead to creation of unsafe work environment.
6.	•	Inadequate identification of process safety controls and their specifications or tolerances.
7.	•	Improper identification of process controls and tolerance limits.
8.	•	Improper identification of process safety precautions/ preparations to be adhered to during the process or before start of the process.
9.	•	Improper identification of safety issues associated with the product during service or application.

Table 5.13 Execution- Skill Vs. Safety-Impact Correlation

Sl. No.	Skill Component	Impact Area (Where it Reflects)
1.	Live Exposure (Experience)	Designing for Safety
2.	Knowledge Bank	
3.	Collective Performance	Ensuring a Safe Environment Across the Organisation
4.	Collective Approach	
5.	Execution Mechanism	
6.	Risk Management (Problem solving)	Quickly Normalising an Unsafe Situation
7.	Communication	Ensuring that Damage is Kept to Minimum
8.	Approach to Accomplishment (Result Orientation)	
9.	Change Management	Quick Response to new Safe-management Techniques/tools to Prevent onset of Periodical Unsafe Situations and to Improve Overall Safety Environment Across the Organisation
10.	Decision Management	Meeting Safety Challenges
11.	Discretion Management	Manoeuvring Unsafe Situations
12.	Innovation	Addressing Safety Requirements Uniquely

Why Accidents Take Place

Purely from fundamental scientific perspectives an accident can be readily visualised as an event taking place at any given point of time. However, unlike other events which are normally planned and executed as per pre-designed execution scheme, an accident is never a planned and executed event. It always remains an unplanned one. Therefore, accidents take place as a result of certain commissions or omissions discussed in Table 5.12 without any specific intention. In fact, as explained in this table, an accident is always an outcome of a combination of many commissions and omissions which is typical of improper and/or incorrect planning and execution. As explained earlier under accident catalysts and promoters, the latent element of *Time* plays a very crucial role in all accidents. We have also seen earlier that the absence of control over this latent element (time) is the key driving force which ensures that an unfortunate incident takes place. Absence of control over time ensures that many reactions and their corresponding response reactions including further catalysed reactions take place at such high speeds that people fail to recognise or know the same or remain helpless spectators for the event. Naturally, they totally surrender to such uncontrolled situations leading to incidence of unfortunate events. On certain occasions, when more knowledgeable people come to know of the seriousness of a situation and apprehend the likelihood of an accident, the negligibly small time factor at their disposal renders them completely helpless to initiate any in-situ corrective actions that could reverse the situation to bring it back to normalcy. And the accident does take place.

While absence of control over the time element is one reason behind accidents, absence of knowledge also plays a decisive role in the incidence of many accidents. In such situations, people would be handling systems whose complete knowledge like what are the key driving forces and what are the secondary forces and what are all the annulling forces is not known to them. As such, they will be playing with part knowledge which ensures that people would not be in a position to intellectually involve and/or interact with the process and hence keep playing with chance elements which may not always come to their rescue. Accidents keep happening.

Emergency Preparedness

Emergency preparedness represents a well thought out action plan or a blue-print of actions to be initiated in accident saturations. Such preparedness should lead organisations to designing and evolving of most appropriate and effective actions that should be put to place at the time of an accident. As explained earlier emergency fighting should aim at minimising injuries, damages and losses. Merits and usefulness of these plans depend only on how efficiently, quickly and effectively they are able to satisfactorily achieve the following key objectives:

1. Taking full control over the situation by identifying means to annul the incident and to immediately bring the situation back to normalcy.
    a. Ensuring and administering, as may be required, that suitably co-ordinated actions and movements are carried out without loss of time so that confusion and chaos do not rule the situation.
        i. Very few organisations realise that in the absence of such pre-thought-out preparedness, confusion and chaos rule accident situations leading to greater losses and damages.
        ii. One of the first and foremost actions that need to be attended on top-most priority is to ensure that no one is hurt in the incident.
        iii. Whenever people are injured in the accident, they should be attended on top-most priority and should be provided necessary help that can give them quick relief. If the situation demands injured people should be shifted to a safe place away from the accident scenario or a secure location away from accident site to prevent further injury.
            - Immediate first-aid treatment should be provided by suitably trained people available in the premises.
            - Additional medical help should be organised at the earliest including shifting seriously injured

people to nearest hospital, as may be required, where full-fledged medical treatment could be provided.

2. Quickly locating the source of problem that triggered the incidence followed by elimination and/or routing out at source, all those reasons so that accidents do not get a chance to continue to make its presence felt for long.
   a. Effectively isolating and/or cordoning-off the source of problem where practical and desirable.
      i. Wherever problem source isolation is not within the ready reach of people or not practical, quenching the intensity of the situation so that the impact gets diluted soon and steadily disappears.
      ii. Knowledge and expertise to quickly decide on the modus operandi is a ready handy tool.
3. Whenever an accident takes place for reasons other than already known and identified and barricaded ones, quickly identifying those fresh/additional reasons and locating their problem sources for initiating necessary action plans so that the situation is quickly annulled and reversed to force accident situations find a natural decay or death.

It goes without saying that evolving an effective emergency preparedness plan calls for a thorough understanding of the mechanism of processes that are being carried out together with details of guiding basic principles. When diligently carried out, this exercise should result in evolving the most appropriate *Annulling Mechanism* namely, identifying the most effective means and methods to successfully handle/fight the situation and to bring it under complete control immediately. Evolution and implementation of an appropriate annulling mechanism will, in turn, depend only on how effective would the organisation be in developing and/or building the right kind of *Scientific Temper* across the entire organisational cross section. (Scientific temper could be built by a well understood, carefully identified, logically developed and sequenced, judiciously analysed and diligently selected thought inputs for the purpose of their interaction. - Very surprisingly and most unfortunately absent in many intellectuals also).

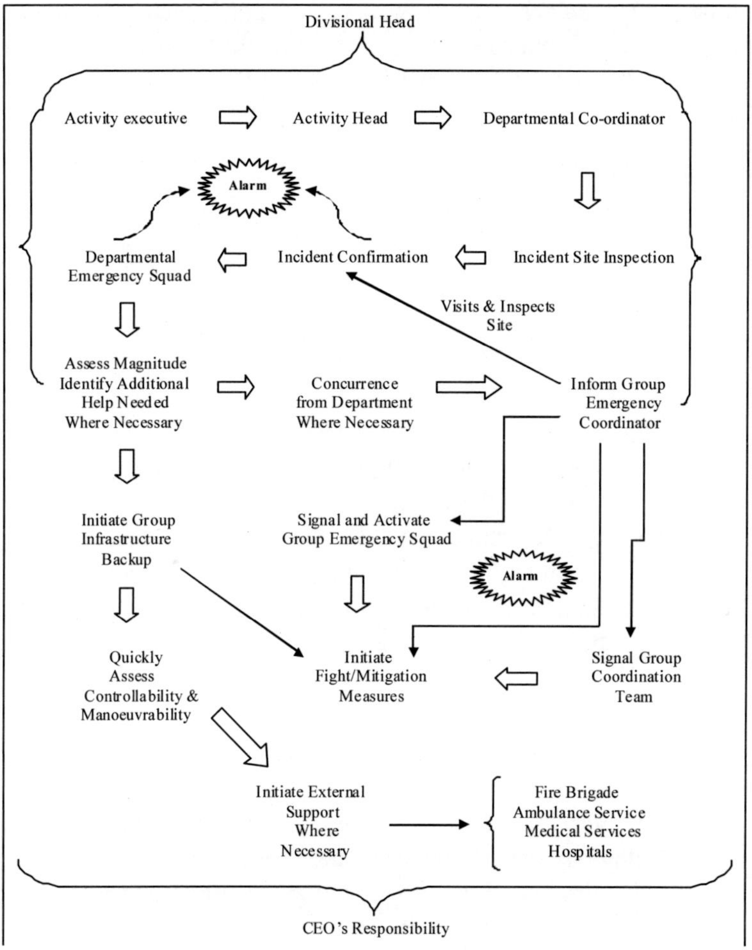

Figure 5.7 Communication/Action Flow During Emergencies

It is well understood fact that any particular situation can only respond to impacts of certain human actions but cannot change the impacting environment on its own thus displaying its ability to correct a situation. Naturally, people involved in manoeuvring a situation should share the additional responsibility to ensure that all processes are guided in the right direction and are conducted in the right way so that accidents do not get a chance to appear on the scene. Designing operations to make them very rugged with lots of cushioning factors not to get impacted by small or minor changes in any of the variable parameters is one of established routes for safe operations. The details given in Tables 5.9 and 5.10 when meticulously followed and practiced, accidents rarely happen.

Accident Management

Since emergency plan refers to post-incident administrative activities it will have to be suitably co-ordinated and carried out as per broad guidelines given below:

- ➢ Well laid out accident-management (incidence-fighting) action plans that do not give any scope for unplanned/instantaneous/ spurious actions.
    - o Only planned, streamlined, synchronised and/or suitably phased out and appropriately coordinated activities should be carried out.
    - o People should not take their own decisions and act accordingly. It would minimise chaos and confusions.
    - o Some actions may have to be taken-up simultaneously but with proper coordination and synchronisation and some actions may have to be suitably phased-out to achieve strategically set objectives.
    - o All decisions should be well defined and well organised to avoid confusions and chaos to rule the scenario.
- ➢ If a disciplined action scenario has to prevail in an accident situation, line of communication, line of responsibility and also the line of actions, whether concurrent or phased-out, will have to be well thought-out, clearly defined and documented. Such a document is generally referred to as *Emergency Plan.*
    - o If this situation has to come to place, line of communication and action sequence will have to be clearly defined. A typical communication scheme is shown in Figure 5.7. Organisational activity nature and structure decide the details of communication mechanism to be practiced.
    - o Control management demands a suitable control structure. A control structure tells us who would do what in an

emergency situation and who would give instruction to whom and who would organise and control all activities and their sequences. Control structure could be drawn on lines similar to the communication chain shown in Figure 5.7. Accident-Nature-Specific independent Control Structures (Fig.5.9) are always beneficial. In fact they constitute fulfilment of a formal requirement.

- o Each of these administrative actions should be backed with well defined responsibility for different actions and should be supported with necessary infrastructure.

Emergency Plan

Emergency plan refers to organisational policies, procedures and practices for coping with an emergency situation either within its own premises or outside in the society. An emergency plan describes a set of well laid out activities that should be executed during emergency situations. All activities which an emergency plan embraces aim at only two key issues namely protecting people and property.

There is a general belief that people working inside a factory and/or business premises know their jobs well and therefore they would ever be prepared to face or handle emergency situations that could come-up within their premises. While it could be true to some extent that people know their jobs well particularly because they are trained well to do their jobs, the belief that they would also know, by-default, how to handle an emergency situation need not always be true. This is primarily because people would invariably be trained to do a good job. They would acquire necessary competence to explore the process of executing a job from different perspectives of efficiency, effectiveness, competitiveness and compatibility with ongoing and contemporary technological developments and innovations. Some executives could also go out of the way to tunnel into annals of new and emerging technological innovations taking place around the world. But, most unfortunately none of these scientific/technological explorations or other details covered during regular training programmes focus on how to handle emergency situations that could come-up during execution of their processes. People would generally be lost in their routine and would be completely caught unawares in case of accident situations.

An emergency plan should highlight the following:

- Well identified, accident-nature-specific, sequence of operations and clearly identified concurrent actions and also clearly defined/identified, action points or fighting locations.
- Well identified accident-specific fighting equipments/facilities and their locations (example: location map of first-aid kits, fire huts, fire tenders, high pressure water hoses, ambulances, medical service centres, clearly demarcated and designated assembly areas for safe gathering of people, accessibility/approach routes etc.) and also other technology-backed infrastructure available for fighting the situation should be described.
    - The type and nature of infrastructure available in-house as well as in other neighbouring industries or in the town should be clearly identified.
    - Evacuation, escape routes and assembly areas should be highlighted.
- Suitably trained and skilled fight-squads equipped with appropriate PPEs.
    - Identification of accident-nature-specific trained fight squads like for example for toxic explosions/bursts, explosive fires, etc. should be clearly defined.
- Well identified/defined methods of incident-intensity dilution and/or diffusion measures for eliminating accident scenario.
- Carrying out well laid out checks for ensuring that accident scenario does not re-emerge once again.
- Preparing necessary reports.
- Initiating appropriate preventive measures to arrest further incidences.

Operation Criticality

Further, as explained below, initially and in all not-well managed emergency situations, chaos and confusions invariably rule the scenario. It is to break this dangerous scenario and to make headway towards rescue and salvage operations a well laid-out emergency plan that defines methods to handle the situation and also specifies the role and responsibility of each individual assigned to handle different aspects of mitigating the damages is called for. The secret of success in effectively handling an emergency operation depends exclusively on how quick are the people in a position to contain the situation and reverse it to one of normalcy especially because time element becomes very critical for their success (Figure 5.8).

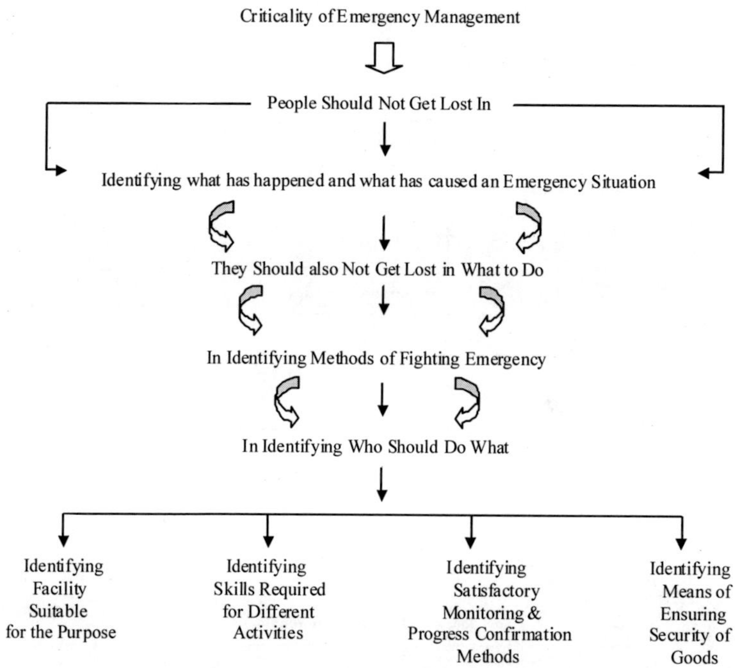

Fig.5.8 Key Elements of Time Management During an Emergency

Emergency Structures

The very fact that an emergency plan aims at minimising the damages caused and/or suffered during an emergency situation, it needs to be very carefully and cautiously handled. This stipulation demands that there should be a proper organisation to administer, supervise and control these operations. This need, in turn, necessitates configuring a formal emergency structure. Such structures are formally known as *Emergency Teams*. While the head of the organisations should be the supreme commando for emergency management, from practical viewpoints configuring accident-nature-specific independent and well trained emergency teams is a basic necessity.

Identifying a formal *Site Emergency Coordinator* would be the starting point in this process. He should be assisted by some more members who could organise, conduct and supervise different

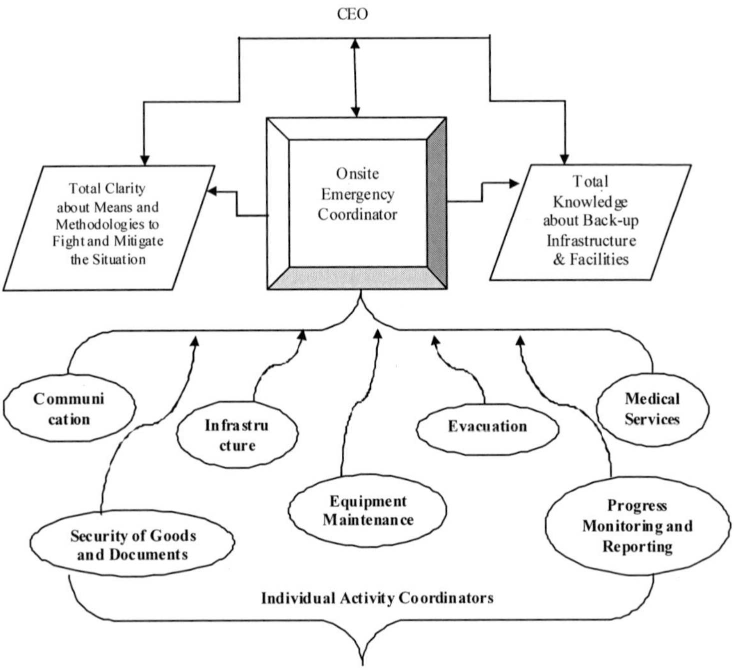

Fig. 5.9 Typical Emergency Team Structure

areas/aspects of emergency management like for example, ensuring proper communication of right data or information is maintained at appropriate levels including issuing warning signals and sirens or evacuation alarms as may be required, monitoring satisfactory progress on different fronts being handled during emergency, ensuring right kind of support infrastructure including provision of suitable mechanical, electrical and electronic support services as may be required for ensuring satisfactory performance of equipments used for fighting emergency situations is organised (in-house or outsourced) and provided, right type of medical help is organised where necessary, organising evacuation (A protective action or a safety strategy that provides for orderly movement of people away from an emergency site) of people to safe shelters as may be required or organising safe custody of precious materials and/or documents, provision of necessary security arrangements for goods under salvage and salvaged materials, etc. A typical *Emergency (Team) Structure* could be as shown in Figure 5.9.

One of the key prerequisites for a site emergency coordinator is that the person should be very conversant with all the processes that are being carried out in the organisation and is also quite familiar with the technology being practiced at different processing centres, and is quite knowledgeable and has good practical exposure to different technological practices and above all enjoys full confidence of top management of the organisation. Similarly, all other associate coordinators also should have necessary competence in the area being handled by them.

Emergency Types

There would be two types of emergency.

- One of them is a local emergency confined only to an individual activity centre or covering an entire isolated activity wing or section, dept. etc.
  - Even when the emergency situation covers an entire section, it rarely happens that all activity centres of the section would be simultaneously involved in the incidence.
  - Except in cases of severe fire accidents where heavily gushing-out smoke engulfs the entire area to totally obstruct ready visibility, locating the source of fire may not pose many challenges.
  - Similarly, wherever other types of shop-floor injuries like a fall injury or an explosion injury, etc. are involved, it would definitely be not a tough task to locate the source of incidence irrespective of the magnitude/severity of the incident.
- The other one is a global emergency where the emergency situation extends its jurisdictional territory far beyond a specific and/or isolated activity section to impact either many

more activity wings in the vicinity or to affect far wider cross section of the organisation.

- Explosive fires involving bursts of fuel gas cylinders, bursting of inflammable liquids stored in pressure cylinders or pressure vessels under the influence of fire, etc. generally belong to this category as the burning flames would be ejected under high pressures to far off places. These thrown out flames would induce forced fire to other combustible materials available in the vicinity of wherever their flame spreads.

Plan Objectives

An emergency plan, whether local or global, as mentioned earlier, should aim at achieving the following objectives:

→ First and foremost objective should be that there should be no injury/damage to people who are either directly handling those activities involved in the accident or who are present in close proximity to the emergency site.

→ All other activities should aim at conserving and saving organisation's precious resources by cutting off material supply chain or arresting the phenomenon or reversing the situation to normalcy as may be desirable.

Tiers of Emergency Plans

Emergency plans could be in three different tiers.

- The first tier always stands for handling an accident involving an isolated activity centre where other activity centres are not readily affected.
- The second tier usually stands for an accident situation where an accident impact covers an entire section or a division and other sections or divisions are quite safe.
- The third tier refers invariably to situations where the entire organisation would be involved or affected, either directly or indirectly, or total capital resources (stocks of raw materials, finished goods, huge stocks of goods-in-process, etc.) are involved.

- Whenever an accident taking place in one of the sections carries a high potential to spread to other places either on its own or with some external support, then it should be treated as a global emergency situation and all other sections will have to jump to action to protect their respective centres.
- This would however, depend on how closely different activity sections are located with respect to each other and the nature of activities being carried out in different close by centres and also the nature of accident itself.

Both first and second tier documents should clearly address when they would seek support from either other sections or from central emergency squad. Similarly, they should address all other requirements of emergency plan for the corporate as a whole.

Responsibilities

Key responsibilities to be handled in an emergency situation include the following:

- Immediate/quick recognition and realisation of the situation.
- Giving information about the incident to the concerned person who is equipped or empowered to take charge of further course of actions.
- Site inspection and confirmation of the incident.
- Raising appropriate alarms, sirens or warning signals to keep others informed about the incident and to initiate necessary administrative supports and procedures as may be required or to put them on their toes to be prepared for jumping to action if called for.
    - o This requirement presumes that levels of alarms, sirens, target audience, etc. are clearly known to the person.
- Organising rescue and relief operations where called for.
- Inspection for entrapment and confinement of people working in isolation and rescuing them as may be required.
- Enforcing and organising evacuation as may be required.
- Assessing magnitude of the incident and evaluating its nature, spreading behaviour and harm potential associated with the accident.

- This requirement presumes that the person assigned this part of action responsibility has necessary competence to make reliable evaluation and assessment of the situation.

- Putting suitably trained squad to the emergency front and assigning them the task of fighting the situation.
  - This requirement presumes that the organisations will always keep suitably trained and skilled people ever-ready to handle emergency situation.
  - This also presumes that the organisation has established a system of updating and modifying its training details as and when additional data/experience gets generated.
  - It also presumes that the person has a ready and free access to trained fight-squads.
- Organising necessary infrastructure support and making it available for fighting the situation.
  - This requirement presupposes that the person has a clear picture of which facility is available in-house and which needs to be outsourced form nearby external sources and further that he is aware of those sources and facilities.
- Continuous monitoring of control process and informing the progress to concerned people.
  - This requirement presumes that the person is clear about how to process the data and how to transmit the same to appropriate levels.
- Maintaining good communication with all concerned people.
- Summarising the details of incident and analysis-outcome.

Details of *who would do what and to what extent, who will coordinate all activities, who will decide as to what should be the course of action, who will coordinate external supports, etc*. are matters of administrative controls and/or procedural practices that could be decided by organisations. But what is important for an emergency plan is its documentation to ensure total clarity about things.

Emergency Response

The type and nature of response that an emergency demands depends only on the nature and scope of activities being carried out in an organisation and on the nature of materials (input, in-process and finished goods, etc.) it processes, handles and stores. It is always a good practice to keep a ready reference matrix (Table 5.14) that specifies the type of responses that one should put to action in case of an emergency. Also refer Table 5.11.

Unlike all other routine activities whose execution mechanism would be quite familiar to people, emergency situation, generally belongs to one of rare category. As such, people may not be very familiar and/or very conversant with the type of responses they should give to those situations, It is therefore advisable that some responses are pictorially depicted and displayed at prominent places in shop-floors.

Whenever situations demand immediate evacuation, people may have to just run for safety and may have to, at once, leave shop-floor premises. *Evacuation is a protective action mechanism that prepares/ helps people for an orderly movement away from an actual or a potential hazard site.* A well identified safe location (assembly area – a designated area located away from the emergency scene where people gather during emergency site evacuation for safety and to receive further instructions) away from active shop-floors should be identified for this purpose and people should be kept well aware of the same. For this purpose, all shop-floors should maintain clearly identifiable exit paths. People should be in a position to quickly reach an exit. Therefore the distance of any exit from any corner in the shop-floor should not be more than about 100 meters. Exits will have to be maintained in such a way that it is clearly visible and readily identifiable from all corners of the shop-floor and exit routes should never carry obstruction of any kind for free movement. Further, it is always desirable that people are lead towards exits throughout by suitable indication lights, preferably with

5.14 Typical Format Showing Emergency Response

Sr. No.	Activity Section/ Division	Type of Emergency	Nature of Response	Infrastructure/ Support Required	Source	Person Responsible for Organising and/or Administering
1						
2						
3						

red fluorescent lights independently energised so that people are in a position to recognise the route and exit even when the main energy supply to the shop-floor gets disconnected.

Emergency Drill

This is another exercise which will always keep people on their toes or at least keep them alert such that they could readily respond to dangerous situations within their own shop-floors or situations that could come-up elsewhere in the organisation premises about which they are not aware. Situations under reference here are those that demand immediate evacuation to eliminate or minimise chances of getting hurt. Immediate evacuations should be notified through special sirens or alarms of different kind and through suitable public address systems located in the shop-floors. These sirens or alarms should be audible from any corner in the shop-floor and should signal a warning to people who are lost in their works and should convey them that they should immediately leave their work spot and shop-floor premises for safety.

It is equally desirable that people are well trained to ensure that before leaving their specific work centres in an emergency situation, they should be in a position to quickly cut-off energy supply to their processing equipments and arrest their movements. Similarly, they should be in a position to immediately cut-off material feeding and/or all feed supplies/service supplies, etc. to their processing equipments. This is to ensure that their work centres also do not contribute to further aggravation of emergency situation that has come-up elsewhere. If these things are not immediately attended to, chances of those work centres also creating emergency situations cannot be ruled out. All these activities will have to be carried out in no time, almost at the flash of a light, and still they should be in a comfortable position to run for safety.

While time element is very critical during evacuation operations, its design should be such that no one is left behind and no other new emergency crops-up. For this purpose, it is necessary that a well thought out list of activities to be carried out before vacating the premises should be prepared and should be periodically rehearsed (mock drills). Periodical rehearsals are called for due to the fact that work environment in shop-floors keep changing for many reasons including for reasons of changes in technology practice environment and execution skill environment. Short-falls noticed during such mock drills should immediately be addressed suitably to ensure that real evacuations in dire necessity during live emergency situations are effective and would ensure that damages are minimised.

Response to Off-site Emergencies

Off-site emergencies generally belong to those emergency situations that come-up outside corporate premises. Incidences of *Natural Calamity* category like flash floods, volcano eruptions, heavy landslides, earth quakes, cloudbursts, cyclones and hurricanes, fire or explosions of fuel tanks/containers, failure of public utility services and emergency services etc. fall under this group. Of late, incidences of civil-disturbance-nature like arson and loots, terrorist attacks, etc. arising from intentional interference with normal life pattern of the society also contribute to creation of emergency situations.

As consciously responsible members of society, all business corporates should have in place, a sound policy and established practices and procedures to respond even to those emergency situations that are external to their work premises but are taking place elsewhere in the society. The way a business corporate likes to borrow certain critical services/facilities from neighbouring industries or from public utility services during their internal emergency, they also should lend their services to other industries and the society when needed.

Governance Audits

Audit Profile

It is a well known fact that an audit is essentially a verification process. It is also a well understood fact that any verification calls for a target audience or a target system or a target operation environment that needs to be verified. Verification target fixes audit definition, scope and the purpose. Since an audit definition is provided by a target audience, audits have to focus on finding answers to issues raised by the target audience. As such, it may not be an uncommon observation that audit scope and purpose is confined to a single pre-identified activity area or a set of a selected few activity areas depending on what drives an audit process. Occasionally, audit scope could also be limited to only a specific, pre-defined conformance verification of an activity and may not cover all the aspects of the same activity centre. Definition or identification of the purpose is therefore very critical for carrying out any audit.

Further, since the purpose behind a verification activity provides the necessary scope for audits, the purpose, by itself, should be suitably qualified through providing a reference base for the verification activity. It is this reference base which can answer questions like "what needs to be verified" and "why a particular aspect should be verified" and "how to ensure whether or not the audit has served the purpose?" A reference base for an audit would always be provided by one or more of the following:

i. Policy of the company.

ii. Documented policy implementation procedures and practices acceptable to and established by the company.

iii. A company standard with reference to either a product or service generated by the company or with reference to execution of an activity.
iv. An industry standard for the activity or its output.
v. A national or an international standard for the activity or its output.
vi. Guidelines fixed by professional bodies.
vii. Requirements set by statutory authorities and law enforcement authorities.

Therefore, when we explore the phenomenon of audit in the context of *corporate-governance*, audit verification refers exclusively to examining the governance mechanism that operates in an organisation with the sole objective of verifying the strengths and weaknesses of the governance mechanism (Fig. 6.1) that operates in an organisation. In the absence of any pre-identified specific-orientation or definition of the purpose, governance audits should be understood as standing for conformance verification of all the twelve areas of governance aspects (CG Components) discussed earlier under governance.

Naturally, the outcome of an audit should result in the following observations with specific reference to the base considered for verification:

1. Analysis of the status of compliance to requirements in each and every individual activity centre of the organisation.
2. Such a status analysis should lead to grouping of corporate activities or activity divisions into following four broad categories based on the degree of compliance to requirements and with collective conformance requirement wherever needed.
    a. Activity areas which are in total conformance to requirements.
    b. Activity areas which carry a high potential to further improve and further strengthen their compliance performance to excel and to set standards for others. Opportunity for Excellence!
    c. Activity areas that are able to maintain only part compliance to requirements.

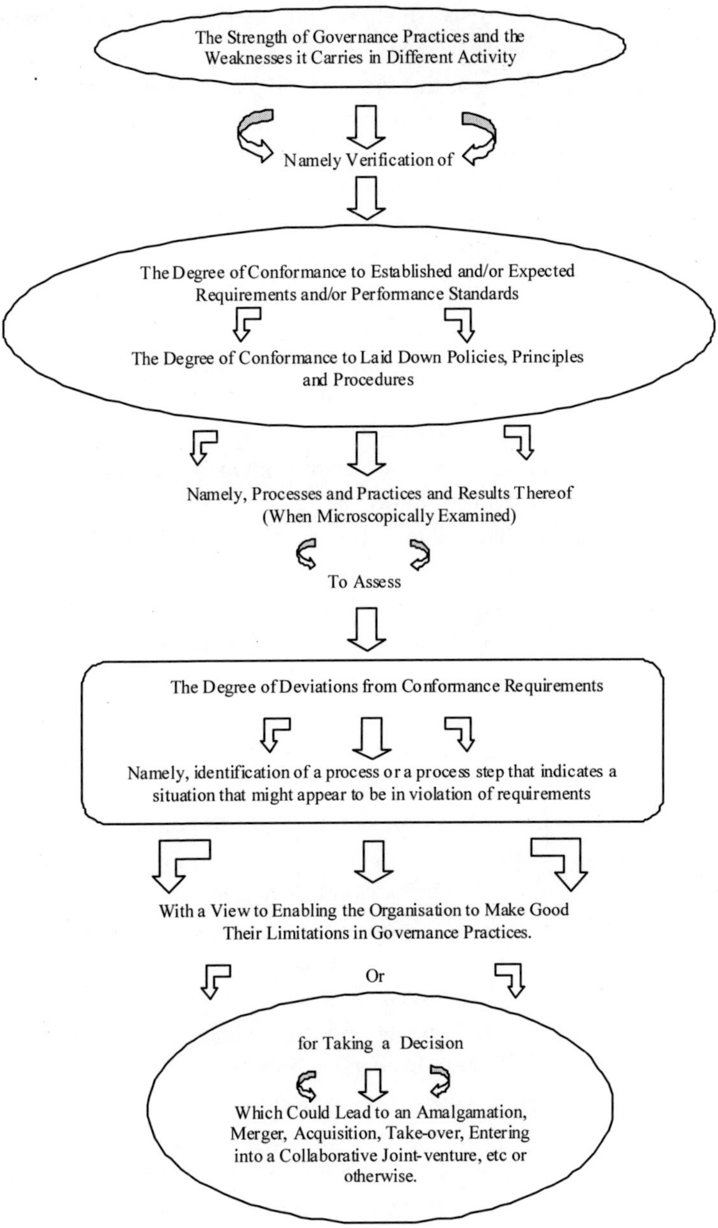

Fig. 6.1 Audit Profile

d. Activity areas which are extremely poor in maintaining compliance to requirements.

e. Activity areas that carry a high potential to cause a major damage to organisatinal reputation and pose severe threat to its existence or smooth operations and therefore need to be revamped immediately to set them right. Opportunity to prevent the impending catastrophe!

3. Carefully identifying the root cause for observed deviations.

   a. Analysing the problem causes and grouping them based on their problem nature and corrective measures:

      i. Problem source lies at company's management in their absence of clarity to certain requirements.

      ii. Problem source lies at company's management in their absence of commitment to conformance, at least in certain areas.

      iii. Problem source lies at the executives who handle different operations.

         - Lack of execution skills.
         - Inability to correctly understand the requirement.
         - Inability to precisely translate the requirements to actions.
           - Inability to design an appropriate operation layout and execution sequence.

      iv. Problem source lies in the infrastructure at the work centre.

         - Inadequacy of infrastructure.
         - Installed equipments do not exhibit the required precision and have many performance limitations.
         - Equipments and other facilities have outlived their utility service life and cannot be maintained in satisfactory working conditions.
         - People do not have right kind of expertise to handle those sophisticated equipments/facilities.
         - Inadequacy of necessary skill-power at the work centre to handle all the required activities of the centre.

4. Identifying the most appropriate corrective actions for ensuring compliance to requirements and initiating those corrective actions.

If the cause of problem for deviation is eliminated at its source or root, then the governance mechanism should keep running smooth.

Types of Audits

Corporates governance is a well recognised system of business management mechanism established and practiced by business corporates for different socio-economic reasons including leveraging certain types of global-marketing and/or social advantages and also to

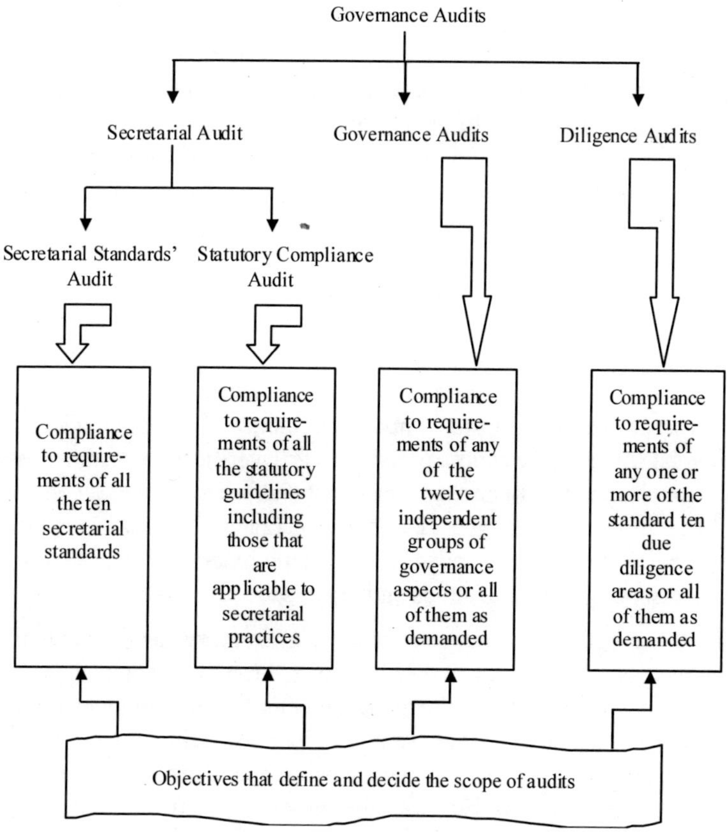

Fig. 6.2 Objective Oriented Types of Audits

address certain types of statutory requirements. Some of these socio-economic reasons or statutory conformance reasons demand business audits from different angles and from different perspectives or viewpoints. As such, similar to audits of any other certifiable management system-standards, governance audits also are carried out with specific objective focus. And, based on objective focus, these are generally grouped into three broad categories as schematically shown in Figure 6.2.

From the view points of statutory and non-statutory angles, governance audits can also be grouped into three categories as shown in Figure 6.3.

Audit Scope

The company act and also the finance acts have mandated two specific areas of audits for business corporates namely the secretarial audit and company audit. Secretarial audit is a process that ensures compliance to rules and regulations, procedural requirements, maintenance of records, etc. according to ICSI secretarial standards. Therefore, in addition to confirming compliance to statutory and other regulatory requirements and guidelines, secretarial audits should also ensure establishment of satisfactory system of appropriate internal checks and controls and a self regulatory corrective mechanism of secretarial practices of the organisation. Therefore, secretarial audits should serve as a means of compliance management for organisations to provide extra comfort to company directors and all stakeholders. In contrast with this, the company audit refers to verification of company's accounts practices, finance management and internal finance controls and to ensure that all types and forms of financial transactions have been carried out as per standard requirements and that there is no fraud and misappropriation of funds and organisational resources.

Since both these audits are mandatory in nature as per company act, reports of these audits will have to pass through the company board and should be presented to the general members of the company during AGMs. The scope of both these types of audits is almost fixed by the act and organisations may not have much scope to decide on the same. These audits generally do not have much scope to embrace other components of governance elements except that the secretarial audit can also probe into the peripherals of funds allocation, expenses, budgeting and planning of corporate social responsibility activity as this area is also covered under secretarial standards and the company has to constitute a CSR committee of the board of directors and its proceedings should be covered by the proceedings of the board meeting. Further, annual report of CSR committee should form a part of company's AGM proceedings.

Therefore, governance audits have still remained a voluntary process at the discretion of business corporates. Unlike the mandated audits whose coverage profile is limited to those specific areas mandated by law, governance audits can always embrace the entire activity gamut of business establishments and depending on the professional competence and expertise of the auditor, management system auditors could bring much higher benefits to the organisation. Organisations could go through the formal mandatory audits for addressing statutory requirements.

Key objectives behind governance audits are:

- To identify and report on compliances status.
  - Statutory compliances – Company law, other legal requirements, competition act, environment protection act, factories act, applicable labour laws, Indian explosives act, public liability insurance act, etc.
  - Compliance to secretarial practices and secretarial standards (ICSI).
  - Compliance to accounts and financial control requirements, finance control mechanisms and internal audits, AFS, CFS, IFRS, adherence to audit standards, etc.
- To identify non-compliances, part compliances and non-satisfactory compliances that carries the potential to attract initiation of legal actions and/or punitive measures.
- To identify practices, activities that carry the potential to either individually and/or collectively defeat requirements of standard governance practices/requirements.
- To identify activities, policies, projects, etc. which carry the potential to dig into basic interests of different categories of

stakeholders right from investors, employees, financiers, collaborators, customers, to society.

- To identify and evaluate deviations, if any, in the practice of CSR.

Scope of Diligence Audits

In contrast with these audits, diligence audits will be more in the nature of investigation and/or exploration into the affairs of the target company. These explorations should positively throw an insight into all those latent activities with a view to unearth and expose miss-representations and misgivings, if any, including exposing latent frauds and misappropriations, etc. These explorations should also result in generation of a potential success (growth) strategy and failure balance sheet for the target company and to highlight areas of concern so that the target company gets an opportunity to bridge the gap, if any, noticed between expectations and actuals before a final decision is taken.

Diligence audits are generally carried out with a view to assessing, analysing and evaluating the situation prevailing in the target company with specific reference to a pre-contemplated objective that could lead to one or more of the following decisions and/or actions.

- To understand the potential performance strengths and weaknesses in the pre-contemplated target area of the company.
- To identify opportunities for investing in a company's capital operations and/or supporting those operations.
- To identify a potential business opportunity for entering into collaborative and/or joint business ventures with the target company.
- To identify critical operations of the target company, assess and quantify the apparent and latent risks associated with such financial participations.

  For this purpose, audit investigations should be carried out to throw a deep insight into target company's financial strengths, commitments and liabilities, cash-flow pattern, etc. As such, whenever a diligence audit is carried out with this objective, the target company has to share with the auditors all its confidential (litigations and legal entanglements), legal (compliance status, compliance limitations and drawbacks, environmental compliances, risks and risk management, performances), financial information (assets including intangible assets, liabilities, credentials, cash-flow, finance control measures, creditors, debtors, etc.) and other useful material data (ethicality of operations and activities, knowledge bank, commitment to honour social responsibility, market strengths and goodwill, company image, technology status, etc.).

A careful study and analysis of some basic information about the target company like company configuration (credibility of promoters and directors, capital investment and capital back-up, board configuration and functioning, investment configuration, etc.), financial data (preceding few years' balance sheets, cash flow statement, profits and loss, creditors, debtors, assets and liabilities, commitments and tax liabilities, important business agreements, internal finance control mechanisms, etc.), market strengths and market data, sales turnovers and unexplored market potential, technology development and acquisitions, insurance and other emergency safety measures, etc. could reveal a true picture of the target company's strengths and weaknesses.

- To quantify the magnitude of confidence that stakeholders can repose in the target company and its various activities.
- To leverage the above information/data for pre-contemplated commercial transactions.
- To identify areas which need to be immediately strengthened and supported to preempt potential legal threats or punitive legal actions and/or to bridge the gap between prevailing performance levels and standard expectations to enhance and further project the prestige/image of the company in the public eye.
- Many times particularly when outright takeover or purchase of another company is contemplated, it is absolutely necessary also to ensure that the technology being practiced there is, either directly developed in-house or formally acquired through proper channels and is not involved in any kind of knowledge-infringement. If this aspect is not confirmed through a carefully

carried out knowledge-audit or intellectual property-diligence audit, the potential purchaser would always carry a high risk. Diligence audits would also serve this purpose if carried out with this specific objective.

Diligence audits are therefore target specific and can be initiated by any of the existing or potential stakeholders like investors, financiers, collaborators or purchasers, etc.

Who should do Audits

The law does not give much scope for organisations in selecting their auditors. Figure 6.3 clearly specifies as to who should do these audits. As per the law, secretarial audit has to be carried out only by a practicing company secretary and the company audit by a practicing chartered accountant. Fortunately, however, companies have the freedom to identify auditors of their choice within the formal guidelines set for the purpose. And therefore, what is left for a general purpose governance auditor is to embrace all other governance component areas which are not specifically covered under secretarial audit or the company audit. In the case of diligence audits, an auditor could be identified from among any of these three categories of auditors depending on the specific activity area of interest for diligence verification.

There are, however, some schools of thought who strongly advocate that the mandatory secretarial audits embrace practically all the aspects of corporate governance and, therefore, it may not be necessary for any organisation to go through another independent governance audit cycle. Another school of thought equally strongly opines that governance audit carried out by a well informed and a well experienced management system auditor would do a much better job as an auditor than any of the mandated and dedicated category auditors. According to this school, unlike those dedicated auditors, a system auditor would generally be exposed to more diverse types of operation environments and would have acquired the skills to easily recognise system deviations as he could more readily read into the minds of his auditee and recognise system tendency to drift towards deviations. Also, these system auditors are always free to avail the services of subject specialists or experts whenever required to help them in certain areas. And as such, they readily bring-in as many different types of expertise into audit scenario as required. Who is a better auditor is not a subject for discussion here. What is important for an organisation is to ensure whether the audits have served the basic purpose well. However, since, a mandatory element is involved here, organisations do not have any option but to go for mandated types of audits and, then, if need be, supplement those observations with the ones from independent system auditors.

Three Stage Audit Preparation

Both company auditors and practicing company secretaries are dedicated auditors and therefore they have a set mechanism and a set sequence of verification of their respective audit areas. Further, scope

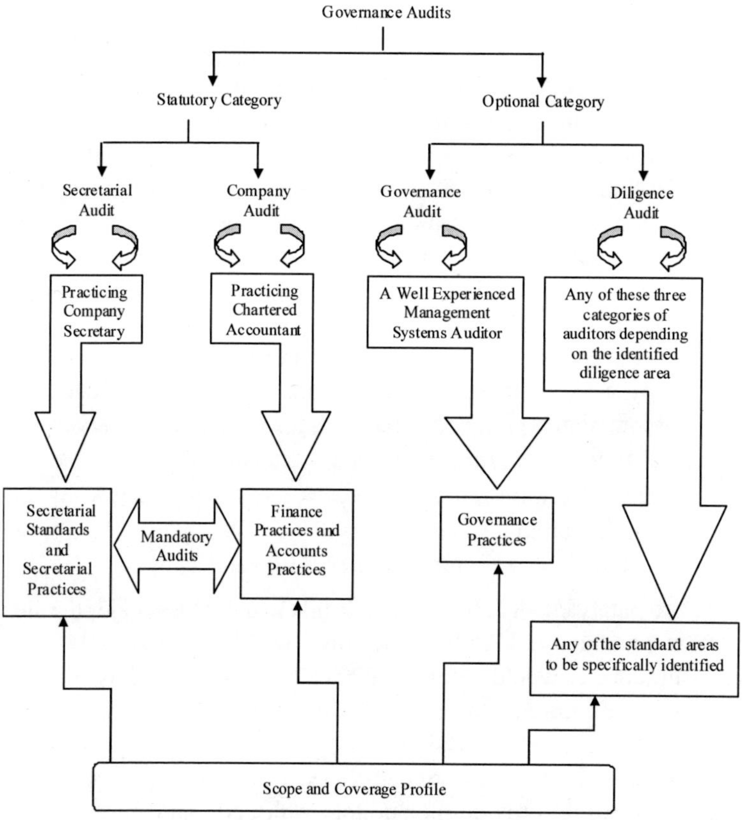

Fig. 6.3 Statutory Stipulation Based Audit Types

of their audits is always fixed and cannot undergo changes. They have always to be carried out within the broad framework set by the act. As such, they do not need additional preparation. Therefore, these details are not separately discussed here. On the contrary, governance audits are comprehensive type of audits with multiple objectives and multiple scopes. For deriving good benefits from these audits, governance auditors have to pass through a preparatory stage which would set the path for a smooth audit.

1. First Stage of Preparation

➢ It is a well known fact that audits are invariably intellectual exercises to be carried out by auditors. If these intellectual exercises have to yield fruitful results, it becomes highly desirable that the entire audit process should be made intelligible to both auditee as well as auditors. The process of transforming audit exercise into one of intelligible category is, by itself, an intellectual exercise and involves a good understanding of the process mechanism or process technology of the target organisation or target activity division. The description process mechanism or process technology refers to both the execution details of activities being carried out based on governing technology as well as to the set guidelines and their governing philosophies. Audit observations and queries seeking clarifications from people should be guided by a good knowledge of the process not from procedural compliance view points but from the view points of associated statutory and/or health and safety considerations.

If this exercise is not properly carried out the result would be disastrous and the audits would not serve any useful purpose. Table 6.1 gives some details of this exercise.

Fortunately enough, for an auditor this will not be a major hurdle. System-Management-Auditor-Training, which are generally very intensive courses would imbibe in them all the required skills. A study of system documents including those that are applicable to administrative, secretarial and finance operations and a couple of short discussions with concerned executives from the target activity section or division would provide the auditors with necessary input for the audit.

Table 6.1 Fist Stage of Audit Preparation

Sl. No.	Some leading probing questions	Outcome of absence of preparation
1.	What precisely needs to be checked?	If these probing areas are not correctly identified And If the answers to these probing questions are not properly generated Then Each of these situations would individually and/or collectively carry the potential to Defeat the very purpose of an audit And, as such, no auditor can afford to skip this activity.
2.	Which specific element of a particular aspect or activity needs to be checked? Why a particular aspect or an element of an aspect should be checked? What is the lead-link for this verification?	
3.	Which are the right target locations and/or target documents for a particular verification? Do these different target locations collectively address the requirement/element being verified? Or do these target locations individually address different facets of the element being verified?	
4.	What are the documents or records that he should check for the purpose? Have those documents been identified and listed together with their target locations? What inference is expected to be revealed by these individual records?	
5.	What inference should be drawn from each of the verifications? Do these individual observations and inferences collectively address the same governance element?	
6.	How to correlate and/or integrate different verification results and/or observations together to draw a useful conclusion regarding a governance element?	

- This understanding should next be further strengthened with an understanding of execution details of each of the target activity centres, preferably with the help of an activity location map prepared for the purpose.
- The next step would be to identify and/or understand the expected statutory conformances as applicable to different target activity centres based on activity nature and scope.

  This activity is preferably carried out with the help of corporate legal register and supported with divisional or sectional legal register and the various statutory licences, permissions, approvals, certificates and grants, etc. The accuracy and the exhaustiveness of this activity are very critical for the success of the audit.

This step should next be strengthened with an understanding of the type of infrastructure required to ensure statutory compliances.

2. Second Stage of Preparation

- The second stage audit preparation refers to preparation of an elaborate audit spread sheet which should give as to what needs to be checked under each of the governance components. This activity involves preparation of an elaborate audit facilitator index (Table 6.2) together with a comprehensive audit-checklist. The effectiveness and usefulness of governance audits depend exclusively on the elaboration and the exhaustive nature of this reference index and also the Comprehensivity of support checklist.

  The index should typically give the following details. Any other useful format can be designed to suit the requirement. When this exercise is well carried out, audit process will be smooth

Table 6.2 Audit Facilitator Index

Sl. No.	Verification Target			Verification Mode or Means					Type of inference to be drawn in relation to governance component
	Aspect to be Verified	Target Activity Centre	Target Location	Personnel Interactions – Interviews, Discussions, Interrogations	Type or Nature of Information Sought	Records and/or Documents to be Checked	Location or Activity centre	Observations to be Made	
CG Component - Law Abidance									
1									
2									
3									

CG Component - Operation Integrity									
1									
2									
3									
CG Component - Operation Transparency									
1									
2									
3									
CG Component - Decision Pattern									
1									
2									
3									
CG Component - Health and Safety Aspects									
1									
2									
3									
CG Component - Compensation Package									
1									
2									
3									
CG Component - Discrimination									
1									
2									
3									
CG Component - Participative Management & Freedom of Expression									
1									
2									
3									

CG Component - Time targeted Response Mechanism									
1									
2									
3									
CG Component - Stakeholders' Interest Protection									
1									
2									
3									
CG Component - Expansions, Diversifications Acquisitions and Takeovers									
1									
2									
3									
CG Component - Corporate Citizenship (Corporate Social Responsibility)									
1									
2									
3									

and auditors would not get lost during the process. If need be this activity could be carried with repeated observations of activities and discussions with executives.

3. Third Stage of Preparation

- Naturally, the immediate next step would be to prepare elaborate and reliable audit-checklists under each one of the governance-component headings to support the above activity step (Table 6.3).

Table 6.3 A Few Typical Audit Checklists

As mentioned earlier, audits are generally focussed activities. Therefore, the centre of focus decides the types of checks to be made in the target area. As such what can be attempted is just a general purpose checklist to serve as a reference base or as a guide for preparing focus-specific elaborate checklists. It is therefore advised that governance auditors should go through the following basic guidelines and prepare their own audit checklists. Most of the points given here below are mere probing area indicators and not necessarily framed questions:

Company Law	
• Are corporate activities designed based exclusively on the broad guidelines set-out in company's memorandum of association or articles of association? • Regulations for management of the company? • Are corporate activities steadily drifting away from the originally declared objectives? If not, are the changes appropriately formalised? Through a resolution in the general body? • Documents to be filed with ROC? • Are all the standard requirements fulfilled? Informing ROC? Marking of changes in all copies? • Registration and associated formalities? • Necessary declarations and affidavits from subscribers to memorandum and their details and first directors? • Document availability at company's registered office? • Permission to change company's registered office, if any? • Holding any investment or property? • Procedures followed for appointment of directors? • Stipulations for directors? Identification number, benefits for self or for relatives of self, interest and concern declaration, vacation of office and removal of directors, if any? • Procedures, frequency and minutes of board meetings? • Independent and women directors on the board appointment procedures, tenure of office, resignation and removal, reappointment, separate meetings? • Four board committees their configuration and details of their functioning? Responsibilities? • Independent directors? Qualification, who could become, code of conduct, mode of appointment, tenure of office, resignation and removal, duties and responsibilities, separate meetings, liabilities, etc. • Role of audit committee and its powers? • Prevention of oppression and mismanagement, Protection of minority shareholders' interest, highlights of protection measures, grievance redressal, IEPF? Role of tribunal and its powers? Removal of the managing director, recovery of undue gains, claiming damages from company or its directors, claiming damages from company's auditors for misleading statements made in audit reports, class action suits, investigation on public interest litigation, etc.	• Criteria for identifying CSR projects? Money spent on CSR projects? Monitoring and controls, CSR domain, eligibility and criteria? CSR corpus, CSR annual report, joint participation in CSR projects, if outsourcing of CSR is practiced, details of source and controls there on? • Are CSR reporting system as per set guidelines? • Are proper procedures followed for company's general meetings and AGMs, notice, quorum, tribunal's intervention, and gap between AGMs, provision for extension of gap, passing of resolutions, scope of special resolutions, preparation of minutes and provision for inspection, approval, and filing of reports with ROC? • Are preparation and Filing of annual returns done properly? Certification by directors and company secretary, contents of returns, action against PCS for false certification of annual returns, etc. • Appointment of KMPs, • Procedures followed for amalgamations, agreements, compromises, etc. and auditor's certificate for the same. • Procedures followed for using company's seal, safe custody, • Procedures and details followed in connection with • Conducting meetings of the board of directors. • Conducting general meetings of company's Members. • Preparing and maintaining the minutes of board meetings, committee meetings and general meetings. • Procedures to be followed for passing of resolutions by circulation. • Broad outlines of the body (contents) of board's report. • Registers and records to be maintained by company secretariat. • Handling issues related with dividends. • Practices to be followed for transmission of shares and debentures. • Procedures to be followed in situations of forfeiture of shares. • Procedures to be followed for affixing of common Seal.

Secretarial Standards

- Appointment of company secretary, duties, roles and responses?
- Do secretarial practices uphold the standard guidelines laid-down for the following activities? Detailed checks on the same.
  - o Conducting meetings of the board of directors.
  - o Conducting general meetings of company's members.
  - o Preparing and maintaining the minutes of board meetings, board committee meetings and general meetings.
  - o Passing of resolutions by circulation.
  - o Broad outlines of the body (contents) of board's report.
  - o Registers and records to be maintained by company secretariat.
  - o Handling issues related with dividends.
  - o Transmission of shares and debentures.
  - o Situations of forfeiture of shares.
  - o Affixing of common seal.
  - Secretarial audit, auditor qualification, audit scope, fraud reporting, board's satisfactory explanations to each and every qualification, observation or adverse remarks?

Detailed checking Under Each of these ⇩ is very critical

Finance and Accounts Controls

- Finance and accounts practice - CFS, IFRS
- Financial year, internal audit and internal financial controls, reports on internal financial controls and its operative effectiveness, coverage of internal financial controls, access of electronic accounts across the country, component approach for depreciation, CFO's role, AFS and CFS, IFRS, key components of IFRS?

Company Audit

- Appointment of auditors, auditor qualification and eligibility, tenure and termination of office, rotation and cooling-off period, formal restrictions on non-audit services, duties, participation in AGM, highlights of audit reports, reporting on frauds, if any?

Competition Act

- Issues related with Anti-competitive agreements, foreclosure of organisations, dominance, controls on combinations, acquisitions, mergers, takeovers, ensuring good socio-economic balance in the society, collective price fixation, limiting production volumes, controlled supplies, discriminatory supply and credit facilities between different customers, clubbed and conditional sales agreements, enforcement of purchase pattern, restricting dealers on selling competitive products, etc.

Environment Protection Act

- Environment statement and assessment of impact of contemplated activities on the environment.
- SPCB consent to operate, controls under air act, prevention of air and water pollution, application category-wise measuring and monitoring of water consumption, controls on effluent quantity and quality, batteries control, ODS controls, manufacturing, storage and imports control on hazardous chemicals, hazardous waste management and controls, prior permission, MSDS, decontamination facility, annual statements, half-yearly medical examination of people,

Factories Act

- Approval. Registration and licence. Stability certificate, periodical licence renewal, permission for linking to public drainage system, maintenance of operation
- Safety aspects, risk management, safety gadgets and PPEs, secured locations for hazardous material storage, LOCKIN-LOCKOUT practices, accident records and associated formalities, Minimum greenery maintenance, etc.

Indian Explosives Act

- Prior permissions for handling, storage, manufacture, imports, sales, etc.
- Safety management plan, packing specifications and packaging methods specifications.
- UN model regulation for transportation.
- Licenses for manufacturing, handling, storage, transportation, etc. of fireworks, controls on fireworks displays, control of cluster of shops, pressure container inspection and approval, control on surroundings, etc.

Public Liability Insurance Act

- Prior obtaining of insurance policies before start of activities involving hazardous materials.
- Liability for paying necessary relief or compensation to accident victims, reimbursement of medical expenses, total or partial disability, etc.
- Contribution to relief fund.

Labour Laws of Concern to Corporates

- Payment of wages and minimum wages, service conditions, contract labour wages and terms of service.
- Service for inter-state migrant workmen.
- Maternity benefits for women workers, engaging child labour, etc.

CG Component - Operation Integrity
a. Accounts and Finance Practices

- Are the figures given in company's balance sheets honest to the core or are they based on manipulated records and figures? Does the company work towards purchasing the goodwill of auditors enabling it to play with accounts figures?
- Any collusion between different executives in preparation of bills, expenses statements, etc? Are expenses statement heads coined in such a way as to confuse others and to manipulate expenses statements to suit some people's convenience and comforts? Does under-billing/overbilling/nil-billing, etc. take place to manipulate situations to somebody's comforts? Do accounts and marketing executives and other executives participate in preparation of fictitious bills and expenses statements including jacking-up of product/service generation costs, staff welfare expenses, etc. to generate black-money to liberally support all forms of corrupt and dishonest practices?

CG Component - Operation Integrity
Public Relations Activities

- Do public relations activities have any set goals, annul plans and a clear definition of purpose, scope of activities, budgeting, etc.? Do they have any set guidelines? Are those executives completely free to select their own activity and activity profile? Are selection and identification of social development projects done only to suit the tastes and desires of some local bigwigs or some other influential people in the society and not necessarily on the true and relative merits or significance of those projects to the local society?
- Are public relations activities designed only to buy goodwill of the general public or some VIPs and influential people or powerful/influential public figures in the society or executives in power whenever an opportunity arises with the sole objective of return of official or social favours from them? Are public events organised only to buy the goodwill of the general public or are they designed to share true achievements and breakthrough with the general public interested in the wellbeing of the company?

CG Component - Operation Integrity
Marketing Activities

- Are marketing activities designed in such a way that they provide a free hand to executives to play around with customer sentiments, market sentiments/situations and the prevailing competitive technology environment and to suitably manipulate product/service prices?
- Do marketing executives practice open pricing policy clubbed with open product distribution policy under the cover of serving the customer better thus entering into a vicious corruption circle? Do marketing executives resort

to intentional short-supplies or nil supplies or delayed supplies or hoarding of products, etc. to create artificial scarcity and to generate extra heavy demand for the product and then leverage the situation to jack-up the prices or to push non-standard products to the market?

- Do marketing executives bribe the customers to influence their purchase decisions? Do marketing executives play around with invoice figures to manipulate the situation to leverage the difference between true prices and invoiced prices for purchasing the goodwill of prospective customers including direct bribes and kickbacks or personal favours?
- Do they resort to differential pricing and distribution to different customer segments to leverage the situation for some non-specified benefits? Do they liberally mix standard, non-standard and sub-standard products together ensuring that customers do not get to know of the same?
- Do product promotion measures share true facts about the products and services or do they aim at creating false impression or appeal in the general public or prospective customers?

CG Component - Operation Integrity
Practice of Technology

- Are people clear about what is expected of them and what all is expected of them and how should they execute the project or do they play around a few routine activities robotically? Are people clearly aware of the various activities associated with the main function and their criticalities to complete the main activity?
- Are people aware of the key purpose behind their activity design and execution plan and do they know the basic principles that work behind the technology they are practicing that would enable them to refine and fine-tune their activity execution and controls there on as and when it becomes necessary including achieving proper orientation with customers' needs?
- Do people intentionally modify execution schemes to address some insane interests either on their own or at someone else's directives to leverage some unholy gains?
- Does the organisation practice remote technology-control so that no one knows what is what? People do not know their technology source and its authenticity?

CG Component - Operation Integrity
Purchase Activity

- Has the organisation established good purchase criteria? What are the parameters that have been considered while fixing the purchase criteria? Do the criteria change periodically? If so what are the factors that would demand a change in purchase criteria? Does the organisation keep the suppliers informed of the criteria fixed for a purchase? Are suppliers involved or consulted in fixing purchase criteria? Are suppliers informed of any changes in the criteria? Are suppliers provided any opportunity to verify and/or challenge the criteria?

- Does a good correlation exist between purchase activity and total utility of purchased products? What are the criteria evolved to correlate between usefulness of a purchased product and the requirements of a consumption centre? Do consumption centres approve such a correlation mechanism? Can the correlation be verified? Do people maintain a good dynamic balance between purchase and consumption?
- Are purchase executives fair to all the suppliers of different categories of materials? Do all suppliers get an equal opportunity to supply their materials to the organisation? How would the organisation verify and confirm that personal biases, preferences and discriminations of purchase executives do not play any role in purchase activities?
- Do purchases executives play into the hands of selected few suppliers and continue to procure materials which exhibit a widely varying coefficient of specification variation (Cv) and bring pressure on consumption centres to use those materials?
- Do people manipulate purchase prices? How would the organisation exert control on these activities?

CG Component - Operation Integrity
Skill-Power Management Activities

- Are SPM activities full of parochialism and acting on whims and fancies of a few individuals but yet make a mere pretention and/or claims of good SPM practices?
- Is a good correlation exists between work centre requirement and skill power development activities?
- Are staff appreciation and promotions directly related with job responsibility and execution skills or other criteria overweigh true merits?
- Does SPM also work towards overall development of staff and staff welfare activities?

CG Component - Operation Integrity
Product/Service Generation Activities

- Does the organisation suffer from investment shyness due to firm belief that investment on infrastructure may not be fully productive and profitable and execution shyness from workmen due to prevalence of firm belief that additional work need not always bring them additional monetary returns? How would the organisation ensure that there is a good balance between requirements of different activity centres and the availability of adequate facilities?
- Does such shyness on both sides of execution result in practice of many operation shortcuts in job executions and the ultimate customer always suffers? How would the organisation ensure that operation shortcuts are not resorted

to by process executives due to inadequacy or non-availability of necessary infrastructure?

- Are people committed to output performance to complete satisfaction of the ultimate end-user or do they care only for some external features of the output forcing customers to take high risks with those products?
- Are process executives concerned with process efficiency and effectiveness and competitiveness of their outputs?
- Does the organisation care to maintain good workforce-friendly product generation environment or care only for output volumes?

CG Component - Operation Transparency

- Are all actions and activities of the company are appropriately documented to ensure that that people have set operation guideline and are backed with clear processes and objectives? How honest are people to their set procedures, actions and activities? Can this be verified or established?
- Do they feel comfortable to demonstrate their actions for verification and confirmation of adherence to set procedures and achievements of set objectives?
- Do people resort to manipulating their records and reports?

CG Component - Decision Pattern

- Can decisions taken across the corporate, whether spontaneous or well deliberated and discussed, without reference to the nature of emergency that forced spontaneous decisions, be verified for the rationale and/or reasoning behind those decisions together with guiding principles or philosophies or the genuineness of intentions behind such decisions?
- Can those decision making executives establish beyond doubts the honesty and integrity and complete freedom from latent insane motives and hidden unethical objectives behind those decisions?
- How would they ensure that those decisions are completely free from both macro- and micro-unethical elements? Do they keep a verification check-list for the same? Who will certify that those decisions are driven by the true un-polluted knowledge that governs those activities for which a decision is taken? How would they ensure that those decisions do not have any adverse impact, either immediate or long-term, on any of the corporate stakeholders including the society and the environment or they do not go against of the established norms and statutory regulations?
- Would those executives check whether their decisions do not adversely affect company's operating finances, and activity effectiveness and efficiencies and also operation comforts of executives or make a dent in company's credibility in the society?
- Does the organisation practice a well designed and a well configured decision and a well structured decision making pattern and do people get collectively involved in decision making process?

- Are the decisions taken by SPM or HR executives free from personal biases, personal opinions, etc., and are free from discriminations?

CG Component - Health and Safety Aspects

- Are executives aware of the type of risks their activities are abreast with? Do they analyse their nature and identify their root-cause? Are those risk sources either eliminated at source or satisfactory remedies identified and organised? Do they maintain a master list of all potential risky operations together with description of the nature risk?
- Are people well aware of the types of health risks they are exposed to, including those that are latent in nature and are cumulative and long delayed in action? Do people know the severity and magnitude of risks they take during activity execution? Do people have necessary execution skills to ensure that they do not get injured or hurt during job execution? Do they get trained to work safe with those risky situations?
- Are process equipments designed to ensure a high degree of operation-safety? Has the process layout been designed to ensure minimum execution risk?
- Are necessary safety gadgets provided and people are trained in their use? Are those safety gadgets well maintained? Does the design of those safety gadgets address the basic risk element?
- Wherever chemicals are used in the process, have the full data on their safety aspects like toxicity, flammability, irritation and corrosive nature, etc. generated? Does process layout and equipment design take care of those risk aspects?

CG Component - Compensation Package

- Does the concept of sharing the returns prevail in the company or does it remain an ever burning issue and an ever-live subject of bone of contention?
- Does the company involve people in the process of working out compensation packages to share thoughts and opinions or it is all pre-decided and enforced unilaterally?
- What mechanism has the company designed to ensure that the process of returns sharing is free from all sorts of personal biases, favouritism and discriminatory practices of a few executives?
- Does the company check whether its business strategies and policies would have an adverse impact on employees' compensation package or on their take-home salary?
- Does the company check whether or not its operation strategies would provide equal opportunities to all employees to prove their efficiency and to explore their own latent unexplored performance potentials and opportunities for growth?
- Does the organisation believe in practicing a transparent rewarding system for the entire cross section of the organisation, from top to bottom, or does it

practice suppression of freedom of expression? How does the company ensure activity and decision transparency?

CG Component - Discrimination

- How does the organisation ensure that all its activities, decisions, policies and procedures are completely free from all sorts of discriminatory practices?
- Does any activity or activity centre get preference over others? Do executives give or receive preferential treatment for their job execution or for sharing certain common facilities or services or staff appreciations and promotions?
- Do executives have a set of standard guidelines to act so that their personal views, beliefs, opinions, impressions or considerations do not get a stake in their decisions and actions?
- Do different cross sections of the local society get identical treatment with specific reference to employment openings and corporate support to development activities?
- In situations of joint business ventures/collaborations or business expansions and diversifications, organisations have to carefully ensure that there will be no discrimination against small pockets of humanity, society and nature through installation of out-dated and/or fully exploited technology.
- How does the organisation ensure that nobody would get a feeling of being discriminated on any account?

CG Component - Participative Management & Freedom of Expression

- Does the company recognise the fundamental truth that it cannot run any business without the participation of many people in the society and therefore many people would be concerned with corporate activities?
- Does the company also recognise the other basic truth that all decisions taken by the corporate need not always be equally acceptable and similarly they need not always bring the same degree of comfort to the entire cross section of its stakeholders and therefore there would always be someone who may like to express his opinion or disagreement with corporate decisions, activities or affairs?
- Does the company provide those stakeholders opportunities to express their concern or views about company's affairs, activities, movements and strategies?
- Do the stakeholders of the company enjoy the freedom of expression? What measures have been taken by the company to ensure that people's freedom of expression is not curtailed at any stage of operations or at any activity centre?
- Does the company believe in taking consensus decisions in consultation with at least a major cross section of the concerned stakeholders? How can the company demonstrate the same?

CG Component - Time Targeted Response Mechanism

- Has the corporate instituted a good mechanism of response to queries received by it from different cross sections of its stakeholders?
- Does such a mechanism address a basic requirement of responses namely they should be timely and should serve the purpose for which a query had been sent?
- What criteria has the organisation identified for fixing the time-target for different types of queries?
- Is the criteria independently validated for its utility for the purpose for which a query has been made? What is the validation mechanism?
- Is the validation mechanism appropriately backed with independent interactions with those people to find out whether the response has served their purpose or whether it was too late to serve their purpose?
- Whenever the response to a query also calls for initiating some action, in-house, are those actions initiated and the query answered to the satisfaction of the person?

CG Component – Stakeholders' Interest Protection

- Are all the corporate decisions and actions verified for their adverse impact, long-term or immediate, if any, on different cross sections of corporate stakeholders?
- Has the company designed a mechanism to verify whether or not its decisions and actions carry the potential to adversely affect the interests, both immediate and long-term, of any of the categories of its wide spectrum stakeholders?
- What are the criteria evolved to identify whether or not a decision and action carries the potential to adversely impact the interest of the groups of corporate stakeholders?
- Has the criteria been evolved, individually, for each category of stakeholders?
- Is the criteria validated with specific reference to one-to-one interaction-based feedback generated, individually, from a good cross section of each category of stakeholders?
- Does the corporate recognise the fact that interests of each category of stakeholders will be unique to itself and need not be common with those of any other category of stakeholders?
- Would the organisation carry out a risk-benefit-analysis of its contemplated decision and action on different category of stakeholders?
- Is the outcome of benefit-analysis used for measuring the degree of satisfaction or the degree of enhancement in the comfort level of each category of stakeholders?
- Is this data periodically validated through regular interactions with different categories of stakeholders?

- Does the organisation quantify stakeholders' interest enabling it to carefully guard and protect those interest areas? Does it also identify a unit for measuring stakeholders' comforts and satisfaction?
- Is such a measure validated through periodical rating of corporate performance by different category of stakeholders? Do such stakeholder ratings have any impact on the parameters considered for measuring stakeholder satisfaction level and the unit of measure identified for the purpose? Can such a correlation be verified?
- Has the corporation evolved a stakeholder comfort-level-index to confirm that it is satisfactorily addressing the aspect of protecting stakeholders' interests?
- Has the organisation established well defined mechanism to measure comfort levels of its various categories of stakeholders?
- Does the organisation use any of the following measures/criteria to assess and quantify the comfort level of its stakeholders? If not, what are the alternate measures/criteria used for each of the stakeholder group? What is the rationale behind selecting or identifying those measures?

  a. **Intellectual Cross Section of the Society**
  Does the organisation consider the following key parameters to evaluate satisfaction level of intellectual cross section of its stakeholders?
     i. Compliance to all legal and statutory requirements.
     ii. Active participation in social development activities and fulfilling other social obligations?

  b. **Investors**
  Does the organisation consider the following key parameters to evaluate satisfaction level of investors?
     i. Enhancement in return on corporate assets.
     ii. Increase in frequency and magnitude of dividends.
     iii. Increase in periodicity in declaration of bonus shares,
     iv. Enhancement in share values and its frequency.

  c. **Employees**
  Does the organisation consider the following key parameters to measure the comfort level of employees?
     i. Degree of transformation of workforce to true knowledge leaders in their respective activity areas:
     (Enhancement in - knowledge wealth across the organisation, ability to take independent and discretionary decisions, ability to design, guide and control the activity, collective approach and team performance attitude, skills in effective risk management, degree of cost-conscience, resource optimisation and process-effectiveness across the organisation, degree of freedom in sharing of information, execution expertise and infrastructural facilities, etc.)
     ii. Enhanced eagerness to root-out problems at source wherever they are noticed

iii. Enhanced degree of knowledge leveraging:
(Enhanced activity effectiveness, better infrastructure utilisation and achievement of enhanced productivity, quick response to external changes and vibrant market environment, frequent technological breakthrough, reduced development time, etc.)
iv. Enhancement in the degree of job satisfaction:
(Increase in - motivation and intuitiveness index, enhancement in performance temperament, prevalence of learning environment for the workforce, competitive cost conscience, sharing of skill-based execution responsibility and sharing of expertise, creating a knowledge driven ever-competitive work environment, absence of activity inappropriateness for want of appropriate data or information, absence of job hibernation in between during the process for want of necessary information or data, complete clarity regarding exact requirements of customers throughout the organisation.
v. Comfort with compensations, recognitions and rewards.
vi. Impression regarding unhealthy competition and prevalence of differential and/or biased treatment.
vii. Steady increase in average service-length of employees in the organisation.

d. **Customers**

Does the organisation consider the following aspects while measuring the comfort levels of customers?

i. Ensuring generation of most appropriate data on customer needs and requirements relevant to customer application environment, application stringency and preparing product delivery schedules to customers' satisfaction.
ii. Getting confirmation from the customer regarding organisation's understanding of customer's requirement and the suitability of the products or services offered to him.
iii. Offering most competitive products to customers and increase in customer coverage-index.
iv. Periodically introducing innovatively novel products that would enhance customers' comforts.
v. Establishing a mechanism to satisfactorily address customers' grievances. How would the organisation confirm that the said mechanism works satisfactorily?
vi. Taking customers' feedback seriously and working towards enhancing value-return to customers through appropriate measures:

(Establishing good correlation between shop-floor activity and customer requirement across the organisation; elimination of product defects, both latent and apparent and other limitations to increase product ruggedness and to widen application range for products, enhancing product utility features; enhancing user-friendliness of the product; widening product application-life-cycle by providing customer demanded additional features and service components, Enhancing product performance capabilities; redesigning and reconfiguring service components to enhance customers' comforts.)

vii. Initiating appropriate BPR based on customer product-positioning and competitive-rating.

viii. Establishing a mechanism to quickly respond to customers' continuously changing demands.

ix. Working on customers' feedback and developing new and improved products.

x. Continuous updation of process technology to ensure that customers always get latest and emerging technology products.

xi. Continuous fine-tuning and refinement of process technology to identify and eliminate all cost additive factors to render the product most competitive.

e. **Suppliers**

How does the organisation measure the comfort level of its different suppliers?

i. Are suppliers, including potential suppliers, made fully knowledgeable about various aspects that are normally considered for evaluation of customer's capability to meet organisations' requirements?

(Methodology followed by the organisation to identify and select suppliers, calculations and formulations adopted for regular performance assessment of suppliers to decide on their continuation or otherwise, clear definition of reasons and specimen worksheets for placing purchase orders on a selected few suppliers in preference to other suppliers, realistic lead-times for different supplies worked-out in consultation with a good cross section of suppliers, provision of opportunity to challenge purchase executive's decision whenever suppliers suspect unethical understanding between purchase executives and some suppliers, provision of opportunity to scrutinise the details of various purchase orders placed by the company on different suppliers at regular intervals giving them an opportunity to improve on their performance levels, provision of opportunity to suppliers' technicians to challenge the reliability and suitability of verification procedures followed by the company, provision of opportunity to suppliers' technicians to demonstrate the shortfall in the practices of the company and to convince company's technicians to revise their verification methods, provision to give a confidential feedback to top management of the company expressing their grievances regarding harassment and discrimination or any other complaints followed by immediate analysis and evaluation of complaints by an independent high-power discipline-enforcement committee with provision for witnessing the proceedings by aggrieved suppliers.)

f. **Society**

What measure does the organisation adopt for measuring the comfort level of the local society? Do any of the following measures have a place in organisation's measures? If these issues are not considered, what are the factors considered for this purpose?

i. Allocation of expenditure for social development activities as a fixed percentage of income.
ii. Preparing an annual plan and an annual budget for social development activities.
iii. Aggressive participation in many social development and welfare activities.
    - Do these activities address any of the following issues of the locality? (Eradicating hunger, poverty and malnutrition; promoting preventive health care and sanitation and making available safe drinking water; promoting education, including special education and employment enhancing vocational skills especially among children, women, elderly, and the differently abled and livelihood enhancement projects; promoting gender equality, empowering women, setting homes and hostels for women and orphans; setting up old age homes, day care centres and such other facilities for senior citizens and measures for reducing inequalities faced by socially and economically backward groups; ensuring environmental sustainability, ecological balance, protection of flora and fauna, animal welfare, agro-forestry, conservation of natural resources, and maintaining quality of soil, air and water; protection of national heritage, art and culture including restoration of buildings and sites of historical importance and works of art, setting up public libraries, promotion and development of traditional arts and handicrafts; measures for the benefit of armed forces veterans, war widows and their dependents, etc.)
iv. Involving in different social welfare activity groups in identifying welfare projects beneficial to a larger cross section of the society.
v. Ensuring most economic use of precious natural resources through adoption of resource-conserving technologies.
vi. Ensuring that posterity is not denied or robbed off of its rightful entitlement to virgin nature and precious natural resources.

g. **Environment**

Does the organisation use any of the following criteria to measure minimisation of injustice done against the environment?

i. Adoption of eco-friendly green and clean technologies.
    - How would the organisation ensure that their technology is eco-friendly and green? What are the criteria applied for this test?
    - Has it identified cut-off levels to declare a technology as green technology?

- Does the organisation have a reference base for such cut-off levels?

ii. Phased-out discontinuation of use of resource-consuming and/or energy and resource guzzling technologies.
- What criteria does the organisation adopt for drawing the borderline between resource guzzling and resource conserving technologies?
- Do they have any reference base for this purpose? Or do they set their own standards?

iii. Taking appropriate measures to ensure that its activities do not leave any adverse or harmful impacts on the environment either immediate or in the long-run.
- How does the organisation identify its adverse impacts on the environment especially the long-term harmful effects?

iv. Adopting environment friendly practices to ensure that its activities do not emit or release polluting gases or discharge any harmful by-products or waste products to cause a loss in environment quality.

v. The company actively participates in educating the general public about environment protection measures by highlighting pollution through different human activities, the environmental burden being perpetrated by uncontrolled human greed for unnecessary material comforts and the need to contain the so called basic needs.

CG Component – Expansions, Diversifications Acquisitions and Takeovers

- Do any of these activities pose a direct challenge to company's guarded value systems and beliefs?
- Do those activities carry the potential to adversely affect company's finances, operations and performances?
- Do those activities pose any legal compliance issues local or international as may be applicable?
- Do those contemplated activities stand the test of time regarding the genuineness of the thought that drives expansions, diversifications acquisitions and takeovers?
- Can they be proved to be free from all sorts of latent objectives and motives?
- Do those contemplated activities carry apparent or latent potential to displace any of the existing organisations, whether small or big?
- Do those activities enable the organisation to re-identify itself with the local society and help it in working for overall development and wellbeing of the local society without resorting to any type of exploitation, whether intellectual, economic, and cultural or resources, etc.?
- Do those activities carry the potential, immediate or long-term, to harm the workforce in terms of their health and safety aspects?
- Are those contemplated activities environment friendly or do any of those activities carry the potential to harm the environment either directly or

indirectly through pollution of ambient or natural air and water, toxic/poisonous chemical contamination of natural water bodies and fertile land, steady deterioration in the quality of natural air, release/emission of gases and vapours with high GWP and ODS concentration, heavy depletion of natural resources, etc.?

- Do those business executions come under the influence of any unethical extraneous considerations like undue inducements, favoritisms, etc.?

Audit Tools

Understanding and/or probing of corporate activities could be achieved through observations followed by some discussions or discussions followed by observations. Both these should be supported with appropriate records. One should not forget that in these audits, interactions take a lion's share because it is only through intelligently carried out interactions or discussions one can get to know of many short-falls and loopholes in operations and practices.

Basic Tools of Governance Audits:
- Observations
- Interactions
- Verification of Records

Close interaction is extremely critical in governance audits especially for verifying certain activity areas like 'compensation package, health and safety aspects, discrimination and decision pattern, operation integrity and transparency, participative management and freedom of expression, timely response mechanism, etc.,' because people would generally hesitate to open their mind on these subjects. It is only people's mind that should give an opening into the true operation philosophies and procedures of the organisation. Operation short-cuts or loopholes would never be recorded. Similarly, how can an auditor verify discriminatory practices in records? Health and safety aspects need to be verified only through careful observations with a back-up of process and/or material knowledge followed by interactions with people who carryout different activities. Operation integrity is another governance component that can never be verified through records. Repeated observations and close interactions backed with a good knowledge of the process technology can only reveal the truth about operation integrity. An experienced, intelligent auditor will be able to dig-out most of these issues through interactions.

Audit Deliverables

Governance audits comprise of four independent processes namely governance audit, secretarial audit, finance control and accounts practice audit and diligence audits. As such, audit deliverables also belong to

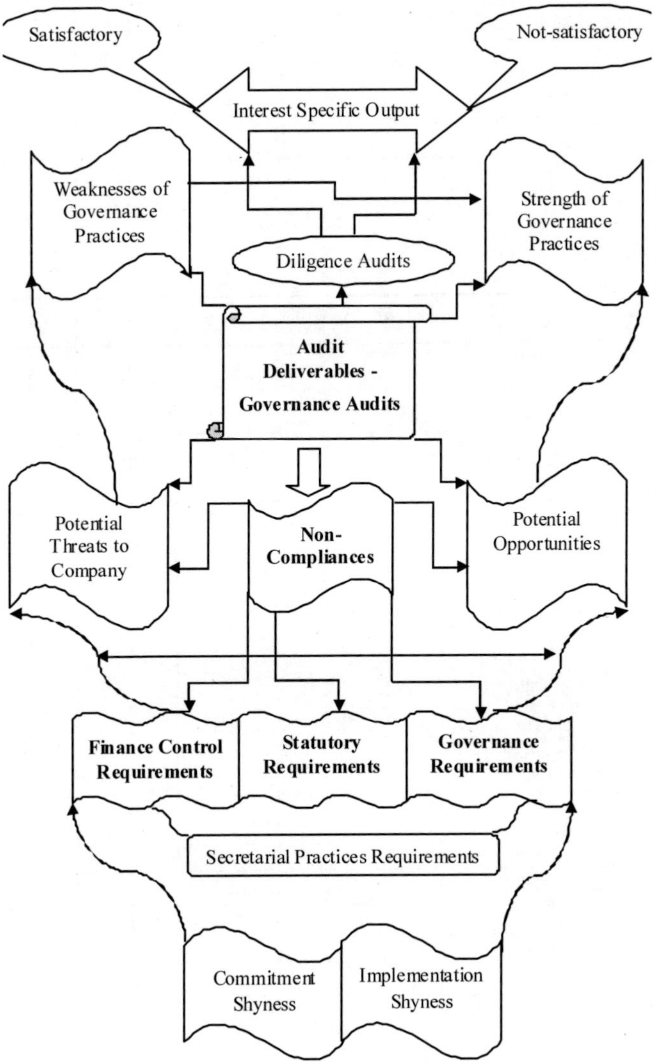

Figure 6.4 Audit Deliverables

Table 6.4 Typical Audit Deliverables

Sl. No.	Audit Process	Verification Aspect/ Component	Identification		Translation to Activity Execution System Design		Execution Commitment		Imple-mentation Commitment		Grading And/or Rating
			Thorough	Partial	Good	Poor	Good	Poor	Good	Poor	
1	Governance System Design and Practices	Legal Requirements									
		Operation Integrity and Transparency									
		Health and Safety Aspects									
		Discrimina-tion and Decision Pattern									
		Other CG Components									
2	Secretarial System Manage-ment	Secretarial Practices									
		Board Configura-tion and Meetings									
		Independent and Women Directors									
		Board Committees and their Functioning									
		CSR Budgeting and Project Execution									
		Other Components of ICSI Standards									
3	Finance Control and Accounts Practices	Annual Returns									
		Internal Audit									
		CFS									
		IFRS									
		Investor Protection and IEPF									
4	Diligence Audits	Requirement Definition									

four distinct groups (Fig. 6.4 and Table 6.4). The table gives a few typical components. Auditors should, however, not confine their report only to these specific areas but should incorporate all the components under each of the audit category in their analysis report and ensure that there is no lacuna in any of the activity area. These components are referred here just to indicate that once they are thoroughly investigated and analysed and if the analysis outcome is positive, the rest of the components under each of the specific category do not normally present a negative picture.

Performance Grading and Rating

Some audit schools prefer to perform an additional exercise of grading and rating the performance in different activity areas as they opine that grading would give a quantitative presentation of the prevailing situation at the time of conducting audits. Different schools follow different schemes for grading an activity performance. Liberal schools compile the answers to each of the probing questions under a specific probing activity area followed by expressing the total numbers of "Yes" answers and the total numbers of "No" answers separately as a percentage of the total numbers of probing questions considered for the area. Wherever the "yes" answer crosses 80 per cent, the particular activity area will be declared as satisfactory with a warning to attend to weaker aspects of areas. Percentages between 60 per cent and 80 per cent will be grouped for "not-satisfactory" category and will be recommended for early improvement actions and those below 60 per cent would be recommended for an immediate corrective action to prevent imminent punitive actions by statutory authorities. These cut-off levels vary from one school to another depending on the exhaustive nature and the type of probing questions they consider for assessing an activity area. Some conservative schools take only + 95 per cent for 'Satisfactory-group" and 85 per cent to 95 per cent for early improvement action and the rest for 'emergency corrective action' category.

Ten Step Audit Process

These audits comprise of basically the following ten key steps.

i. Identifying and understanding the scope of audit to be carried out.

This is the starting point of an audit. Since these audits are carried out with different but specific objectives, it is necessary that a clear definition of the scope of audit is generated first. The objective should be unambiguous. Otherwise, the audit can go astray. It is only the clarity of objective that fixes the type of interactions and observations to be made and records to be verified.

ii. Once the objective and the scope is clear, auditors have to start on the preparatory homework namely following the three step audit preparation as relevant to the audit area and audit scope under consideration.

   The starting point for this activity is a carefully conducted tour of the activity area for a first observation especially wherever elaborate activity execution details prevail. This tour will give an idea of the nature of activity being carried out by different people and also to some extent the role of different executives in completing the activity cycle. This tour would further enable the auditors to correlate the definition and the scope of audit with the activities and also fixes/refines the type of probing questions to be generated and asked during personal interactions, actual shop-floor people to be identified for discussions and the type of records to be verified. This type of homework would set the route for a good verification process that can lead to drawing reliable inference. Further, in situations of elaborate execution activities, this tour would also help in identifying the legal aspects and their impacts associated with the job execution.

iii. Identifying key personnel for personal interactions.

   People to be identified for interactions should be from both managerial level and also from the execution level that could either demonstrate an execution process and/or explain the details to auditors' satisfaction.

iv. Formal discussions with key operating personnel.

   The key purpose behind this interaction would be to know legal implications, if any, associated with the activity, to check operation integrity and transparency behind their activities.

v. Listing out and verifying the relevant records.

vi. Visual observations of actions wherever felt necessary.

This is primarily to confirm the preliminary observations made earlier and to ensure that there is no latent legal impact and health impact areas..

vii. Summarising observations and inferences.

This step of audit activity is a highly involved process and calls for an elaborate analysis of the various observations made during visual inspections and the data generated during verification of records and personnel interactions. The outcome of this activity should result in generation of summary of first set of inferences as per format given in Table 6.4.

viii. Discussing the summary of observations and inferences with key personnel.

Auditors should always remember that during the visual observations and/or personnel interactions they could even miss certain finer aspects of execution that could lead to drawing incorrect inferences regarding certain aspects of activity. It is for this purpose that the first inference should be discussed with the auditee who could give additional input by way of clarifications.

ix. Based on the input from key personnel on preliminary audit observations, re-verifying additional records or operations, if need be and preparing final audit observation reports.

Wherever called for, auditors could revisit the activity centre and reconfirm their earlier observations. Similarly, they could also re-verify the records. This exercise would provide the auditors an opportunity to correct and/or refine their inferences, wherever called for, to make their inferences closer to reality.

x. Follow-up with concerned activity centre for redesigning their activity execution details and for fine-tuning operations.

Though this step is generally considered as a repetitive activity, it is very critical for ensuring that the audit observations made and inferences drawn do drive the activity centre to refine and modify their execution details to ensure total satisfaction to different statutory expectations.

Some Salient Aspects of Companies Act, 2013

Sl. No.	Focus Area	Key Aspects/Emphasis	Act Reference
1.	Enhanced Management Responsibility	Enhanced stringency in directors' and management's responsibility Strict vigilance and heavy penalty for insider trading activities Active participation in CSR made mandatory Provision for public scrutiny on CSR activities All listed companies should have at least one independent director Companies with more than 15 directors should have at least one woman director AGM to be conducted only during working hours between 9 A.M. and 6 P.M. excluding national holidays Provision for electronic voting by members Only physical presence of members to be counted for meeting quorum Removal of provision for issuing shares at discounted price Removal of provision for accepting deposits from public or investors Mandatory credit rating for deposits from public No buy-back within 12 months' interval from pervious buy-back Only public companies can issue securities in accordance with SEBI act and rules Provision for accepting deposits from members through a board resolution and subject to credit rating, deposit insurance and 15 per cent deposits in scheduled banks. Stringent restrictions on related party transactions regarding contracts and/or arrangements/agreements with regard to purchase, sales, goods or service supplies, agency arrangement, office of profit, etc, that may adversely affect the interests of investors. Provision for aggrieved shareholders to guard their interest.	

		Protection of Investors' Interests	Following actions could be initiated through the Tribunal. ⇩ • Preventing the company on pursuing all those actions that are prejudicious to company's interests and shareholders' interests. • Termination of all such activities injurious to company's health. • Removal of MD or other executives responsible for unacceptable activities and recover damages. • Claim damages/compensation from company's auditors/audit firm for making wrong or misleading statements in audit reports and/or for not reporting fraudulent actions in the company. • Annulling resolutions passed to alter memorandum of articles by suppressing certain facts and stopping the company and its directors acting on such resolutions. • Restraining the company from acting contrary to resolutions passed by shareholders. • All forms and types of assets should be valued only by a registered valuer.	Section 188 & Section-241 - 246
		Independent directors should submit a statement, a statement confirming their independence namely not having any direct or indirect interest in company's or its ancillaries and associates, affairs, not related with company's promoters or directors, not having any relatives working for or in the company, not worked for the company for a minimum of previous three years, not having worked for affirm which has transactions with the company, not worked as independent director continuously for the previous 6 years and having a having gap of at least three years if worked earlier.		Section 149
		To be selected from the data bank maintained for the purpose by an external agency or by a notification of central govt.		Section 150
		Should ensure independent judgement on all critical deliberations and decisions of company's board especially on issues of strategy, performance, risk management, resources, key appointments and standards of conduct for the company.		
		Ensure maintenance of highest standards of ethics, integrity and probity in all activities of the company.		
		Should ensure objectivity in evaluation of board's performance and company's management.		

<table>
<tr><td rowspan="9">2.</td><td rowspan="9">Independent directors</td><td colspan="2">Should objectively evaluate management's performance and goal achievement including the board members and also the chairperson of the company</td><td rowspan="6">Schedule IV & Section 149</td></tr>
<tr><td colspan="2">Should ensure total integrity and saneness of all financial transactions, data and controls exerted thereon to further ensure that risk management mechanism is robust</td></tr>
<tr><td colspan="2">Should safeguard interests of types of stakeholders without reference to their stake-value and numbers</td></tr>
<tr><td colspan="2">Should ensure that all forms of conflicting interests across the company and of stakeholders are suitably balanced and appropriately moderated as may become necessary in the interest of the company</td></tr>
<tr><td colspan="2">Should ensure that remuneration to senior managerial personnel and company's directors are appropriate</td></tr>
<tr><td colspan="2">Should ensure timely inflow of appropriate data/ information from company's management to the board</td></tr>
<tr><td rowspan="3">Corporate Social Respon-sibility</td><td>Should frame CSR policy and identify appropriate projects together with budgeting for the same</td><td rowspan="3">Section 135</td></tr>
<tr><td>CSR projects should give preference to local areas and local issues</td></tr>
<tr><td>Should keep strict vigilance and monitor progress on CSR activities</td></tr>
<tr><td rowspan="8">3.</td><td rowspan="8">Increased Accountability
⇩
Better Reporting and Control Mechanism
⇩</td><td colspan="2">Uniform financial year ending 31st March for all companies for purposes of performance review, assessment and reporting</td><td rowspan="4">Section 129</td></tr>
<tr><td colspan="2">Mandatory preparation of consolidated financial statements for all associates, subsidiaries, ancillaries, joint ventures, etc.</td></tr>
<tr><td colspan="2">Severe penalty for violations</td></tr>
<tr><td colspan="2">Should give true and fair picture of company's financial status</td></tr>
<tr><td colspan="2">Provision for revision of financial statements under special situations after getting permission from appropriate govt. agencies. Strict control on reasons for revising financial statements</td><td>Section 130</td></tr>
<tr><td colspan="2">Provision for voluntary revision of financial statements after approval from Tribunal under genuine and pressing conditions</td><td>Section 131</td></tr>
<tr><td colspan="2">Provision for maintaining books of accounts in electronic form in specified format</td><td>Section 128</td></tr>
<tr><td colspan="2">Statutory recognition of CFO as a key managerial person</td><td>Section 128</td></tr>
<tr><td rowspan="3"></td><td rowspan="3"></td><td colspan="2">Defined criteria for auditor selection</td><td>Section 139</td></tr>
<tr><td colspan="2">Auditor cannot audit more than 20 companies</td><td>Section 141</td></tr>
<tr><td colspan="2">Auditor service tenure is defined and restricted
Audit tenure limited to five years at a time with five years</td><td>Section 139</td></tr>
</table>

		cooling-off (gap/interval) period in between two audit assignments		
		Audit companies can continue for two successive tenures of five years duration each		
4.	Stringent Audit Controls ⇩ Increased Accountability of Auditors	Clear reference to items to be specified in audit reports	Financial health of the company, usefulness and genuineness of mechanism devised for maintenance of books of accounts, effectiveness and adequacy of internal financial controls, impact of pending litigations, if any, on company's financial health and status, delays in depositing requisite amounts in IEPF, etc. Comments on internal modes and means.	Section 143
		Fraud reporting	All types and kinds of frauds/fraudulent operations and unholy practices to be positively reported to appropriate government agencies within 30 days of audit conclusion.	
		Specific restrictions on auditors/ audit firms	Auditor or audit firms cannot render certain listed services to the company ⇩ Accounting and book keeping, internal audit, design and implementation of any other services and financial packages, actuarial services, investment advisory services, investment banking services, rendering of outsourced financial services, all types of management services; and other services to be prescribed from time to time.	
5.	Mandatory Internal Audits	Internal audits to be carried out only by a CA or CWA		Section 138
		Audit outcome and observations especially internal financial control mechanisms and their usefulness effectiveness to be compulsorily reviewed and reported in directors' annual report to the general body		
		Severe penalty for violations		
		Company auditor should comment on methods and means followed for internal audits and on the reliability of its outcome and observations		

Bibliography

Andrea Westall (ed.), 1996. "Competitiveness and Corporate Governance", Institute for Public Policy Research, London.

Balachandran, V. and V. Chandrasekaran, 2013. "Corporate Governance, Ethics and Social Responsibility" PHI Learning, New Delhi.

M. H. Bala Subrahmanya, 2009, "Industrial Policy and Management", Bengaluru, Indian Society for Technical Education (ISTE) Working Professionals Learning Project (WPLP).

Barbara Ley Toffler, 1990, "Managers Talk Ethics: Making Tough Choices in a Competitive Business World," Chichester, John Wiley & Sons.

Copeland T, Koller T, and Murren J, 1990, "Valuation Measuring and managing Values of Companies," New York, USA, John Wiley and Sons.

B. N. Ghosh, 2112, "Business Ethics and Corporate Governance," New Delhi, McGraw Hill Education (India) Pvt. Ltd.

Bob Tricker, 2012, "Corporate Governance Principles, Policies and Practices", U. K. Oxford University Press.

Fernando A.C., 2009, "Corporate Governance Policies and Practices," Delhi, Dorling Kindersley.

Francis Cherunilam, 1996, "Business and Government," Mumbai, Himalaya Publishing House.

Francis Cherunilam, 2010, "Business Policy and Strategic Management," Mumbai, Himalaya Publishing House.

J. Fred Weston, Kwang S. Chung and Susan E. Hiau, 1990, "Integers Restructuring and Corporate Control", New Delhi, PHI Learning Pvt. Ltd.

John A Pearce II, Richard B Robinson and Amita Mittal, 2012, "Strategic Management Formulation, Implementation and Control," New Delhi, Tata McGraw Hill Education Pvt. Ltd.

Kesho Prasad, 2014, "Corporate Governance," New Delhi, PHI Learning Pvt. Ltd.

H. R. Machiraju, 2013, "Corporate Governance," Mumbai, Himalaya Publishing House.

Marie Jennings, 1990, "The Guide to Corporate Citizenship," Cambridge, Director Books.

Mary C. Gentile, 2005,"Handbook of Responsible Leadership and Governance in Global Business," edited by Jonathan P. Doh and Stephen A. Stumpf, Edward, pp. 221–240, Northampton, MA, Elgar Publishing Inc.

Mruthyunjaya, H.C., 1993, "R&D in the Private Sector: Prospects and Retrospects", Bangalore, Navakarnataka Publications,

Mruthyunjaya, H.C., 2001, "Strategic Steps to TQM", Saket Industrial Digest, Ahmedabad; "Managing Knowledge to Enhance Corporate Performance", Mumbai, Udyog Pragati:The Journal for Practising Managers; "Cutting Across the Competition Edge", Delhi, Quality World.

Mruthyunjaya, H.C., 2005, "Competence Management in a competitive Environment" , Quality, Six Sigma and CSR, 2004, Appreciating the Human Capital, Increasing Long-term Value for Shareholders through Quality Strategies, Delhi, IOD Publication; "Strategic Steps to TQM", Saket Industrial Digest, Ahmedabad;

Mruthyunjaya, H.C., 2011, "Knowledge Management and Corporate Social Responsibility" in "Knowledge Management," New Delhi, PHI Learning Pvt. Ltd.

Mruthyunjaya, H.C., 2013, "Business Ethics and Value Systems," New Delhi, PHI Learning Pvt. Ltd.

Richard T. De George, 1993, "Competing with Integrity in International Business," New York, Oxford University Press.

Reiman, BC., 1989, "Managing for values A Guide to Value Based Strategic Management." Oxford, U.K, Basil Blackwell Ltd.

Robert A.G. Monks and Nell Minow, 2112, "Corporate Governance," New Delhi,Wiley India Pvt. Ltd.

Robert Monks and Nell Minow, 1991," Power and Accountability," London, Harper Collins.

V. Shunmuga Sundaram and H. Balanagagurunathan, 2007, "Corporate Governance: Concepts and Practices," Varanasi, Kushal Publications and Distributors,

Subhash Chandra Das, 2012, "Corporate Governance in India An Evaluation," New Delhi, PHI Learning Pvt. Ltd.

Swami (Dr.) Parthasarathy., 2013, "Corporate Governance Principles, Mechanisms and Practice," New Delhi, Biztantra.

Van Herck, G., 1982, "Corporate Monopoly Power and Risk," European Economic Review 17, January.

Viscusi WK, Harrington J.E., and Vernon JM., 2005, "Economics of Regulation and Anti-trust," fourth Edn., Massachusetts, The MIT Press.

T. J. Von der Embse and R. A. Wagrey, 1988, "Managerial Ethics Hard Decisions on Soft Criteria," SAM Advanced Management Journal, Winter, p – 6.

Index

13,13200 ECB
CWMC/1952